Managing
Information
in the Public Sector

Managing
Information
in the Public Sector

Jay D. White

M.E.Sharpe
Armonk, New York
London, England

Library of Congress Cataloging-in-Publication Data

White, Jay D.
  Managing information in the public sector / by Jay D. White.
      p. cm.
Includes bibliographical references and index.
ISBN 978-0-7656-1748-4 (cloth : alk. paper)—ISBN 978-0-7656-1749-1 (pbk.: alk. paper)
  1. Public administration—Information technology. 2. Public administration—Information
resources management. I. Title.

JF1525.A8W55 2007
352.3′8011—dc22   2006038942

Printed in the United States of America

The paper used in this publication meets the minimum requirements of
American National Standard for Information Sciences
Permanence of Paper for Printed Library Materials,
ANSI Z 39.48-1984.

∞

BM (c)   10   9   8   7   6   5   4   3   2   1
BM (p)   10   9   8   7   6   5   4

Contents

List of Exhibits and Figures

Exhibits

Figures

Preface

A little over ten years ago I began teaching a master's-level course titled "Managing Information in the Public Sector" at my university. Like any new course, it started out in the category of "Special Topics," but it eventually became a permanent course as an elective in our MPA program because student responses to the course were positive and my faculty felt there was a need for such a course.

I am not really sure how good I was as an instructor for the course in those early years. I had an interest in information systems from a management perspective, and some undergraduate courses in FORTRAN and COBOL programming and master's- and doctoral-level courses in cybernetics and general systems theory. So, I came to the field from two different directions: the dirty trenches of programming and the high-level, and often esoteric, perspective of the master disciplines informing the field of information systems. I had also authored a few articles and book chapters on public information systems, which gave me some sense that I knew what I was talking about.

For years I have been trying to teach the course using conventional introductory management information system textbooks that one finds commonly used in MBA programs. While many of those textbooks are good, they seldom contain much reference to what is going on in the public sector. I found that I had to supplement that component of the course with my own reading and research. Then about five years ago my career in higher education went digital, and I found myself teaching the course in a totally Internet-mediated fashion. The first couple of semesters of doing so were a lot of hard work.

The basic problem was this: In a face-to-face classroom setting, if a student were to ask me a question, like "Could you explain the systems development life cycle?" I would pause and then, off the cuff, carry on about the life cycle at great length until I got a sense that the student's question was answered satisfactorily. This was a relatively easy thing to do while looking at the student and the rest of the class. However, I found that when such a question appeared on the discussion board of Blackboard, the software system we use to deliver our distance education, I spent a lot more time responding in much greater detail than I would in the classroom, including providing primary and secondary references to whatever topic was in question, hoping that I had given a full answer to all of the students. Over time, those responses became the source of much of the information in this book.

I also found myself preparing lecture notes about unique features of information management in the public sector, such as procurement and contracting processes for technology acquisitions and the development of enterprise architectures as blueprints for public agency information management. Those notes also became source material for a good portion of this book. It got to the point where my lecture notes effectively eliminated the need for a general introductory text in management information systems. The notes covered all of the basics of managing information from a general perspective along with public-sector managerial and policy concerns.

Then it dawned on me that there might actually be a need for a book that provides a public-sector view of information management along with the basics of information technology and technology management in general. So I floated the idea past Executive Editor Harry Briggs from M.E. Sharpe, and M.E. Sharpe was interested. So, that is the story behind this book.

The book is not intended solely for classroom use. It is written in such a way that any public administrator can pick it up to learn more about information management, the related technologies supporting the management of information, and some of the public policy and public management issues arising from the use of information technologies in public agencies at all three levels of government.

I would like to thank my colleague, Ronald J. Bauers, who teaches an introductory course in management information systems in the College of Business Administration at the University of Nebraska–Omaha (UNO). He was kind enough to read the manuscript for clarity and technical correctness. He also found the public-sector perspective quite informative. Then, of course, my heartfelt thanks go out to scores of MPA students who have "suffered" through early drafts of chapters in this book and who were kind enough to tell me when they did not understand what I had written. I would also like to thank my colleagues in the School of Public Administration at UNO who forgave me for missing some meetings when I was engrossed in writing. Finally, my wife Faith deserves a considerable degree of thanks since she put up with me locked away in my home office writing this book for many months.

Managing
Information
in the Public Sector

1

Why Study MIS in the Public Sector?

The field of management information systems has grown independent from its origins in computer science, management, accounting, and business administration. Stand-alone academic departments, schools, and colleges of information systems (IS) or management information systems (MIS) have emerged to provide generic teaching and research for the field. With MIS being its own autonomous field of academic study and professional practice, why should programs in public administration or public policy offer their own courses in management information systems when the MIS field offers generic knowledge and skill? Why not simply turn to these MIS programs? Well, there are many reasons to mention.

First and foremost, information is a vital organizational resource. It is just as important as people and money. While this may seem obvious today, it has not always been so. For example, during the 1980s and early 1990s, the National Association of Schools of Public Affairs and Administration (NASPAA), which accredits master's programs in public administration and public policy, held a rather narrow view of information management. Its standards for common curriculum components mentioned that all programs should pay some attention to computers and computing technology.[1] This was often interpreted to mean that a master's program should expose students to the use of software application programs for statistical analysis such as SAS or SPSS, or that some programs might rely on other departments within a university to offer courses in software programming languages such as FORTRAN or COBOL or survey courses in management information systems.

While knowledge of what computers are and what they can do as well as knowledge of the use of software programs are a part of understanding information technology, it is a very old and very narrow view of information management. Today, NASPAA has embraced the modern view that information is an organizational resource important in its own right. This view is

3

reflected in the organization's current statement about common curriculum components, which says that students should learn about "information management, technology applications, and policy" alongside the management of financial and human resources.[2]

The second reason public administration and policy programs should offer courses in MIS is that managing information in the public sector is significantly different in many respects from managing information in the private sector, technically, politically, bureaucratically, and financially. One might argue that technology is technology no matter where it is applied. That might be true in some cases, but some of the operations of government differ significantly from the business activities of the private sector. For example, a standard off-the-shelf accounts receivable system developed for private-sector firms might not be suited for a public agency's collection of user fees. In those situations, experience has shown that it is sometimes difficult to adapt software developed for private-sector applications to public-sector practices.

Then the political and bureaucratic environments in which technology decisions are made can differ significantly. For example, the acquisition and implementation of many technology solutions in the public sector are influenced by political decision making not found in the private sector. Politics and procurement laws have a tendency to slow down acquisition decisions and decisions to improve existing systems. When budgets are tight, politics often leads to the acquisition of less than desirable technology solutions. While private firms can be just as bureaucratic as public agencies, bureaucratic rules and regulations significantly affect technology decisions in the public sector. Nowhere is this more evident than in contracting for technology and technology services. The procurement procedures of many government entities are often excruciatingly slow and cumbersome, so much so, that many times when a system is finally acquired, it is already out of date.

Yet another difference between the sectors has to do with the cost of technology and the people needed to manage and support it. Many times public agencies simply cannot afford "bleeding edge" or even "cutting edge" technology. Revenues and budgets simply cannot pay for it. So, many public agencies have to deal with less than state-of-the-art technologies. As far as personnel are concerned, the vast majority of public agencies simply cannot afford the high cost of managerial and technical support personnel for information systems because the salaries for these positions are usually much higher in the private sector. This limitation creates unique problems in managing the public management information technology workforce, especially such things as reliance on outside consultants, vendors, and even outsourcing the technology functions of agencies.

Beyond these two overarching reasons to study the management of information and technology in the public sector, a host of other reasons can be grouped under four general headings: information systems misfortunes, big bucks, big failures, and the "ITernal Triangle" of information management.

Public-Sector Information Systems Misfortunes

Unfortunately, information and its related technologies are not well managed in the public sector. Problems with information systems persist across all three levels of government (federal, state, and local) as well as in the private sector. The following examples of IS misfortunes in the public sector highlight the need for more effective management oversight.

The Illinois State Toll Highway Authority began installing electronic toll lanes in 1993.[3] In 1995, with 40 percent of the system operating and $17.5 million spent, the Authority tossed the existing system for one they thought would be better. But the new system failed. Half of the 30,000 electronic devices placed under the windshields of cars that automatically deduct money from drivers' accounts simply failed to work.

In the late 1990s, the City of St. Paul, Minnesota, wanted to acquire an integrated payroll, human resources, and benefits package.[4] After spending a considerable amount of time and $1.6 million to do a requirements analysis for the new system, they scrapped the idea because the planned system would cost too much to install and run.

In 1988 Congress ordered the states to build similar child support enforcement systems so they could share information because "deadbeat parents" often move from state to state.[5] A handful of vendors began building fifty-two different systems. Why? Because each state handles its child support enforcement paper processes differently, and getting the states to conform to a single reporting system has been near impossible.

In 1987 the California Department of Motor Vehicles began spending $60 million on an automated "one-stop shopping" vehicle registration and licensing system that never left the start-up stage.[6] It was abandoned when its projected cost exceeded six and a half times its original estimated cost and its anticipated delivery date was pushed back to 1998.

In 1994, the automated baggage-handling system for Denver's new international airport held up the opening of the airport for nine months because of bugs in the software, adding millions of dollars to the already expensive project and requiring the expenditure of millions more dollars to repair the system once it was up and running.[7] Management knew about the bugs but apparently could not do anything about them. Some of the airlines serving the airport resorted to traditional non-automated baggage-handling systems.

In 1995, the State of Florida attempted to develop an automated welfare-eligibility-benefits determination system. The system would cost the state more than $200 million over five years,[8] which was more than double the original budgeted amount for the system. Criminal charges for mismanagement were filed against the welfare agency's MIS director but were later dropped.

Hawaii's budget for its Information and Communication Services Division is 40 percent lower than it was in 1992, and the Division has no authority over any of the state's other agencies.[9] Technology acquisitions over $25,000 have to be put out for bid. By the time the bids go out, the desired technology is already obsolete. Obsolescence due to lengthy bidding and procurement processes is not a problem unique to Hawaii. It plagues most public agencies.

Illinois does not have a centralized department dedicated to information management.[10] Each agency does its own thing in an uncoordinated fashion, often needlessly duplicating IT investments and applications across state departments. This is not a problem unique to Illinois. It affects many federal agencies, states, and local governments as well.

Nebraska's human resource system tells virtually nothing about its employees except their leave status.[11] The State has no strategic information systems plan, but it does have a Chief Information Officer. Unfortunately, the CIO has no authority over other agencies. The State does have mainframe computers, which they have operated for thirty-plus years, but they are antiquated and function poorly.

In a much-publicized IS failure, the Federal Aviation Administration (FAA) had spent twelve years and more than $2.5 billion on a new Advanced Automation System designed to modernize the nation's air traffic control system.[12] Eventually the scope of the system was scaled back drastically, and the FAA terminated its contract with IBM because of excessive cost overruns.[13]

More recently, the Federal Bureau of Investigation scrapped a $170-million Virtual Case File automated management system because of over 400 problems with the software that would prevent the system from working.[14] Management knew about those problems but continued developing the system for two years and invested an additional $17 million to test the system knowing that they were probably going to pull the plug on it some time in the future.

While some of the problems associated with these examples were technical in the sense that they included software difficulties, the major concern in all of these examples is simply poor management of technology, people, and money, as well as inadequate organizational policies and procedures to manage information and technology.

In general, every state is trying to operate using antiquated hardware and software systems that run slowly and frequently break down. Every state has paperwork information systems that are costly to run and could be automated. Also, the use of information technology in the states and localities is fragmented and disjointed. It is not uncommon to find two or more agencies each paying hundreds of thousands to millions of dollars for the same system. There are also incidences where one state agency has a fully functional system to handle some application that could be used by other state agencies but is not.

The Government Performance Project, funded by the Pew Charitable Trusts, grades each state annually on a variety of management performance issues, including how each state manages money, people, infrastructure, and information.[15] In 2005, the overall grade for all states for the management of information was a "B–" with twenty-six of the states receiving grades of "C" or below—not a very commendable record for information management for over half of the states.

Things are not that much better at the federal level of government. The General Accounting Office (GAO) has, over the years, offered many warnings about how poorly information technology is being managed in the various executive agencies. For example, in 1994 the GAO observed the following:

> Without action by federal executives, the gap between public expectations and agency performance will continue to expand. Program risks will continue and unique opportunities for improvement will remain unexploited. Many low-value, high-risk information systems projects will continue to be developed unimpeded and undermanaged as leaders blindly respond to crises by purchasing more technology. Most federal managers will continue to operate without the financial and management information they need to truly improve mission performance. Moreover, many federal employees will struggle unsuccessfully, under increasing workloads, to do their jobs better as they are hampered with information systems that simply add on another automated layer of bureaucracy. Given these risks, sustained Congressional attention is vital to reinforce the link between accountability for returns on information-related investments and the satisfaction of real public needs.[16]

Since that 1994 observation the GAO, recently renamed the Government Accountability Office, has published several reports indicating that information technology is poorly managed across a wide variety of agencies. Many agency information systems are antiquated and need to be extensively modernized. Strategic planning for managing information technology investments is minimal but is getting some attention. Policies and procedures to effectively manage information resources are minimal, but new emphasis is being placed on improving and enforcing these policies and procedures. Training in information technology management is minimal, but efforts are underway to improve this as well as to attract and retain highly qualified information technology professionals, even though they can earn much higher salaries and benefits in the private sector. The role of the chief information officer to direct and oversee agencies' information resources was recently recognized and established but still needs to be strengthened.[17] The U.S. Office of Management and Budget recognized only in 2004 that many duplicate and redundant investments in technology solutions have been made across agencies and it has issued directives to stop this.[18]

Overall, the managers of localities, states, and federal agencies are keenly aware that their information technology infrastructures and their management systems for dealing with information and technology need to be greatly improved. As we will see, the failures to effectively manage information technology investments in the public sector outweigh the successes.

Big Bucks

Governments spend a lot of money on information technology and related professional services to support that technology. It is relatively easy to get a fairly accurate picture of what the federal government spends on IT. In January of 2006, the GAO reported that federal agencies had requested over $65 billion for IT-related investments for fiscal year 2006.[19] INPUT, a technology market research firm, projects the federal budget for IT for fiscal year 2007 to be $75 billion and will increase to $93 billion by fiscal year 2011. While this may seem like a tremendous amount of money—and it is—it actually represents a slowdown in the growth of IT spending because of several federal government performance and measurement initiatives.[20]

Estimates for state and local government spending on technology and services are a little more difficult to pin down because there is no single clearinghouse for such information. One has to rely on studies conducted by market research firms to get a picture of IT expenditures. For example, in August of 2005, *Datamonitor* estimated that all state and local governments will increase their spending on technology to $62.4 billion by fiscal year 2009. The greatest increases will be in services such as consulting, systems integration, outsourcing, and consolidation, as opposed to direct hardware or software purchases.[21] Commenting on this report by *Datamonitor*, an article in *Federal Computer Week* reports the $62.6 billion projection for fiscal year 2009 is an increase of over $55 billion actually spent in fiscal year 2004. The article also breaks down the figures between the states and localities. State spending on IT will rise from $27.8 billion in fiscal year 2004 to $33.5 billion in fiscal year 2009, while local spending on IT will rise from $27 billion in 2004 to $28.9 billion in 2009. Also reported in *Federal Computer Week* is that more of this money will be spent on technology services, consulting, and outsourcing as opposed to actual hardware and software.[22]

Although the exact dollar amounts are hard to pin down precisely, these estimates represent a tremendous amount of taxpayer dollars. How successful are governments in managing this money? Unfortunately, no comprehensive or conclusive answer to this question exists, but some indicators and cases suggest government investment in information technology can be risky and wasteful.

Big Failures

Several major surveys of private- and public-sector organizations have clearly demonstrated that most new IT project initiatives are often plagued by failures, meaning that they were not completed on time, did not stay within budget, or did not offer the promised functionality of the new system, or some combination of all three marks of failure. For example, a 1995 study conducted by the Organizational Aspects Special Interest Group (OASIG), a United Kingdom–based IS research organization, concluded that "7 out of 10 IT projects fail in some respect."[23] A 1997 Canadian study conducted by KPMG, an international accounting firm, concluded that 61 percent of the 174 IT projects studied failed. Three-quarters of them went over schedule by 30 percent. More than half exceeded their original budgets substantially, and unbudgeted project expenditures ran into billions of dollars annually.[24]

In 2001, the Conference Board conducted a study of 117 companies that attempted an enterprise resource planning (ERP) implementation. ERP is an IT industry term for a set of integrated software packages that support a wide variety of an organization's back-office operations such as accounting, finance, and human resources. The study found that

- 34 percent were very satisfied;
- 58 percent were somewhat satisfied;
- 8 percent were unhappy with what they got;
- 40 percent failed to achieve their business case within one year of going live;
- the companies that did achieve benefits said that achievement took six months longer than expected;
- implementation costs were found to average 25 percent over budget;
- support costs were underestimated following the year of implementation by an average of 20 percent.[25]

Perhaps the most notorious study of IT project failures comes from Standish Group International, a market research firm, with their classic and quite famous 1994 study titled the *Chaos Report*.[26] It tells the story of tremendous information technology failures across both public and private organizations. For example, the report estimated that private companies and government agencies spent $81 billion on software projects that were cancelled before becoming operational and $59 billion on projects that were completed long after their original start times, often overbudget, and with less functionality than promised. Of the companies and public agencies surveyed, only 16 percent reported successful software projects, defined as coming in on time and on budget, with all of the promised functionality. Fifty-three percent were "challenged," meaning that they came in either overbudget, late, or with less functionality than promised, or with some combination of all three indicators of failure. Remarkably, 30 percent of the projects were "impaired," meaning that they were started but not completed. Indeed, no public or private project estimated to cost more than $10 million succeeded. Half of these big-dollar projects failed completely. The plug was pulled before going live after considerable start-up expense. The other half of the projects experienced time and cost overruns, and in the end, did not provide the original desired functionality, meaning that the systems did not do all that they were supposed to do.[27]

As part of its research, the Standish Group conducted several case studies to uncover some of the reasons for the high failure rate. They focused on the California Department of Motor Vehicles, mentioned earlier as one example of failure. In 1987 the DMV set out to modernize their driver's license and registration process through automation. By 1993 the automation effort was scrapped after the DMV had already spent $45 million. The reasons given for the failure were: "no monetary payback, lack of support from executive management, no user involvement, poor planning, poor design specifications, and unclear objectives."[28]

More recently the Standish Group found successful technology projects have actually decreased since 1994 from a 34 percent success rate to a 28 percent success rate today. The number of projects that were cancelled before completion moved from 15 percent to 18 percent, and 51 percent were late, overbudget, and lacking in promised functionality.[29]

Why is this happening? The answers are the same as they were ten years ago: lack of top management support, lack of user involvement, more big projects as opposed to small projects, lack of planning, poor project management, unrealistic schedule and cost estimates, lack of risk management, and the dreaded requirements creep. Requirements creep happens when customers and clients begin to ask a new system to do a lot of extra things, not originally specified within the scope of work.

As the *Chaos Report* indicates, IS failures are not confined to the public sector; they happen frequently in the private sector, too. What makes the public sector so important for anyone in public administration or public policy is the obvious lack of stewardship of the taxpayers' dollars.

A major case in point is the U.S. Federal Bureau of Investigation's failed case management system, as noted earlier. Shortly after September 11, 2001, the FBI began developing an electronically based Federal Investigative Case Management System to replace its largely paper-based way of doing business. The project was scrapped in the spring of 2005 as the FBI realized that the system would not perform as desired. The FBI had already spent $170 million on the project. The Justice Department's inspector general recently reported that the project suffered from poor management decisions, a lack of adequate project management oversight, and inadequate IT investment practices. The problem was not in the technology: It was poor management practices that cost the taxpayers so much money.[30]

The ITernal Triangle of Information Systems

It is easy to blame the technology for information systems failures, but in reality the failures often have more to do with poor management functioning and the lack of an organizational culture to support effective information management. This situation is depicted by the ITernal Triangle of Information Systems (see Figure 1.1). It portrays the tensions that exist among people in organizations with different interests in technology.

At the top are elected or appointed officials who frequently do not understand what technology can do for an agency. They may also become reluctant to acquire new technologies that they do not understand and they tend to avoid risks associated with costly technology adoptions. Generally, they do not adequately understand the management of information in public agencies. Consequently, they may be reluctant to initiate and strongly support IT innovations, which is almost always a prerequisite for IT innovation success.

At one corner of the triangle are the information technology personnel. They are usually schooled in computer science or programming languages. Often they do not understand government's business. They understand only the technology, not the information needs of managers and workers. They will not readily support or easily contribute to IT innovations or reforms requested by managers or workers because they have difficulty understanding the business case for the requested improvements. Some prefer to be left alone to play with their technology. Some may have a computer or data processing outlook that lacks a strategic agency mission vision for the use of technology. They may also become highly defensive about the role and importance of their departments, especially when they see technology innovations emerging in

Figure 1.1   **The ITernal Triangle of Information Systems**

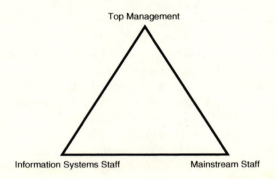

Top Management

Information Systems Staff   Mainstream Staff

Source: Richard Heeks and Anne Davies, "Different Approaches to Information Age Reform," in *Reinventing Government in the Information Age*, ed. Richard Heeks (London: Routledge, 2000): 39. Original Source: A.V. Knight and D.J. Silk, *Managing Information* (London: McGraw-Hill, 1990.

the hands of mainstream staff and end users who sometimes choose to go their own ways, developing their own IT-based applications.

At the other corner of the triangle is the mainstream staff. Those who are not computer literate are usually threatened by IT, especially by its jargon, which can be quite confusing at times. They may also fear the changes that new technologies can bring about, especially if the nature of their work changes as a result. Those who are computer literate often embrace technology innovations and reforms on their own. They want to do it by themselves using inexpensive personal computers and off-the-shelf software to develop their own business applications. Sometimes they may even resent IT personnel, seeing no need to coordinate with them, especially when the IT department wants to control technology acquisition and use. They may even view IT personnel as an interference in their day-to-day business functioning. As they acquire and use their own technology, it is often done in a piecemeal fashion, resulting in duplication of effort or applications that do not operate optimally, or applications that do not share vital data with IT department applications.

Naturally, in organizations experiencing this type of technology culture, one would expect to find a lack of strategic vision for what technology can do, conflict among various groups of workers and managers over technology use, tensions over centralized versus decentralized decision making about technology acquisitions and use, and an overall lack of coordination. No wonder there are so many horror stories about IS misfortunes and technology failures.

The Purpose of This Book

The purpose of this book is to provide any manager in the public sector with a broad understanding of the management of information and its supporting technologies. Hence this book examines ways that information is managed and mismanaged and how it should be managed in public organizations. This process involves understanding the nature of information; how information is used to support operational, tactical, and strategic decision making; and how various related computer and information technologies lend support to the proper management of information. This is not a book on computer hardware or software, although you will become acquainted with some of the basics of technology that all public managers should know. You will not learn how to operate a computer, write application software, or use application software. Instead, this is a book about management and political issues concerning the use of information in the delivery of public services. In other words, this book is every public manager's guide to managing information and technology. One might even call it a survival guide.

More specifically you will have the opportunity to:

1. Appreciate the importance of information as an organizational re-source.
2. Acquire an understanding of how information should be managed in public organizations.
3. Explore several major issues about the proper management of infor-mation in the public sector.
4. Address some of the ways that the information revolution is transforming the administrative and public policy dimensions of government.
5. Understand some of the broader political, social, economic, and ethical issues related to information management in the delivery of public services and in the enhancement of democracy.
6. Develop an understanding of some of the major technologies that support the management of information.
7. Acquire the language and ability to communicate effectively with information systems professionals.

Overview

To this end, you will be exposed to the following topics and issues in this book's chapters.

Chapter 2. Information Technology for Decision Making

In the early days (the 1950s, 1960s, and 1970s) computers were used mainly to keep track of transactions, store data, and generate reports. Periodic and exception reports were used by lower- to mid-level managers to make decisions, but only in a very rudimentary way. A periodic report, produced, say, once a month, provided some information about the performance of some function within an agency. The information was usually of limited value, not particularly up-to-date, and not in a format that was easy for managers to use in decision making. In the late 1970s, as technology became more sophisticated, managers discovered that technology could be used to make more timely, accurate, and relevant decisions of an operational, tactical, and strategic nature. Decision support systems, group decision support systems, executive information systems, and expert systems were developed to greatly enhance decision making at all levels of management. This chapter will describe each of these decision systems, provide examples of each, and note their relative strengths and weaknesses. This chapter will also introduce the problems associated with legacy systems—old, cumbersome, and ineffective systems—that cannot be easily replaced and must be maintained for the daily operations of an agency. Problems in dealing with legacy systems will appear in several places throughout the book.

Chapter 3. Hardware and Software Issues

Technology comes in the form of hardware and software. A brief history of the types of computers and software programming languages will be presented as a backdrop to dealing with two major managerial issues. First is the controversy over commercial off-the-shelf software (COTS). The IT community is divided over whether it is appropriate to design and use a software system for a specific task in a specific type of organization or try to adapt commercial, general-purpose software for an agency's specific and sometimes unique needs. Making this decision is a major management challenge that can be very costly if the wrong direction is taken. Second is the issue over open source software. Unlike proprietary software (such as almost all Microsoft products), open source software is distributed with its source code, which allows programmers to change and adapt the software to meet an agency's specific needs, to improve the security of the software, and to debug operating problems with the software. Many governments worldwide are opting to go with open source applications, much to the concern of many commercial software vendors.

Chapter 4. Managing the Agency's Data Resources

With the development of database technologies and database management systems, managers gained the ability to more quickly and easily store and process data in such a way as to make information relevant to timely and accurate decision making. In particular, we now have the capability to develop data warehouses containing vital information about the internal operation of an agency as well as information external to an agency. With these data warehouses, technicians, and sometimes even managers themselves, can use data mining technologies to discover and explore patterns in the data that can lead to new insights into the operations and functioning of an agency or some segment of the population that the agency represents.

The ability for government agencies to build data warehouses and conduct data mining raises serious privacy issues for the public. Nowhere is this concern more evident than in the Defense Department's attempt to develop the Total Information Awareness program, which would have captured vital personal information about virtually all citizens and visitors to the United States. Some argued that this project would severely violate the privacy rights of citizens; also of concern to some was the fact that this project was led by Admiral John Poindexter of the infamous Iran-Contra Affair.

This chapter will explore the opportunities and pitfalls associated with database innovations and explore the possible privacy threats associated with government data mining. It will cover the role of database managers and data administrators in public agencies, present the importance of data warehouses and data mining, and finally discuss the privacy issues associated with government data mining.

Chapter 5. The Telecommunications Revolution

In the old days of mainframe and microcomputers, people had to bring their work to the computer itself to get their data processed into something they could use. With the advent of client/server computing, supported by developments in telecommunication devices and networking technology, information systems capabilities were radically improved. Now, with a personal computer hooked up to a network, workers can share data as well as software applications throughout an agency. In effect, it is like having the power of a mainframe or minicomputer sitting on everyone's desk.

The greatest impact that technology has had on society is not in the realm of computing capabilities but rather on the much broader realm of telecommunications. With the advent of new technologies and the breakup of American

Telephone and Telegraph (Ma Bell), we have seen a revolution in telecommunications communication devices that rely on computer and information technologies. Nowhere is this change more evident than in the now-ubiquitous use of cell phones and the growing use of WiFi and Internet technology to enhance communication possibilities nationally and internationally.

This chapter will explore the impact of telecommunications technologies on society as well as on the operations of government agencies. It will briefly explain the basics of telecommunications. Then it will provide a case study of a telecommunications implementation in a public school district to highlight some managerial concerns about telecommunications options. The chapter will wrap up by addressing several managerial and public policy issues related to telecommunications.

Chapter 6. The Internet Revolution

With the growth of the Internet, governments have discovered that many information services and some transaction services can be provided electronically through the development of local, state, and federal web sites that serve as portals for the public's access to information and services. Governments have also discovered that web sites can be used to enhance opportunities for the public to engage in democratic discourse and, in some cases, explore the use of the Internet to facilitate voting in elections. This chapter will present some historical and technical background on the Internet. Then it will explore the issues associated with e-government, e-democracy, and e-voting. Some of the issues are quite controversial, such as whether e-government is actually effective, if e-democracy will destroy representative democracy and lead us back to what some call the tyranny of direct democracy, or whether e-voting is safe and secure and actually improves voter turnout.

Chapter 7. Systems Development and Implementation

There is probably no area of management information systems where one can get into more difficulties than in systems development and implementation. This is immediately evident in the requirements analysis phase in which IT personnel try to figure out the information needs of end users without a full understanding of what the end users do, and end users try to specify what their requirements are without an understanding of what the technology can do for them. Inadequate requirements analysis is often stated as the source of all subsequent problems with a technology application. To complicate matters, several approaches to systems development exist—the waterfall model (also known as the systems development life cycle), prototyping, rapid systems development, agile development, joint applications development, and end user development. Each method has its virtues and drawbacks, both of which will be explored in this chapter.

Logically, implementing a new information system is clear and simple. Nevertheless, this is another area where a lot of things can go wrong due to poor or uninformed managerial decision making. This chapter will explore the options for implementing systems, noting their pros and cons.

Chapter 8. Transforming Government with Technology

Three private-sector IT innovations have a great potential for transforming governmental business processes: enterprise resource planning (ERP), business process reengineering (BPR), and customer relations management (CRM). ERP is an ugly and misleading name referring to software products that promise to integrate data across all of an agency's business functions so that the data can be shared by all functions. ERP systems have met with some success and quite a few failures in both the public and private sectors. Nevertheless, they are still being marketed heavily by major application service providers (ASPs), usually in conjunction with reengineering efforts. Depending upon one's point of view, BPR is either the most important approach to managing information to come along or it is just a questionable fad. The basic idea behind BPR is to simply ignore the way processes were carried out in the past, and create them anew without regard to old ways of doing things. BPR was quickly embraced by the reinventing-government movement because it promises to fundamentally change the way government conducts its business. This chapter will explore this controversial approach to systems design and implementation. CRM is more of a strategy, although one that often relies on technology for businesses to better serve their customers. It is being adopted in the public sector, where it is often renamed "citizen" relations management to improve government services to citizens. All three of these approaches to transforming government operations will be introduced in this chapter.

Chapter 9. End User Computing Issues

Three topics are unique to the end user: privacy issues, telecommuting, and ergonomics. Privacy has already been addressed on a macro policy scale with the issues surrounding data warehousing and data mining, but there are more micro managerial issues at hand. What is an employee's right to privacy? What management policies work or do not work to ensure the privacy rights of the employee and the agency? These questions will be answered in this chapter. The federal government and many states and localities have vigorously adopted telecommuting policies that allow government employees to work from home, but telecommuting is not for every position or for every person. There are situations in which it works and those in which it does not work. This chapter will describe several government efforts to set effective policies that allow for telecommuting. Ergonomics is the science of designing working conditions along with technology to make work physically and mentally safe, as well as more productive. Some of the things that governments are doing to make technology work ergonomically will be addressed here.

Chapter 10. Acquiring Technology Solutions

A major area in which management problems occur is in the acquisition and procurement of technology and technology services, especially outsourcing technology services. This chapter will address the unique challenges that governments face in purchasing hardware, software, and other technologies, as well as in contracting for technology services, especially outsourcing. The latter process is at the cutting edge of government management practices as agencies at all levels of government are discovering that in some cases it is much cheaper to rent than to own not only technology but also the personnel to support the technology and the management of the agency's information. Yet outsourcing is controversial in the sense that agencies can lose control over vital information resources; there are also political issues associated with outsourcing public technology functions to firms in foreign countries. This chapter will provide a conceptual background on the logic of government contracting and procurement. It will then describe what is going on with procurement and contracting at the federal, state, and local levels of government. Finally, it will address the outsourcing movement that is occurring at all three levels of government.

Chapter 11. Information Security

Most IT experts believe that the security of any information system can be breached. This weakness can have critical consequences for a public agency because of the sensitivity of the data about people that many agencies store. This chapter will discuss the general concept of information security, followed by a discussion of the various threats to security and their severity, ending with a discussion of what the federal government is doing to try to ensure the security of government information. Unfortunately, as we will see, the federal government is not doing much substantively to secure private information about the citizens of the United States.

Chapter 12. Managing Information Strategically

The recognition that information is a vital organizational resource has led the IT community to realize that it must be managed strategically. Technology, data, and information are not merely operational or tactical concerns. This is evident in the emergence of information resource management (IRM), the new leadership role of chief information officers (CIOs), the creation of enterprise architectures (EA), and the emergence of knowledge management (KM) strategies in public agencies.

With the recognition that information is a vital organizational resource, the public sector, followed by the private sector, adopted the term *information resource management* (IRM) in the late 1970s and early 1980s, and many organizations in both sectors began creating IRM job functions, positions, and departments within agencies. As the recognition of the importance of information increased, the job position of chief information officer was created in order to elevate the importance of managing information to the same status as chief financial officers or chief operating officers. The federal government, followed by the states and many localities, began creating CIO positions in the mid- to late 1990s in efforts to centrally manage all of an agency's information and technology assets. This chapter will examine the CIO leadership initiatives.

An enterprise architecture (EA) is a comprehensive framework used to manage and align an organization's business processes, information technology, software and hardware, local and wide area networks, people, operations, and projects with the organization's overall strategy. An EA strives to answer the following types of questions: What are the organization's business processes, and how is IT supporting those processes? Is the current architecture supporting and adding value to the organization? How might an architecture be modified so that it adds more value to the organization? Based on what we know about what the organization wants to accomplish in the future, will the current architecture support or hinder those goals? Ultimately, this structured process helps to guide an organization to make sound, targeted decisions about how to manage its information-related assets for maximum effectiveness. Under the direction of the President and the Office of Management and Budget, the federal government has made several strong EA initiatives that will be described in this chapter. This chapter will also summarize the many managerial and political issues presented in this book as EA has emerged as a comprehensive approach to all things technical and managerial when it comes to information.

Knowledge management (KM) begins with the realization that most organizations do not know what they know. In other words, knowledge exists in organizations, usually in the minds of its employees, but management does not have a clue about what that knowledge is, where it is in the organization, who has it, and how important it is. So the subfield of knowledge management tries to capture the knowledge of an organization and inventory it, because knowledge is vital to an organization's success. In recent years, the federal government has made several KM initiatives that will be examined in this chapter.

Summary

With this knowledge in hand, you will become a savvier public administrator when it comes to dealing with the management of information and its related technologies and technology issues. Indeed, you will understand the strategic importance of information technology as well as the human side of information management—the side where most of the problems as well as most of the opportunities for success reside. Although technology is vital in the sense that it supports the use of information in organizations, we will see that most of the problems associated with managing information are not technical. Instead, they are managerial and organizational, meaning they have to do with missions, strategies, structures, policies, procedures, decision making, leadership, and communication. Nevertheless, all managers need to know something about the basics of technology including hardware, software, and types of information systems. This book provides both a historical perspective on the development of information technology and an understanding of what technology can do today and in the future. The following chapters will focus on some of the important management issues related to acquiring, implementing, maintaining, and using technology solutions in public organizations.

2

Information Technology
for Decision Making

The first computers were designed to perform mathematical calculations with great speed and nothing more. Fundamentally today's computers still do nothing more than solve complex mathematical equations, but they do it in a way that supports a wide range of government and business applications that enhance decision making. This chapter will present those applications within a framework of the types of decisions found at various levels within a public agency. At the operational level, the day-to-day activities of frontline workers are supported by batch and transaction processing systems. Mid-level managers can use decision support systems to assist them with their tactical decision making. Top management can turn to executive information systems to help them make strategic decisions. Following the discussion of each type of information system for managerial decision making, two additional types of information systems will be introduced: knowledge work systems and legacy systems. Knowledge work systems reflect fundamental changes in the nature of work and the economy. Legacy systems pose major problems for IT professionals and public managers. Finally, an extended example will show how information systems have evolved over the years to support operational, managerial, and strategic decision making.

Operational Transaction Processing Systems

The earliest information systems for government and commercial uses featured batch and transaction processing systems and were available only on mainframes.[1] These systems are still in use today on mainframe, mini, and networked terminal or PC-based client/server technology environments. ("Client/server" is an IT industry term used to describe telecommunication networks of terminals, mini computers, possibly even mainframes and PCs that generally share data and applications within a single organization.) These systems are found at low operating levels of public organizations. They handle the routine, day-to-day operational transactions of an agency. For example, a caseworker in a social service office may see several new clients in a day. Records, usually in the form of paper reports or applications, are filled out and stored in a file for each client. In older applications, the information contained in those paper forms might be entered into a computer system at a later time by data entry personnel or by the caseworker creating an electronic file for each client. This is known as batch processing in which a group of related transactions are batched together, meaning that they are all stored and executed at the same time. In our example, all of the transactions related to all of the clients seen in the agency would be batched at a later time, usually at night by a technician or at the end of the workday or work week by a caseworker.

If this were a real-time transaction processing system, all of the information related to a client could be processed and stored immediately by the caseworker, working at a terminal or a PC connected to a mainframe computer or a mini computer. However, the nature of this work does not usually require real-time updating of information, which tends to be a more costly feature of this type of information system. Therefore, batch processing is usually sufficient for operational systems that are not time sensitive.

Most of us encounter batch processing systems on a frequent basis, even if we are not aware of them. Automated teller machines (ATMs), debit cards, and credit cards are perfect examples. Whenever someone uses one of these conveniences a transaction occurs, but rarely is the transaction completed in real time. For example, when you use your ATM card to get cash, your receipt shows a deduction of some amount of money from your account. Actually the money is still there; it will not be withdrawn until some time later when the bank batches all of its transactions for a specified time period. Imagine someone sitting at a terminal at a very remote location from your bank, perhaps in another country, entering a series of keyboard commands that will batch hundreds of thousands, if not millions, of ATM transactions, perhaps late at night. That is when your cash will actually leave your account. The banking industry feels that this is an acceptable delay in processing ATM transactions. The technology is available to allow banks to process ATM transactions in real time, but it is simply cheaper to do it in a delayed batch mode.

Note that in the prior social services agency example, we could be talking about a purely paper-based system without the aid of any electronic technology whatsoever. In this case, the client's file is updated and stored in a filing cabinet where it rests until it can be retrieved again to change some data if necessary. The introduction of a computer-based system simply creates electronic files in which relevant data are stored for later retrieval and processing if necessary. This system offers the following advantages:

1. Reduces the amount of paperwork associated with a wide variety of operational activities.
2. Reduces the number of errors associated with maintaining data in paper form, although there are possible problems with errors in data entry that can be minimized by electronic data error checking.
3. Increases the speed in which data can be retrieved for use in a face-to-face meeting with a client.
4. Increases the speed in which data can be updated in a client's file.
5. Greatly enhances the ability to generate reports for low-level operational control.

Transaction processing systems, as in this example, become the repository of data relevant to a specific function or unique work process of any organization. Data can be drawn from such systems in order to generate reports that allow frontline workers and supervisors to keep control of a variety of functional processes.

Historically, there are two types of reports: periodic reports and exception reports. Periodic reports provide summarized data at specified time intervals and in fixed formats that are difficult, if not impossible, to change. For example, a social service transaction processing system could produce monthly reports indicating the number of clients served and the various types of services they received. An exception report can be programmed to be generated automatically if a value exceeds a specified threshold. For example, an exception report might be triggered if a caseworker's case load exceeds a certain ceiling, or if the number of clients receiving a specific program service (e.g., Food Stamps) reaches a specific limit. Such reports allow operational personnel to take control of basic organizational processes.

The obvious advantages of electronic reporting are the reduction in time and person hours to produce such reports, reduction in errors, and the fact that such reports are generated in a standardized format for easier interpretation. In pre-technology days, it could take literally hundreds of person hours to manually go through all of the paper files to collect and record the desired data. Such work was prone to errors in reporting. It could also generate summary reports that were not standardized, meaning that only some, not all, of the required summary data would be presented or that irrelevant summary data would be presented.

Reports generated from operational systems do have their limitations. They are periodic, which means that in some cases workers might have to wait an unreasonable amount of time for the data to be presented to them. A quarterly or even monthly report may not be timely enough to deal with an immediate problem. It can also be extremely lengthy and costly in programming time to modify periodic reports so that they present different data. In a similar sense, operational systems do not easily lend themselves to ad hoc queries. Sometimes it is impossible to request a unique report from an operational system, simply because the programming code will not allow it. When it can be done, it is usually very expensive in terms of programming resources and time. This problem can be bypassed by having a clerk or technician sift through mountains of raw data and manually extract the desired data for decision making, but this step can be a lengthy and costly process that is prone to human error. Fortunately, as will be shown in chapter 4, with the advent of database technology, the data in operational systems can be offloaded into a unique database where it can be more easily accessed and manipulated to generate useful reports in a much more timely fashion.

The basic concepts behind transaction processing systems presented with this social services example can extend to a vast array of government operations that deal with citizens (e.g., record keeping by law enforcement agencies, courts, cities, counties, states, etc.) and to a host of internal operations that support the daily functioning of an agency (e.g., accounting, inventory, budgeting, capital asset management, human resource management, etc.). Operational processing systems are good at entering and processing data. They are limited in their reporting of data, however, and they provide no convenient electronic way of analyzing data. Hence the roles for decision support systems.

Decision Support Systems

Decision support systems (DSSs) are notoriously difficult to define precisely.[2] They can range from simple spreadsheets to complex systems comprising their own databases and mathematical modeling software for statistical analysis, linear programming, goal programming, and a host of other more specialized modeling techniques. We can get a more general and useful sense of them by saying that a decision support system is designed to assist mid-level managers in making semistructured decisions: decisions in which there is some degree of uncertainty and an absence of routine, programmed decision-making procedures.[3] This usually means that the system has access to relevant data from within and outside of the organization, it has a user-friendly interface, it sits on the desk of the manager (meaning that it is usually PC-based), and it has application software that allows the manager to conduct "what if" analyses. Decision support systems are almost always designed for relatively narrow and unique applications in public agencies, such as revenue forecasting, inventory management, or scientific research, among other things.

The following is a general example of what a decision support system can do. Many financial services firms make investment decision support systems available to their customers, and even potential customers, on their web pages.

A potential investor can make a selection of a variety of investment vehicles (stocks, bonds, mutual funds, etc.), enter a dollar amount for an investment, and then perform "what if" analyses. For example, the investor can adjust the general inflation rate to see what would happen to an investment if the inflation rate increased by some percentage. Or he or she could enter a desired rate of return on an investment, say a mutual fund, and see what might happen to that fund over a five-, ten-, or fifteen-year period. Or he or she could play with the Federal Reserve's interest rate to see what possible changes might do to a selected investment. Conceptually and from the point of view of the end user, this is what a decision support system can do. It allows you to play around with different scenarios by changing certain parameters to let you see what might happen if one or more of the parameters changes.

Despite the difficulty in defining precisely what a decision support system is, governments are investing significantly in them. A market research study conducted by Federal Sources, Inc., in 1999 found that "the federal government will spend about $383 million on services, software and hardware aimed at refining the output of information systems to support decision-making processes. That investment will swell to more than $6 billion by 2003."[4] State and local governments are also finding many uses for decision support systems.

A survey of decision support system applications from 1988 until 1994 found that decision support systems are being used in a wide variety of government applications, as shown in Exhibit 2.1. From this list and our imagination, we can see that there are many potential application areas in the public sector that can benefit from decision support technologies.

Decision support systems are usually designed for the use of one person or several persons working independently. Group decision support systems (GDSSs) were developed to allow several people to work collectively on one or more problems or tasks. They allow a group of interested people to share information about a specific organizational or public policy problem and to communicate with one another. Depending upon how the group decision support system is built, it might also have unique databases and mathematical modeling capabilities allowing the users to do "what if" scenarios. However, the emphasis in group decision support systems is on communication among the interested parties.

In the early 1980s, when the idea of group decision support systems emerged, it was assumed that the communication among the interested parties would take place over network technologies like local and wide area networks and would be supported by specialized GDSS software packages.[5] This assumption was before the widespread emergence of the Internet and e-mail systems. Today, GDSSs are greatly enabled by the Internet, web-based technologies, and e-mail clients. Parties with an interest in a problem that might

Exhibit 2.1
Some Examples of Decision Support Application
Areas in the Public Sector

- Allocating inspection resources
- Facilitating the quality improvement process
- Analyzing energy policy
- Facility and equipment planning
- Assessing flood risks
- Hurricane mitigation planning
- Cost-benefit-risk analysis of safety backfit for nuclear power reactor
- Improving decision practice in youth probation service
- Decision conferencing for systems planning
- Managing pavement rehabilitation
- Designing a service territories network
- Manpower planning and scheduling
- Developing national economic policy
- Planning nuclear emergency evacuation
- Environmental planning
- Planning statewide highway networks
- Evaluating multistage investment in coal production
- Planning and evaluating NASA space projects
- Evaluating motor vehicle taxation legislation
- Proactive debt management
- Tracking criminal histories
- Scheduling the Olympic Games
- Strategic decision and information system for government cabinet

Source: S. B. Eom, S. M. Lee, E. B. Kim, and C. Somarajan, "A Survey of Decision Support System Applications," *Journal of the Operational Research Society* 49 (1998): 109–120.

be addressed by a GDSS can have access to web pages and chat rooms on the Internet dedicated to the problem and the decision support system.

Some Examples of Public Sector Decision Support Systems

Some examples of decision support systems in government that illustrate a wide variety of application areas follow.

The State of Colorado uses a DSS as part of its water-management system.[6] It was developed by the Colorado Water Conservation Board and the Colorado Division of Water Resources. The system helps in making informed decisions regarding future use of water within the State of Colorado. The DSS comprises a variety of models, databases, and documentation along with a series of application scenarios that include Spatial Database, Water Resource Planning, and Evaluating Operational Strategies. The DSS allows managers and policy advisors to make informed decisions about the use of water in the Colorado, Rio Grande, South Platte, and Arkansas river systems.

The University of Arizona's Department of Agricultural and Economic Resources offers ranchers a DSS to assist in cow-culling decisions.[7] The major components of the DSS include biological factors, market factors, costs of production, management alternatives, joint consideration of biological and market factors, the value of pregnancy testing, and managing herd composition. Values are entered for season, sale calf at side, cost of replacement, current calf price, and cull value. Returned is a decision graph that advises the rancher whether to "keep and breed immediately," "replace with bred heifer," "keep and breed in 6 months," "cull and don't replace," "pregnancy test and replace," or "pregnancy test and cull."

The City College of San Francisco uses a DSS to manage student enrollment.[8] The DSS is designed to help administrators, faculty, and staff with data and information for program review reports, campus and school planning projects, grant proposals, faculty and classified position requests, scheduling of classes, and proposals to either expand or contract current class offerings. The DSS consists of three database modules: Student Demands for Courses and Sections; Enrollment Productivity; and Student Headcount, Characteristics, and Student Success. The DSS offers two options for retrieving data: from reports compiled by members of the Office of Research, and from databases that can be easily queried by the user and that produce data tables that can be either printed or downloaded to a computer.

In Vermont, the Chittenden County Regional Planning Commission (CCRPC) and the Chittenden County Metropolitan Planning Organization (CCMPO) developed a DSS to aid in examining the relationships between land use and transportation.[9] The project includes the development of a DSS to analyze interrelationships between transportation infrastructure and land use and development patterns. There are two main modules used in the system, the snapshot module and the forecasting module. The snapshot module creates an analysis based on a single point in time. The forecasting module predicts the location of future housing and employment based on transportation accessibility and local land-use policies. The snapshot module of the DSS is a support tool to help stakeholders and decision makers create plans through issue identification, alternatives analysis, and goal setting; implement plans by evaluating development consistency with goals; and achieve plans by measuring cumulative progress toward goals. The forecasting module has a standardized set of indicator measurements that are used regularly to gauge actions and compare results across alternative land-use and transportation scenarios.

Decision support systems are ubiquitous in public organizations worldwide. They have and will continue to help to support tactical decision making for mid-level managers and other professional specialists in public agencies. However, they are not particularly useful for executive-level strategic decision making.

Executive Information Systems

Executive information systems (EISs) are a logical and practical extension of DSS for top management strategic decision making.[10] An EIS puts highly aggregated data about an agency and its external environment on the desktops of high-level public executives where they can perform analytical operations similar to a DSS but with a much broader scope—a comprehensive view of the entire agency and the strategic position of the agency within its political, economic, social, and cultural environments. It allows top-level executives to monitor the performance of their agencies in accordance with a variety of key performance indicators identified by the executives, conduct analyses of what is going on in the agency, and "drill down" through the aggregate data to get at issues or potential problems.

EISs differ from traditional information systems and DSSs in several ways. First, they are specially tailored to an executive's information needs, which might include broad performance indicators for various programs in an agency such as the number and types of clients served. Second, they are able to access data about specific issues and problems. Third, they can access a broad range of internal, and sometimes external, data relevant to the functioning of the agency. Fourth, they are, or at least should be, extremely easy to use, requiring minimal training. Fifth, executives access information using simple keyboard commands, mouse pointers, or touch screens. Sixth, executives should be able to do, as opposed to request, various types of analyses themselves, such as trend analysis, exception reporting, or drilling down, without having to rely on others to do it for them. All they have to do is press a key or click a mouse, and the analyses are done for them. Seventh, they can present information in graphical as well as textual form. Eighth, they minimize hard-copy reports while keeping high-level executives updated. With an EIS, qualitative information is obtained without producing volumes of paper.

A final distinguishing feature of an EIS is its drill-down capability. This feature allows an executive to point to an icon or press a key to acquire more detailed information about an issue or potential problem. For example, the director of a state's correctional agency might notice an unusually high number of inmate incidents at a certain facility. An EIS could provide that executive with the ability to make an inquiry that would explain the reasons for the high number of incidents by providing more detailed data about the number and nature of the incidents at that facility, leading to a quicker and more knowledgeable response on the part of the executive. For example, this drill-down feature might point to an unusually high number of violent incidents in a particular holding facility as compared to other holding facilities. This can lead the director to make inquiries about what is going on in that particular holding facility.

Most executive information systems highlight the areas of the agency that are going astray. Color codes can be used to display data that are in an acceptable or unacceptable range as defined by the executive. This technique allows the system to track important project assignments within an agency. An EIS often allows access to external as well as internal information. Both types of data play a vital role in executive decisions. Depending on the mission of the agency, external factors such as economic trends, crime rates, vehicle accidents, bird migration, or just about anything can be incorporated with the internal data. Typically, it is the inclusion of these factors, both internal and external to an agency, that drives the successful development of an EIS.

Two Examples of EISs in the Public Sector

Executive information systems can be used to manage parts of an agency's operations or almost all of the agency's operations. An example of each will be presented here.

The Notes System at the General Services Administration

In 1994, the U.S. General Services Administration (GSA) had an EIS named the Glenn Asset Management System up and running, built on what the agency called its Notes System.[11] It is designed to manage many gigabytes (GB) of data about the government's huge inventory of real estate. At the click of a mouse, a manager can navigate through 4 GB of data about 16,000 government properties worldwide. The manager can make ad hoc queries that generate a variety of reports. For example, a manager can input the name of a specific government building and find out what agencies actually occupy it. He or she can retrieve financial information about the building as well as photographs of the building. Maps of the government's many properties can also be obtained with a click of a mouse.

Aside from the immediate availability of tremendous amounts of information about the government's property holdings, some of the unique things about this system are that it extracts data from a wide variety of disparate transaction processing systems, it is PC-based, and it is built on a client/server architecture that allows the data to be accessed from various locations. Furthermore, the EIS was built entirely by combining several commercial off-the-shelf software products, meaning that the system did not have to be built from scratch, which kept down the cost of the system. Furthermore, the interfaces were built in such a way that any manager could easily learn how to use the EIS within a short time.

The MEDITECH System at the Nebraska Medical Center

The Nebraska Medical Center, the largest health care facility in the state, uses an EIS to manage its entire operation. The system is called MEDITECH and is provided by Medical Information Technology, Inc., of Westwood, Massachusetts.[12] The system offers hospital executives and department managers from both multiple- and single-facility health care units a powerful management tool to gather and analyze information from throughout their health care networks. The EIS produces user-defined reports instantaneously, enabling decision makers at all levels to view integrated financial, clinical, and statistical information from all departments, facilities, and units.

The system collects and displays financial, administrative, clinical, and patient information. Screen displays or printouts may include information from a single department or present information from multiple departments throughout the entire health care organization. The information contained in the system is updated automatically. It assembles information from the following application areas:

- Registration
- Case Mix Management
- Patient Care System
- Order Entry
- Laboratory
- Billing/Accounts Receivable
- General Ledger
- Accounts Payable
- Payroll/Personnel
- Materials Management
- Cost Accounting
- Staffing and Scheduling
- Pharmacy
- Physicians' Practice Management

Executives and managers have several options in viewing standard and individualized reports. The system makes accessing and viewing information practically effortless. Users simply identify the categories of information they want on a particular view. The system displays the data in tabular and graphic formats automatically. Once in a particular view, the user has several options for changing the display or the breakdown of data.

The system includes a number of features that enable users to gather and analyze information at various summary levels and in different time periods.

- Depending upon the specific application, data are captured on either a daily or periodic basis. Users can change the time scale on a view to quarterly, fiscal year, fiscal year to date, or any desired range.
- The system has a drill-down capability. Executives can view increasingly specific information by drilling down through multiple levels of detail. Point-and-select operations and windows of choices instantly move users to additional detail, saving valuable time and effort.
- The system also has a history option in which information is displayed in the time scale currently associated with the view. Additionally, the net change and percent change in data values over the time period are calculated and displayed in tabular and graphic form to clarify trends.
- The system has a breakdown option in which detailed selected information is displayed. For example, the number of admissions may be broken down by physician, location, or service. Users drill down to detail based on how the data are stored in the feeder applications.
- A time-slice option enables information from one time period to be compared to prior data in another time period. Additionally, the net change and percent change in data values between the two columns are calculated and displayed for all the data fields on the view.
- Finally, the selection option allows users to view only the data that are relevant to their interests, thus avoiding data overload.

Overall, this EIS provides the medical center executives with the most timely and accurate data about the performance of the entire center as well as its various units or divisions. This application offers a tremendous amount of executive control over operations as well as providing information to assist in the long-range planning and strategic decision making of the institution.

Other Examples

EISs have been used extensively in large private-sector organizations since the early to mid-1980s. The public sector has seen only a modest initiation of

EISs, primarily because of their initial high cost to develop. Yet the use of EIS in the public sector is growing because public managers are becoming aware of their advantages and the costs of such systems are coming down.

The following are just a few examples of the use of EISs in the public sector.[13] In 1990, the Correctional Services of Canada implemented an EIS to transform mountains of transactional information into summary data that provide executives with key performance indicators and other indicators such as inmate population increases and budget deficits. The U.S. Naval Computer and Telecommunications Command uses an EIS to monitor all of its programs, data requirements, and information technologies as part of their mission to provide information management capabilities to the Navy and joint Department of Defense communication programs. The Federal Highway Administration's EIS automatically updates the agency's financial data each day. Executives can review summaries of key agency information including data highway plans, motor carrier safety, research studies, highway performance, and bridge investigation. The data are presented in graphical format and are updated daily from mainframe databases.

No one really knows how extensively governments are using executive information systems. A 2001 report in the *Government Finance Review* says that nearly $5 billion were projected to be spent across both the public and private sectors, and that a variety of governments were in the process of investing in executive information systems (e.g., State of Minnesota, State of Maryland, State of Utah, Texas Education Agency, Maricopa County, City/County of San Francisco, City of Albuquerque, and City of Philadelphia).[14]

Issues Related to Executive Information Systems in the Public Sector

Several managerial issues are related to the use of EIS in the public sector. First is cost. As noted before, the early EISs were very expensive. They were built for mainframe and mini computer applications and sometimes required the acquisition of new hardware, which added even more to the cost of the system. The early high costs of EISs put them out of the hands of all but the biggest and richest government agencies.

The second issue has to do with realistic expectations about how important it is for top executives to have immediate, up-to-date, and accurate information about the performance of their agency and the environment in which they operate. While sound arguments could be made that some units in the Defense Department or the Department of Homeland Security desperately need executive information systems, in a multitude of other public-service activities, executive decisions can be supported simply by traditional written reports, computer-generated reports, memos, e-mails, phone conversations, and face-to-face meetings. Just because the technology exists and is becoming more affordable does not mean that the local animal control authority needs an EIS. There are gray areas between these two examples where managers need to do careful cost-benefit analyses to determine the appropriateness of acquiring an EIS.

This point leads to a third issue. Some of the benefits of an EIS are intangible. The phrase, "build it and they will come," does not apply to EISs, because some public managers simply will not use them. Those executives reside at the corner of the ITernal Triangle where they resist, if not fear, technology innovations. For this reason alone, some EIS development efforts result in systems that never get used. In response to top executives' reluctance to use an EIS, developers have learned that it is best to start small by building a modest prototype of the EIS. Then, in a series of iterations, they show it to the executives in order to get feedback about what information the executives want and how they want it to be displayed. This process can add significant cost to the in-house development of an EIS, but it helps to assure acceptance of the final application.

It takes a tremendous amount of knowledge and skill on the parts of the technical developer and the senior executives to build an effective EIS. The developer needs to learn the business of the agency and the executive needs to articulate the right key performance indicators. The latter are particularly important, because if they are not right, the EIS will produce irrelevant information. Executives need to spend time with developers, discovering what types of screens or written reports are generated and what useful data might be presented by them. Otherwise, the data are of little use for decision making.

The development of an EIS leads to a fourth issue: build it in-house or go outside? In the early days of EIS, public managers had no choice but to build in-house. This endeavor was costly because it often involved hiring programmers with unique skills at a hefty price. Today, in-house development is not as much of an issue because a variety of vendors offer commercial off-the-shelf EIS packages that can be adapted to an agency's particular needs. The most notable of these venders are Adayturn, Inc., Business Objects, Inc., Comshare, Inc., Cognos, Inc., Hyperion Solutions, Corp., SAS Institute, Inc., and OutlookSoft. All of them claim to offer executive information systems that run on a variety of hardware platforms. Although we do not have a precise understanding of how pervasive executive support systems are in government, if these vendors can be believed, the public sector will see a significant growth in the use of EIS to aid top managers in strategic decision making.

Knowledge Work Systems

Back in 1959, in his highly influential book, *Landmarks of Tomorrow: A Report on the New "Post-Modern" World*, the famous management consultant Peter Drucker identified the emergence of a special class of workers in our modern society—the knowledge worker.[15] Drucker saw a forthcoming fundamental change in the nature of work. The importance of agrarian, industrial, and even service work would give way to the supremacy of knowledge work. A knowledge worker is anyone who works for a living at the tasks of developing or using knowledge. For example, a knowledge worker might be someone who works at any of the tasks of planning, acquiring, searching, analyzing, organizing, storing, programming, distributing, marketing, or otherwise contributing to the transformation of information from one form to another, and those who work at using the information that is produced by them or someone else.

Technology has fostered a tremendous growth in knowledge work. Nowhere is this more evident than in the software that comes with a new personal computer. No matter the computer maker, one is likely to get software applications for word processing, spreadsheets, databases, calculators, and web surfing, all of which are used extensively in knowledge work. Furthermore, the work of the vast majority of government workers is knowledge work as seen in the acquisition, processing, transmission, and communication of data and information using the previously mentioned information technologies, as well as DSSs and EISs, which can be classed as knowledge work systems because they process data for knowledgeable decision making.

The premier example of knowledge work technology is the expert system.[16] Expert systems are a special class of information technology decision-making systems used at the operational levels of some public organizations. Expert systems are derived from the field of artificial intelligence. They are designed to replace the decision-making capabilities of human experts in narrow areas of application such as making medical diagnoses or financial forecasts or decisions in situations where there are so many rules to follow that only an "expert" on those rules has knowledge of how to apply them. Expert systems comprise a database and a set of heuristics—rules of thumb—obtained by knowledge engineers from experts' patterns of thought, or inferences, when solving problems. In other words, they emulate the thought processes of human experts in various problem-solving situations. They are used in highly specialized domains of decision making where knowledge engineers are able to capture the thought patterns and inference rules of experts and convert them into specialized computer programs for solving problems and suggesting possible courses of future action, sometimes with estimates of the probability of the success of those actions.

Expert systems are particularly useful in situations where there are many rules that must be followed that no one person could possibly remember or master them all. For example, the government of New South Wales Australia uses an expert system called "HR eXpert" to navigate through the highly complex rules governing their public employment system in order to determine accurate wages and benefits for their public employees.[17] Another example is the expert system called "Logist" used by the Israeli Ministry of Finance to determine wages, benefits, and retirement eligibility.[18] Human resource systems are often mired in many complex rules that even seasoned human resource specialists may not recall or understand. Hence the need for such automated IS-based assistance in decision making. Expert systems also prove to be very useful when seasoned human experts retire or leave an agency, only to be replaced with a novice who may not have knowledge of all of the rules and how to apply them in a particular decision-making situation. Here expert systems can be queried by the novice to sift through a mountain of rules and regulations to come up with a proper decision that the novice would not be able to arrive at alone.

Legacy Systems

Most public- as well as private-sector organizations that have data processing systems dating date back to the 1970s or even the 1980s face the problem of legacy systems. A legacy system is usually old, utilizes mainframe and mini computer platforms, and has systems software and applications software written in ancient programming languages like machine language, assembler language, or COBOL (see chapter 3 for a discussion of programming languages). This can mean that the systems are often very slow and prone to crashing. Nevertheless they are crucial to the day-to-day operations of the agency, which means that they cannot be shut down, they are extremely difficult to modify, and they are often incompatible with newer systems, making the sharing of data virtually impossible. They are also very costly to maintain. If the public agency is large, it may have hundreds, if not thousands, of legacy systems that cannot communicate with one another and often perform redundant tasks. Finally, they can be expensive to replace.

A case in point is the U.S. Naval Marine Corps Intranet (NMCI) project that was begun in 2000.[19] (An intranet uses the Internet as the "backbone" of what is virtually a private telecommunications network made secure using a variety of technologies.) In the beginning NMCI was an effort to replace over 9,000 legacy software applications with a single network. The intranet uses the World Wide Web as the backbone for a network of 360,000 noncombat, shoreline desktops, or computer seats, across the nation and in Puerto Rico,

Iceland, and Cuba. The original contract was outsourced to Electronic Data Systems (EDS) in 2001 at a price tag of approximately $6.9 billion. The cost of the contract subsequently increased to $8.8 billion over ten years as the developers began finding more legacy system applications—approximately 100,000—than originally expected. It has become the largest outsourcing contract in the history of the federal government and has garnered a tremendous amount of attention from the IT industry electronic trade papers such as *Government Computer News* and *Federal Computer Week*.

Why spend so much money to replace those legacy systems? They were antiquated, inefficient, and ineffective. Furthermore, top management had no idea of how many legacy systems actually existed, because over the years many base commanders had the authority to acquire their own hardware and software applications. This led to a tremendous redundancy in applications and an inability to share data across applications. The idea of a single intranet that would reduce the number of applications down to less than one hundred and make them accessible at 360,000 locations seemed to make sense. And it does, but at a hefty price.

While the NMCI experience is an extraordinary case in terms of its size and scope, thousands of public agencies at all levels of government are facing the problems of having to deal with legacy systems. With mixed results and little success, they are trying either to maintain them—because they cannot be turned off; otherwise, the work of the agency would grind; to a halt—or to integrate them with newer applications, with little success, or to replace them with cutting-edge technology, which is an enormous monetary challenge. We will encounter the difficulties associated with legacy systems again when we consider such topics as systems development, implementation, and acquisition.

From Operational to Executive Decision Making: An Extended Example

The following is an extended example of the evolution of transaction processing systems that shows how information technology has evolved to enhance managerial and executive decision making. The example is student grading and record keeping in a state university setting, a function usually performed by the registrar's office. In the days before computers, all of the information relevant to a student was contained in a paper-based file. When it came time for an instructor to submit a student's grade, he or she used a paper form that contained places to record the grades for all of the students in a class. The form was then submitted to the registrar's office where clerks recorded each student's grade in each student's file. This was a laborious task, requiring the clerk to take a class grade sheet, find the file for each of the students in the class, and then record the grade in the file. If the student was registered in four to five classes, the student's file would have to be handled four to five times. Imagine the amount of work and time this would take for a university with an enrollment of 20,000 students.

At this point a number of time-consuming activities would begin. A grade report for each student would be prepared showing the grades received for each class taken during that semester. A copy would go into the student's file in the registrar's office. Then the grade report would be sent by mail to the student and a copy would be sent to the appropriate academic department where it would be placed in yet another (and often redundant) student file. This process often took weeks. Then all of the grades for all of the students would have to be averaged, by hand, to determine each student's overall grade-point average. This value would determine if the student should be placed on the dean's list or on probation, or dropped from the program. Such information from a purely paper-based data processing system might not appear until well into the next semester, which would be very inconvenient for a student who had flunked out of the university but was still enrolled in classes because the fact that the student had failed did not emerge from the paper-based system before the beginning of the next semester.

Fortunately, operational-level data processing systems have eliminated the enormous amount of time and work in entering, storing, and reporting grades. Some may remember the early class grade reports that were filled out by the instructor with a "number 2 pencil" and then optically scanned into the processing system where the grades would then be recorded in the electronic files of the students. Today, at one university, if not more, the instructors submit their grades from the keyboards of their personal computers through a web portal maintained by the registrar's office. Oddly enough, this method saves the work of clerks scanning in grade sheets, but it creates extra work for the instructors. In this particular application, the students' grades are not updated in real time. After the instructor submits the grades via the web portal, a window appears to inform the instructor that the grades will not be available until the next day. This means that the grades are batched overnight. Although this process creates more work for the instructor, the student has access to his or her grade the next day via the same web portal. Students no longer have to wait weeks to find out what grades they got in their classes.

Old approaches to registering for classes are another example of outdated, inefficient, ineffective, and time-consuming paper-based data processing. Many people can remember the days when they were students at a university. Registration meant standing in very long lines for very long periods of time, waiting until you reached the counter to hand in your registration form. In some cases you discovered that a particular course you wanted was full. This meant that you had to step out of line, fill out another registration form, get back into line again, and hope that the other section of the course was not full. Today, these operational transactions can be completed electronically via the registrar's web portal. Within a certain period of days or weeks before the beginning of the next semester, students can register for classes from a terminal or from a PC via the Internet and the web portal at virtually any time of day. The output screens display immediately what sections are available, what prerequisites are required, and ultimately what classes the student can actually register for.

These batch and transaction processing systems have revolutionized student record keeping, reporting of grades, and registering for classes. As we shall see shortly, they also form the basis for decision support and strategic decision EIS making.

Administrators also had trouble with these old registration systems. It took many person hours of work, at times weeks, to get all of the students registered in the right classes and valid class lists distributed to the various departments and ultimately the entire teaching faculty. For this reason, many departments would have no idea of how many students were enrolled in their courses for that semester unless they required each member of the faculty to obtain a class list for each class, showing the student's name, identification number, degree program in which they were enrolled, as well as contact information. This meant that a staff person would have to compile his or her own paper-based information system detailing how many students and which students were enrolled in the current course offerings. When the official class lists arrived in the department after several weeks, their content had to be checked against the department's unofficial class lists to see if the right students were enrolled in the right courses. One might find some students enrolled in courses for which they did not have the right prerequisites. Consequently these students would be pulled from the courses, which could have affected the timely completion of their studies.

This old, paper-based way of doing the university's business did not support managerial decision making well. It made it difficult to advise students which courses to enroll in in future semesters. It also made it difficult to predict the demand for future course enrollments, which affects decisions about how many sections of a course to offer. For example, suppose a department sets a cap of twenty-five students in a master's-level course. Without good historical data on the demand for that class, it is difficult to determine how many sections to offer. If student demand is high and not enough sections are offered, students' programs of study might be unreasonably extended. If student demand is low and too many sections of a course are offered, an instructor's time might not be allocated efficiently or effectively.

This situation forced some academic departments to duplicate the functions of the registrar's office. With the advent of PCs, the chairperson of a department might direct a departmental secretary or other person to create the department's own database of students, including such data as student name, ID number, address, phone number, place of employment, course enrollments, and grades. This database would duplicate what was already in the registrar's system, but it did allow for much greater local control. Over time, the data would build up and the departmental chair could have reports generated on such things as historical enrollment trends. To the extent that databases and spreadsheets were used to generate these reports, they represented rudimentary decision support systems that allowed the department heads to plan more effectively for future course offerings. In some cases, the spreadsheet reporting might also reveal that few if any students were enrolled in a particular area of specialization. This information might lead to a decision to stop offering that area of specialization and direct resources to specializations with greater demand. In other cases, the spreadsheet reporting might reveal significant increases in enrollments over the past several semesters, leading to decisions about raising entrance requirements to stop the flood of new students, or about going to central administration to ask for additional faculty resources to cope with increases in student demand for course offerings. In a university setting, these are typical mid-level managerial decisions that can be supported by a rudimentary decision support system consisting of a database and spreadsheets.

Today, with sophisticated student information systems, these ad hoc departmental decision support systems are no longer needed. A campuswide student information system means that student records need to be kept only once and in one place via an electronic filing system that only authorized users can access, either from central administration (e.g., for student loan or financial aid information) or from departments (e.g., checking on a student's cumulative grade-point average, or finding a student's address or phone number). Grades can be recorded directly by an instructor using a web portal, and the grades that are entered are batched overnight. Cumulative grade-point averages are computed immediately and posted on a web page that the students can access the next day. Students register for classes online from their homes or offices, at any time of the day, knowing immediately whether or not there is space in a preferred section. Administrators can track enrollment in the next semester's classes on an hour-by-hour basis, giving them the opportunity to make immediate decisions about adding additional sections or dropping an underenrolled class. This flexibility can allow faculty resources to be allocated in a timely fashion and can enable the administrators to make important decisions about their program offerings using timely and accurate historical data.

Finally, executives in the upper echelons of the university can make strategic decisions by analyzing the university's internal data across all programs, departments, schools, and other units to discover where additional resources need to be placed or where funding for low-demand programs might be reduced. In times of state revenue shortfalls and budget cutting, this capability gives university executives hard numbers upon which to make decisions. When combined with external databases containing data about future high school graduations, projections about future enrollments can be made. If those projections show a decline in potential future enrollments, university executives can take such actions as marketing the university to the youth of the state, adjusting tuition rates, forming partnerships with junior colleges, or offering alternative forms of program delivery such as distance education programs. While the student information system might not have an official EIS designation, university executives have the data and the analytical tools to do just what a formal EIS is designed to do.

Summary and a Look Forward

The preceding example summarizes how information technology has evolved to support frontline operational, mid-level tactical, and executive strategic decision making in a public organization. In the next chapter, we will consider the types of hardware and software that are used to enhance this type of managerial decision making. Then, in chapter 4, we will see how databases, database management systems, and data warehouse and data mining technologies are enhancing the business intelligence of public-sector management information systems.

3

Hardware and Software Issues

Unless your personal computer (PC) or agency mainframe or mini has crashed on you, or if you or your technical staff could not get an expensive piece of software to work properly, it might be hard to imagine real issues associated with the selection and use of hardware and software, either for you personally or for a public agency. Well, there are. The types of hardware (mainframes, minis, micros, or networks) that an agency has or acquires will often determine what software will run on them. Different hardware platforms from different vendors can create the problem of non-interoperability—the inability to share data across platforms. Also, differing software applications may be unable to share data. Imagine your disappointment when you discover that the new database management system your agency has acquired will not share data with your existing spreadsheet applications.

Beyond these fundamental issues about what software runs on what hardware are two major issues that all public managers should know about. First is the decision between building a software application from scratch or acquiring a software package for an application that has already been developed by a vendor. We encountered this question in the previous chapter when we discussed executive information systems. This question can be extended even further: To what extent can a commercial off-the-shelf software (COTS) product be adapted to the specific needs of an agency? For example, can an agency adequately use Microsoft Access to satisfy all of its database needs, or does the agency need a more specialized and more expensive database system designed for a unique function such as a juvenile justice case-management system?

The second issue is the question about whether to use proprietary software or open source software. With proprietary software, the developer or vendor keeps the licensing rights to the software and will not share the source code—the kernels of software programming that allow an end user to actually use the application software without having to know the programming language that created and supports the application software package. This means that the user usually has to pay a lot of money for the software and cannot modify the software to meet the user's unique needs. Open source software, on the other hand, is usually cheaper and sometimes free, and comes with the source code so that modifications in the application software can be made. Both of these issues are hot topics in public administration IT circles today.

This chapter will first cover the basics of computers, including the difference between data and information, and the various types of computers, programming languages, operating systems, and types of software. Then the controversies over commercial off-the-shelf software and open source software will be addressed.

Basics of Computers

This book is not intended to be a comprehensive or in-depth introduction to the workings of computer technology. Nevertheless, some basics need to be covered to ensure a reasonable foundational knowledge of data, information, and technology.

Data versus Information

Computers process data, not information. Although the terms *data* and *information* are often used interchangeably, they are really two different things. Data, the plural of *datum*, are raw facts about some thing or some organizational transaction. They are numerical representations of the attributes or characteristics of things, people, places, and events. Data do not become information until they are perceived by a person, is understood by a person, and is useful to that person within some practical context such as sending an e-mail or writing a report. This means that data need to be aggregated, manipulated, and organized into something (e.g., a report) that can be studied and evaluated by a person within a meaningful context. Then you have information. Technically speaking, computers only process and store data. They do not process or store information. They can, however, present data to a person who may then transform the data into information. This distinction will be paramount in chapter 12 when we explore the emerging field of knowledge management.

Types of Computers

It is useful to distinguish among six types of computers: mainframe computers, mini computers, personal computers, supercomputers, networked computers, and special-purpose devices. According to some criteria used to differentiate the types of computers, the distinctions tend to become somewhat blurry. For example, in terms of speed, some high-end personal computers approach the processing capabilities of mini computers, and some large mini computers approach the processing capabilities of mainframes. Nevertheless, the distinctions among the six types of computers are still conventional in the field of information systems.[1]

Most everyone knows that mainframe computers came first. Indeed, the name "mainframe" did not emerge until mini computers were introduced in the late 1960s and early 1970s.[2] The first mainframes were designed simply to be calculators and nothing more. All they did was add, subtract, multiply, and divide, but they performed these computations much faster than humans. Interestingly enough, the term *computer* has it origins in people, not machines. Around 1822, Charles Babbage introduced his idea for a Difference Engine. It was conceived as a mechanical device that would perform logarithmic and trigonometric functions needed for the design of railroads, textile mills, steamships, bridges, and other industrial devices. As designed, it consisted of rotating wheels and a crank that was to be powered by a steam engine. It would replace many people who worked day and night computing these mathematical functions. Indeed, these workers were called "computers" in their official job descriptions, giving computers in general a human name. Unfortunately, the machine was never actually built because the technology was not available at that time. Then Babbage turned his attention to another device that he called the Analytical Engine. It was also designed to perform calculations, but this time Babbage introduced the idea of punched cards as a means of putting the data into the machine. As a demonstration project Ada Lovelace, the daughter of Lord Byron and long-time friend of Babbage, wrote a program to make the calculations. The programming language was named *Ada* in honor of Lady Lovelace.[3]

The first computers were largely mechanical. Arguably, the abacus developed by the Babylonians about 3000 B.C. could be considered as the forerunner of the first computer, or at least the first handheld calculator.[4] In more modern times, 1890, Herman Hollerith, who worked for the U.S. Census Bureau, developed machines that could read data from holes punched into cards that were fed into the machine.[5] This method greatly reduced human error in making calculations and greatly increased the speed of calculation. Following this success, a variety of commercial punch-card devices developed by International Business Machines (IBM) and Remington greatly increased the speed of mathematical calculations. These machines used electricity to drive mechanical parts that read in the data punched into the cards; then they added, multiplied, and sorted the data and fed out other cards with the punched results.

The first all-electronic computer was the Electronic Numerical Integrator and Computer (ENIAC).[6] It was built during World War II for the U.S. Army by J. Presper Eckert and John William Mauchly of the University of Pennsylvania. It was a special-purpose computer, used only to do the calculations for ballistic firing tables. It was also a giant computer consisting of over 17,000 vacuum tubes and took up an entire large room. Programming was a laborious task consisting of plugging wires into a control panel connected to the vacuum tubes. Because of all of the vacuum tubes, the machine ran very hot and the room in which it was contained needed to be kept cool. It was also a "one-off" machine that was turned off after the war and was never used again.

The first general-purpose commercial computer, the UNIVAC I, was developed by Eckert and Mauchly after the war.[7] A general-purpose computer does more than simply calculate numbers. The early ones supported a limited range of scientific research and administrative functions for large universities and businesses and federal government agencies. Eckert and Mauchly sold their corporation to Remington Rand, which, in turn, delivered the first UNIVAC to the U.S. Census Bureau in 1951. Subsequent models went to the U.S. Air Force, the U.S. Army, the U.S. Navy, the Atomic Energy Commission, the A.C. Nielsen Company, the Prudential Insurance Company, General Electric, DuPont, and Pacific Mutual Insurance. The existence of this miraculous device came to the attention of the general public because the Columbia Broadcasting Company (CBS) used it to predict the outcome of the 1952 presidential election.

Where was IBM in all of this? When IBM started in 1911, its primary business was producing punched-card tabulating machines.[8] The company got into the mainframe market in 1953 with its first special-purpose computer, the 701 Electronic Data Processing Machine. It was nothing more than a very fast calculator used primarily by government agencies, research institutions, and corporations in the defense industry for research purposes. It was not until the mid-1960s that IBM introduced its popular general-purpose System/360 series mainframe computer for government and commercial applications. What made the System/360 series so popular was that IBM made a range of models from small to large. This flexibility allowed IBM to market relatively low-cost models to government and business that could be easily and relatively cheaply upgraded if needed as customers slowly began to discover new applications for automated systems. With the System/360 series and numerous subsequent models that had different numerical designators and greater computing power, IBM became the dominant force in mainframe computing. Many public agencies at all levels of government are still using mainframes acquired in the 1960s, 1970s, and early 1980s to support their operations.

The mini computer emerged in the mid- to late 1960s and developed through the 1970s in response to demand for a cheaper computer. Firms such as Hewlett-Packard (HP), Digital Equipment Corporation (DEC), and Honeywell-Bull (Bull) stepped in to fill this void. Unlike mainframes, which could handle hundreds or even thousands of users simultaneously, mini computers could only support up to about 200 users simultaneously. Also, they were not as fast as mainframes, but there were many government and business applications that were well suited for this type of machine. During the latter part of the 1990s, use of mini computers began to diminish somewhat as network technology developed, allowing microcomputers to be linked together in a client/server configuration.

The distinguishing feature of the microcomputer, or personal computer (PC), besides the microchip technology that made it small, was that it could be used by only one person at a time. Also, it was nowhere near as fast or as powerful as the mini computer or the mainframe. IBM introduced its first PC in 1982 in response to the market that Apple Computer and Commodore created in the late 1970s. The IBM clone (Dell, HP, Gateway, and others) grew to dominate the personal computer market. As PCs became more powerful, they were able to act as servers in a client/server network, approaching the power of a mini computer.

Client/server architecture consists of a server connected to numerous clients. The client is an application that runs on a microcomputer (PC) or workstation. A server can be a mainframe, but it is usually a mini computer or a very powerful microcomputer that can serve as a file server for data storage, as a print server that commands one or more printers, or as a communications server that links together a series of microcomputers. Client/server architectures also can contain database servers that handle only database processing and queries. Today, client/server systems are ubiquitous in the public sector, yet one still finds mainframes and minis supporting the operations of public agencies, often as legacy systems.

Then, there are supercomputers that are expensive, fast, and designed for specific applications requiring tremendous numbers of mathematical calculations.[9] They are owned only by very large corporations, universities, research institutions, and research-based government agencies. They are used for calculation-intensive tasks found in scientific research such as mathematical modeling and simulations. The major difference between a supercomputer and a mainframe is that a supercomputer puts all of its power into running only a few programs at the same time. As such, it is not suited for managerial applications, which involve slower computations and multiple simultaneous users.

Finally, there are hosts of special-purpose devices that do not look like computers but that technically are because they accept input, process data, and produce output. Examples include handheld devices for reading water meters, machines for sensing changes in weather conditions, devices that steer ships or fly airplanes, machines for medical research and medical record keeping, personal digital assistants (PDAs), and, of course, the ever-popular cell phone. PDAs combine computing, telephone, fax, instant messaging, Internet, and networking features. Of course, cell phones are mobile communications devices, but many of them also provide access to the Internet, e-mail, and even PCs. Public managers, and especially knowledge workers, are finding that both PDAs and cell phones are becoming indispensable productivity tools, as will be noted in chapter 5, which deals with telecommunications.

Programming Languages

Programming languages are the instructions that tell the computer what to do with the data that are stored in it. Some programming languages support end-user software applications such as word processing or spreadsheet packages. There are a wide variety of programming languages, only a few of which will be mentioned here.

Initially, mainframes were programmed in machine language, which was extremely difficult to understand because it consisted of nothing but numbers represented by 1s and 0s—the binary logic of all computers. Even today, all computers must have a machine language in order to run, but users never see it. Fortunately, higher-order languages, closer to English, were created to translate the programming code into machine language. For example, assembly language is the next level of programming code that creates the machine language. Instead of being all numbers, it consists of names and variables. Higher-level languages such as FORTRAN, COBOL, BASIC, C, C++, and Java are written in English (as well as other human languages) and can be mastered by computer programmers. Another piece of software called a compiler translates these program commands into assembly and machine languages.

The oldest higher-level language, FORTRAN, which stands for formula translator, was developed in the early 1950s primarily for scientific applications. It was designed to handle complex mathematical equations. COBOL followed in the late 1950s. COBOL stands for Common Business Oriented Language, and, as noted by its name, it was designed for business applications. Programmers familiar with FORTRAN often complained that COBOL was too bulky because it contained many instructions in English words, which slowed down the speed of programming but met the needs of government and business applications. BASIC stands for Beginner's All-Purpose Symbolic Instruction Code. It was also written for business applications, and, as intended, it was easy to learn. C is another higher-level programming language developed in the 1970s for business applications. It is particularly useful for microcomputer applications because it requires much less memory than other languages. Today we have advanced versions of C called C+ and C++. Java was designed to run on a variety of hardware platforms, making it an all-purpose programming language. It is also well suited to web-based applications. It is the programming language that was used to create Microsoft Internet Explorer and Netscape Navigator.[10]

Fortunately, today most computer users do not have to learn a programming language to actually use a computer. The graphical user interface (GUI) and keyboard commands do the programming for them. This does not signal the demise of programmers, however. They are still needed to create the interfaces for the user and to perform other important programming functions such as creating new applications. Actually, there is not a lot of original programming being done in the public sector today. Aside from real cutting-edge applications such as nanotechnology, computer programs have already been written for most common operational and managerial applications. This leaves most programmers in public agencies with the task of maintaining and modifying existing programs. In fact, a lot of their time is devoted to caring for aging legacy systems. Industry estimates suggest that as many as 70 percent of all operational and managerial applications are still written in COBOL.[11]

Operating Systems

The operating system is the most important program on a computer. It performs such tasks as recognizing input from a keyboard, sending output to the display screen or printer, keeping track of files and directories, and managing a variety of other devices. On large systems, the operating system allows more than one person to use the computer at the same time, more than one program to run at the same time, and different parts of the same program to run at the same time. Various types of operating systems are available for various machines. UNIX and Linux are available for mainframes, minis, and workstations. DOS, OS/2, Windows, and Linux are available for personal computers. The various early Windows operating systems such as Windows 95, Windows 2000, and Windows ME were designed to run "on top of" a basic DOS program. These versions of Windows tended to be unstable and often crashed. Windows XP was introduced a few years ago to solve the stability issue and other problems. Unlike prior Windows programs, XP did away with the underlying DOS platform, which has annoyed some experienced PC users who like to work with the blank DOS screen and the amber or green DOS prompt (">") where they can enter commands from their memory.[12]

Types of Software

Two types of software are crucial to computers: system software and application software.[13] System software comprises low-level programs that actually manage the functions of the computer, such as the operating system and utility programs that manage specific devices like printers and disk drives. In today's modern technology environments, they are hidden from the user by a friendly interface.

Windows XP is an example of system software. The interface makes it extremely difficult, if not impossible, to get to the operating system underneath. The Command Prompt command allows the user to get to something that looks like the old DOS that supported earlier versions of Windows. This feature gives the user a limited range of line commands with which to tell the computer to do something, for example, "md" for make a directory, "copy" to copy files, or "move" to move files. Users who grew up with PCs sometimes find the XP user interface irritating because they are used to telling the computer to do something from a blank screen, a simple DOS prompt, with a keyed-in command like "run." Of course the users had to learn those commands, but often they became very proficient, giving them the feeling of more control over the operation of the computer.

In a PC environment, application software, also known as end-user programs, includes such things as word processors, spreadsheets, databases, database management systems, e-mail clients, and so on. They are written for specific tasks and are usually designed to be easy to use. In a mainframe, mini, or network environment, a vast array of commercially available application software packages can handle such functions as general ledger, fund accounting, accounts receivable, accounts payable, billing, asset management, inventory, payroll, and employee benefits. A wide range of more specialized software packages including database management, decision support, executive information systems, network management, e-mail systems, records management, fleet management, fund accounting, budgeting, inventory management, computer-aided dispatch systems, integrated client management systems, and the like is available. The list of potential applications can go on and on.

The most important development in software in the last ten years has been the emergence of enterprise resource planning (ERP) software.[14] This rather ugly name for a concept can become even uglier when implemented. The idea behind ERP is to have all of an agency's software applications "talking to one another"; in other words, they can all share the same data.

The ERP concept emerged from the fact that, over many years, public agencies acquired different software packages for different applications such as accounting, inventory, payroll, and human resources. Often those packages were written in such a way that they could not share data. The idea that they should be able to share data led to the creation of a new class of software vendors who called themselves "integrators" and who began selling the idea that all of an organization's data should be integrated, not only in databases ,but also in transaction processing systems themselves. This is something of a dubious notion because it hard to think of a reason why anyone would want to link the data in their inventory system with the data in their payroll system. Nevertheless, integrators began selling modules for unique functions like payroll in the hope that managers would like the one module and buy another in the future. Having all of your applications sharing the same data seemed like a good idea until it came time to implement the ERP system. Many full-scale ERP implementations failed in both the public and private sectors. Chapter 8 will deal with the benefits and limitations of ERP systems.

Commercial Off-the-Shelf Software

A controversy rages within the software industry about the efficacy of commercial off-the-shelf (COTS) software; namely, can it be modified to meet the client's unique needs? The answer is a qualified "maybe."[15] To get a sense of this issue, let us use a simplified hypothetical example. Suppose you have just purchased a new notebook computer and find, in a very unlikely case, that it did not come with word-processing software. Now you are faced with a decision: Are you going to build your own word-processing software or are you going to go out to a store and buy a word-processing package? Of course you are going to buy it because you do not have the knowledge, expertise, or time to develop your own word-processing application.

In the early days of computing, public agencies usually had no choice but to build their own software applications from scratch because there were no vendors selling prepackaged software for the agencies' unique needs. This meant hiring costly programmers and software engineers to develop the applications for the agency or contracting out for such services, which was also expensive. Today a host of vendors offer prepackaged software applications for numerous government operational and managerial functions. These applications can be cheaper, but they are still expensive and may or may not suit all of an agency's needs, even if the vendor claims that the programs can be easily adapted to an agency's unique requirements.

Let us continue with the simple example. Now you have to go out and buy a word-processing application. Which one? Microsoft Word? Corel Word-Perfect? How do you know which one of the applications you will like? You don't. You would have to buy both and try them out. This is absurd because each of these packages is expensive. You could toss a coin, consult a friend, or maybe even ask for a demonstration. The latter is not typical for an individual end user, however.

Public agencies face exactly the same dilemmas when they have to choose software applications to run on their mainframes, minis, or client-servers. As in the private sector, a host of vendors offer prepackaged software applications for numerous public-sector applications. How does one choose?

Well, a public manager can do several things that will be briefly mentioned here and presented in greater detail in chapter 10 on acquiring technology solutions. If technical people are on hand who can help managers specify the operating requirements of the new system, a request for proposals (RFP) can be put together to see if some vendors will bid on the project. A manager can hire independent consultants who have knowledge of the various products that vendors offer and who will study the situation and advise on the best software application package to acquire. Vendors' web sites can be reviewed for advertisements about their application software offerings and checked for testimonials and case studies about successful implementations in other organizations. Naturally, one should be wary about the information (sometimes read "hype") that vendors put on their web sites. Or management can go back to the very beginning and hire a host of expensive programmers, systems architects, and software engineers to build the system from the bottom up. This scenario is highly unlikely in today's environment of budget shortfalls and political demands for outsourcing to the private sector.

If management ultimately goes with a prepackaged software system, they might find that it meets their requirements completely and they will be satisfied. Or they might find that it meets only some of their requirements and they will be unsatisfied. Or they might find that it fails to meet even a modest threshold of their minimum requirements and they will be very unsatisfied. Or they might find that it far exceeds all of their requirements and adds a lot of additional functionality, leaving them to wonder if they paid too much for the "Best of the Breed" software application that may have features they may never use.

Note that the term *requirements* has been repeated here frequently. Requirements analysis is one of the most important aspects of systems development and systems acquisition. As will be seen later in chapter 7, it is something that is very difficult to do for two reasons: One, managers and sometimes IT professionals simply do not know what their technology requirements are. They simply do not know what a computer-based automated system can do for them. Two, when buyers begin to learn what a technology product like a new software application can do, they begin asking for additional requirements. Some of these requirements may be needed; others may be frivolous.

The latter is known as "requirements creep," and it can be expensive as un-needed requirements are added by the vendor at the request of a naïve client. By analogy, the situation can be expressed by "Can it make coffee, too?" Vendors are all too often happy to satisfy additional requirements because these additions mean increased revenue for the vendor, and at an increased cost to the agency.

Once the decision has been made that a commercial off-the-shelf software application will be acquired, the issues turn to whether it can be adapted successfully to meet the agency's specific needs. Again the answer is a qualified "maybe." The following is an example of a successful adaptation of such software in a foster care unit of a municipal social service agency.[16]

A Case Study

A foster care unit of a municipal social service agency was facing the challenge of dealing with an ineffective payment system for foster care providers. The city had 4,000 children in foster care. Some of them were in institutional homes while about 80 percent of them were in individual or group homes. The annual payment made to these caregivers was approximately $75 million. When a child was placed in a care facility, the social worker would fill out a payment authorization form that would go to a different unit in the agency and a check would be issued to the individual caregiver. If a child remained in care for more than sixty days, a semipermanent account was set up to give the foster parent automatic recurring payments.

Unfortunately, the existing system had problems. Sometimes the case-workers failed to complete the payment authorization forms or were slow in completing the forms, delaying payments to the foster parents. Other times foster parents would receive duplicate checks, and, worst of all, when a child left foster care, the foster parents would continue receiving payments. The agency found that it was difficult and expensive to collect these erroneous payments. Furthermore, the payment system was only partly automated, meaning that the validity of the payments had to be checked by hand, a lengthy paperwork-intensive process.

Naturally, the management of the agency was concerned about these problems, so with the aid of two outside consultants they studied the situation and decided that they wanted a fully automated system that would do the following:

1. Provide online access to data about children who had been placed in the foster care system and the type of care that each child received;
2. Provide online access to data about foster care providers;

3. Automatically calculate the amount to be paid to each provider for each child every month;
4. Maintain online historical information about payments both by child and by foster care provider;
5. Automatically detect possible duplicate payments prior to disbursement; and
6. Print disbursement checks to foster care providers with supporting documentation indicating the children and the time periods for which payment was being made.[17]

Management then considered three approaches to developing the new system: build it from scratch using Microsoft Access, purchase a dedicated payment system that was designed for a similar process in another political jurisdiction, or purchase an off-the-shelf commercial accounting software system and adapt it to their needs. The first alternative would be too time consuming and might require hiring additional skilled staff. The second alternative was feasible but about ten times more expensive than the third. So they examined three commercial general-purpose accounting software programs: Great Plains Dynamics, Solomon for Windows, and MAS 90. All three are COTS software packages designed for specific accounting functions for a variety of private-sector organizations.

Management selected the Great Plains Dynamics package because it could be modified easily to meet the transaction processing needs of the agency. The accounts payable module was modified to capture data about each foster care provider. The payroll module of the system was modified to accept data about each child. Then a data entry screen had to be modified to capture the unique data related to this application. In the end, the foster care unit got an automated payment system that satisfied the stated initial requirements. The system took only a few months, instead of years, to build, and cost substantially less than the dedicated software system in use in other political jurisdictions.

This was a success story. There have been failures as well as other successes. The point is that a potential application situation needs to be analyzed carefully along with competing software products to determine whether one should build from scratch, buy a predesigned dedicated system, or try to modify a COTS system. This decision is a concern during systems development and implementation, which will be the subject of chapter 7.

Open Source versus Proprietary Software

There is tremendous controversy over the use of open source versus proprietary (or closed source) software within the public administration information system community.[18] Open source software is either free or comes at a very low price. It also comes with a core source code that allows programmers to adapt the software to an agency's specific needs and debug it if necessary to get the software operating properly. Proprietary software, on the other hand, is usually much more expensive and does not come with the source code so it cannot be adapted easily to unique situations nor can it be debugged easily. Most of the major software vendors, most notably Microsoft, offer only proprietary software. These vendors maintain that they have intellectual property rights to their software products and that they are better equipped to debug their products and make improvements to them.

Open source software is more than just the software itself. It is a philosophy about how software should be developed and distributed. That philosophy is clearly stated in the official definition of open source software maintained by the Open Source Initiative, which is a nonprofit corporation dedicated to the development of such software. Their definition of open source software follows in Exhibit 3.1.

According to the Open Source Initiative, the basic idea behind open source software is simple: "When programmers can read, redistribute, and modify the source code for a piece of software, the software evolves. People improve it, people adapt it, people fix bugs. And this can happen at a speed that, if one is used to the slow pace of conventional software development, seems astonishing."[19]

One of the major players in the open source game is Red Hat, Inc., which markets a variety of software applications using the Linux operating system. Other players include the Apache Software Foundation, which offers a variety of applications, most notably the Apache web browser as an alternative to Microsoft Internet Explorer. Then there is Mozilla, which also offers a web browser, Firefox, and an e-mail client called Thunderbird that compete with Microsoft Internet Explorer, Outlook, and Outlook Express. Also, OpenOffice. Org offers free word-processing and spreadsheet software to compete with Microsoft Word and Corel WordPerfect. It is not as powerful as Word, but as one IT consultant has put it, "some office workers need the massive Microsoft Office Suite, but millions of government workers don't, so why pay for it and deal with the license hassles?"[20]

There are a variety of reasons why both public and private organizations are turning to open source software. Not all of those reasons have to do with the "free" nature of those programs, although developing countries such as Peru, Venezuela, and China are attracted to the low cost and have passed legislation mandating the use of open source software. Yet many wealthier, developed nations in Western Europe, the United Kingdom, Australia, New Zealand, and, of course, the United States are also interested in these systems, partly because

Exhibit 3.1
Definition of Open Source Software

The Open Source Definition
Version 1.9

Introduction

Open source doesn't just mean access to the source code. The distribution terms of open source software must comply with the following criteria:

1. Free Redistribution
The license shall not restrict any party from selling or giving away the software as a component of an aggregate software distribution containing programs from several different sources. The license shall not require a royalty or other fee for such sale.

2. Source Code
The program must include source code and must allow distribution in source code as well as compiled form. Where some form of a product is not distributed with source code, there must be a well-publicized means of obtaining the source code for no more than a reasonable reproduction cost—preferably, downloading via the Internet without charge. The source code must be the preferred form in which a programmer would modify the program. Deliberately obfuscated source code is not allowed. Intermediate forms such as the output of a preprocessor or translator are not allowed.

3. Derived Works
The license must allow modifications and derived works and must allow them to be distributed under the same terms as the license of the original software.

4. Integrity of the Author's Source Code
The license may restrict source code from being distributed in modified form only if the license allows the distribution of "patch files" with the source code for the purpose of modifying the program at build time. The license must explicitly permit distribution of software built from modified source code. The license may require derived works to carry a different name or version number from the original software.

5. No Discrimination Against Persons or Groups
The license must not discriminate against any person or group of persons.

6. No Discrimination Against Fields of Endeavor
The license must not restrict anyone from making use of the program in a specific field or endeavor. For example, it may not restrict the program from being used in a business or from being used for genetic research.

7. Distribution of License
The rights attached to the program must apply to all to whom the program is redistributed without the need for execution of an additional license by those parties.

8. License Must Not Be Specific to a Product
The rights attached to the program must not depend on the program's being part of a particular software distribution. If the program is extracted from that distribution and used or distributed within the terms of the program's license, all parties to whom the program is redistributed should have the same rights as those that are granted in conjunction with the original software distribution.

9. The License Must Not Restrict Other Software
The license must not place restrictions on other software that is distributed along with the licensed software. For example, the license must not insist that all other programs distributed on the same medium must be open source software.

Source: Open Source Initiative, www.opensource.org/docs/definition.php (accessed May 22, 2006).

of cost, partly because of enhanced interoperability among applications, and partly because of a desire to be independent of proprietary vendors such as Microsoft.[21] China has serious political reasons for favoring open source software. They have no interest in relying on Western firms for their software systems, and they are concerned about the security of those systems. In 2004 almost 70 percent of all software purchases in China were open source–based products, and the national government had mandated that all national and local government agencies use only open source software.[22]

A major survey on open source use, known as the "Free/Libre and Open Source Software: Survey and Study" (FLOSS), was conducted in 2002.[23] It was supported by a consortium of universities, research institutes, and governments from the United Kingdom, Spain, Argentina, Brazil, Bulgaria, China, Croatia, India, Malaysia, and South Africa, with the University of Maastricht, Netherlands, serving as the coordinator. One thousand four hundred and fifty-two companies and public institutions with at least one hundred employees in Germany, Sweden, and the United Kingdom were surveyed. The study found that, along with cost savings, the highest-ranking reasons to use open source software were higher stability, better security, improved performance, and greater functionality.

In the United States, public agencies at all levels are turning to open source software. States and local governments are finding open source software attractive because of IT budget constraints and increasing hardware and software licensing constraints, and because they can contract out the writing of software code, which is less expensive than maintaining in-house professionals to change and develop applications.[24] Federal agencies are also beginning to adopt open source software applications, but slowly, partly because most of their existing applications are already written in proprietary software programs.[25]

On July 1, 2004, the Office of Management and Budget (OMB) released a memo to all senior procurement executives and chief information officers reminding them that according to OMB circulars A-11 and A-130 and the Federal Acquisition Regulation (FAR):

> These policies are intentionally technology and vendor neutral, and to the maximum extent practicable, agency implementation should be similarly neutral. As this guidance states, all agency IT investment decisions, including software, must be made consistent with the agency's enterprise architecture and the Federal Enterprise Architecture. Additionally, agencies must consider the total cost of ownership including lifecycle maintenance costs, the costs associated with risk issues, including security and privacy of data, and the costs of ensuring security of the IT system itself.[26]

The memo went on to warn about complex licensing agreements associated with proprietary software, and the very mention of open source software in the memo has been taken as an official "go ahead" to move in the open source direction.

According to the market research firm INPUT, state and local governments are "warming up" to the idea of open source software.[27] They observe that widespread adoption of open source software should reduce overall state and local software spending and that the move to open source also enhances the ability to manage the confidentiality and integrity of publicly held data. In 2004, Massachusetts became the first state to publicly endorse a mandatory open standards policy, even after many complaints from the proprietary software industry. Other states have been pursuing open source solutions but without the fanfare of Massachusetts.[28] Finally, state and local governments are also motivated to go the open source route because vendors such as Microsoft are announcing that, in the near future, they will no longer support their older products like Windows 98. This leaves the states and localities little option but to move to open source software, which they themselves can support because they have access to the source code.

Does open source signal the demise of proprietary software? Not likely. Users in the public and private sectors usually continue to go with products with which they are familiar and from companies that they are used to dealing with. Nevertheless, open source will continue to see gains in the public sector.

Summary and a Look Forward

This chapter has introduced some of the basics of hardware and software, as well as some of the issues associated with the selection of different types of hardware and software. The issues of commercial off-the-shelf software packages and proprietary versus open source software will be addressed again in the chapters on systems development and implementation (chapter 7) and acquiring technology solutions (chapter 10). In the next chapter we will address the logical and practical extension of application software, namely databases and database management systems that have made tremendous improvements in managerial decision making, as noted in chapter 2.

4

Managing the Agency's
Data Resources

An agency's data can be stored on paper, in files, in filing cabinets, or electronically in batch and transaction processing systems as we saw in chapter 2. The advantage of the latter is that these systems can produce periodic reports more quickly and with fewer errors than using only a paper-based system. They are limited, however, in the nature and type of data presented in the reports, and it is difficult and expensive to redesign the content of periodic reports. Also, data contained in periodic reports may not be as timely as some managers may want. The data in the report could be a week or two, or perhaps a month or two, old, or even older. Thus the data might not be timely enough for the worker or manager, depending upon the urgency of his or her decision situation.

In response to management's desire for more timely and accurate data, the 1960s saw the development of database (DB) technology and database management systems (DBMS). Generally and simplistically, but factually, a database is nothing more than a place to store data. The data can be drawn from a transaction processing system via a floppy disk or magnetic tape, or they can be hand-entered using punched cards or a keyboard. A database usually stands between the agency's transaction processing systems and the user of the database in the sense that data are offloaded from the transaction processing system and placed into the database where they can be more easily manipulated. The major advantage of a database is the ability to generate a variety of reports to support operational, managerial, and strategic decision making with the use of database management software that contains a suite of software applications allowing for data queries and report generation.

The original databases were large, complex, and designed to run on mainframes and mini computers.[1] They required a tremendous amount of technical knowledge and expertise to build and run. This was not a task for a worker or a manager; professional IT staff were required in order to ask for specialized reports. In the 1970s and 1980s, database capabilities became distributed. Using client/server network technology along with terminals, workstations, and PCs, technical personnel could access a database from a remote location to enter and retrieve data and to generate their own reports as requested by workers or managers. In the 1990s, database management packages such as Microsoft Access and Corel Paradox became available for PCs, allowing any user to create his or her own databases and generate customized reports. Today, distributed, mainframe-, mini computer–, and PC-based database applications are used by most public agencies, both large and small.

Over the past several years database technology has expanded into two new and powerful—and sometimes controversial—technologies: data warehousing and data mining. A data warehouse is a special database containing data from inside and outside of the organization. Using specialized data-mining software, patterns in the data can be mined to discover associations that no one could anticipate in advance. For this reason, data mining has become known as knowledge discovery in databases (KDD).[2] Both technologies have become controversial because they have the potential to violate the privacy rights of public employees and citizens.

The first part of this chapter will deal with some database basics. We will not get very technical because database technology is complex and is the domain of highly trained specialists. The second section will discuss database management systems, the often-complex software programs that manage the data in databases. The third section will discuss the important role that database managers and data administrators play in public agencies, especially as they interface with end users and managers. The fourth section will focus on data warehousing and data mining. The fifth section will address the privacy issues arising from public and private data-mining efforts.

Database Basics

A database (DB) is a collection of data stored in such a way that a computer program called a database management system (DBMS) can quickly extract desired pieces of data and present them to a user in a report form that makes the data meaningful to the user.[3] This section will introduce the following basics that underlie the development and operation of databases and database management systems: the building blocks of databases, data models, query languages and report generators, data dictionaries, data manipulation languages, centralized and decentralized database structures, and database machines. This brief introduction to the technology of databases will help to explain why they need to be managed by professionals educated and trained in database management.

The Building Blocks of a Database

Traditional databases are organized by characters, fields, records, and files. A character consists of a single alphabetic, numeric, or other symbol, such as the number "2." A field is a single piece of data about some entity such as a person, place, object, or event comprising related characters such as a person's name or date of birth. A record is one complete set of related fields such as a person's name, date of birth, sex, and Social Security number. A file is a collection of records such as all the names, dates of birth, sex, and Social Security numbers of a relevant group of people. The generic example that is frequently used to illustrate the logic of a database is a telephone book. The phone book represents the file that contains a list of records, each of which consists of three fields: a name, an address, and a telephone number, each of which represents a unique character.

A phone book represents a file that contains many records. Each record refers to a person. The attributes of that person are called fields. The fields would be the person's name, address, and telephone number, each of which represents a unique character. Each field comprises bits and bytes. A bit, which stands for *binary digit*, is the smallest unit of data in a computer, represented by 1s and 0s. A byte, which stands for *binary term*, is a collection of bits that can represent a single character such as a letter or a number. For example, "01001010" is a collection of bits into a single byte that stands for the letter *J*. In this example, each letter of a person's name would be a byte; each number in a person's address as well as each letter in the name of the street would also be a byte composed of a collection of bits, and each of the numbers in the person's telephone number would represent individual bytes composed of a series of bits.

Does this sound complicated? Well, it is for most people, except for the computer scientists who devised this way of representing data in a computer and the programmers who write the code that stores the data. Fortunately for end users of computers, all of this processing goes on behind a user-friendly graphical interface, and public agencies have specialists on hand who know how to manage data at this fundamental level.

Data Models

In a database environment, four basic types of data models are used to logically represent the structure of the database: the hierarchical model, the network model, the relational model, and the object model. The term *model* is used to represent the logical view of the database, not its actual physical structure. The user or programmer does not really need to know about the actual physical structure of a database, that is, where the data are actually physically located, but he or she does need to know about the database's logical representation because each mode offers advantages and disadvantages.

The first databases were built for mainframes. They used a hierarchical data model structured like a tree that presented a one-to-many relationship among the records. An analogy would be a family tree with the senior parent as the top record and numerous children who have grandchildren, all of whom would be subsequent records arranged in a hierarchy. In early mainframe applications, such data models were fast and highly efficient in generating routine, prespecified reports, but they became difficult to work with when lower records needed to be associated with one another. In that case, the system had to move down the hierarchy and back up again to associate lower-order records with one another, slowing down the speed of report generation. While fast and efficient in handling prespecified reports for routine types of transactions, the hierarchical model does not handle ad hoc requests very well. Modifying the structure of a hierarchical model to create new reports is also difficult, requiring considerable sophisticated programming.

The network model emerged from the hierarchical mode as a more flexible alternative. Instead of featuring the one-to-many parent-child relationships, the network model allows each record to have many parent and child relationships, forming a many-to-many relationship that resembles a lattice structure. This structure made generating predefined reports easier and faster. On the downside, however, the many-to-many structures make this model more complex to use. Data can be retrieved only using predefined relationships in the network, making ad hoc reporting difficult. This model also requires complex programming.

Today, many database models are relational.[4] A relational database stores data in tables, which are composed of columns and rows. Each column in the table represents a field and each row in the table represents a record. A field is a single item of information about a person, place, or thing. A record is a group of related fields that contain all of the information about a person, place, or thing. A table is a group of related records, and each record contains the same fields.

To understand the functioning of relational databases in greater detail, consider the following example of an inventory database. Recall that relational databases store data in tables composed of columns and rows. Each table in the database is used to store information about a particular entity, or type of "thing." For instance, in an inventory database there would be a table that describes Customers, a table that describes Products, a table that describes Orders, and a table that describes Suppliers.

One of the goals of relational database design is to reduce data redundancy. Ideally, information about each customer, product, order, or supplier would appear in the database only once. For instance, instead of repeating the names and addresses of all of the Suppliers over and over in the Products table, a field in the Product record would be reserved for a brief numeric reference to a corresponding record in the Suppliers table. In a very large database, this method saves a great deal of disk space.

The relational model also increases data integrity. In a relational database, a Supplier's address could be updated in just one place, and the change would appear immediately in all queries, screens, and reports. In a hierarchical database, someone would have to open up each of the product files to change the supplier's address. Or else there might be some scheduled program that runs at night to replicate the change throughout the database. If the scheduled process didn't run, or if the supplier's name were misspelled in some of the files, then the database would contain conflicting information about the Supplier in various files, violating data integrity and producing inconsistent queries and reports. In this example, one piece of inconsistent data could lead to problems such as invoices that don't add up right, payments that are delayed, and/or shipping manifests with inaccurate product counts. This problem would be very difficult to find and resolve.

Relational databases offer quick and easy retrieval of information using a structured query language (SQL). The major advantages of relational databases over the other models are that they provide considerable flexibility in handling ad hoc information requests, they are easier for programmers to work with, and in a PC environment end users can use these databases with little training and effort. On the downside, relational databases cannot handle large amounts of transactions as quickly or efficiently as the hierarchical and network models. For example, an academic department in a public university setting might maintain a small database on its students using Microsoft Access, but the university's database on, say, 25,000 students is probably maintained in a network or hierarchical database on a mainframe or a mini computer.

The object-oriented database model is relatively new and is gaining in popularity because of the expansion of the Internet and web-based technologies, especially multimedia applications.[5] In this model the data describing the attributes of an entity are encapsulated into an "object" that also contains the programming operations that can be performed on the data. This structure allows the model to handle very complex types of data such as graphics, text, and audio. This ability is its major advantage over the other data models, but only for very specialized multimedia or graphical applications.

Centralized and Distributed Databases

In mainframe, mini, and networked applications, databases can be centralized or distributed. A centralized database is one in which all of an agency's relevant data are contained in a single, centrally located database. Early on, managers would have to request the generation of reports from the IT staff. As technology developed with terminals, workstations, and PCs connected to the centralized database, staff and managers gained the ability to generate their own reports, which raised a special concern for the IT staff. Rightfully, they did not want end users to compromise the integrity of the data in the database by deleting it, adding to it, or changing it. This concern led to the implementation of many technical controls to maintain the integrity of the data.

Distributed databases emerged with the advent of network and client/server technologies. In this model, data could be distributed across a variety of locations in different but interconnected databases. This method resolved concerns about having to request reports from a central location where there might be a backlog of requests. However, it also introduced further worries about maintaining data integrity, which brought about even more sophisticated technical controls.

Another way to distribute databases is to duplicate the central database at various locations. This method provides personnel at the various locations immediate access to needed data and reports. It also alleviates the IT personnel's fears because if something were to go wrong with the one centralized database, duplicates would be available as backups. This also means, however, that strict controls have to be put into place to make sure that personnel working on the distributed databases maintain the central data standards and definitions. Security also becomes an issue as possibly sensitive data becomes widely distributed. So, security controls need to be implemented.

Database Machines

In large data-rich public organizations one usually finds entire computers dedicated solely to database management functions. Database machines are specially designed computers that hold the actual databases and run only the DBMS and related software. Connected to one or more mainframes or minis via a high-speed channel, database machines are used in large-volume transaction processing environments. Database machines have a large number of DBMS functions built into the hardware and also provide special techniques for accessing the disks containing the databases, such as using multiple processors concurrently for high-speed searches. They can also serve as repositories of data for data warehouses that allow for data mining, a topic that will be subsequently addressed as a major advancement in decision support systems and what some industry people call "Business Intelligence."

Database Management Systems

Databases by themselves are of little use. A database management system (DBMS) is needed to create the database, maintain it, query it, and produce reports. A DBMS usually comes with a suite of software programs for managing the database. These programs include a data definition language (DDL), a data manipulation language (DML), a data dictionary, query languages and report generators, and other utilities. The DDL is used to create and modify data. It also defines the data and the relationships between the data. The DML is used to process and update data. Some of the most popular database management systems are the IBM DB2 and Oracle RDBMS, both designed for mainframes, minis, and networks, and Microsoft Access, designed for personal computers.

Data Dictionaries

All database management systems contain a data dictionary. The dictionary contains a list of all of the files in the database as well as the number of records in each file and the names and types of each file. As such, the data contained in the data dictionary are really metadata, or data about data. The data dictionary does not contain any of the actual data in the database. It simply provides a guide to the data in the database. A data dictionary also includes software that manages the data definitions about the structure, data elements, and other characteristics of an organization's databases. Without this guide, the DBMS cannot access the data in the database. Most database management systems keep the data dictionary hidden from users to prevent them from accidentally destroying its contents.

Structured Query Language and Report Generators

The major advantage of databases and database management systems is the fact that they make getting to the data and generating reports easier and quicker than in a conventional transaction processing environment. Using a database and DBMS requires the use of structured query language (SQL) and report generators. SQLs are also data manipulation languages.

SQL is the standard query language for requesting information from a database. The original version, called SEQUEL (structured English query language), was designed by IBM in 1974 and 1975. SQL was first introduced as a commercial database system in 1979 by Oracle Corporation. SQL is pretty much standardized by the American National Standards Institute (ANSI) and the International Organization for Standardization (ISO), but it does have several variants. More recently, SQLs have been developed to support personal computers networked together in a distributed database system. The SQLs embedded in Microsoft Access and Corel Paradox are invisible to the user because they reside behind a GUI. This structure allows the user to point and click while making a query or generating a report. The user-friendly interface allows most PC-based end users to easily learn to create their own databases and extract their own reports, but in mainframe and mini computer database environments, workers and managers usually still rely on technical personnel such as database managers and database technicians to query the database and generate needed reports.

Most SQLs have report generators associated with them to allow the results of the queries to be presented on screen or in a printed report. Most generators enable users to specify the formats of their reports and the data contained in them. Most also allow users to present the results of their queries in tabular and graphical forms such as histograms, bar charts, and pie charts.

Summary of Databases and Database Management Systems

The preceding discussion of some of the elements of databases and database management systems only scratches the surface of a highly complex set of technologies that rightfully belong only in the hands of expert database managers and data administrators. Before addressing the function of these professionals in public organizations, some of the benefits database management systems offer can be reviewed.

- A DBMS reduces data redundancy. When data reside only in transaction processing systems, they are often duplicated across a variety of applications, leading to redundancy. Storing the data in a database in a single location reduces that redundancy.
- A DBMS offers data independence. The data are located in the database where they can be accessed by other applications. Changes to the data in the database can be made without affecting the programs that access the data.
- A DBMS integrates data from multiple files. Through data modeling the relationship between data elements can be prespecified, allowing for a logical, not physical, view of the data.
- A DBMS retrieves data rapidly. The logical relationships and query languages allow data to be retrieved quickly, often in seconds or minutes instead of hours or days as when using conventional programming languages like COBOL or C.
- A DBMS improves security. With the data residing in one place, controls for protecting the data can be put into place more easily.

- A DBMS supports operational and analytical activities. Reports can be extracted from databases much more easily than from transaction processing systems. This capability facilitates the day-to-day operations of an agency and allows agencies to analyze their data in different ways.

Database Managers and Data Administrators

Most large public agencies have several database managers and one or perhaps more data administrators. Both types of IS professionals have become essential in public organizations because of their specialized knowledge and expertise.

Simply put, database managers manage databases. They usually manage several databases that support an agency's functioning. In large public agencies one might find a financial database manager, a personnel database manager, an operations database manager, and so on, depending on how many unique databases exist in the organization. These people are responsible for data modeling, developing and maintaining data dictionaries, selecting and using SQLs, maintaining databases, and managing centralized and distributed databases. While the term "manager" is used in the job title of the database manager, the actual job of the database manager is primarily technical in nature.

In contrast, the database administrator is usually a high-level executive who is responsible for such things as establishing and enforcing policies and procedures for managing data as a strategic resource; collecting, storing, and disseminating data in standardized formats; implementing a data-planning activity for the agency; developing policies and setting standards for agency database design, maintenance, and security; and selecting database management software and data dictionary software.[6] Thus the job of a data administrator is to manage the organization's data so that it is timely, accurate, relevant, and not redundant. They are analogous to inventory managers who deliver the right parts in a timely fashion.

Data administration has become a crucial function of most public agencies. Actually, it is more than just a mere function: It has become a philosophy or outlook on the management of data as an organizational resource. As an example, the following is the Arizona State University's official statement concerning the role of the data administration for the institution:

> Data Administration is the process of managing the institutional data in order to provide reliable, accurate, secure and accessible data to meet strategic and management needs at all levels of the enterprise. It is the purpose of this process to improve the accuracy, reliability, and security of the institution's data; reduce data redundancy; provide ease of access, assuring that data are

easily located, accessible once located, and clearly defined; and to provide data standards. It is also the purpose of the Data Administration function to educate the user community on institutional data policies and to encourage the responsible use of data.[7]

This statement reflects the importance of data administration to this public university.

Many other public institutions and agencies have embraced similar positions on data administration, recognizing that data are a vital organizational resource. Consider the scope of data administration depicted in the "Purposes and Principles of Data Administration" at the Forest Service of British Columbia, Canada, presented in Exhibit 4.1. The Forest Service's statement of the data administration purposes and principles ends with the following observation about the importance of data: "Information is intrinsic to the business requirements of the ministry and is thus an important corporate resource. The quality and reliability of ministry data must meet basic standards or continually be improved, so that appropriate decisions can be made based on verifiable information."[8] These statements clearly indicate that data administration is not simply a business function. It is a philosophy about how an organization's data should be strategically administered.

Note also that the language of the corporate world has crept into the vocabulary of public management information systems with such phrases as "business requirements" and "marketing." One can speculate that in Canada this reflects themes from the New Public Management movement. Similar corporate language also appears in the policies and procedures of public agencies in the United States, partly because of the New Public Management movement and partly because of political pressure to make government run more efficiently and effectively, supposedly like the private sector.

Data Warehouses and Data Mining

As database technologies developed and databases got larger and larger, the concepts and practical applications of data warehouses and data mining emerged. Data warehouses hold large amounts of an agency's historical data drawn from the agency's databases and transaction processing systems. If the amount of data is extremely large, the data are broken down into unique data marts within the data warehouse. For example, a large social service agency might maintain a data warehouse comprising a variety of data marts representing different programs like Food Stamps or Title XX or Child Protective Services. Usually the data marts reflect the various functions or programs of an agency.

Exhibit 4.1
Purposes and Principles of Data Administration

Data Administration Purposes

- Increase the ministry's ability to exploit information so that it can better meet its business objectives.
- Promote an integrated view of the business by providing a vision for the totality of the data resource.
- Help the ministry identify its future information needs.
- Keep the sense of perspective about data on the business, not on technology or automation.

Data Administration Principles

- Manage ministry data as a corporate resource.
- Model the inherent logic in ministry data structures and make the models available to ministry staff.
- Communicate through standard message protocols (e.g., standard codes, standard data names, standard metadata structures, etc).
- Identify future issues so that any required data structure changes can be planned for well ahead of emergency situations.
- Coordinate shareable data and related application system components across the ministry.
- Promote data sharing and integration across the ministry.
- Market information as a vital resource for all areas of the ministry, and market the management of information as an essential and worthwhile effort by all staff.

With the introduction of a special technology called Online Analytical Programming (OLAP) in the mid-1990s, the data in a data warehouse can be analyzed very quickly, much more quickly than in a normal database, because the data in the warehouse is structured for analysis, not report writing.[9] The difference will become evident soon. Microsoft, IBM, SAP, and SAS Institute are among the major providers of OLAP applications.

Data warehouses and OLAP allow for data mining. Data mining has been defined as, "The nontrivial extraction of implicit, previously unknown, and potentially useful information from data."[10] It involves the discovery of previously unknown patterns in large data sets using statistical analysis tools and artificial intelligence. Data-mining software is one of a number of analytical tools for analyzing data. It allows users to analyze data from many different dimensions or angles, categorize it, and summarize the relationships identified. Technically, data mining is the process of finding correlations or patterns among dozens of fields in large relational databases.

The private sector has been using data mining for some time now to discover things about their customers. For example *Time Magazine*[11] reports that

- A credit card company using a system designed by Teradata, a division of NCR, found that customers who fill out applications in pencil rather than pen are more likely to default.
- A major hotel chain discovered that guests who opted for X-rated flicks spent more money and were less likely to make demands on the hotel staff. . . . These low-maintenance customers were rewarded with special frequent-traveler promotions.
- Victoria's Secret stopped uniformly stocking its stores once MicroStrategy showed that the chain sold twenty times as many size-32 bras in New York City as in other cities and that in Miami ivory was ten times as popular as black.

While large-scale information technology has been evolving separate transaction systems and analytical systems such as decision support systems and executive information systems, data mining provides the link between the two. Data-mining software analyzes relationships and patterns in stored transaction data based on open-ended user queries. Several types of analytical software are available: statistical, machine learning, and neural networks.

Generally, any of four types of relationships are sought:

- Classes: Stored data are used to locate data in predetermined groups. For example, a restaurant chain could mine customer-purchase data to determine when customers visit and what they typically order. This information could be used to increase traffic by having daily specials.
- Clusters: Data items are grouped according to logical relationships or consumer preferences. For example, data can be mined to identify market segments or consumer affinities.
- Associations: Data can be mined to identify associations. For example, people who buy imported wine are likely to also buy imported beer.
- Sequential patterns: Data are mined to anticipate behavior patterns and trends. For example, an outdoor equipment retailer could predict the likelihood of a backpack being purchased based on a consumer's purchase of sleeping bags and hiking shoes.

The federal government is becoming heavily involved in data-mining activities. A 2004 report from the Government Accountability Office (GAO) found a widespread use of data mining in the federal government.[12] Their survey of 128 federal departments and agencies showed that 52 are using or are planning to use data mining. A total of 199 data-mining efforts were reported; 68 were planned and 131 were operational. The data-mining efforts are used to improve service or performance; detect fraud, waste, and abuse; analyze scientific and research information; manage human resources; detect criminal activities or patterns; and analyze intelligence and detect terrorist activities. Among the agencies and departments that have data-mining efforts underway are the Departments of Defense, Homeland Security, Justice, and Education, and the National Aeronautics and Space Administration.

Some examples of how federal agencies are using data mining to enhance decision making and improve the performance of government follow: The Department of State uses data mining to detect fraudulent use of government credit cards among its employees. The Internal Revenue Service uses data mining to distinguish between criminal tax evaders and those who simply make errors on their returns. The Department of Agriculture uses data mining to uncover fraudulent crop-loss claims. The Marine Corps uses data mining to predict turnover in its uniformed personnel. The Navy uses data mining to determine the appropriate number of training personnel available. The Navy also maintains a data warehouse on all parts for all of its ships to predict failure rates and reduce downtime on ships. The Department of Education maintains a data warehouse that keeps track of legitimate and fraudulent Pell Grant payments. The Department of Health and Human Services has built a data warehouse to keep track of the nation's blood supply and to watch out for potential blood supply shortages. The U.S. Marshals Service maintains a data warehouse that it mined to determine appropriate workforce levels. The list of data warehousing and data-mining activities of federal agencies goes on and on.

State and local governments are also turning to data warehousing and data-mining technologies. As early as 1995, the State of Massachusetts began building a centralized data warehouse. Executives faced the challenge of not being able to analyze data across a host of legacy systems designed only for transaction processing and periodic report generation. Now up-to-date information is fed into the data warehouse from the state's accounting, payroll, cost reporting, and budgeting systems, allowing analysts to investigate cross-organizational issues and compare program finance inputs with program service outcomes.[13] Iowa is also considered a leader in data warehousing. Instead of having several data warehouses serving the needs of individual agencies, Iowa decided to create a centralized data warehouse to serve all state agency needs for analytical, query, and decision support systems. That warehouse was mined in 2002 to collect more than $20 million in unpaid taxes, representing a 673 percent return on investment.[14] In New York City, the Department of Criminal and Juvenile Planning used a data warehouse to reduce its annual analytical query costs from $215,000 to just $2,690.[15]

Quite a few other municipalities and states are also turning to data warehousing and data mining to do sophisticated analyses and queries for a variety of programs and applications. As one observer put it:

> Often residents receive services—such as food stamps, subsidized childcare and mental health counseling—from multiple agencies and programs, but few local governments are aware of the redundancy. That is because each department or agency collects information in its own computer system and does not share or compare information with other departments. As a result, a single client or family may be receiving overlapping services from multiple agencies or departments at a high cost to the city or county.
>
> Creating a data warehouse can help determine exactly how many residents are receiving services, how much overlap exists in agency client bases and how many agencies are assisting each person or family. That type of information can help caseworkers provide better service to clients. Also, it can help managers design better programs and allocate resources based on an accurate picture of the client population and needs. A data warehouse also can be instrumental in detecting cases of fraud and abuse.[16]

Unfortunately, there is no central clearinghouse, governmental body, or other organization that keeps tabs on what the states and localities are doing in terms of using data warehouses and data mining to enhance what has become known as "Business Intelligence" within the IT industry.

Privacy Issues

Data mining by either public or private organizations raises serious questions about a citizen's right to personal privacy. The GAO report on federal data-mining efforts noted that some of those efforts involved the warehousing of and mining for personal information. For example, the report states that

> Agencies also identified efforts to mine data from the private sector and data from other federal agencies, both of which could include personal information. Of 54 efforts to mine data from the private sector (such as credit reports or credit card transactions), 36 involve personal information. Of 77 efforts to mine data from other federal agencies, 46 involve personal information (including student loan application data, bank account numbers, credit card information, and taxpayer identification numbers).[17]

The report did not, however, make any mention of any possible legal or ethical implications of mining for personal data of citizens.

Privacy advocacy groups such as the Electronic Privacy Information Center (EPIC) have raised serious questions about the ethical and legal implications of government agencies collecting personal information about citizens and what those agencies might do with that information.[18] Nowhere has this been more evident than in the uproar a few years ago around the Defense Department's Total Information Awareness (TIA) program. TIA was a program of the Information Awareness Office (IAO) of the Defense Advanced Research Projects Agency (DARPA). As originally conceived, TIA would contain massive amounts of personal information on every person in the United States. This information would have included such things as every purchase a person makes with a credit card, every magazine subscription someone buys, everyone's medical history and prescription purchase, every web site that a person visited and all e-mail sent or received, every academic grade a person received, every bank deposit made, every trip a person might book, and every event a person might attend. What is at issue here, according to opponents of TIA, is that the program would be a major violation of U.S. citizens' Fourth Amendment rights under the U.S. Constitution. Opponents felt that TIA would lead to unreasonable searches of private information without probable cause. Pentagon officials apparently felt differently.[19]

The arrogance of some Pentagon officials was shown in at least three ways. First was the very name of the program—Total Information Awareness—which was later changed to Terrorism Information Awareness after the Pentagon received some political heat from the American Civil Liberties Union (ACLU) and EPIC, as well as from several senators and congressional officials. Second, the program was headed by former admiral John Poindexter, who was convicted in 1990 of five felony counts of lying to Congress, destroying official documents, and obstructing congressional inquiries into the Iran-Contra Affair, which involved the secret sale of arms to Iran in the mid-1980s and diversion of profits to help the Contra rebels in Nicaragua. In 1991, that conviction was overturned by an appeals court that determined that Poindexter's right to privacy was violated. Placing someone like Poindexter, whose moral judgment is questionable, in charge of TIA was a red flag for civil liberty and privacy rights groups. Third was the emblem of the program, which featured a creepy eye sitting on top of a pyramid looking over the world. It also contained the motto, "Scientia est Potentia," which is Latin for "Knowledge is Power." Eventually, the emblem was removed from the TIA web site.[20]

Due to political pressure from civil liberty groups, privacy groups, and politicians, funding for TIA was eventually withheld, but federal and state data mining to supposedly combat terrorism lived on in Matrix, which stands for Multistate Anti-Terrorism Information Exchange. It was a pilot project supported by grants from the U.S. Department of Justice and the U.S. Department of Homeland Security that allowed law enforcement agencies in participating states to have access to a database containing a vast amount of data on citizens. Only 2.6 percent of the 1,866,202 queries of the database had anything to do with terrorism or national security. The vast majority of the queries had to do with ordinary crimes. As a pilot, "proof of concept" project, it was terminated in April of 2005.[21]

A *Congressional Research Service Report* to Congress points out two inherent problems with data mining: mission creep and privacy concerns. "Mission creep is one of the leading risks of data mining cited by civil libertarians, and represents how control over one's information can be a tenuous proposition. Mission creep refers to the use of data for purposes other than that for which the data was originally collected. This can occur regardless of whether the data was provided voluntarily by the individual or was collected through other means."[22] A hypothetical case in point would be information collected about a person's medical history that, by virtue of data sharing, which could happen but should not, ultimately prevents that person from obtaining additional life insurance or medical insurance.

As far as privacy issues are concerned, the report notes that observers and experts generally disagree over whether data mining should actually be carried out by the government at all, whether adequate technical controls are in place to ensure the privacy and security of the information that is collected, and whether existing policy and procedure statements are strong enough and clear enough to protect the personal information contained in both public- and private-sector data warehouses. The report goes on to recommend, "As data mining efforts move forward, Congress may consider a variety of questions including, the degree to which government agencies should use and mix commercial data with government data, whether data sources are being used for purposes other than those for which they were originally designed, and the possible application of the Privacy Act to these initiatives."[23]

Despite the demise of TIA and Matrix, privacy groups like the EPIC are still concerned that the federal government is still heavily involved in numerous smaller data-mining surveillance projects. They note heavy increases for surveillance activities in the President's 2006 Budget.[24] The recent GAO report on government data mining confirms that federal agencies are still collecting personal information about citizens. But it is not just the government that is collecting information on citizens. Private firms are in that business, most notably ChoicePoint, which provides government agencies access to large quantities of data on citizens.[25]

Advances in hardware (DBMS machines and computers devoted entirely to data warehouses) and software (OLAP and other software query languages) have greatly enhanced the ability of public workers, managers, and executives to make more accurate and more timely decisions in a wide range of possible application areas. Yet these advances bring serious concerns about the public's right to privacy versus the common good of protecting our citizens from crime and terrorism, proving that technology advances bring forth important issues that require public administrators and political officials to perform delicate balancing acts.

Summary and a Look Forward

This chapter has taken us on a long journey, beginning with the tiniest building blocks of a database to national issues of privacy rights. Along the way, we have seen how public agencies store and manage their data resources for operational and analytical purposes. Databases and database management systems have significantly improved managerial and executive decision making over older transactional processing systems. With the advent of data warehouses and data-mining technologies, decision making has been greatly enhanced at the operational, mid-, and executive levels of public agencies. But with the advent of data-mining technologies comes the potential problem of violating the privacy rights of citizens. While privacy issues are an important public policy issue for citizens, they also become important managerial issues for public agencies. The questions become: What is a public employee's right to privacy in the agency in which he or she works? What policies regarding employee rights to privacy should management establish? These are issues that will be addressed in chapter 9. In the next two chapters, we will be dealing with technical matters as well as managerial and public policy issues related to telecommunications and the Internet, both of which can contribute to privacy concerns because any data that can be transmitted are data that someone else could possibly capture.

5

The Telecommunications Revolution

Many of us have been living through a telecommunications revolution. Not that many years ago there were no cell phones, no cable or satellite television companies offering hundreds of programming channels, no high-definition digital televisions, no global positioning systems, and no Internet. Due in part to the breakup of AT&T (Ma Bell), the telecommunications industry has experienced tremendous growth and competition. This growth has given us a wide range of telecommunications devices for our personal convenience, our entertainment, and our work. If the monopoly had not been broken up, AT&T would have had little incentive to innovate and we might still be using black, corded, rotary-dial, bakelite phones.

Computers and information technology are at the center of this revolution, creating opportunities as well as issues for public administrators and elected officials. This chapter begins with some of the basics of telecommunications technology as it relates to managing information in the public sector. Then it presents examples of some of the challenges public managers face in implementing telecommunications technology in the context of an actual implementation of a network for a school district. The third section addresses some of the current managerial and public policy issues related to the use of telecommunications technology in government.

The Basics of Telecommunications

Telecommunications is both simple and complex. Its simplicity is evident in the basic definition of telecommunication as merely the transmission of data from one point to another for the purpose of communication.[1] Its complexity arises from the types of data that are transmitted (e.g., voice or video) and the media used to move the data (e.g., copper wire, coaxial cable, fiber optic cable, radio waves, or satellite signals). The basic elements include telephones, cellular phones, telecommunications media, and types of networks, network processors, protocols, servers, and network typologies.

Telephones

The most common telecommunications technology in use in government today is the simple telephone, but telephony technology is far from being simple.[2] Most public agencies at whatever level of government use Private Branch Exchange (PBX) technology. PBX harkens back to the days when operators would manually plug phone cables into sockets to connect two parties together on a phone line, allowing the parties to have a conversation. In those days it was called a Private Manual Branch Exchange (PMBX); this was soon replaced with electronic switching systems called Private Automatic Branch Exchange (PABX). Today it is simply called a PBX.

Both public and private organizations still use PBX technology because it is cheaper to own the phones, wiring, and switching devices. This setup avoids the high cost of having each phone in an agency directly connected to a common carrier like a local telephone company. It also allows users to dial extension numbers instead of full phone numbers to connect with another party inside of the same building or group of buildings. This capability avoids the toll charges that would be associated with having each phone connected directly to an outside common carrier or telephone company, only to be routed back into the agency again.

Agencies that have multiple physical sites or locations can connect their internal PBX systems together using what are called "trunk lines," which can be owned by the agency or leased from a common carrier like the local phone company. The latter case is called a Centrex system, in which a local phone company handles the routing and switching of calls at a central exchange (hence Centrex) separate from the agency. Trunk lines are also provided by common carriers to call numbers outside of the agency's PBX, usually by first dialing a "9" or some other number to get an outside line. They are called "trunk lines" because they carry many separate phone lines within single cables or trunks.

Most of the world is covered by a public switched telephone network (PSTN) system consisting of hundreds of thousands of circuit-switched networks owned by thousands of telephone companies. A circuit-switched network consists of a dedicated communications channel between two nodes, which allows for a physical electrical connection that carries an analog signal. The connection stays open for the entire duration of the call. Early telephones used analog technology in which the sound vibrations of the human voice were turned into electrical vibrations and then transmitted over copper wire and turned back into sound vibrations at the other end.

Today most telephone service is digital; analog sound waves are sampled at some interval and then digitized into 1s and 0s for transmission. For a time, integrated services digital network (ISDN) protocols allowed for the transmission of both voice and data digitally over copper phone lines. Since the late 1980s some phone companies have added digital subscriber line (DSL) capabilities to the public switched network to allow for more digital communication via the use of cable modems for high-speed Internet access. Phone companies have added asymmetric digital subscriber line (ADSL) capability as a form of DSL. It allows for even faster transmission rates for voice and data. Asymmetric means that data can be downloaded much faster than it can be uploaded. Most consumers prefer greater download speeds, allowing them to retrieve such things as files and photographs much more quickly and giving them faster access to web pages.

Digital phone service for both voice and data uses packet switching instead of circuit switching. In packet switching, voice or data is broken up into little packets of data, sometimes called payloads, that also include the addresses for their intended destination. Recall that in circuit switching the connection is open for the entire length of the phone call or data transmission. In packet switching, the transmission line is open only long enough to send some of the packets toward their destination. The speed at which this occurs is so fast that the person on the other end of the line recognizes no distortion in the voice or data. Packet switching optimizes bandwidth—the amount of data carried in a communications line—and allows for multiple connections between parties or hosts at the same time. On the Internet, the packets that make up an e-mail may travel over many different networks until all of them reach their intended destination. Packet switching enhances the speed at which voice and data are transmitted.

It may seem rather mundane to start a discussion of telecommunications technology with a discussion of telephones since they are so ubiquitous and usually not problematic. Nevertheless, since the beginning of the postal service, the Pony Express, and the telegraph, the telephone represents the primary technology for communication in government, and as we shall see, the logical structure of a PBX system is often modeled in more advanced telecommunications technologies. Now we face the biggest advancement in telephone service—the cellular phone.

Cellular Phones

Since the 1980s the popularity of cellular phones has increased tremendously, so much so that people are giving up their landlines in favor of cell phones. In some European and Asian nations as many as 90 percent of people use cell phones; in the United States about 50 percent of the population uses cell phones, but the number of new users is growing rapidly, especially in the thirteen- to seventeen-year-old age group.[3] While they are personally convenient, they also have their applications in government and business as well, as we will see in the third section of this chapter.

Cellular phones are a prime example of what is known as a disruptive technology.[4] A disruptive technology is a new innovation in a technology or service that replaces an existing technology that once dominated a market. A disruptive technology usually begins by filling a void in an existing market (e.g., mobile cellular communication) that an older technology (e.g., landline phones) cannot. Another example would be digital photography, which is replacing traditional chemical-based film photography. Cellular phones are disruptive because they are replacing landlines. They are also disruptive because they are placing new demands on governments and industry, as we shall see later.

Cell phones rely on computer technology.[5] They contain their own microprocessors to handle keyboard functions and visual displays, their own operating systems to enable cell phone functioning, and their own read-only memory (ROM) to store data such as phone numbers, notes, and reminders. Some models also take pictures, connect to the Internet, provide e-mail access, offer text messaging, allow web surfing, play music (MP3 players), contain gaming features, and offer global positioning satellite functioning. With the addition of more features and functionality, cell phone technology has generated a new name for what was originally a simple communications device, namely a personal digital assistant (PDA), which has many of the functions of a personal computer but in a handheld size. In fact, a variety of handheld devices such as Blackberrys are the personal computers of choice among many public employees, especially those who work in the field—and as many as 40 percent of state and local government employees work in the field.[6]

Technically, cell phones are actually radios. They use radio wave technology to send and receive sounds in much the same way as a radio receives signals and broadcasts them as sounds through a speaker. Cell phones originally used analog technology. Analog signals are continuously variable, and fluctuations in the signal carry meaningful data from one point to another. Cell phone manufacturers and service providers are converting to digital signals because analog signals cannot be easily compressed. Converting an analog voice signal into the 1s and 0s of binary digits and compressing it allows for more voice signals to be carried over telecommunications media.

Telecommunications Media

Landline telephones and cellular phones require media to transmit voice and data. Telecommunications media may be bounded or unbounded. *Bounded* implies a physical wired connection between devices. *Unbounded* means wireless communication. Both types of media are common in government.[7]

Bounded Media

There are three forms of bounded media: twisted pair, coaxial cable, and fiber optic cable. Twisted pair refers to conventional copper telephone wires, consisting of two wires twisted together and wrapped in a rubber or plastic cover in order to shield out electromagnetic interference. This form is the oldest and still most widely used telecommunications media for both voice and data because it is cheap to acquire and install. Unfortunately, this type of media is limited in the amount of data it can carry, suffers from electrical interference, and offers little security. It provides the slowest speed of data transfer at 56 kilobytes per second (56Kps) when connected to a modem. Yet twisted pair remains the media of choice for most public agencies for normal phone service in wiring offices in single buildings because it is inexpensive.

Coaxial cable uses copper or aluminum wire that is insulated to minimize interference and distortion. It can carry a much larger volume of data faster, about 100 Mbps (million bits per second), which is equivalent to over 1,800 voice calls at once. It allows for high-speed transmission and is often used in offices and local area networks (to be discussed in the next section). It can be laid underground and is not affected by water. Coaxial cable is, however, more expensive than twisted pair. It is a favorite medium for networks within a single building or among closely adjoining buildings.

Fiber optic cable uses many very fine filaments of glass, as thin as a human hair, wrapped in a protective jacket. Signals are converted to light form and fired by lasers in bursts. Fiber optic cable is more expensive than twisted pair and only slightly more expensive than coaxial cable. The major advantage to fiber optic cable is that it can transmit both digital and analog signals, increasing communication ability and capacity at data transmission speed reaching into the gigabyte range. It does not suffer from electrical interference and has a much lower error rate. It is also extremely secure because attempts to tap into the cable can be detected easily. On the downside, it is much more expensive than twisted pair, installation is difficult because it requires splicing the cables together to make a connection, and it requires additional expensive communications equipment.

During the early 1970s, the U.S. military moved quickly to implement fiber optic communications to support strategic and tactical maneuvers. During the 1980s, telephone companies began to implement fiber optic trunks nationally. Today, most of the United States and the rest of the modern world are wired in fiber optic cable for phone service, except for many instances where copper wire still enters homes and offices from a junction box located outside on the street. The world's transcontinental long-distance phone service is supported in large part by fiber optic cables running under the oceans, avoiding the poor quality of voice transmission formerly provided by satellite technology.

Unbounded Media

Unbounded media for wireless communication can include microwave radio signals, communication satellites, cellular phones, high-frequency radios, and wireless local area networks. Microwave signals are transmitted through the air as high-speed radio waves in a single line-of-sight direction between relay stations. Because microwave signals do not bend around the curvature of the earth, they must be relayed to microwave stations about every thirty miles. They do offer high-volume voice and data transmission.

Satellites can beam voice and data from the earth to an orbiting satellite, from satellite to satellite, and back again. They allow for high-volume and long-distance transmission of data and voice and can be quite cost effective when moving a large amount of data over long distances. On the downside, putting satellites into orbit is expensive and the signals can be subjected to interference by solar activity and weather conditions. Also, satellite transmissions are insecure: Anyone with the right equipment can listen in. For this reason, the U.S. military and the militaries of other nations prefer fiber optic cable.

Radio waves allow cellular phones to communicate data, voice, and images. The term *cell* comes from the fact that small geographic locations of only a few square miles are isolated into a cell. Each cell has its own transmission tower and relay devices. Since the early 1980s, mobile phone networks have spread rapidly throughout the world. Their establishment costs are low compared to traditional wired telephones. They form the basis for a variety of mobile technologies. As noted, cell phones were originally analog. Today more and more service providers are switching to digital transmission, which makes the voice quality of cell phones much clearer and crisper.

Wireless local area networks (WLANs) utilize high-frequency radio waves as an alternative to wired local area networks (LANs).[8] WLANs transmit and receive data over the air, without the use of any cable, combining the benefits of data connectivity and user mobility. Installation is fast and easy, eliminating the need to run coax or fiber through walls. Their range is limited to several hundred square feet. They are excellent for home or office applications because desktop and notebook mini computers do not need to be wired to a printer or a modem, allowing for greater mobility within an office or home setting. WLANs are essentially similar to personal area networks (PANs), which will be discussed next as a type of network.

Types of Networks

Telecommunications networks have been traditionally classified by size from local area networks, metropolitan area networks, wide area networks, and more recently personal area networks.[9] There is, of course, the biggest network (or network of networks) in the world—the Internet—which will be the topic of the next chapter. A local area network (LAN) can cover a building or a group of buildings. A larger network, called a metropolitan area network (MAN), obviously extends the size of the network to a city or perhaps a university campus. A MAN usually uses coaxial cable, fiber optic cable, or wireless technology for communications.

Then there is the wide area network, or WAN, which covers a wide geographical area. WANs can be used to connect LANs together. They can be built for a particular organization using leased telephone lines and are, therefore, private. Telephone companies and Internet service providers such as Cox Cable and Time Warner offer cable connection to support WANs, making the data transfer faster because cable can carry more data more quickly than telephone lines can.

Most recently, personal area networks (PANs) have become available. These networks link personal computers to printers and other output devices like projectors and screens and to input devices such as personal digital assistants (PDAs). They can also provide access to the Internet. PANs are usually found in the home, but they can also be used in an office. PANs are very similar to WLANs, discussed earlier. The major difference between the two is that a PAN serves the telecommunications needs of one person in a single geographic area, like an office or a home, while WLANs can serve many people in a building or group of buildings. Many public, as well as private, universities are adopting WLAN technology so students, faculty, and staff do not have to search for a place to plug in their notebook computers for access to the Internet or university computing services.

Network Processors

A variety of devices process data on a network. The most obvious one is a modem. A modem, short for modulator-demodulator, is a device that enables a computer to transmit data over telephone or cable lines. It converts analog waves into digital impulses and back again.

In addition to the modem is the multiplexer, which allows multiple simultaneous transmissions of data through a single communication channel terminal. At one end of the channel, a multiplexer merges the data from several terminals into one transmission. At the other end, a multiplexer receives the merged transmission and then separates the individual transmissions. Frequently a multiplexer and de-multiplexer are combined into a single unit capable of processing both outgoing and incoming signals.

Then there are switchers, routers, hubs, and gateways. A switch is simply a processor that makes the connection between telecommunications circuits in a network. A router is a processor that connects networks based on different rules or protocols so that a message can be sent to its proper destination. A hub is a switching device that allows servers, printers, workstations, and personal computers to access a network and share its resources. A gateway is a special type of processor that connects networks that use different protocols. It can translate data from one protocol to another, ensuring interoperability.

Protocols

Protocols are agreed-upon formats for transmitting data between two devices, usually written in an application programming language or "hard wired" in a hardware device.[10] The protocol determines how the data will be represented, authenticates the data, performs error checking, compresses data, and signals the beginning and end of a message. Protocols also determine whether transmission will be synchronous or asynchronous, and whether data will be transmitted in half-duplex or full-duplex mode.

In synchronous transmission, data moves in a constant, steady stream. In asynchronous transmission, data moves intermittently. By analogy, two people can talk at the same time in a phone conversation. This is asynchronous transmission. In synchronous transmission, the first party would have to wait for the other party to finish speaking before the first party could speak.

The difference between full-duplex and half-duplex transmission is similar. Full-duplex transmission allows data to be transmitted in both directions at once. Half-duplex transmission allows data to be transmitted in only one direction at a time. By analogy, full-duplex is like a telephone conversation where two people can talk and be heard at the same time, while half-duplex is like a walkie-talkie conversation where only one person can speak at a time. A variety of standard protocols are available. Selection of a compatible set of protocols is essential; otherwise, data will not be transmitted. Unfortunately, because of different protocols some devices cannot be connected to share data. Furthermore, because of a lack of industry standardization of hardware, software, and communication devices, incompatibility problems often arise in communications networks. The goal of most communication protocols is standardization—one of the reasons why network administrators are vitally important in any public agency.

Fortunately, the telecommunications industry provides several standard protocols from which to choose. Transmission Control Protocol (TCP) coupled with Internet Protocol (IP) have become the standard for Internet connections. TCP allows two computers to make a connection and exchange data and makes sure that the data gets to its intended destination on the network. IP controls the packets of data that are transmitted on a network under the control of TCP. Both TCP and IP have been configured to work with Ethernet.

Ethernet is a local area network protocol that was developed in the late 1970s by Xerox, Digital Equipment Company (DEC), and Intel.[11] It is commonly used on bus or star network typologies (see the next section). In early and present basic common configurations it can support the transmission of data at 10 million bites per second (10 Mbps). It has become such an industry-wide standard for connecting devices to a computer that it is almost always built into the motherboard of desktop and notebook personal computers under the name of Network Interface Card, or NIC. Advanced versions of Ethernet can transfer data at even greater speeds. "Fast Ethernet," also called 100Base-T, can carry 100 Mbps, while Gigabit Ethernet can transfer data at 1 gigabit (1,000 megabits) per second, a considerably high speed.

Servers

Computer networks require the use of servers to carry out a variety of tasks. Servers are computers that are dedicated to handling server tasks. They are called "servers" because they provide a variety of services to clients on a network.[12] For example, *file servers* store files on a network for use by the clients on the network. A *printer server* controls the printers on a network. A *database server* is a computer that allows client access to a database on a network. *Web servers* provide access to web pages on a network or on the Internet using hypertext transfer protocol (HTTP), the standard protocol for using the World Wide Web. *Mail servers* keep track of e-mails on a network, directing them to their proper destination. *File transfer protocol* (FTP) *servers* control the movement of files on a network or on the Internet. Other types of servers carry out various other unique tasks.

Proxy servers are a special class of server. A proxy server stands between a real server and a client application. Its job is to intercept all of the requests to the real server and try to fulfill those requests if it can. If it cannot, it sends the request to the real server. This setup improves the performance of a network by saving common and repeated requests from clients. For example, within an agency's e-mail system, a proxy server may collect and hold all requests for the client's e-mail server, thereby taking the workload off of the main server and speeding up access to e-mail. Proxy servers are also used to filter or block clients from accessing certain web pages on the Internet.

Figure 5.1 **Bus Network**

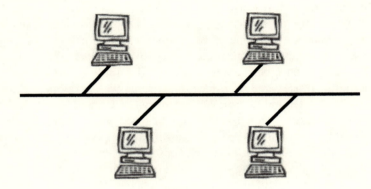

Network Typologies

A variety of network typologies is available to implement telecommunications architectures, each with its own advantages and disadvantages.[13] A network typology refers to the way in which computers and other devices are wired together. Five basic typology configurations are used: bus, ring, star, tree, and mesh.

In a bus network all of the computers and other devices are connected to a single line (copper wire, cable, or fiber). All data travel along this single bus line as if it were a public transportation bus. (See Figure 5.1.) This configuration contains no host computer or file server. It tends to be an inexpensive installation, and if one of the computers fails, the other computers will continue to operate individually, but if there is a break in the cable the entire network will go down. The computers on the network will no longer be able to share data or applications. For example, if something happens to the cable that goes to the centralized printer, none of the computers on the office bus network will be able to submit print jobs to the central printer.

A star configuration features a central unit that is linked to an array of other computers and devices. (See Figure 5.2.) The central unit can be a mainframe or a mini, or even a high-powered micro, that can serve as a file server in client/server architecture. This configuration is popular in large organizations with centralized data-processing operations.

Many users can access the central unit at the same time. The major disadvantage of the star configuration is that if the central unit goes down, the entire network fails to operate and all communications stops. Another disadvantage is the high cost of the cabling to link the nodes to the central unit. An advantage, however, is that if one of the computers attached to the central node of

Figure 5.2 **Star Network**

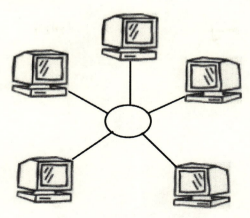

the star goes down, the rest of the computers or other devices attached to the central machine will continue to function normally.

Client/server technology was a major breakthrough in the management of information. It allows a powerful central computer to act as a controller and a server upon which application software and data files can reside. Client computers can call upon the server when an application or data file is needed. The server sends it to the client where the user can work with it to meet the user's needs. This means that a person sitting at a client can have access to a centralized database as well as the application software to work with the database. The database and the often-expensive application software do not have to be duplicated on all of the client computers in an agency, thus significantly reducing costs. The client/server model that came with star network configurations became the paradigm for distributed computing.

The ring network is more like a bus network, except the transmission medium (copper wire, coaxial cable, or fiber optics) is formed to make a loop. Computers and other devices are tied together in a ring, making this a decentralized approach to configuration. (See Figure 5.3.) The ring network is usually more reliable than a star network because if one computer goes down, the other computers can continue to function. They can also continue to share data and communicate with one another along the network, bypassing the malfunctioning computer if the ring network is wired to do so. If it is not so wired, and one computer goes down, the entire network goes down. Individual computers may continue to operate on their own but they will not be able to share data or applications.

The tree typology combines the bus and star typologies. (See Figure 5.4.) A switch controls an array of other computers and connects them to the bus,

Figure 5.3   **Ring Network**

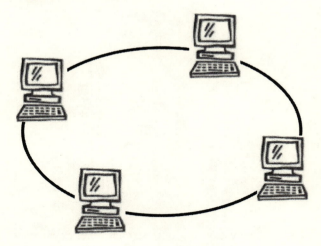

Figure 5.4   **Tree Network**

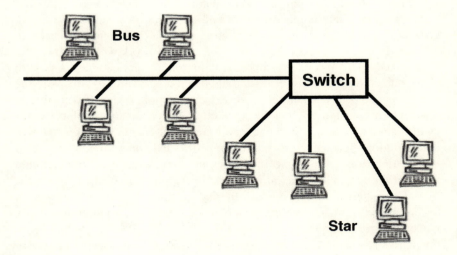

and one of the computers serves as a file server. This configuration is popular on college and university campuses where computer labs represent the tree branch that is connected to the main bus via a switching device. Students can work locally in the labs on a variety of tasks such as word processing and then connect to the university's bus line to gain access to the library, the Internet, or other university computing services such as e-mail.

Figure 5.5 **Mesh Network**

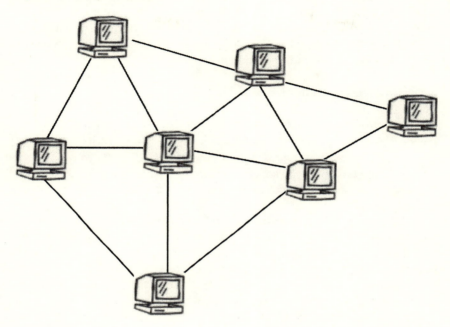

Mesh typology uses lots of cables to connect every computer or device with every other computer or device. (See Figure 5.5.) It is expensive to wire up, but if any cable fails, there are many other ways for the other computers or devices to communicate with each other. The cabling can be expensive because there is so much of it, but it is a very reliable configuration. Indeed, as we will see in the next chapter, the Internet was set up in much the same way, at least logically, so that computers in a nationwide or global network could continue to communicate with one another even in the event of a nuclear war.

Telecommunications Applications in Government: An Example

How do public agencies use telecommunications? This is a simple and rather obvious question with somewhat complicated answers. An immediate response might be, "Well, of course they use telephones" or "Well, they use e-mail." Of course they do, but what kind of telephones? Wired or wireless? How do they use e-mail? Do they use America Online? Some small agencies do. Do they use Microsoft Outlook and Outlook Express? Yes, some smaller agencies do. Actually, most large agencies use larger scale e-mail applications such as Lotus Notes because these applications interface well with their existing hardware and software architectures and provide additional features such as notebooks, calendars, and "to do" lists. This is not the place to recount the obvious uses of telecommunications technology in government, but it is a good place to demonstrate how a public agency—a local school district—dealt with telecommunications implementation issues.

A School District's Wide Area Network

A school district in a relatively small town with 2,770 students faced the following technical and managerial challenges.[14] The school district consisted of five schools, the central office for the Board of Education, and a bus garage, representing a total of seven locations spread over several miles. The schools had computer labs for students and computers available for the faculty and staff to use.

Management wanted to establish a wide area network that would connect all seven locations and provide the following services: (1) e-mail communication for faculty, staff, and students; (2) access to the Internet for research purposes; and (3) electronic file sharing as opposed to using paper hard copy. Resources for establishing the network were limited, but funding was expected from federal grants and the city's operating budget.

The first managerial decision they faced had to do with communication media. Fiber optical cable would have been optimal for its high speed and high volume of data transfer except for the fact that it was too expensive to run the cable over the required distances between the seven locations. So, they decided to go with leased lines from a common carrier, a much less expensive option. Although basically a matter of technology requirements, this decision falls appropriately into the managerial realm because of the cost considerations.

The next decision had to do with the choice of a network operating system. Like stand-alone computers, which must have their own operating systems, networks, too, need their own operating systems. Microsoft Windows NT 4 was selected as the server operating system because the technical staff was familiar with it. They could have chosen Novel Netware, the chief rival to Windows NT 4, but the staff was familiar with Windows products. NT 4 is similar to Windows 95 in terms of its graphical interface, but it is primarily designed to run network applications on one or more servers in the network.

Typical of most network configurations, Windows NT was installed on a server, a computer, also known as the Primary Domain Controller (PDC). One of the functions of the PDC was to control access to the network. A database had to be developed containing approved user names and passwords. When someone logged on at a remote location, the authentication of the user went through the central PDC.

Internet access was provided by Microsoft Internet Information Server (ISS), which came packaged with Windows NT. ISS handles all of the protocols necessary to access the Internet and the World Wide Web. Apache, an open source Internet information server, could have been chosen as an alternative, but obviously Microsoft ISS was already at hand.

With Internet access, the managerial issue of monitoring the use of the Internet and controlling what sites can be accessed by the students, teachers, and staff arose. Obviously, the management team wanted to filter out objectionable material such as pornographic web sites as well as web sites offering illegal and legal copies of music files and videos. The legal downloading of music files by the students would severely overload the network given the massive size of those files. A proxy server designed specifically to block access to web sites was installed to handle the filtering.

Next, the issue of selecting communications protocols arose. Fortunately for the school district, these decisions were easy because they chose TCP/IP, which has become an almost universal standard for network and Internet communications, allowing for asynchronous and full-duplex transmissions at relatively high baud rates. In this respect, TCP/IP easily fit the needs of the school district.

Then management turned to issues about e-mail services. Staying within the Microsoft family, they chose Exchange 5.5 for e-mail service and Outlook 98 for the e-mail clients on each computer. Microsoft Exchange Server is a full-featured e-mail server that can be placed on a network. Its primary rival in the marketplace is IBM Lotus Notes/Domino Server. Exchange allows an agency to create its own internal e-mail system without having to go outside of the agency and onto the Internet, although it does allow for contact with the Internet. In this respect, it is analogous to the old and still standard PBX internal telephone system.

This choice of e-mail technology required the school district to adopt standardized protocols for e-mail service, namely, SMTP and POP3. SMTP stands for Simple Mail Transfer Protocol. It is one of the earliest and simplest protocols for sending e-mail and has become an almost universal standard for all e-mail applications. It contains a given set of rules for routing e-mails to their appropriate destinations within a network. On the other end, POP3, which stands for Post Office Protocol Version 3, is an equally universal standard set of protocols for receiving e-mail. A major advantage of POP3 is that messages are downloaded from the server onto individual computers, thus freeing up space on the server.

Another set of important decisions had to be made in the design of the network. Management had a choice between point-to-point connections or frame-relay connections. Point-to-point would have required dedicated twisted pair connections from each of the sites to the local phone company where data transmissions on each line would be digitally switched to another twisted pair connection to arrive at its proper destination at another site. This setup would have meant that each site would have had to maintain a dedicated line to each of the other six sites, which would have added up to many twisted pair connections at each of these sites. The lease cost of this many lines was cost prohibitive.

Frame-relay requires only one connection to a frame-relay node at the local phone company or Internet Service Provider (ISP). The connection, or line, can be owned by the agency but is usually leased, as it was in this case. The local phone company or ISP then routes the data transmissions over its own existing media (twisted pair, coaxial cable, or fiber optic) until the data reaches its intended destination, which would be another computer on the school district's network. The school district shares the existing transmission media with other customers of the local phone company or ISP. This choice was a much less costly solution for the school district because it avoided a lot of point-to-point hard wiring. It would have been even less expensive for the school district to use conventional modems and ISDN lines. ISDN allows for voice and data to be transmitted in digital form over conventional circuit-switched public telephone networks owned by the phone company and leased by the agency. Unfortunately, this technology could not carry the amount of data required by the district. So, the school district found a suitable way to build a WAN that was a middle-ground solution between an expensive fiber optic WAN and an inexpensive but inadequate WAN built on leased lines.

Alternatives to the School District's WAN

The school district had two other options to build their WAN not mentioned in the case study from which this example is drawn. They could have created an intranet or a virtual private network (VPN), both using existing Internet technology.

An intranet can emulate both LANs and WANs, providing virtually all of the same services of LANs and WANs. It uses the same concepts and technologies as other networks such as servers, clients, protocols, e-mail, and file transfers, except that these concepts and technologies are implemented on the existing Internet.[15] Intranets do need two additional technologies: firewalls and gateways. A firewall may be implemented as hardware or software in a network configuration. It guards against unwanted intrusions into an existing network. It controls traffic between what are called "zones of trust." By itself, the Internet has no zone of trust: anyone with the right technology can access it. With a firewall, a network administrator can establish very strict zones of trust for the intranet, thereby controlling who has access to the intranet, the Internet, web sites, e-mail, and file transfers. The gateway would control all access to the intranet and the Internet. It is usually installed on a single computer on the network to manage the flow of all network traffic.

If the school district had chosen an intranet to provide its networking capabilities, each computer on the network would have to have its own access to the Internet. This could become a complex endeavor depending on the number of computers involved, requiring many Internet connections. This choice could also become a costly endeavor, depending upon how the local phone company or ISP charged for the use of Internet connections.

The school district probably did not go this route because intranets seem to be best suited to organizations that have to span wide geographic locations, perhaps nationwide or even globally. An example would be the U.S. Navy Marine Corps Intranet project, which is currently being built (see chapter 10) at a cost exceeding $10 billion. For the Navy and the Marine Corps, it makes sense to have each of their stations or bases function as LANs connected into one giant intranet over the existing Internet. This structure provides for local control and management of the LANs along with connectivity and interoperability with all of the other LANs in the intranet.

The other option is a virtual private network (VPN), which also uses the existing Internet as the "backbone" of the network.[16] In this case, each of the seven sites in the school district would be configured as a LAN, and each LAN would be connected to the other LANs via the Internet. This type of network configuration would also require firewalls and gateways, as well as a host of security features involving cryptography (the science of securing information) and encryption of transmitted data, authentications, and passwords. The security features make this type of network "virtually private."

Issues in Telecommunications

Several issues are associated with the ever-expanding use of telecommunications technology in government. They include public employee use of cellular phones, voice over Internet protocol (VoIP) technology, 911 emergency services, municipal initiatives to blanket cities with universal WiFi access, and regulatory issues about who has the right to offer telecommunications services.

Public Employee Use of Cellular Phones

The use of cell phones by public employees who need to be in contact with their office may not, at first glance, seem controversial. But first consider the costs associated with providing pagers and cell phones to federal employees who work for the U.S. Department of Transportation's Federal Aviation Administration (FAA). In 2000 it was reported that the FAA spent $60 a month to give an agency-owned pager or cell phone to one of its employees for official use.[17] This expense could add up to a lot of money on a per-year basis considering at the time the FAA had about 6,000 technicians located across the country. Indeed, just the Logistics Center of the FAA spent over $70,000 a year in 2000 on mobile communications devices, wireless devices, pagers, and cell phones. Aside from cost, some FAA officials were also concerned about how to control the use of the cell phones by employees in the field. The agency cell phones should be used for official business only, no private business. This meant that they needed to develop a way to monitor the use of the cell phones—an additional cost in terms of time, money, and personnel.

Management came up with a simple solution: Each approved employee would be allowed to use his or her personal cellular phone for FAA business and would receive a monthly voucher in the amount of $30 to pay for the FAA business–related calls. Over time, that amount could be adjusted in much the same way that public employees receive reimbursement for gas mileage while using their personal automobiles. In cases where a public employee exceeded the monthly amount of $30 for business-related calls, the employee would be allowed to submit a reimbursement request.

The Logistics Center expects to save 45 to 75 percent annually on the use of mobile devices with this simple solution that also offers the following other benefits:

- An immediate return on investment since there is no cost for phones
- Significant operational and administrative cost saving over the current process
- No vendor switch-over costs, with a simple transparent transition process
- The use of one-piece telecommunications equipment per individual pager or cell phone
- Participants no longer having to carry equipment that is restricted from private use[18]

While this case may appear to be a rather mundane example of cost savings for one among hundreds of agencies in the federal government, consider the potential size of the cost savings if these policies were extended to a broader range of not only federal agencies but state and local governments as well.

Voice over Internet Protocol (VoIP)

On January 10, 2005, *Government Computer News* presented a brief, nonauthored comment titled "The Lowdown on VoIP."[19] In a few short sentences it announced that soon phone calls could be made over the Internet at significantly reduced costs. Since then, Voice over Internet Protocol (VoIP) has been a leading topic in that magazine as well as its sister magazine, *Federal Computer Week*.

VoIP is a cutting-edge technology that has the potential to greatly decrease the cost of phone calls, especially long-distance phone charges.[20] It takes the analog audio signals that you hear on a phone and turns them into digital data that can be transmitted over the Internet. This technology can turn a standard Internet connection into a way to make free phone calls by using free VoIP software to bypass the telephone company, although companies such as Vonage and AT&T CallVantage are offering VoIP service but at significantly lower rates than for traditional long-distance service.

VoIP has three configurations. The first, and most basic, is the computer-to-computer connection. It requires a computer, a microphone, speakers, a sound card, a cable or DSL modem, and VoIP software, which is either free or relatively inexpensive. The only downside to this configuration is that the user is tied to the computer when making phone calls.

A second configuration requires the use of an analog telephone adaptor (ATA). It allows you to connect a standard phone to a computer or an Internet connection. Like a modem, an ATA converts analog phone signals into digital form and back again. VoIP via ATA technology is not completely free. Firms like Vonage and AT&T CallVantage provide these special phones for free, but users must pay a monthly fee for services. The firms also supply the necessary software for your computer.

The third configuration is an Internet Protocol Phone (IP phone). They look just like regular phones expect that they plug into an RJ-45 Ethernet connector, allowing your IP phone to connect directly to your router. They also come with the necessary software built into the phone to enable transmission. The next step will be WiFi IP phones that can be used wherever a WiFi hotspot is available.

Public agencies at all levels of government are moving quickly, but also sometimes cautiously, to convert their legacy public switched telephone service to VoIP. In 2000 the Census Bureau took the lead in experimenting with VoIP technology. It was looking to replace its antiquated telephone systems that were no longer available from AT&T. They installed 5,000 IP phones at their Washington, DC, headquarters and added an additional 1,500 IP phones at three national call centers and 12 regional offices.[21] Then, in September of 2004, the Department of Defense completed its testing of CISCO's VoIP technology and gave it the go-ahead to start converting all of its phone systems to VoIP. This will allow the DOD to control all of its telephone service without having to rely on common carriers.[22] Subsequently, the U.S. Army discovered that "going wireless" was a lot less expensive for its networks at its Pohakuloa Training Area in Hawaii.[23] The alternative would have been to bury fiber optic cable at a cost of $150 a linear foot.

Because VoIP uses the Internet, it does not use conventional telephone circuit switching. As noted earlier, in data networks, data (e.g., an e-mail or a file) is broken up into individual packets that flow through a chaotic network along thousands of possible paths. In circuit switching, the dedicated line is kept open all of the time during a connection. In packet switching a connection is made just long enough to send the packet to a destination. Then the connection is closed. Each packet has an address telling it where to eventually arrive. It may be sent from one computer to a router, then on to another router, and then another router, and so on, until it finally arrives at its proper destination. In VoIP, what is spoken is broken up into many different packets that travel over many different connections until they finally arrive at the intended destination where the data in the packets are put back together again to form the sound of a human voice. Packet switching is very efficient. It lets the network route the packets along the least congested and cheapest lines. It also frees up the two computers communicating with each other so that they can accept information from other computers as well.

States and localities are also looking to VoIP to reduce their local and long-distance telephone costs. Industry analysts project tremendous growth in this area because many state and local governments are already "wired" into the Internet and Internet phone companies are offering VoIP package plans to state and local governments at attractive savings over traditional circuit-switched landline phones. For example, in 2003 the Arizona State Legislature passed a bill requiring all state agencies to replace their legacy PBX systems with VoIP systems.[24] In one department, the Arizona Department of Commerce, the total cost for replacing its existing phone system was $250,000, but it was able to recover those costs. The new VoIP system saves $50,000 a year in handset rentals and premium phone service charges, and an additional $80,000 a year in salaries. The old system required a dedicated phone system supervisor, who is no longer needed.

As an interesting aside, right after Hurricane Katrina blasted its way through Louisiana, the Baton Rouge General Hospital found itself with no internal or external telephone service.[25] They were in a crisis mode because they could not communicate between rooms, offices, labs, and floors, or with the outside world. With the help of the hospital's own technical staff and the donated services of their local technology outsourcing provider, Dell Computers, Vonage, and a local Radio Shack, they were able to set up VoIP phone and data transmission service. Within a day they had established an internal VoIP system that resembled an old PBX system as well as a limited system to make long-distance phone calls over Vonage's commercial VoIP long-distance service.

VoIP technology does have some disadvantages. It will not work if there is a power outage. Landlines will work during power outages because they carry their own power in the phone line. VoIP service providers may or may not offer directory assistance of phone white pages. Finally, VoIP does not ensure the ability to make emergency 911 calls.[26]

911 Emergency Services

With the advent of both cellular phones and VoIP comes the issue of having access to 911 emergency services. With conventional landlines, emergency service workers in call centers (police departments and fire departments) almost always have the ability to trace and pinpoint the location of the phone from which the call is coming—not so with cell phones and VoIP.

In 2001 nearly a third of all 911 emergency calls were placed from wireless phones.[27] At that time it was impossible for dispatchers to locate the source of those calls. The Federal Communications Commission responded by requiring all wireless phone service providers to provide the technology to pinpoint the location of those calls. The industry responded in two phases. Phase One would allow dispatchers to pinpoint the broad geographic cell from which the call was made but not the precise location of the phone itself. This capability would locate the call within a twenty- to thirty-mile radius of a typical relay cell. Phase Two will narrow the location of the phone call down to a range of 160 to 1,000 feet.

By 2003 the Government Accountability Office reported that the implementation of wireless 911 numbers was still many years away.[28] Although the deadline set for Phase Two implementation was in the year 2006, the GAO reported that only twenty-four states had plans to implement Phase Two in 2005, while the rest of the states could not estimate the date for full implementation of Phase Two. This is another example of how a disruptive technology can create a ripple effect that governments must respond to in a timely and costly manner.

WiFi

Municipalities and counties across the nation and in other nations are moving quickly to implement wireless local area networks (WLANs) using "wireless fidelity," or WiFi, technology. Cities initially started building wireless networks to support their day-to-day operations. For example, in 2004 the City of Lincoln, Nebraska, installed five WiFi access devices in the Health Department, a waste-water treatment facility, two Parks Department buildings, and a parking garage to enhance mobile communications among these facilities.[29] Industry analysts predict that in just a few years, most cities, even small ones, will have all of their core business applications supported by wireless technology.[30]

The wireless revolution in local government is taking place in small cities. For example, Grand Haven, Michigan, a city with a population of only 11,000, partnered with Ottawa Wireless, Inc., and installed several hundred WiFi "hotspots" across the city to create a VPN so the city can connect its departments and the city's hospital. The city's management went one step further by offering its citizens unlimited access for $19.99 a month.[31]

A host of other cities have started to offer free or relatively inexpensive WiFi access to their citizens. For example, Philadelphia plans to offer wireless service to the public. The city will spend about $15 million to cover the city in a wireless network that will cost about $2.5 million a year to maintain.[32] Citizens will have easy access to wireless hotspots all over the city. Alexandria, Virginia, is another city that is offering WiFi service at no cost in a limited public area in the historic downtown section of the city. The city government hopes that this amenity will promote tourism, economic development, and the image of Alexandria as a high-tech community.[33] City officials claim that they have built the pilot project in such a way that it will not compete with private Internet service providers.

Many other cities are also moving in this direction. At the forefront are cities such as Corpus Christi, Texas; Cleveland, Ohio; Taipei, Taiwan; Portland, Oregon; Mangaratiba, Brazil; Düsseldorf, Germany; Gyor, Hungary; Jerusalem, Israel; the Principality of Monaco; Seoul, South Korea; Osaka, Japan; and Westminster, London, United Kingdom. These cities have been named the leading "Digital Communities" by the Intel Corporation.[34]

Regulatory Issues

The fact that the city of Alexandria, Virginia, publicly states that their WiFi project does not compete with commercial ISPs brings us to the important issue of who should provide both wired and wireless Internet service? This is a hotly debated issue at the moment. The ISPs (both telephone and cable companies) argue that governmental entities have no business being in the business of offering free or low-cost access to the Internet for the public, even if it serves specific public interests. On the other side, cities, counties, and states, as well as public interest groups, argue that the private sector is either unwilling or unable to provide Internet access to the public at reasonable rates or in certain geographic localities like remote rural areas where Internet access has the potential to spur economic development.

This is especially true when we are talking about broadband service. Many rural areas are not served by high-speed Internet cable companies or high-speed Internet satellite companies. These communities have to rely on the local telephone companies who may offer only slow-speed Internet connections or more costly but faster DSL Internet connections. Farmers and small agricultural businesses as well as for-profit and not-for-profit environmental firms rely heavily on Internet access to acquire data related to their respective businesses. Many of them have to put up with slow-speed access to the data that they need and, in some areas, no access at all. (These issues will be raised in the next chapter as part of the controversy over the digital divide.)

Currently, fourteen states prohibit local governments from offering wired or wireless Internet access even though the transmission media may already be in place. As of the writing of this book, two competing bills in Congress are focused on this issue. The McCain-Lautenberg Bill, the Community Broadband Act of 2005 (S 1294), would limit the efforts of the states to stop local government from offering broadband service to citizens. The Sessions Bill, the Preserving Innovation in Telecom Act of 2005 (HR 2726), strictly prohibits all state and local governments from providing any Internet access in competition with commercial providers.[35] At the moment, it is not clear how this public policy issue will be resolved.

Summary and a Look Forward

This chapter has covered a lot of territory from the technical basics of telecommunications technology to some of the managerial and public policy issues associated with the use of telecommunications technology by governments, businesses, and the public. The length of the chapter is testimony to the fact that telecommunications technology plays a deep and broad role in our daily lives both personally and professionally. The same can be said for the place of the Internet in our personal and professional lives, as will be shown in the next chapter. As evidence of this, consider how many of the notes and citations to this chapter refer to web pages as well as conventional printed media. Following a discussion of the Internet revolution, attention will be returned to more "nuts and bolts" issues of developing and implementing technology solutions for public agencies.

6

The Internet Revolution

The previous chapter made several references to the Internet without formally defining it. A formal definition was not called for because most people in modern societies are well acquainted with the Internet and the World Wide Web (WWW, or web). Certainly the majority of this book's readers are regular users of the Internet and the web. This chapter will provide some background on the Internet and the WWW before addressing some of the major managerial and public policy issues raised by its existence: namely e-government, e-democracy, e-voting, and the digital divide.

Background on the Internet

Contrary to what Al Gore once said, and what some people believe, he did not create the Internet. He was not even in Congress in 1969 when the Internet was started under the name of ARPANET, nor was he in Congress in 1974 when the term "Internet" was first used. Gore did, however, support the development of the Internet while he was in Congress.[1]

ARPANET was the product of the U.S. Defense Department's Advanced Research Project Agency (DARPA). It evolved from earlier work in the 1960s on packet switching technology.[2] Recall from the previous chapter that in packet switching, data is broken up into little packets, sent to a destination over many different networks, and put back together again when it arrives at the intended destination. This process was the basic scientific and technical idea behind what became the Internet. The early ARPANET used Network Control Protocol (NCP) as its transmission protocol from 1969 to 1982. Then NCP was replaced with the now widespread TCP/IP (Transmission Control Protocol/Internet Protocol) discussed in the previous chapter.

The Internet was also created for political and military purposes. When the USSR launched *Sputnik*, the first orbiting satellite, in 1957, politicians and military officials became worried about how military installations would be able to maintain communications in the event of a nuclear attack. The idea was to construct a computer-based communications system of many networks so that if one of the networks went down, messages could still be transmitted via other networks using packet-switching technology. The first physical network, built in 1969, consisted of four nodes, located at the University of California at Los Angeles, the Stanford Research Institute, the University of California at Santa Barbara, and the University of Utah, using satellite communication. Then in 1974, SATNET was established, linking the U.S. computer network to European networks via satellite. It was also in 1974 that the term *Internet* was first used. In 1984 ARPANET was split into two networks: MILNET for military purposes, leaving ARPANET for scientific research purposes. ARPANET finally became known simply as the Internet.

The Internet is a network of more than a million computers worldwide. Any person with a computer, the right software, and a connection to the Internet can become a part of the Internet. In the early days of ARPANET one needed to use a mainframe computer in a university, research institute, government agency, or major corporation to access what became the Internet, and one had to have considerable knowledge about how to use the related software to support the communications. Today, almost anyone can learn to use the Internet in a few minutes.

The Internet consists of the World Wide Web, electronic mail (e-mail), file transfer protocol (FTP), Internet Relay Chat (IRC), and USENET (a news service). Each will be briefly explained.

People tend to confuse the Internet with the World Wide Web (WWW). The WWW is actually a technology that "sits on top" of the Internet to allow for communication enabled by web browsers such as Internet Explorer, Netscape, and Firefox. It is best understood as an interface or service that simplifies the use of the Internet. It was invented in 1989 by Sir Tim Berners-Lee who coined the term "World Wide Web."[3] He built the first web browser while working at CERN, the European Particle Physics Laboratory. Mosaic was the first fully developed web browser, implemented in 1993 for general-purpose use. Currently, Microsoft Internet Explorer and Netscape Navigator have the lion's share of the market, but Mozilla Firefox is gaining favor among people who are comfortable with open source software.

E-mail is self-explanatory. Most people in modern societies send and receive e-mail daily. Receiving unwanted e-mail (spam) has become a major problem in most of the world. As we shall see in chapter 11 on information systems security, e-mail is often the source of malicious pieces of software like worms, Trojans, and viruses that can cause damage to a computer's file system, hard disk, or operating system.

The Internet is also used to transfer files among people. FTP, or file transfer protocol, allows for the direct transfer of documents, musical recordings, and videos from one computer to another via an FTP server, directly via the Internet, bypassing the WWW. Web pages use the Hypertext Transfer Protocol (HTTP) to transfer parts of web pages from one web page to another computer via a browser communicating across the WWW.

Internet Relay Chat (IRC) is a special Internet application that allows for the creation of thousands of channels on the Internet that a person can create or join to have conversations with other people (chats) around the world regarding an unlimited range of topics.[4] With the right software, which is easily downloaded from the Internet, anyone can create a channel on any topic on IRC. mIRC is presently the most popular IRC client.

USENET, derived from UNIX User Network, is a system of newsgroups where people can post messages on any conceivable topic as well as pictures, videos, music files, and software.[5] People can respond to those messages, creating the potential for a dialogue, and they can also send their own pictures, videos, music files, and software to a variety of newsgroups. The newsgroups were originally used by scientists to communicate with one another. Today newsgroups span every possible interest from people who own Persian cats to people who make pipe bombs.

One often hears that no one owns the Internet. To a great extent this is true. No single public or private entity controls the Internet, but a few organizations have significant influence over the Internet and the WWW. On the corporate side there are thousands of companies involved with the Internet such as ISPs, telephone companies, and telecommunications companies that provide part of the Internet backbone (coaxial cable or fiber optic cable mostly). Some guess that UUNET owns 30 percent of the backbone with AT&T coming second. The parent company of UUNET is MCI WorldCom. Then there is America Online, Netscape, MSN, Yahoo, and Mozilla, but they do not wield much power on their own. Some governments, such as those in China, Myanmar, Indonesia, and Australia, tightly control citizen access to the Internet, but most governments do not, especially the United States, because the Internet is seen as a boon to the economy and keeps the citizens happy.

There are, however, some organizations that have a strong influence over the Internet. For example, the Internet Corporation for Assigned Names and Numbers (ICANN) is a U.S. nonprofit firm that controls domain name registration. It has been operating under a Memorandum of Understanding (MoU) with the U.S. Department of Commerce since 1998.[6] While each nation has control over its own domain names, ICANN acts as a clearinghouse for all domain name registrations. ICANN also controls the root servers that store the master files of domain names such as .com, .net, and .org. There are ten root servers in the United States, two in Europe, and one in Japan. The United

Nations also has an interest in the Internet. Their Working Group on Internet Governance would like to take control of the Internet, but that is unlikely given the relative power of other groups and organizations.

The Internet Engineering Task Force (IETF) is a very unusual group of people.[7] Thousands of people belong to it, but it does not have a membership roster nor do members pay dues. It is not a corporation and has no formal structure, but it does have a variety of subgroups composed of computer scientists, network managers, and computer technicians working on a variety of tasks designed to enhance the Internet. It meets three times a year, and anyone can attend the meetings. Its first meeting was held in 1986. Much of the work of the IETF is conducted via the Internet through e-mail, web sites, and newsgroups. Its stated mission is to

- Identify and propose solutions to pressing operational and technical problems in the Internet;
- Specify the development or usage of protocols and the near-term architecture to solve such technical problems for the Internet;
- Make recommendations to the Internet Engineering Steering Group (IESG) regarding the standardization of protocols and protocol usage in the Internet;
- Facilitate technology transfer from the Internet Research Task Force (IRTF) to the wider Internet community; and
- Provide a forum for the exchange of information within the Internet community between vendors, users, researchers, agency contractors, and network managers.[8]

As this indicates, the IETF offers considerable technical support for the maintenance and development of the Internet.

The IETF is affiliated with the Internet Society (ISOC). The ISOC is a nonprofit membership society of more than 100 member organizations and over 20,000 individual members from over 180 countries. Since 1992 it has served as a global clearinghouse for information about the Internet and as a facilitator of Internet development and innovations. Its stated goals and purposes include

- Development, maintenance, evolution, and dissemination of standards for the Internet and its internetworking technologies and applications;
- Growth and evolution of the Internet architecture;
- Maintenance and evolution of effective administrative processes necessary for operation of the global Internet and internets;
- Education and research related to the Internet and internetworking;

- Harmonization of actions and activities at international levels to facilitate the development and availability of the Internet;
- Collection and dissemination of information related to the Internet and internetworking, including histories and archives;
- Assisting technologically developing countries, areas, and peoples in implementing and evolving their Internet infrastructure and use;
- Acting as liaison with other organizations, governments, and the general public for coordination, collaboration, and education in effecting the above purposes.[9]

The free and open nature of the Internet is reflected in the ISOC guiding principles:

- Open, unencumbered, beneficial use of the Internet.
- Self-regulated content providers; no prior censorship of online communications.
- Online free expression is not restricted by other indirect means such as excessively restrictive governmental or private controls over computer hardware or software, telecommunications infrastructure, or other essential components of the Internet.
- Open forum for the development of standards and Internet technology.
- No discrimination in the use of the Internet on the basis of race, color, gender, language, religion, political or other opinion, national or social origin, property, birth, or other status.
- Personal information generated on the Internet is neither misused nor used by another without informed consent of the principal.
- Internet users may encrypt their communication and information without restriction.
- Encouragement of cooperation between networks: Connectivity is its own reward; therefore, network providers are rewarded by cooperation with each other.[10]

With this stated philosophy it is easy to see that the people most closely involved in maintaining and developing the Internet want it to be open to anyone. They want a true open society that is not under the control of any public or private body.

The web portion of the Internet also has its own supporting organization called W3C, or the World Wide Web Consortium.[11] It was founded in 1994 by Berners-Lee, who serves as its director. Its members include more than 350 organizations worldwide including all of the major technology firms. The W3C has several long-term goals. First, it believes that the WWW is for everyone so it strives to make the web available to people all over the world. Second, it strives to develop the web so that it may be accessed by a variety of devices—computers, cell phones, PDAs, and many other devices. Third, it wants to develop the web so that it becomes an enormous depository of knowledge on any and all subjects. Fourth, it wants the web to be a secure and safe place for people to work collaboratively on a vast range of projects.

From all of this we can see that no one owns the Internet or the web, but it does have its many supporters. It looks like both will continue to grow and remain free for everyone to use.

So how many people use the Internet? Internet World Stats offers some recent data on Internet usage.[12] The United States leads with 205,326,680 Internet users as of March 2006. China follows with 111,000,000 users. The remaining top-ten countries are Japan (86,050,000 users), Germany (48,721,997 users), the United Kingdom (37,800,000 users), South Korea (33,900,000 users), Italy (28,870,000 users), France (26,214,173 users), Brazil (25,900,000 users), and Canada (21,900,000 users). Measured in terms of the percentage of the population using the Internet (penetration rate), Iceland comes in with a 75.9 percent population penetration rate, followed by Sweden (74.9 percent), Hong Kong (72.5 percent), Denmark (69.4 percent), United States (68.6 percent), Canada (67.9 percent), South Korea (67 percent), Netherlands (65.9 percent), Australia (65.9 percent), Switzerland (63.5 percent), and the United Kingdom (62.9 percent). For all of the top-ten countries the total percentage of the population using the Internet is 66.4 percent, leaving the rest of the world at only 8.1 percent. Overall, only 12.7 percent of the world's population is using the Internet. This discrepancy indicates that internationally there is still a significant digital divide between those who have Internet access and those who do not. For the top-ten countries, the digital divide is much narrower and will become even smaller as technology gets cheaper and telecommunications infrastructure is built up.

E-Government

E-government is about delivering information and services to the public over the Internet and the web mainly through the use of web pages and web portals. Type the name of a city, even a small- or medium-sized city, into a search engine like Google and you are likely to find that the city has a web site. On that site you might find information about the city itself, such as its population; its history; the names, addresses, e-mail addresses, and phone numbers of its elected and appointed officials; phone numbers and addresses of various city departments; and information about public hearings, council meetings, and the city's budget. You might also find that it is possible to pay for certain city services like electricity, water, and permits online. In some cities you might also find that you can participate in public discussions about public issues, and you might be able to cast a vote in a nonbinding referendum on a particular policy issue. This is electronic government and electronic democracy at work. Both are very new, originating in the late 1990s. Both are enabled by the Internet, the WWW, and related telecommunications and networking technologies. In addition, both are controversial in terms of their potential benefits to society and their costs to society.

They are also different. *E-government* refers to the use of the Internet and related technologies to provide citizens with relevant public information and public services. *E-democracy* offers citizens the opportunity to engage in public discourse about specific public policy issues. In some circumstances, e-democracy can also mean providing citizens the opportunity to cast their votes electronically, either at a polling place or even from home, in a referendum or a general election. It is convenient to think of the difference between the two in terms of the old dichotomy between politics and administration. E-democracy allows the citizen to engage in the political process and public discourse; e-government provides governments the opportunity to offer administrative services to the public perhaps more effectively and efficiently than out of the offices of a city or a state or federal agency. Both e-democracy and e-voting will be discussed in subsequent sections of this chapter.

E-Government Worldwide

Darrell M. West of the Center for Public Policy at Brown University has conducted extensive research on the growth of e-government worldwide.[13] In the summer of 2005 he and his associates analyzed 1,797 national government web sites for 198 nations. Subnational units like municipalities were not included in the study. Some of his more interesting findings follow:

- Nineteen percent of government web sites offer services that are fully executable online.
- Eighty-nine percent of web sites this year provide access to publications and 53 percent have links to databases.
- Eighteen percent (up from 14 percent in 2004) show privacy policies, while 10 percent have security policies (up from 8 percent in 2004).
- Nineteen percent of government web sites have some form of disability access, meaning access for persons with disabilities, up from 14 percent in 2004.
- Countries vary enormously in their overall e-government performance based on our analysis. The most highly ranked nations include Taiwan,

Singapore, the United States, Hong Kong, China, Canada, Germany, Australia, and Ireland.
* There are major differences in e-government performance based on region of the world. In general, countries in North America score the highest, followed by Asia, Western Europe, Pacific Ocean Islands, Middle East, Eastern Europe, South America, Russia and Central Asia, Central America, and Africa.[14]

Overall, he concludes that many governments are making steady progress in building e-government capacity, but there are no huge leaps forward.

West's conclusion is supported by research conducted by Accenture, a management research and consulting firm. In their 2004 global study of e-government initiatives they observe that growth in the maturity of e-government web sites has slowed down considerably.[15] They have identified several attributes that most e-government web sites share: (1) they are becoming more citizen centric in the sense that the sites are designed from the point of view of the user, not an agency employee who has an insider's view of what is going on; (2) they are responding more to businesses than to citizens in general; (3) they are broadening the number of overall services provided to businesses and citizens; (4) more of the web sites are providing single portals as access points to a variety of different public agencies; and (5) they are engaging in a variety of activities to foster citizen and business use of the government web sites.

Accenture also provides a yearly ranking of the quality of e-government services globally. For 2004, as in the past three years, U.S. services came in second behind Canada's, tying with Singapore's.[16] Canada's e-government services rank first for several reasons. One, they provide one portal for citizen access to all national, provincial, and local governments, something that the United States finds hard to do because of its federalist structure. Two, the Canadian government actually asks citizens what information and services that they want to access via the Internet using extensive public surveys. Three, Canadian e-government services are marketed actively through television, radio, and print outlets. Four, Canadian e-government services are available through wireless access via mobile devices such as cell phones and PDAs. Fifth, and finally, Canada has a national Chief Information Officer (CIO) who has the authority to make sweeping decisions about the use of technology nationally and subnationally. The United States has an administrator for information technology and e-government in the Office of Management and Budget, but that person's power is very limited. That person is more of an influencer than an enforcer.

The United Nations Online Network in Public Administration and Finance (UNPAN) casts a slightly different light on global readiness. Its 2005 survey of e-government readiness examined 191 UN member nations. One hundred and seventy-nine had government web sites that promoted citizen awareness of public policies and programs. The United States is the world leader, followed by Denmark, Sweden, and the United Kingdom. Among the top twenty-five countries were South Korea, Singapore, Estonia, Malta, and Chile. Countries found to be at the lowest levels of e-government maturity were located in South and Central Asia as well as Africa, where one-third of the world's population resides.[17]

Although the statistics differ somewhat in their rankings of various nations, we can conclude that many industrialized countries worldwide are moving forward in initiating e-government programs. Growth in the forward movement has slowed down somewhat, but it seems that modest incremental progress is still being made. It also appears that nations begin by offering e-government information and services, and then some progress to offer greater citizen participation in public decision making by offering e-democracy services such as public policy discussion forums or chat rooms.

U.S. Federal E-Government Initiatives

While the United States federal government ranks relatively high among other nations with regard to providing e-government services to its citizens, when looked at closely it may not be doing a very good job because of the decentralized nature of federal agencies.

On July 18, 2001, the Office of Management and Budget initiated a task force to develop the federal government's e-government strategy.[18] In conducting their background research, the task force found that the federal government offers over thirty-five million web pages online at over 22,000 web sites. Unfortunately, most of these web sites are agency centered rather than citizen centered; in other words, they are not citizen friendly. They use the language of the bureaucracy rather than the language of the citizen to try to communicate information that citizens often find difficult to understand since most do not speak the language of bureaucracy. Most of these web sites are also redundant, leading to wasted resources and excessive electronic red tape and confusion. The task force described the situation as follows:

> The Task Force's analysis found that redundant and overlapping agency activities have been major impediments to creating a citizen-centered electronic government. Of 28 lines of business found in the federal government, the assessment revealed that, on average, 19 Executive Departments and agencies are performing each line of business. Each agency typically has

invested in both online and traditional approaches, regardless of other departments' redundant efforts. That translates into many duplicative reporting requirements, while requiring citizens to wade through thousands of Web sites and dozens of call centers to find and obtain service. For example, a community attempting to obtain economic development grants could file over 1,000 forms at more than 250 federal bureaus, each form containing much similar data. The Task Force found that this "business architecture" problem creates underlying redundant activities and processes, resulting in unnecessary burdens and costs on citizens, state and local governments, businesses and federal employees.[19]

The task force also observed that the agencies studied have been working for two years to get 6,600 paper-based transactions (representing millions of transactions per year) online, but only hundreds were currently available.[20]

The task force has taken a highly enlightened approach in making its recommendations for building the e-government capacity of the federal government. In the spirit of business process reengineering, they realize that it is foolish to simply automate inefficient and ineffective paperwork processes. To be truly citizen centric, the agencies need to streamline processes before putting them on the web. They have focused their attention on twenty-four initiatives in four categories:

- The Government-to-Citizen (G2C) initiatives will fulfill the vision of one-stop, online access to benefits and services (such as Recreation.gov). They will also bring modern relationship management tools to improve the quality and efficiency of service delivery.
- The Government-to-Business (G2B) initiatives will reduce the burden on businesses by adopting processes that dramatically reduce redundant data collection, provide one-stop streamlined support for businesses, and enable digital communication with businesses using the language of e-business (XML).
- The Government-to-Government (G2G) initiatives will enable sharing and integration of federal, state, and local data to facilitate better leverage of investments in IT systems (e.g., geographical information) and to provide better integration of key government operations, such as disaster response. The G2G initiatives also improve grant-management capabilities, as required by the Federal Financial Assistance Improvement Act (P.L. 106-107). These initiatives will also support "vertical" (i.e., intergovernmental) integration requirements for Homeland Security.
- The Internal Efficiency and Effectiveness (IEE) initiatives bring commercial best practices to key government operations, particularly supply

chain management, human capital management, financial management, and document workflow.[21]

Despite the recent administration's emphasis on e-government and various initiatives to enhance e-government services by the federal government, access to relevant web sites by citizens is complex, confusing, and time consuming.

What Do Federal, State, and Local E-Government Initiatives Offer the Public?

It is difficult to get a comprehensive picture of federal, state, and local e-government initiatives, except to say that all of the states and many, but certainly not all, local governments have a web page or web portal, and although the federal government has one point of access—FirstGov, the U.S. government's official web portal—it still has thousands of web sites scattered across a wide variety of agencies. Precisely what information and services each web site provides is generally unknown. It would be possible to compile an inventory of all federal, state, and local government web sites and the information and services they provide by carefully examining over 11,000 web sites inventoried on "State and Local Government On the Net" or the same thousands of government web sites listed on FirstGov, but that task would be beyond the scope of this book.[22]

Fortunately, Darrell M. West and his team of researchers from Brown University conduct annual surveys of federal, state, and local web sites to see what kinds of services they provide and to evaluate their services. The following are some highlights from *State and Federal E-Government in the United States, 2005*.[23] In June and July of 2005, Brown and his associates conducted a similar survey of 1,620 government web sites consisting of 1,599 state government web sites, 48 federal legislative and executive sites, and 13 federal court sites. Briefly, here are some of the findings for all three levels of government.

In the category of online information almost all of the federal and state sites provide phone numbers and addresses of elected or appointed officials and various agencies, departments, or other units of government. Ninety-eight percent of the web sites provide a variety of publications, and 67 percent provide access to a variety of databases. A small number of sites offer audio clips (12 percent) and video clips (18 percent). Similarly, almost all of the city web sites also provide phone numbers and addresses. Eighty-one percent offer publications, 61 percent offer databases, 10 percent offer audio clips, and 12 percent offer video clips.[24]

Although electronic services such as filing income tax returns or purchasing licenses or permits lags behind information services, these services show strong growth. For example, in 2000, 78 percent of federal and state agency web sites offered no services. That number dwindled to 27 percent in 2005. In comparison, in 2000 only 2 percent of the web sites offered three or more services. This jumped to 54 percent in 2005. Fifty-nine percent of the web sites accepted credit card payments for services, up from 25 percent in 2004. For the cities in 2001, 87 percent offered no services compared to 60 percent offering no services in 2004. Only 16 percent of the cities offered four or more services in 2004 with 23 percent offering one to three services. This means that 40 percent of the largest cities do not offer any electronic services and 40 percent offer only a few services. This seems odd because municipalities have the potential to offer a wide variety of services electronically, like paying for utilities, paying for parking tickets, paying for permits and licenses, and accessing library records and renewing books.[25]

Information privacy and security are on the minds of many citizens. In 2005, 69 percent of the federal and state web sites contained statements about privacy policies as compared to only 7 percent in 2000. Fifty-four percent of the web sites contained security policy statements in 2005 as compared to only 5 percent in 2000. For the cities in 2004, 53 percent contain some privacy statement and 32 percent contain some security statement. Going deeper into the privacy and security issue we find something of a contradiction. In 2005, 65 percent of the federal and state web sites say that they prohibit the sharing of personal information, but 62 percent of the web sites share information with law enforcement agencies. Similarly for the cities, in 2004 30 percent prohibit the sharing of personal information, but 31 percent do share personal information with law enforcement agencies. The study does not mention who they prohibit from sharing information on citizens, nor does it mention how the web sites share information with law enforcement agencies.[26]

If a government web site is going to be useful to the public, the public should be able to read and understand the information contained on the site. The 2005 survey shows that the federal and state web sites failed miserably in communicating with the general public. Sixty-seven percent of the web sites require a twelfth-grade reading ability while half of the American public reads at the eighth-grade level or below. Only 10 percent of the web sites were designed for citizens who read at the eighth-grade level or below. Furthermore, only 18 percent of the federal and state web sites provide foreign language access, while only 17 percent of the city web sites have foreign language access. It would appear that readability and lack of foreign language access creates a unique version of the digital divide, different from merely not having access to the Internet. To add to this divide, consider that only 44 percent of federal web sites, 40 percent of state web sites, and 21 percent of city web sites meet the accessibility criteria for the disabled as established by the W3C. So, it would appear that web sites at all three levels of government are not meeting the needs of citizens with poor reading skills, language barriers, and disabilities.[27]

Generally, public agencies at all three levels of government are putting a lot of effort into building e-government web sites. For now most of them simply provide information to citizens. Some are beginning to provide services through which citizens can make limited transactions with an agency on its web page. The agencies at all three levels are not paying much attention to people who have personal barriers to web site access and use. Some public agencies are beginning to move to customer relations management (CRM) software solutions to improve access to government web sites. CRM is discussed in chapter 8 as a strategy and technology that has the potential to radically transform the way that government deals with its citizens.

Are these efforts by government agencies to offer information and services to citizens actually more effective and efficient than traditional "store front" operations or do they simply duplicate what agencies at all three levels of government are traditionally doing with their offices that are open to the public? At the moment there is no comprehensive answer to that question. Certainly some local, state, and federal agencies' e-government web sites have provided enhanced access to information and sometimes transaction services to its constituents, but the fact that not all of the citizenry has "gone digital" means that many public agencies still have to maintain public offices to deal with citizen inquiries and transactions, leading perhaps to costly duplications of services. The tremendous push behind e-government suggests that one day most public agency information, services, and transactions will ultimately be almost entirely online.

The Promises and Pitfalls of E-Democracy

While e-government develops, there is still some ambiguity about e-democracy. It has met enthusiasm with those who favor more direct democracy and reluctance with those who favor representative democracy. For our purposes here, e-democracy will be defined as the use of the Internet and related technology to foster democratic discourse among citizens and between citizens and elected or appointed officials over public policy issues. It does not include the provision of services or routine information (like addresses and phone numbers of elected officials or government agencies). It also does not include electronic voting, which, of course, is part of the democratic process; e-voting will be treated as a separate topic.

The Internet and related technologies, often called Information Communications Technologies (ICT), have great potential to allow citizens and elected or appointed officials to share information about public policy issues and to engage in a dialogue about those issues. The United Kingdom and Switzerland are two nations that have actively embraced e-democracy initiatives nationally and locally. In the United States, the city of Minneapolis has been a pioneer in e-democracy. In the United Kingdom, there has been considerable effort to get all elected officials "on the Web" so that they can communicate with their constituents. This goes for all members of parliament and all local council representatives. Chat rooms, discussion boards, and weblogs have been set up as places to discuss national and local policy issues. Nonbinding referenda have taken place so that elected officials can "consult with" their constituents.

The response to all of this on the part of the elected officials has been mixed at best. Some embrace it, some ignore it. Aside from any personal "techno-fear" aversions on the part of some elected officials to using Internet technologies, there is the broader issue expressed by some that e-democracy is a threat to true representative democracy. Those against e-democracy hold to the notion that they know what is in the best interest of their constituents, so they do not need to consult with them. Some have expressed fears that e-democracy will result in the return to direct democracy along with the rule of the mob and demagoguery. Because of these nontechnical issues, e-democracy has been slow to catch on in the United Kingdom, but it has taken a foothold and will probably continue to grow.

The *eGov Monitor Weekly*, a weekly electronic newsletter, summarizes the e-democracy initiatives in the United Kingdom as follows:

> Tools are being developed for online consultations between the government, citizen, action groups and business. But the results are limited. There is much discussion and interaction between groups and citizens and, to a certain extent, between government and the citizenry. However eDemocracy is evolving within society more on the level of group-to-group and peer-to-peer interactions with participants using ICTs (Internet communications technologies) to enhance and better their lives. The latter is a form of eDemocracy that has minimal influence from government, except to the degree that people might use online or offline government information to further their work. Community and online groups work well when these people are driven by individual interest, no matter what the cause.[28]

E-democracy is more advanced in Switzerland, which has always had a very strong "near" or "semi" direct democracy movement.[29] In the nineteenth century, the people of the Swiss cantons and the Federation led the way by introducing elements of direct democracy—referendums and popular initiatives—into their constitutions. Somewhat later, individual states in the United States also adopted similar forms of direct democracy. These elements give citizens a voice in important political decisions as well as the right to vote in elections.

Interest in direct democracy has also been growing in other countries. In 1994, there were almost 160 national referendums in the world (not counting those in Switzerland). A high proportion of these took place in the countries of Central and Eastern Europe and in South America. Therefore, from a comparative perspective, Switzerland's direct democracy is not unique, as is often claimed, though it is an exceptional case. Together with individual states in the United States, Switzerland has developed a system in which popular initiatives and referendums give citizens the opportunity to participate regularly in the political decisions of their parliaments. In addition, Switzerland is the only country that enables its people to participate in decision making at all levels of government, from local to national. Furthermore, in Switzerland, citizens have an a priori right to vote on every conceivable issue, from speed limits on motorways to the abolition of the army.

The mechanisms that allow Switzerland to be considered a "near" direct democracy are: the popular initiative, the optional referendum, and the mandatory referendum. The popular initiative gives citizens the right to propose an amendment or addition to the Swiss constitution. In order to be valid, 100,000 signatures of people eligible to vote must be collected over a period of eighteen months. If the number of valid signatures is sufficient, the initiative is put to a popular vote. The optional referendum gives citizens the right to demand that any bill approved by parliament be put to a nationwide vote. In order to be valid, 50,000 signatures must be collected in 100 days. If the number of valid signatures is sufficient, the new law must be approved by a popular vote. Under the mandatory referendum, all constitutional amendments approved by parliament must be put to a nationwide vote. Voters are also required to approve Swiss membership of certain international organizations, such as the United Nations and the European Union. With such a rich tradition of near direct democracy, we will see in the next section that Switzerland has taken the lead in Internet voting.

Minneapolis was a pioneer in e-democracy. In 1994 the City of Minneapolis initiated what is now called Minnesota E-Democracy.[30] Accessed through discussion boards, the initiative was originally designed to be a free and open forum for discussion of any public policy issue that any citizen might wish to raise. It became very popular very quickly, but this enthusiasm soon became a problem. The discussion boards grew in vast numbers as did citizen comments. Some of those comments were relevant and worthwhile. Many others were simply "off the wall" and sometimes downright rude. It became very difficult to follow the public debates. To use an analogy, the problem was this: In many cities across the nation you might find an individual who attends every city council meeting and who demands to speak on every issue before the council, even if he or she has no clue as to the nature of the issue.

Through Robert's Rules of Order and other mechanisms, councils limit the amount of time that such "cranks" may speak; otherwise, the work of the council would never get done. Minneapolis discovered that there were way too many such "cranks" within the State of Minnesota who clogged up the discussion boards with trivial, meaningless, and off-topic comments. What was originally envisioned as a universally free forum for public discourse turned into an electronic mob scene. The people who ran Minnesota E-Democracy had to establish rules for participating in the discussion boards and, in some cases, had to prevent some people from having access to the discussions. A valiant attempt at direct democracy ran into its old nemesis—mob rule—and totally free public discourse had to be curtailed.

What does all of this portend for the advancement of e-democracy overall? Well, in countries such as the United States and the United Kingdom where representative democracy is firmly entrenched there may be opportunities to expand public discourse on policy matters through the use of carefully monitored discussion boards, but the technological impetus for a return to direct democracy seems lacking.

E-Voting

The popular phrase "build it and they will come" may or may not apply to Internet voting. While it is technically possible to allow citizens to vote in general elections from their home-based microcomputers, cyber cafés, or public places like libraries, the practice is far from widespread at this time. The primary concern about Internet voting is security. It is possible that an electronic election could be hacked. Therefore, security measures are of utmost concern. For this reason, political jurisdictions in the United States have been cautious about instituting Internet voting. There have been some experiments in state and local elections in 2002. In some cases the votes were counted; in other cases they were not. Some counties of Washington, California, Arizona, and elsewhere have held some nonbinding Internet voting experiments. Perhaps the most talked about Internet voting experiment was the 2002 Arizona Democratic presidential primary in which approximately 85,000 votes were cast and counted electronically.[31]

Nowhere have security issues been made more vivid than in the case of the Secure Electronic Registration and Voting Experiment (SERVE), an Internet-based voting system built by Accenture and its subcontractors for the U.S.

Department of Defense's Federal Voting Assistance Program (FVAP).[32] The experiment tried to address the problems that Americans abroad (military and civilians) have in dealing with absentee ballots. The problem with absentee voting lies in obtaining and returning paper ballots from a distant location. It can be a frustrating process that may depend on slow or unreliable foreign postal services.

A team of experts were brought in to assess the security of SERVE in 2003. Their report released in January 2004 offers the following observations:

- DRE (direct recording electronic) voting systems have been widely criticized elsewhere for various deficiencies and security vulnerabilities: that their software is totally closed and proprietary; that the software undergoes insufficient scrutiny during qualification and certification; that they are especially vulnerable to various forms of insider (programmer) attacks; and that DREs have no voter-verified audit trails (paper or otherwise) that could largely circumvent these problems and improve voter confidence. All of these criticisms, which we endorse, apply directly to SERVE as well.
- But in addition, because SERVE is an Internet- and PC-based system, it has numerous other fundamental security problems that leave it vulnerable to a variety of well-known cyberattacks (insider attacks, denial-of-service attacks, spoofing, automated vote buying, viral attacks on voter PCs, etc.), any one of which could be catastrophic.
- Such attacks could occur on a large scale and could be launched by anyone from a disaffected lone individual to a well-financed enemy agency outside the reach of U.S. law. These attacks could result in large-scale, selective voter disenfranchisement, and/or privacy violation, and/or vote buying and selling, and/or vote switching even to the extent of reversing the outcome of many elections at once, including the presidential election. With care in the design, some of the attacks could succeed and yet go completely undetected. Even if detected and neutralized, such attacks could have a devastating effect on public confidence in elections.
- It is impossible to estimate the probability of a successful cyberattack (or multiple successful attacks) on any one election. But we show that the attacks we are most concerned about are quite easy to perpetrate. In some cases kits are readily available on the Internet that could be modified or used directly for attacking an election. And we must consider the obvious fact that a U.S. general election offers one of the most tempting targets for cyberattack in the history of the Internet, whether the attacker's motive is overtly political or simply self-aggrandizement.
- The vulnerabilities we describe cannot be fixed by design changes or bug

fixes to SERVE. These vulnerabilities are fundamental in the architecture of the Internet and of the PC hardware and software that is ubiquitous today. They cannot all be eliminated for the foreseeable future without some unforeseen radical breakthrough. It is quite possible that they will not be eliminated without a wholesale redesign and replacement of much of the hardware and software security systems that are part of, or connected to, today's Internet.

- We have examined numerous variations on SERVE in an attempt to rec-ommend an alternative Internet-based voting system that might deliver somewhat less voter convenience in exchange for fewer or milder security vulnerabilities. However, all such variations suffer from the same kinds of fundamental vulnerabilities that SERVE does; regrettably, we cannot recommend any of them. We do suggest a kiosk architecture as a start-ing point for designing an alternative voting system with similar aims to SERVE, but which does not rely on the Internet or on unsecured PC software.

- The SERVE system might appear to work flawlessly in 2004, with no successful attacks detected. It is as unfortunate as it is inevitable that a seemingly successful voting experiment in a U.S. presidential election involving seven states would be viewed by most people as strong evi-dence that SERVE is a reliable, robust, and secure voting system. Such an outcome would encourage expansion of the program by FVAP in future elections, or the marketing of the same voting system by vendors to jurisdictions all over the United States, and other countries as well. However, the fact that no successful attack is detected does not mean that none occurred. Many attacks, especially if cleverly hidden, would be extremely difficult to detect, even in cases when they change the outcome of a major election. Furthermore, the lack of a successful attack in 2004 does not mean that successful attacks would be less likely to happen in the future; quite the contrary, future attacks would be more likely, both because there is more time to prepare the attack and because expanded use of SERVE or similar systems would make the prize more valuable. In other words, a "successful" trial of SERVE in 2004 is the top of a slippery slope toward even more vulnerable systems in the future.

- Like the proponents of SERVE, we believe that there should be better support for voting for our military overseas. Still, we regret that we are forced to conclude that the best course is to not field the SERVE system at all. Because the danger of successful, large-scale attacks is so great, we reluctantly recommend shutting down the development of SERVE immediately and not attempting anything like it in the future until both the Internet and the world's home computer infrastructure have been fundamentally redesigned or some other unforeseen security breakthroughs appear.

- We want to make clear that in recommending that SERVE be shut down we mean no criticism of the FVAP, or of Accenture, or any of its personnel or subcontractors. They have been completely aware all along of the security problems we describe here, and we have been impressed with the engineering sophistication and skill they have devoted to attempts to ameliorate or eliminate them. We do not believe that a differently constituted project could do any better job than the current team. The real barrier to success is not a lack of vision, skill, resources, or dedication; it is the fact that, given the current Internet and PC security technology and the goal of a secure, all-electronic remote voting system, the FVAP has taken on an essentially impossible task. There really is no good way to build such a voting system without a radical change in overall architecture of the Internet and the PC, or some unforeseen security breakthrough. The SERVE project is thus too far ahead of its time and should not be reconsidered until there is a much-improved security infrastructure to build upon.[33]

On the basis of this report, the SERVE project, which cost $22 million, was not implemented.

The experts' conclusions reflect the same cautions expressed by the California Internet Voting Task Force in 2002:

- The implementation of Internet Voting will be a complex undertaking with no room for error. This task force recommends a phased-in approach to developing an Internet Voting System that will allow election officials and voters the opportunity to identify any possible problems before they occur.
- Phase One of the task force's recommendation would provide for the use of Internet Voting technology in a supervised setting like a traditional polling place. In this phase, voters would not yet gain the advantage of voting from any place at any time, but the integrity of the voting and tabulation technology will be verified through the use of Internet Voting Machines.
- Phase Two of the task force's recommendation would allow voters to cast Remote Internet Ballots. The authentication of voter identity would take place with a combination of manual and electronic procedures that would provide at least the same level of security as the existing voting process.
- For the foreseeable future, Internet Voting should be viewed only as a supplement to, not a replacement of, traditional paper-based voting.
- The design of any Internet voting system must be at least as secure against fraud as the current absentee ballot process in every respect.

- All election activities stem from voter registration, which is a paper-based system maintained locally by fifty-eight county election offices. Until digital signatures and digital identification are a common aspect of everyday life for all Californians, online registration and the eventual collection of online petition signatures for initiative, referendum, and recall campaigns should not be made available.
- Until the voter registration rolls contain a digital signature or biometric identification for all registered voters, requests for Remote Internet ballots must be made on paper with a manual signature that can be compared against the manual signature on the voter's registration card. Voters will be provided a digital signature for voting purposes once the manual signature on the Internet ballot request and the paper voter registration card are verified.
- Internet voting systems must be designed to protect the secrecy of the ballot, while providing election officials with an audit trail that can be used to conduct recounts of election results.[34]

While officials in the United States are cautious about implementing Internet voting, their counterparts in the United Kingdom and Western Europe are much more aggressive. As mentioned earlier, the United Kingdom has many advocates of e-democracy. Several political jurisdictions in the United Kingdom have experimented with Internet voting for referenda.

While not pervasive today, Internet voting systems are likely to increase in the near future. Consequently, it is a good idea to establish some criteria for such systems. Jim Adler, president and CEO of VoteHere.net, offers the criteria presented in Exhibit 6.1. These proposed criteria certainly seem to complicate e-voting, more so than conventional voting. Yet the overall pace of technological innovations would suggest that one day Internet voting will be commonplace, as the following example for Switzerland suggests.

The Swiss conducted the first federal online voting experiment in September of 2004.[35] Twenty-two thousand voters in four Geneva municipalities—Anières, Cologny, Carouge, and Meyrin—were given the opportunity to vote online on three referenda: whether to introduce a statutory paid maternity benefit nationwide, whether to extend a Swiss Post service, and whether to ease the country's naturalization laws. To vote online, a polling card number was keyed in before the system sent an electronic ballot. Voters were issued with a PIN code and also had to enter their birth date and place of origin in order to be recognized by the system. The electronic voters' registration system was designed to ensure that only one ballot per person could be cast. The experiment was considered a success by Swiss government officials. About 22 percent of the voters chose to cast their votes electronically, and turnout in the four Internet-voting municipalities reached 58 percent, a few percent-

Exhibit 6.1
Criteria for Internet Voting

- Eligibility—Only authorized voters can vote.
- Uniqueness—No voter can vote more than once.
- Privacy—No one can determine how anyone voted, including election officials.
- Soundness—No one can change, add, or delete votes without being discovered. In the most sound systems, the final vote tally may be perfect, either because no inaccuracies can be introduced or because all introduced inaccuracies can be detected and corrected. Partially accurate systems can detect but not necessarily correct inaccuracies.
- Verifiability—Anyone can independently verify that all votes have been counted correctly. The verifiability property can be further classified into individual verifiability and universal verifiability. A system is individually verifiable if it allows voters to verify their own votes and, possibly, correct any mistakes they might find without sacrificing their privacy. The problem with this level of verifiability is that the burden is on the voter to verify his or her vote—an unreasonable requirement for the average voter. Systems that are universally verifiable allow anyone to verify the entire election, including election officials, observers, and voters. All voters can make sure their vote has been taken into account in the final tabulation.
- Non-coercibility—No voter can prove that he or she voted in a particular way. This property is important for the prevention of vote buying and extortion. Voters can sell their votes only if they are able to prove to the buyer that they actually voted a certain way.
- Revisability—A voter can change his or her vote within a given period of time. This is typically not allowed in civic elections.
- Convenience—Voters may cast their votes quickly, in one session, with minimal equipment or special skills.
- Flexibility—This attribute allows a variety of ballot question formats, including open-ended questions. Flexibility is important for write-in candidates and some survey questions. Some voting protocols are inflexible because they allow for only single-bit (yes/no) votes.
- Mobility—No restrictions, other than logistical, are placed on the location from which a voter can cast a vote.
- Efficiency—The election can be administered with a reasonable amount of resources.

Source: Jim Adler, president and CEO of VoteHere.net, www.votehere.net/ada_compliant/ourtechnology/whitepapers/primer.html (accessed May 29, 2006).

age points above their average turnout of the last five years. Swiss authorities believe that online voting will become a third option alongside postal voting and conventional polling-place voting. The experiment was not without its detractors, however. The Swiss information technology community opposed the experiment because of concerns about the security of the system.

So what is the future of Internet voting? Despite concerns about security it looks like the Internet and related technologies will be used with greater frequency in the future to allow citizens to cast their votes online, whether it be from home, a cyber café, or a public polling place. The present concern about security may be ameliorated by advances in strong encryption and other security-enhancing technologies. Questions about whether Internet voting will increase voter turnout remain unanswered.

The Digital Divide

One of the greatest obstacles to e-government, e-democracy, and Internet voting is the digital divide. The divide is enormous when viewed globally. The statistics on who has access to the Internet speak for themselves. The "haves" are clearly North America, the United Kingdom, much of Western Europe, China, South Korea, Japan, some Asian countries, Australia, and New Zealand. The rest of the world, including most of the nations of Africa, Russia, and former Soviet Republics are the "have nots." The spread of technology ensures that eventually this gap will close, but no one can say just when this will occur. Consider that 80 percent of the people in the world have not heard a dial tone, let alone surfed the web.[36] Even within the "haves" there are segments of people who do not have access to the Internet and hence no access to e-government, e-democracy, and e-voting.

The digital divide is a complex issue because of the timeliness and accuracy of the data that defines the divide, and because of rapid changes in technology that also define the divide in different ways. The best data about the digital divide in the United States were collected from the Department of Commerce's 1998 census data, by the Department's National Telecommunications and Information Administration (NTIA). In *Falling Through the Net*, NTIA reports that

> Overall, we have found that the number of Americans connected to the nation's information infrastructure is soaring. Nevertheless, this year's report finds that a digital divide still exists, and, in many cases, is actually widening over time. Minorities, low-income persons, the less educated, and children of single-parent households, particularly when they reside in rural areas or central cities, are among the groups that lack access to information resources.[37]

A closer look at the 1998 data will show some of the disparities among groups that do and do not have access to the Internet. Only 38.9 percent of rural households had access to the Internet. Although rising rapidly, only 23.5 percent of black households and 23.6 percent of Hispanic households had Internet access. People over fifty years of age were the least likely to be Internet users. People with a disability were less likely by half to have access to the Internet, and those with vision problems or manual dexterity problems were even less likely to use the Internet. Looking at actual computer ownership, both black (32 percent) and Hispanic (33.7 percent) households fell behind the national rate of 51 percent of all households.

How accurate are these data today? We just do not know, but we can guess that Internet access either from home or from a public place like an Internet café or library has increased for all groups given that the technology has become cheaper to buy. The divide may have dwindled even more, taking into consideration that PDAs and cell phones can now access the Internet. The divide may have become a non-issue for some groups.

Because of changes in technology, the digital divide is actually being redefined in terms of broadband access versus telephone access. According to the Consumer Federation of America we are now facing a second-generation digital divide between those who have broadband access and those who have only dial-up access. A report titled *Expanding the Digital Divide and Falling Behind on Broadband: Why a Telecommunications Policy of Neglect Is Not Benign*, published jointly with the Consumers Union, explains that "Half of all households with incomes above \$75,000 have broadband, while half of all households with incomes below \$30,000 have no Internet at home."[38] Now the issue is who has high-speed access and who does not, and it is a public policy issue. The Consumer Federation and Consumers Union are critical of the Bush administration's reluctance to support or subsidize universal access to high-speed Internet.[39] They report that

> the U.S. is falling behind other nations and the digital divide is growing . . . the U.S. has fallen from third to thirteenth in broadband adoption. When per-capita income is taken into account, the U.S. is performing poorly in getting high-speed Internet to American households. Cross national comparisons of price show that Americans pay between ten and twenty times as much, on a megabit basis, as consumers in Korea and Japan pay. Three years ago the price gap was half as large. There has been almost no increase in the percentage of households with Internet access at home. Penetration has been stuck at around 60 percent.[40]

A Library of Congress Report (2004) summarizes the broadband digital divide issue as follows:

Some policymakers, believing that disparities in broadband access across American society could have adverse economic and social consequences on those left behind, assert that the federal government should play a more active role to avoid a "digital divide" in broadband access. One approach is for the federal government to provide financial assistance to support broadband deployment in underserved areas. Others, however, believe that federal assistance for broadband deployment is not appropriate. Some opponents question the reality of the "digital divide," and argue that federal intervention in the broadband marketplace would be premature and, in some cases, counterproductive.

Legislation introduced into the 107th Congress sought to provide federal financial assistance for broadband deployment in the form of grants, loans, subsidies, and tax credits. Similar legislation has been introduced into the 108th Congress. In assessing this legislation, several policy issues arise. For example, is the current status of broadband deployment data an adequate basis on which to base policy decisions? Given the early stages of broadband deployment, is federal assistance premature, or do the risks of delaying assistance to underserved areas outweigh the benefits of avoiding federal intervention in the marketplace? And finally, if one assumes that governmental action is necessary to spur broadband deployment in underserved areas, which specific approaches, either separately or in combination, are likely to be most effective?[41]

The questions raised in this report are yet to be resolved.

A September 2004 report from NITA titled *A Nation Online: Entering the Broadband Age* shows that there is a significant transition from dial-up to high-speed Internet access.[42] The number of U.S. households with broadband service more than doubled from 9.1 percent in September 2001 to 19.9 percent in October 2003, and the proportion of dial-up users declined from 40.7 percent to 34.3 percent. Yet there still seems to be a divide between urban and rural net surfers. Only 24.7 percent of rural households had high-speed access as compared to 40.4 percent of households in urban areas. Data in the report also indicate that blacks, Hispanics, and people with disabilities lag behind whites in their overall use of the Internet whether it is via dial-up or high-speed connections, and the same relative disparities exist for those groups who use broadband technologies. Interestingly, the NITA report states that the Bush administration has established a goal of universal and affordable high-speed Internet access by the year 2007. This runs contrary to the opinions of the Consumer Federation of America and Consumers' Union.

So, what can we make of all of this confusing data about the digital divide? Well, the United States ranks behind several other nations when it comes to overall Internet access as well as high-speed access. Within the United States, black, Hispanic, rural, disabled, and low-income groups of people lag behind the overall white population when it comes to Internet access of all kinds, as well as high-speed access. Also the lack of high-speed broadband access for some segments of the population is becoming a major public policy issue.

Summary and a Look Forward

As we have seen, the Internet has brought with it many considerable advantages and opportunities and will probably continue to do so. It has also brought with it several public management and public policy challenges that still plague administrators and policymakers, from seemingly mundane management decisions about what types of routers an agency should acquire to establish an agency's intranet to large policy issues such as the potential for the promotion of more e-government information and services, e-democracy, and e-voting. The technology is in existence or is still being developed to enhance public agencies' use of the Internet to provide information, services, opportunities for enhanced democratic discourse, and even voting, but the exact future of such activities is still unclear, not for technical reasons, but because of political, public policy, and public management concerns. The next chapter on systems development and implementation will take us back inside of the world of IT managers and technicians who have to build and implement information systems to enhance the performance of public agencies.

7

Systems Development
and Implementation

The information systems failures mentioned in chapter 1 usually begin during systems development and may be carried forward into system implementation. For this reason it is absolutely essential that public managers know about the various approaches to systems development and implementation, which will be the topics of this chapter.

There are several different approaches to systems development: the waterfall method, prototyping, rapid applications development, agile software development, joint applications development, end user development, and the Software Acquisition Capability Maturity Model. The advantages and disadvantages of each will be presented here. Public managers should pay particular attention to the selection of one or more of these approaches because quite often the situation or problem at hand will dictate which approach to use. The selection of the wrong approach can lead to disaster.

Each of the approaches may apply to the development of new information systems consisting of hardware and software decisions, or to modifications of existing systems including hardware and software, or to just software acquisition or development by itself without reference to new hardware acquisitions. This distinction is important because many contemporary systems development improvements involve only additions to or modifications of software; an entire software acquisition capability maturity model will be addressed in this chapter. For now, it is best to think of the approaches to systems development as involving decisions about the development of software applications for existing hardware foundations, although hardware choices may also be needed in some circumstances.

This chapter will present the major approaches to systems development and implementation in the following order: the waterfall method, prototyping, rapid applications development, agile software development, joint applications development, end user development, the Software Acquisition Capability

Maturity Model (SA-CMM), types of system implementation, and finally systems maintenance. Some of the major similarities and differences among the major approaches will be noted.

The Waterfall Method

The waterfall method is also known as the systems development life cycle (SDLC) and has been around in one form or another since the mid-1960s.[1] The term "waterfall" reflects the top-down approach of the SDLC as the systems development process proceeds from one step to another until the process has been completed, with each step being considered as a "deliverable," in project management terms, that requires someone's approval or "sign off." Each stage in the life cycle cascades downward in a linear fashion until the project is completed.

Given its long history, the steps in the SDLC have been enumerated in slightly different ways at different levels of detail, but the steps are pretty much all the same. Here the steps in the SDLC will be presented from the official *Department of Justice Systems Development Life Cycle Guidance Document*, which can serve as a model for all other depictions of the waterfall approach.[2] Exhibit 7.1 presents the steps in the SDLC officially used by the Department of Justice (DOJ).

Other renditions of the SDLC portray the various steps with either less or greater detail. The DOJ model is fairly comprehensive without going into too much detail and gives a good sense of each of the steps as enumerated by a public agency.

The DOJ also insists on strict management controls for the entire life of the project. These include:

- Life Cycle Management should be used to ensure a structured approach to information systems development and operation.
- Each system project must have an accountable sponsor.
- A single project manager must be appointed for each system project.
- A comprehensive project management plan is required for each system project.
- Data Management and security must be emphasized throughout the life cycle.
- A system project may not proceed until resource availability is assured.[3]

As one can see from the ten steps in the process and the management controls, the SDLC is indeed a very structured approach to building and

Exhibit 7.1
U.S. Department of Justice Systems Development Life Cycle

Steps in the System Life Cycle

1. Initiation Phase
The initiation of a system (or project) begins when a business need or opportunity is identified. A Project Manager should be appointed to manage the project. This business need is documented in a Concept Proposal. After the Concept Proposal is approved, the System Concept Development Phase begins.

2. System Concept Development Phase
Once a business need is approved, the approaches for accomplishing the concept are reviewed for feasibility and appropriateness. The Systems Boundary Document identifies the scope of the system and requires Senior Official approval and funding before beginning the Planning Phase.

3. Planning Phase
The concept is further developed to describe how the business will operate once the approved system is implemented, and to assess how the system will impact employee and customer privacy. To ensure the products and/or services provide the required capability on time and within budget, project resources, activities, schedules, tools, and reviews are defined. Additionally, security certification and accreditation activities begin with the identification of system security requirements and the completion of a high-level vulnerability assessment.

4. Requirements Analysis Phase
Functional user requirements are formally defined and delineate the requirements in terms of data, system performance, security, and maintainability requirements for the system. All requirements are defined to a level of detail sufficient for systems design to proceed. All requirements need to be measurable and testable and relate to the business need or opportunity identified in the Initiation Phase.

5. Design Phase
The physical characteristics of the system are designed during this

phase. The operating environment is established, major subsystems and their inputs and outputs are defined, and processes are allocated to resources. Everything requiring user input or approval must be documented and reviewed by the user. The physical characteristics of the system are specified and a detailed design is prepared. Subsystems identified during design are used to create a detailed structure of the system. Each subsystem is partitioned into one or more design units or modules. Detailed logic specifications are prepared for each software module.

6. Development Phase
The detailed specifications produced during the design phase are translated into hardware, communications, and executable software. Software shall be unit tested, integrated, and retested in a systematic manner. Hardware is assembled and tested.

7. Integration and Test Phase
The various components of the system are integrated and systematically tested. The user tests the system to ensure that the functional requirements, as defined in the functional requirements document, are satisfied by the developed or modified system. Prior to installing and operating the system in a production environment, the system must undergo certification and accreditation activities.

8. Implementation Phase
The system or system modifications are installed and made operational in a production environment. The phase is initiated after the system has been tested and accepted by the user. This phase continues until the system is operating in production in accordance with the defined user requirements.

9. Operations and Maintenance Phase
The system operation is ongoing. The system is monitored for continued performance in accordance with user requirements, and needed system modifications are incorporated. The operational system is periodically assessed through In-Process Reviews to determine how the system can be made more efficient and effective. Operations continue as long as the system can be effectively adapted to respond to an organization's needs. When modifications or changes are identified as necessary, the system may reenter the planning phase.

---

10. Disposition Phase

The disposition activities ensure the orderly termination of the system and preserve the vital information about the system so that some or all of the information may be reactivated in the future if necessary. Particular emphasis is given to proper preservation of the data processed by the system, so that the data is effectively migrated to another system or archived in accordance with applicable records management regulations and policies, for potential future access.

Source: U.S. Department of Justice, *The Department of Justice Systems Development Life Cycle Guidance Document*, Chapter 1, Section 1.2 (January 2003), www.usdoj.gov/jmd/irm/lifecycle/table.htm (accessed May 30, 2006).

---

implementing systems. It is favored in those situations where large software (and sometimes also hardware) systems need to be designed and built under strict managerial controls that supposedly ensure that the project will not go over budget or over the promised delivery time, and that the project will have almost all, if not all, of the intended functional requirements. Herein lies its paradoxical downfall. It is often too structured, which leads to very lengthy development and implementation times, often causing a project to go over schedule and perhaps over projected costs, and by the time the system is finally implemented some of the business requirements (what the end users want the system to do) can change.

Linearity is a convenient fiction in planning and developing an information system. Nowhere is this more evident than in the requirements analysis and design phases. During requirements analysis, systems analysts and designers are supposed to be talking with end users about what they want the system to do. In some cases, the end users may not have the foggiest idea about what they want the system to do. In other cases, they may have only a vague idea, which usually leads to an abstract and not very concrete vision of what the system is supposed to do. This uncertainty can lead to a system that does not do what the end user really needs it to do. To avoid this outcome, one needs to ignore the assumption of linearity and have the systems analysts and designers return to the end users, usually several times, to get a very concrete understanding of what the system should do to satisfy the needs of the end user. This violates the linearity rule of the SDLC and can lead to extended development times as designers repeatedly return to users to find out what features they may want in the system.

Then there is probably the greatest systems development sin of all: not consulting with the end user at all. This can happen when the analysts and the designers talk only to top- and mid-level managers about what they want the system to do. If top- and mid-level managers have firsthand knowledge of the work that will be performed, this situation may not pose a problem, but such acquaintance with the day-to-day work is rare. Also, not talking with the end user can create a tremendous barrier to end user acceptance of the system because they have little or no ownership (sometimes called "buy in") of the new system. According to the Standish Group, end user involvement in the design of a system is the leading criteria for systems development success, with clear statements of requirements coming as the third success criterion.[4] Not communicating with the end user would be the single greatest contributing factor to systems development failure. It should be evident that it is difficult to obtain a clear statement of system requirements without talking to the people who already do the work and who will be using the new system.

On the other hand, talking too much with the end users can cause another type of problem called requirements creep. This occurs when the end users begin to realize what the new system can do for them. Then they start asking for additional features, such as displaying three or four different types of screens of data, or producing three or four different types of reports containing different types of data. Carried to an absurd extreme, it is like asking the analysts and designers if the system can "make coffee, too." Requirements creep can indeed add some valuable extra functionality to a system, but it can be carried too far, causing a project to go over budget because vendors are only too happy to add more features at an additional cost. At some point in time, management must step in to prevent unnecessary requirements creep. That could be the responsibility of the project manager or the person heading up the steering committee for the project.

The linearity assumption should also be ignored during requirements analysis and design if management suspects that the analysis and design staff do not have a clue about the nature of the work performed. Imagine what a nightmare it would be if the analysis and design staff has no knowledge of the work processes and the end user staff have no knowledge of what an information system might do for them. The two "partners" in the design effort would have little to say to each other. Most vendors try to get around this by claiming to have technical experts who are also familiar with the work processes of agencies because they have worked on similar systems in similar agencies. In the best of all possible worlds this might be true, but it is essential for top management to make sure that the vendor has specific experience working with similar systems in similar agencies. If this is not the case, expect a long learning curve for both the IT professionals and agency staff as each gets to know something about the other's business.

Another extremely important issue can arise in the analysis and design phases—automating an already inefficient and ineffective paperwork process. This is where the seeds of business process reengineering should be sown, a topic for chapter 8. For now it will simply be introduced.

Suppose an agency has an existing paperwork process for handling some aspect of the day-to-day business activities of the organization. One should not go in and simply automate that existing paperwork process. If that paperwork process is inefficient or ineffective, the result will likely be an automated and, hence, a very fast but still inefficient or ineffective system. This is the time to step back and look at the nature of the work itself: What data need to be collected? How many times do they need to be collected? Where should they be stored? Who should receive them? How should they be represented on display screens or in electronically produced reports? Are there steps in the existing work process that are redundant? Are there steps in the work process that are unnecessary and can be eliminated? Are there steps in the work process that should be included but are not? In other words, before any requirements are collected and any design work done, the work itself needs to be examined to eliminate any inefficiencies and to identify opportunities to make the work process more effective. This is not a job for the IT staff but rather for persons who are experts at workflow analysis. Sometimes these experts can be found within an agency's own staff. At other times an agency might have to rely on the expertise of an outside consultant who knows how to analyze a work process to do away with inefficiencies and enhance the effectiveness of the work process before the process is automated.

A Case of What Can Go Wrong in Systems Development

The following is an actual example of what can go wrong in a systems development project. It illustrates the importance of following some of the steps in the SDLC and making informed management judgments about the anticipated requirements of a new information system.

In the early 1990s, a state health department decided that it was time to automate its medical and financial records.[5] The state health department consisted of 125 semiautonomous county health departments, not an uncommon occurrence in a decentralized and federalized system of governance such as that in the United States. Each county maintained its own paper-based records on patients in various forms. The design of the forms differed in each county. Some of the larger counties were already automated, but their systems had difficulty sharing data because their applications software differed. The automated systems that did exist did not work well. Some of the systems did not allow for data-entry errors to be corrected. Others allowed for corrections but only by starting from the beginning—in essence, they required the redoing of the entire data-entry process. At times, some of the systems would crash inexplicitly, leaving the workers unable to complete their work until the system came up again. When it came time to collect the forms from the 125 county offices, the central staff faced the monumental chore of sifting through hundreds of different forms looking for data on patients that would be in different places on different forms. To make matters worse, the handwriting on the forms was often difficult to read. Needless to say, the central information system was prone to error because of the difficulty of entering the data correctly.

Beyond these internal problems was the important issue of service delivery. Some of the patients seen in one county office had moved to other counties. If a patient needed service in the other county, a new file was established for the patient in that county; rarely did the patient's old file in the other county find its way to the new county to which the patient moved. This break in communication created considerable redundancy in data collection for those patients who were on the move. Management recognized the value of having patients' medical records move with them if they moved to a new county, but the current system did not support this. This lack of support, along with the chaotic and nonstandardized reporting system, led management to decide to automate all 125 offices and create a standardized reporting system.

The first mistake that management made in developing the new system was to come up with only a broad and general statement of requirements for the new system. They wanted the existing automated systems to share data. They wanted all 125 offices to be automated. They wanted data on the patients to be shared electronically across offices, and they wanted the county offices to share their data with the central office. They knew that this data sharing would require a client/server architecture, but beyond that they did not have much of a clue as to what the new system should do.

This was about as specific as management got in stating its requirements. Little was said about what data would be collected or how or by whom, or how the data would be entered into the new automated system. Nor was much said about what the data collection reports and the data presentation reports would look like. Those decisions were left up to the staff of the health department and the vendors during the design stage, causing delays, as well as changes, in the design of the system. According to the SDLC, these decisions should have been made during requirements analysis, not during the design stage where decisions like these can cause delays in the design and costly changes to the design itself. If the changes were not made during the design phase, they would have to be dealt with during the system maintenance phase, which requires a lot of reworking of the original design resulting in considerably more wasted time and money.

The health department did not have the personnel on staff to develop this new system internally. They put out a request for proposal (RFP) and subsequently signed a multimillion-dollar contract with an established vendor. That vendor soon realized that they did not have all the expertise to develop the new system, so they had to call in yet another vendor that had more experience with client/server systems. The addition of the new subvendor led to several redesign efforts that pushed the implementation of the new system way beyond its original "go live" date.

During the design and redesign phases another major mistake was made. No one looked to see if the existing paperwork processes that they were automating were, in themselves, efficient or effective, and whether they contained the information about the patients that management deemed necessary. No one looked at the nature of the workflow to see if it could be improved before it was automated.

Then the dreaded requirements creep occurred as the health department's staff began to learn what the technology could do for them. They began asking for changes to the system that was already in development, resulting in additional design work that was not within the terms of the original contract. This creep created a great deal of tension and animosity between the health department staff and the original prime contractor. It also added to the cost of the new system, which ultimately went over budget and over schedule. In the end, the health department was not happy with the system that they eventually got.

It is important to point out that in this case the technology was not at fault. The second vendor understood the client/server technology and how to develop it for the health department's needs. The fault rests with poor management decisions and an inability or a reluctance to follow some of the steps in the SDLC. The requirements should have been specified in detail before entering into the design phase; the health department's change requests should have been made during the requirements analysis; and the workflow process should have been examined and optimized according to the capabilities of the available technology.

Advantages and Disadvantages of the SDLC

Although the management and the vendors in the project just described could be faulted for not strictly following some of the steps in the SDLC, there are inherent problems in the waterfall model. For one thing, it is too rigid. It does not allow for the incorporation of new ideas about what a new system can do once the development and implementation process moves out of the requirements analysis phase, and sometimes new and useful ideas do emerge as a system is in the design phase. For another thing, it is often too complex and too time consuming, especially if one is looking to develop a relatively small system. It takes a lot of planning and a lot of money to fully implement the SDLC. In fact, in some large-scale SDLC projects the end users' requirements might change during the life of the systems development process due to changes in work processes mandated by management or by legislative action. Then there is the problem of accurately estimating the costs associated with each of the phases of development. This is a particularly vexing problem when an entirely new system is being built and there is little history upon which to estimate costs. Then, of course, the linearity assumption is often ignored and sometimes with just cause, as we shall see in the other approaches to systems development. Oddly enough, the inventor of the waterfall model, W.W. Royce, described it as an iterative model, but his followers insisted on the linearity assumption.[6]

When to Use the SDLC

Despite these limitations, the waterfall method should be given serious consideration when faced with new and large systems development, especially when the work that is actually performed is of a very routine and certain matter, requiring only standardized output screens and printed reports. It is better to have a complex, lengthy, and sometimes too rigid method than no method at all, and, of course, the steps in the SDLC can be relaxed somewhat if the situation calls for it. Because of the distinct stages in the model, it is relatively easy to track the progress of the project. This allows for project management methodologies to be applied to the development of systems. In turn, this means that specific milestones and deliverables can be identified. All of this affords greater control of the systems development and implementation process. The SDLC is also very useful in uncertain environments because it lends itself to the application of risk-management methods that identify potential risks and develop contingency plans if something were to go wrong.

Prototyping

Prototyping is pretty much the opposite of the waterfall model, and it is usually, but not always, confined simply to software development as opposed to the acquisition and testing of hardware.[7] It generally begins with requirements analysis in which the systems analysts and designers sit down with the end users and begin to explore the requirements of the end users. Based on a preliminary initial examination of requirements, a prototype of the system is developed and returned to the end users for evaluation. At this point the end users may ask for modifications to input screens, output screens, and printed reports to ensure that they have the data that they need and that the data are presented in a usable format.

Prototyping is an iterative process. The analysts and designers may sit down with the end users many times until the end users are satisfied with the development of the system. At this time, the prototype becomes the fully functional system. In this situation, the developers and users will be working with an actual system, usually consisting of input screens, output screens, and report generators that are modified until they meet the users' needs.

In some situations the analysts and designers will be dealing only with mock-ups of the actual systems—perhaps paper-based pictures of input screens, output screens, and reports that the end users can evaluate. This avoids the usually high cost of actually building the system (e.g., writing programming code). A downside to using mock-ups is that the end users usually do not understand why it may take a long time to get an actual working system once the final mock-up is approved because they may not appreciate the time it takes to design and code the actual system.

When actual usable systems are developed using the prototyping method, at some point the prototype becomes the actual accepted new system. It may not have all of the requirements or "bells and whistles" that the users actually want, but it will probably deliver a certain degree of acceptable functionality that most users will be satisfied with. Oftentimes of providing all of those additional bells and whistles becomes just too costly.

When to Use Prototyping

Prototyping as an approach to systems development works well when management wants to make sure that all of the requirements are clearly specified and that the final system does what the end users want it to do. Of course, this method also helps to ensure that the end users will actually accept and use the new system. Prototyping is best used in the development of relatively small systems that are not mission critical. The progress of the prototyping needs to be carefully managed to ensure that the iterations are completed in a timely fashion. While usually faster than the SDLC, prototyping can take an extended length of time if it is not carefully monitored.

Rapid Applications Development

Prototyping is at the heart of another systems development approach called rapid applications development (RAD), but RAD is more than just prototyping.[8] It has a somewhat different philosophy, usually expressed as the ability to build a system very quickly, usually within sixty to ninety days, as opposed to several months or years. The rationale behind RAD is that some basic system requirements can be fulfilled much faster than all of the desired requirements, which can be added later. In this way, the users get at least a partially functioning system in much less time than it would take to get a fully designed and implemented system, and the cost of development is usually a lot less than that of the prototyping method. Of course, the end users must be willing to negotiate about the quality of the delivered system since it may not do everything the end users want, at least initially. End users may have to be patient as additional features are added in the future.

Beyond iterative prototyping, RAD usually employs the use of CASE tools and time boxing. CASE stands for "computer-aided software engineering," which involves the use of specialized software programs that do nothing but write new software code for new software applications. These tools eliminate the need for a programmer to actually write the software code by hand for a new application. They also allow the programmer to borrow and modify existing program code from similar preexisting applications and apply it to the new application. Special types of CASE tools, sometimes called "computer-aided prototyping systems," or CAPS, are used exclusively for prototyping activities. CAPS speed up coding time and reduce coding errors. Both of these features of CASE tools reduce both the time and the cost of producing usable code for a new application. Time boxing is an IT industry code word for putting a desired feature of a new system into a "time box" for later development. It speeds up the delivery of a new system, but the system lacks fully desired functionality. It also allows management to control for requirements creep since each additional requirement is in a "time box," and management can decide when and if to add the requirement in the future.

When to Use RAD

RAD is a useful systems development approach to use when an agency needs to develop a new system quickly. The system should meet the minimum number of user requirements, and the agency should be willing to wait for additional requirements or improvements to be added at a later time. In addition to reducing the time to "go live," RAD is usually a less expensive approach to systems development than other systems, which can be a plus when agency budgets are tight.

Agile Software Development

An expansion on RAD is agile software development, which is a conceptual framework for software development and a collection of software development

Exhibit 7.2
Principles Behind the Agile Manifesto

We follow these principles:
1. Our highest priority is to satisfy the customer through early and continuous delivery of valuable software.
2. Welcome changing requirements, even late in development.
3. Agile processes harness change for the customer's competitive advantage.
4. Deliver working software frequently, from a couple of weeks to a couple of months, with a preference to the shorter timescale.
5. Businesspeople and developers must work together daily throughout the project.
6. Build projects around motivated individuals. Give them the environment and support they need, and trust them to get the job done.
7. The most efficient and effective method of conveying information to and within a development team is face-to-face conversation.
8. Working software is the primary measure of progress.
9. Agile processes promote sustainable development.
10. The sponsors, developers, and users should be able to maintain a constant pace indefinitely.
11. Continuous attention to technical excellence and good design enhances agility.
12. Simplicity—the art of maximizing the amount of work not done—is essential.
13. The best architectures, requirements, and designs emerge from self-organizing teams.
14. At regular intervals, the team reflects on how to become more effective, then tunes and adjusts its behavior accordingly.

Source: "Principles Behind the Agile Manifesto," http://agilemanifesto. org/principles.html (accessed May 31, 2006).

methods. Like RAD it uses prototyping, time boxing, and a variety of CASE tools. Unlike RAD, it holds to the philosophy that a systems design change can be made at any point in the developmental process, even after formal requirements analysis and design has been accomplished. For this reason its followers call it an adaptive process rather than an iterative one like RAD or a linear one like the SDLC.

Agile got its start in 2001 when a small group of programmers got together at a conference in Utah and drew up a manifesto to support their approach to software development.[9] The manifesto clearly describes the philosophy behind this approach to software development, as shown in Exhibit 7.2.

This philosophy is a far cry from the rigidity of the waterfall model and even appears extreme when compared to prototyping and RAD. Indeed, followers of agile software development distinguish what they do by calling it adaptive rather than iterative, which characterizes prototyping and RAD. It has been called "cowboy programming," which means do anything you want to do, follow no specific method, and forget about documenting what you are doing. This is not quite true for RAD, however, since as a method it does use some very well-defined processes and procedures.

Extreme programming (XP), one of the methods of software engineering sometimes used in RAD or agile systems development and implementation, is highly controversial. It was introduced by Kent Beck and others in 1999 as an approach to software development that can meet the challenges of rapidly changing business requirements.[10] It involves small teams of developers and end users who work closely together to design specific functionalities for a system in the simplest way possible, along with repeated testing of the system and improved design of the system based on the repeated tests. XP sidesteps the lengthy requirements analysis and design phases of the SDLC and moves directly to building small parts of the planned system until all of the parts are finally put together to form the completed total system. XP is based on twelve principles presented in Exhibit 7.3.

As an approach to systems development XP has its fair share of critics.[11] They complain about the lack of detailed specifications, the lack of up-front design, and the incremental nature of the design activity that appears to take place "on the fly." They note that organizations are reluctant to embrace this approach to systems development because they fear they will not be able to control the activities of the designers and programmers. Despite these objections quite a few software developers and engineers are pursuing extreme programming. What will come of it in the future is not known at this moment. It is important to point out that XP is just one approach to systems development under the broader rubric of agile systems development. Other, more conservative approaches to actually writing the code and developing the systems can be used.

When to Use Agile Development

When should the management of a public agency choose to use the agile development approach? It is appropriate for systems that are not mission

Exhibit 7.3
The Twelve Principles of Extreme Programming (XP)

- The Planning Process—The desired features of the software, which are communicated by the customer, are combined with cost estimates provided by the programmers to determine the most important factors of the software. This stage is sometimes called the Planning Game.
- Small Releases—The software is developed in small stages that are updated frequently, typically every two weeks.
- Metaphor—All members on an XP team use common names and descriptions to guide development and communicate on common terms.
- Simple Design—The software should include only the code that is necessary to achieve the desired results communicated by the customer at each stage in the process. The emphasis is not on building for future versions of the product.
- Testing—Testing is done consistently throughout the process. Programmers design the tests first and then write the software to fulfill the requirements of the test. The customer also provides acceptance tests at each stage to ensure the desired results are achieved.
- Refactoring—XP programmers improve the design of the software through every stage of development instead of waiting until the end of the development and going back to correct flaws.
- Pair Programming—All code is written by a pair of programmers working at the same machine.
- Collective Ownership—Every line of code belongs to every programmer working on the project, so there are no issues of proprietary authorship to slow down the project. Code is changed when it needs to be changed without delay.
- Continuous Integration—The XP team integrates and builds the software system multiple times per day to keep all the programmers at the same stage of the development process at once.
- 40-Hour Week—The XP team does not work excessive overtime to ensure that the team remains well-rested, alert, and effective.
- On-Site Customer—The XP project is directed by the customer who is available all the time to answer questions, set priorities, and determine requirements of the project.
- Coding Standard—The programmers all write code in the same way. This allows them to work in pairs and to share ownership of the code.

Source: The Twelve Principles of Extreme Programming can be found on a web site called Extreme Programming (XP) FAQ, www.jera.com/techinfo/xpfaq.html (accessed May 31, 2006).

critical, for systems where there will be a high degree of change in requirements as the system is being built, where senior developers are on hand to
work on the system, and in organizations that can tolerate a high degree of
chaos. On the other hand, agile development is not appropriate for mission-
critical systems that have the support of only junior developers and that will
have few changes in requirements. It is also not appropriate for organizations
where things are usually done in an orderly fashion. To the extent that many
public agencies, at all three levels of government, have been characterized as
being overly bureaucratic, slow moving, and inflexible, it would seem that
agile system development may not be particularly effective in these types of
environments.

Joint Applications Development

The joint applications development approach is similar to RAD in that it also
uses iterative prototyping, CASE tools, time boxing, and other developmental
time-reducing techniques, but it is more of a management philosophy than
a method or technique. It relies on the creation of joint development teams
consisting of systems analysts, systems developers, programmers, end users,
and managers who work closely for extended periods of time on the development of a new system, almost always with the use of a group facilitator who
keeps track of the team's progress.

The basic philosophy behind JAD is expressed on the Human Resources
web site of the University of Texas at Austin.

The JAD process is based on four simple ideas:

1. People who actually do a job have the best understanding of that
   job.
2. People who are trained in information technology have the best
   understanding of the possibilities of that technology.
3. Information systems and business processes rarely exist in isolation—they transcend the confines of any single system or office and
   affect work in related departments. People working in these related
   areas have valuable insight on the role of a system within a larger
   community.
4. The best information systems are designed when all of these groups
   work together on a project as equal partners.[12]

The fact that JAD is a management process as opposed to an IS technology
technique, like RAD, is underscored by the fact that it is explained on the
university's Human Resources web site.

As the web site explains in great detail there are several explicitly identified roles for relevant people to play in joint applications development; roles that differ significantly from the traditional SDLC approach to systems development. They include the project sponsor, project leader, record keeper, timekeeper, and of course the end user client. Each role has a host of clearly designated responsibilities. Some of them are as follows.

The project sponsor is directed to make sure the end user clients are part of the process. He or she helps identify the scope and functionality of the new system, makes sure that technical support is on hand, and monitors the work of the project team. The sponsor also makes the needed hardware and software available, and makes sure that members of the team are given time off from their regular duties to perform the work of the project team. In effect, the sponsor becomes the champion of the project; a much-needed role in system design and development success.

The project leader is responsible for making sure that the right people are part of the team and that the roles for the various team members are filled and understood. The leader schedules meetings, establishes agendas for meetings, assigns tasks and monitors their completion, facilitates team meetings, and makes sure that the record keeper is maintaining the records of the team meetings properly. Although not in the words of the University of Texas at Austin, their designated project leader assumes many of the traditional roles of the formal project manager who is essential for effective systems development success.

Obviously the job of the record keeper is to keep accurate and thorough notes of each meeting. They also summarize and condense the notes into an understandable document and check the accuracy of those notes with the project sponsor and others involved. Finally, they disseminate the notes to all relevant parties after they are checked for accuracy. In effect, record keepers become the historians of the project, keeping everyone abreast of what decisions have been made in the past and why those decisions were made.

The timekeeper makes sure that meetings begin and end on time. He or she also makes sure that the meetings finish up early enough so that what transpired during the meetings can be summarized and shared with the rest of the team for their confirmation and future agenda setting as the project develops.

The end user clients are very important members of the JAD team. They attend meetings to provide information on work processes, help make decisions about how work process might be changed, identify critical requirements and distinguish them from simple "wants" that might be nice to have but may not be necessary. They are also asked if there are any current problems with existing processes that should be fixed before a new automated system is put into place. They also test the new system in its model or prototype form to see if it is doing what needs to be done correctly and they make recommendations about how to improve the model or prototype. They also assist in the development of the documentation that explains how the new system should work, and they are also responsible for participating in the development and implementation of the training needed for the new system.

These designated roles for all of the parties involved make joint applications development very different from the waterfall model of the SDLC, which made the IT personnel the focal point of development instead of the end user clients. This difference is further underscored on the university's web site by instructions on how the IT staff and the end user clients should communicate with one another. On the one hand, the IT analysts are instructed to encourage the users to speak up about the nature of their work. They are told to ask the end user clients what they do and how they do it to accomplish a work process, and strive to get a complete understanding of the work that must be accomplished. The analysts are explicitly admonished not to use overly technical terms, particularly technology jargon. They are also told to check with the clients for possible problems even if the client may not be mentioning any problems. Finally, they are encouraged to be gentle when telling the end user clients that some asked-for features may be too impractical or too expensive to provide.

The end user clients, on the other hand, are told not to be bashful and to speak up about what they need to get their work done. They are instructed to provide the analysts with an understanding of how the work should be done and to educate them on the nature of the work with examples of what should be done so the analysts will actually have an appreciation for the nature of the work performed. End user clients are urged to ask for features that they need to get their work done, features that will make their work easier, sometimes even in small ways. If the analysts begin to speak in "computerese" the clients are told to "bring them gently back down to Earth." They are also told to bring up possible problems with the new system when they see them, and not to assume that they will get worked out later. In the end, the end user clients have a very expanded voice in the design of a new system.

The explicitly stated roles of each of the parties along with the rules for communication between the parties can often lead to the synergistic effect that advocates of JAD hope for—a fully functional automated system that does what it is supposed to do and is accepted by the end users, and ultimately improves the efficiency and effectiveness of some work process of an agency. The roles and rules go a long way in avoiding almost all of the rigidity and pitfalls of the traditional SDLC.

The features of JAD presented by the University of Texas at Austin can also be found within the IT industry in general as well as in other public and private organizations. The interesting thing about the JAD approach to system development is that it really does not do away with all of the major steps in the

SDLC. It does however make those steps more flexible as well as iterative and it incorporates a modified form of prototyping. More importantly it recognizes the importance of all of the parties to the development process—managers, IT specialists, and end users.

When to Use JAD

When should JAD be used to build information systems? Given the comprehensiveness of this approach to systems development, its emphasis on communication, and its overall management focus, it is tempting to say that JAD should be used all of the time. In many cases this would be true, particularly because it can incorporate some of the valuable features of the SDLC, RAD, and agile development if appropriate. It would, however, be overkill, due to its scope and comprehensiveness, when faced with the development of a small system that would serve only a few users. An example would be an electronic meter-reading system for a public works department. Another example would be a small database developed by one or two end users using off-the-shelf software like Microsoft Access.

End User Development

The last example brings us to end user development (EUD), a highly controversial approach to systems development because end users who have an understanding of their own work processes (usually called work domains, or simply, domains) develop automated systems without the advice of the IT professional. Information systems applications that easily lend themselves to end user development include spreadsheets, spreadsheets that can be turned into decision support systems, databases and database management systems, and web pages that can used by one person or shared within an agency. The primary motivating force behind the development of such end user systems is the fact that Microsoft and other software vendors make these systems relatively easy to build for a non-IT professional. It is estimated that in 2005 in the United States there were as many as 55 million end user developers as compared to 2.75 million professional software developers.[13]

There are obvious pros and cons associated with EUD. The pros include improved decision making and improved productivity because of the better availability of data, and an increase in the satisfaction of the end user with the completed work. EUD can also avoid possible miscommunications and conflict between end users and IS development staff. (Recall the ITernal Triangle of IT presented in chapter 1.) Associated with this is the belief that the end user knows more about his or her work processes than do the IT professionals. If end users are "computer savvy," they can learn to customize their own software applications to better serve their own decision making.

The cons include frequent failure to back up data, incorrect or incomplete requirements analysis, lack of testing to remove bugs in the software that could cause errors in the data that is reported out, and a mismatch between tools and applications, such as trying to force a spreadsheet program to do the work of a database program. In addition there are costs associated with the end users selecting the appropriate technology, installing it, learning it, programming it, and debugging it, especially when all of this distracts from their own domain work responsibilities. For example, should a social service caseworker be taken away from his or her clients to develop an automated case management system using a commercial off-the-shelf product like Microsoft Access? Maybe. Maybe not. It all depends on how important it is for that caseworker to develop a new case management system that others might eventually use. The problem is: Who should be making these decisions? The caseworker? The caseworker's supervisor? Middle managers? IT staff? There is no easy answer.

There can be serious tensions in public agencies between IS staff and end users over EUD.[14] IS staff may fear that end users are incompetent to build effective systems, and they worry about bugs and errors in the end user systems that are built. End users may resent the intrusion of IS staff into their own developmental work, or they may find the IS staff unresponsive to their needs. CIOs who take an enlightened approach to EUD encourage end users to build or modify their own applications, and they encourage IS staff to be as helpful to the end users as possible.

When to Use EUD

End users should be allowed to develop their own applications when and if it makes their own work in their own work domains more efficient and effective. The classic example would be allowing an end user to develop his or her own spreadsheet or database application for his or her own personal use or the use of a few other people. If the system that is developed appears to have promise for more widespread use, it should be turned over to IT professionals for debugging and testing before it is released. EUD is certainly not appropriate for large systems development projects.

The Software Acquisition Capability
Maturity Model (SA-CMM)

The Software Acquisition Capability Maturity Model (SA-CMM) is yet another approach to systems development.[15] It is an extremely comprehensive model consisting of five stages that an agency goes through to achieve a state of optimized maturity in the process of acquiring hardware and software and developing software applications. It was initially developed between 1994 through 1996 as a joint effort between the Department of Defense and the Software Engineering Institute at Carnegie Mellon University. It was revised in 2002 to keep pace with changes in the IT industry.

The SA-CMM may be considered to be a total systems approach to developing an information system. Its scope far exceeds the steps in the SDLC or any of the processes and procedures of the other approaches to systems development presented here. Because much of the SA-CMM deals with the acquisition of hardware and software from vendors, managing contracts with vendors, and performing project management and risk management functions in the development and implementation of information systems, discussion of the SA-CMM will be presented in chapter 10 on acquiring technology solutions.

Types of System Implementation

When all of the systems development work is nearing completion, it is time to think about implementing the new system.[16] Implementation should begin with developing a cutover proposal, which is nothing more than a written recommendation from the project team to management that it is time to implement the new system. Before implementation, a few tasks need to be performed, namely developing manuals and providing training. Manuals containing information on how to use the new system should be prepared and distributed to the people who will be using the new system. These manuals should be written in consultation with a sample of the users of the new system to ensure that the directions contained in the manuals are easily understood. Then, the people who will be using the new system should be trained. Training should take place very close to the time of the actual cutover. It is usually a waste of time to train people on a new system more than a week or two before the new system is implemented because most people simply forget what they learned in a training session after some time has passed.

With this groundwork laid, management can follow one of four basic cutover approaches: pilot, immediate, phased, and parallel. A *pilot cutover* is a trial system that is usually implemented in a single location, like an office or a geographic area. For example, an automated eligibility-determination system for a social service agency might be piloted in one or two local offices before it is implemented agency wide. The pilot allows the developers to see how the users react to the new system and possibly change some features of the new system if necessary or feasible. If changing the system is not possible, the pilot will reveal things that might need to be included in manuals and training sessions. Obviously a pilot cutover may take a considerable amount of time, especially if it is feasible to make changes in the system or if the manuals need to be changed or if new training needs to be delivered.

Obviously, an *immediate cutover* would be a lot simpler. You simply turn the old system off and the new one on. This might work well for small-scale system changes, but it is usually not recommended for any large-scale changes. Even something as simple as changing from one word-processing system to another would not work well under immediate cutover because end users would have to learn new sets of commands. While something as simple as this might be considered a modest annoyance, it can cut into worker productivity. In this case, it would be advisable to engage in *parallel cutover,* allowing end users to work with both word-processing systems until they have become accustomed to the features of the new system.

Finally, new systems can be *phased in,* meaning that different modules of the system are added at different times or in different locations. For example, a new accounts payable system might be added first, followed by an accounts receivable system, then an accounting system, then a budgeting system, and so on. Phased-in implementation is popular when an organization is planning on integrating a variety of application systems that have the potential benefit of sharing data.

Systems Maintenance

Once the new system is implemented, it enters the maintenance phase. If the new system has been properly planned, analyzed, designed, and implemented, maintenance is usually a simple matter. It may involve some simple debugging of the system or adding minor enhancements. If any of the preceding design and development steps have been skipped or been done poorly, maintenance can become a nightmare, as technicians can spend tremendous amounts of time trying to fix the new system to make it do what it was envisioned to do. Unfortunately, possible issues about system maintenance that might arise during the design and implementation phases are often overlooked, causing headaches like system crashes and added costs like hiring additional support personnel to keep the system up and running and doing what it was originally designed to do. There is not much more to say about the maintenance phase from a managerial perspective since it is primarily the domain of technical experts. If a system has been designed and implemented properly, maintenance should be a fairly straightforward matter.

Summary and a Look Forward

As can be seen from all of this, there are several ways to design and implement an information system. Some of them include choices about hardware and software; others simply involve choices about software development. In either case managerial decisions have to be made about the right approach to use. Such decisions are situational; they depend on the size and scope of the project and the available budget. Public managers should understand the pros and cons of each approach and have competent IT professionals on hand to advise them on which approach to use. Such knowledge and expertise may be found in-house or acquired from an outside consultant or a vendor. One must be careful about vendors. They may overstate their claims of knowledge about an agency's business processes, as we shall see in the next chapter that deals with business process reengineering, enterprise resource planning, and customer relations management.

8

Transforming Government with Technology

Information technology has the potential to radically transform the way public agencies do their business. Enterprise resource planning (ERP), business process reengineering (BPR), and customer relations management (CRM) are three of the most important developments in the IT industry affecting government and business that emerged during the 1990s. All three promise to revolutionize the way that public and private organizations operate by increasing the efficiency and effectiveness of their work processes. ERP is a rather ugly name for a suite of software programs that promises to integrate all "back office" operations such as accounting, finance, human resources, and specialized transaction processing systems by allowing cross-functional sharing of data. BPR is a management philosophy (some might call it a fad) that advocates radical changes in the ways that private and public organizations do their business with information technology being viewed as the primary enabler of change. Customer relations management (CRM) software is not really software, although special software and technologies are sometimes involved. More broadly, it is a managerial approach to serving customers and citizens more effectively. Usually called a "front office" application, it has migrated to the public sector as agencies try to enhance electronic services to citizens and become more citizen centric in an effort to improve services.

Public managers often think about undertaking these three strategies at the same time in an effort to increase organizational efficiency and effectiveness. For this reason they will be discussed together in this chapter. Note, however, that they can be undertaken separately. This is an important point to underscore because each has the potential to radically change the way an agency conducts its day-to-day business. Also it would not be wise to consider undertaking more than one of these strategies at a single time since each has the potential to radically change the daily operations of a public agency. While all three are products of the early 1990s, their influence on both government and business are still being strongly felt today, and this will continue into the future.

Enterprise Resource Planning

The IT industry is famous for its arcane jargon, and ERP is the epitome of "computerese."[1] It is a name given to a software concept that has little to do with planning or resources, but a lot to do with the enterprise, whether it be a private or a public organization. Since ERP was originally designed for private-sector use, it will first be explained within the context of private-sector examples; then it will be discussed in the context of the public sector. The following scenario will set the stage for understanding some of the reasons behind ERP software projects and some of the problems that emerge from using this technology.

A Hypothetical Example from the Private Sector

Imagine a large manufacturing firm in the 1960s, when businesses began to automate many of their functional processes. Computers and software were purchased over the years by this firm to support a variety of functions such as accounting, finance, inventory, payroll, human resources, manufacturing, marketing, sales, fleet management, and so on. Due to a lack of centralized management planning and control, imagine that all of these applications ran on different hardware platforms and used different systems software and different applications software provided by a variety of vendors. Consequently, none of these systems would be able to share data electronically.

In the IT industry, such stand-alone information systems are called "stovepipe" systems as a reflection of their impenetrable nature and rigidity. To share data between different functions, data would have to be manually offloaded from one system and then manually entered into the other system—a time-consuming and error-prone task, frequently requiring data to be cleansed and converted from one form to another to make the data fit different hardware and software systems. This method also meant that middle and top management would have to rely on manually generated reports in order to make tactical and strategic decisions. Also, old legacy stovepipe systems do not easily lend themselves to decision support systems (DSS) and executive information systems (EIS) add-on applications. Their primary value was simply operational-level transaction processing.

Now let us narrow this hypothetical example. Suppose a salesperson takes an order from a customer for 10,000 widgets. The order is written on an order form and placed in an in-basket where it sits for a few days until it can be batched along with a lot of other orders. When it is batched, another paper report is delivered to the warehouse, where it is placed in yet another in-basket to sit for a few more days until it is batched along with a bunch of other orders. Yet another paper report is generated, showing that the firm has only 5,000 widgets. So, another paper request is sent to manufacturing, where it sits in an in-basket for a few days until manufacturing codes it into its own automated system, only to discover that it will take ninety days to make the additional widgets because they have to purchase parts from several suppliers, which entails generating even more paper-based requests that need to go to the purchasing department. In the meantime, the finance department has received its own paper-based notice of the pending sale. They key it into their own system and discover that the customer is habitually late in paying for its widgets. Yet another paper report is sent up the organization demanding payment on delivery. Finally the salesperson gets a call telling him that he will have to tell the customer that the widgets will take ninety days to deliver and payment must be made on delivery. The angry customer cancels the order and goes to another supplier. The firm has just lost a customer because its processes were inefficient and ineffective even though they were automated.

While hypothetical, this example is also realistic. It is also the reason for the emergence of ERP software in the private sector. The idea behind ERP is to get all of a firm's stand-alone stovepipe automated systems "talking to one another," in other words, enabling them to share data when appropriate. The key here is "when appropriate." ERP systems can be very expensive because they often involve replacing old legacy systems, including both hardware and software. A total ERP implementation would be a daunting and expensive endeavor. For this reason, ERP integrators usually offer their systems in modules that can be implemented incrementally so that only a few stand-alone functional systems can share data. In our hypothetical case, sales, the warehouse, manufacturing, and finance would be likely candidates for an ERP system with perhaps a human resources system added at a later date.

Public-Sector ERP

One of the ways to introduce the use of ERP systems in the public sector is to see what some of the vendors (usually called "integrators") are offering public agencies in the way of ERP solutions to their business practices. Some of the major ERP integrators working the public sector have been Data Management Group, SAP, Oracle, PeopleSoft, and J.D. Edwards. Emphasize here "have been" because ERP vendors are notorious for merging with other vendors and changing the names of the firms. Sometimes it is hard to tell just who is in the game.

The Data Management Group's web page gives a general idea of what ERP can do for public agencies:

- Enterprise Resource Planning (ERP) systems solve the challenges of governmental agencies using incompatible systems and disparate business processes, hindering their ability to exchange information, by giving agency managers and government policy makers the resources they need to make timely, informed decisions.
- It attempts to integrate all departments and functions across a company onto a single computer system that can serve all those different departments' particular needs.
- Building a single software program that serves the needs of people in finance as well as it does the people in human resources and in the warehouse is a difficult task. Each department typically has its own computer system and is optimized for the particular ways that the department does its work.
- Data Management Group can assist in the selection and implementation of an ERP system, combining all departments together into a single, integrated program that operates from a central database so that the various departments can more easily share information and communicate with each other.[2]

In a similar fashion, the SAP Public Sector web page promises that agencies can integrate such functions as accounting, financial management, human resource management, capital asset management, procurement, tax revenues and management, grants management, financial analytics, workforce analytics, and records management, just to name a few functions.[3]

All of this should give some sense of the potential benefits of ERP applications in government, and governments are responding accordingly. In the late 1990s, brief references and news notes to ERP began appearing in *Washington Technology* and *Government Computer News*, two of the public sector's leading professional print and online newspapers. Then, in 2002, an article appeared in *Washington Technology* announcing that "Half of all U.S. federal, state, and local government agencies still rely on (legacy systems), and about 70 percent of those are looking to implement ERP in the next five years."[4] The article went on to suggest that governments would spend billions of dollars on ERP systems in the next several years.

More recently, in 2005, INPUT expects the federal government market for ERP systems to grow 33 percent from $5.8 billion in 2005 to $7.7 billion in 2010.[5] The market report went on to indicate that the growth in the ERP market for the federal government is being driven by several factors. First is the president's management agenda, which includes the strategic management of human capital, competitive sourcing, improved financial performance, expanded e-government initiatives, and the integration of budgeting and performance measurement. Second are initiatives by the Department of Defense. The U.S. Navy expects to spend $3 billion on ERP projects to replace legacy systems while the U.S. Army is in the process of implementing an ERP project that would include over 135,000 end users.

Most state and local government ERP projects tend to be smaller in scale, yet still quite a lot of ERP implementation activity exists among the states and localities as well as in other countries. For example:

- State of Kansas—one of the first to attempt an ERP implementation in 1994 using PeopleSoft to integrate human resources, payroll, and benefits.
- City of Phoenix—integrated financial systems with web applications in 1998.
- County of Sacramento, California—integrated some financial and payroll functions in 1998.
- Multnomah County, Oregon—integrated financial and payroll functions in 1998.
- State of Arkansas—currently spending $30 million to integrate some of their financial and human resource functions with SAP R/3.[6]

These are just a few examples of what states and localities are doing in the way of ERP implementations. Scores of other ERP implementations are taking place all over the United States and in many other countries. The following two examples will illustrate some of the complexities of implementing ERP systems in state governments.

Large-Scale ERP Implementation: A Case of Rough Going

In the early 1990s, the State of Louisiana was one of first states to begin a large-scale ERP design and implementation.[7] The ERP project was named the Integrated Statewide Information System (ISIS). As envisioned, it would integrate such functions as purchasing, contract management, inventory management, budget development, executive information systems, decision support systems, human resources, payroll, accounts receivable, debt management, investment management, and property inventory—quite a large undertaking. The state selected SAP R/3 ERP software, hired an outside consulting firm to help with the design and implementation of the system, and purchased both hardware and software from a variety of vendors.

While Louisiana's ERP system was not a failure, there was some rough going during design and implementation. The magnitude of changing the data from the legacy systems to the new system was a monumental task, involving converting data from several legacy systems, designing and redesigning input and output screens as well as designing and redesigning printed reports. To make matters worse, because of the decentralized nature of the Louisiana state government agencies, the developers had to ask—not tell—the various agencies to provide their data in a timely and useful manner, which did not always happen. Consequently, numerous and significant errors in the new ERP system had to be detected and worked out to avoid the age-old problem of "garbage in, garbage out." This process took a lot of unplanned time and money to accomplish.

Considerable attention had to be paid to the performance of some of the modules in the new system. For example, the old system could process payroll in four hours. The new system took thirty-seven hours to process the same payroll. Modifications had to be made in the database and the software to bring the performance standards of the new system to the standards of the old system. This fix took an inordinate amount of time and resources because it required the involvement of many different managerial and technical professionals.

Training became a problem because 3,200 people had to be trained on a system that was changing daily because the design of the system was changing, and, in some cases, training had to be delivered after the system went live, not before. There were also people trained in the use of the new system who would never use that training because they were retiring, but they took the training nonetheless, wasting training and personnel resources.

Although not a failure, Louisiana's ERP implementation was riddled with a number of headaches for the IT professionals as well as general managers. Several mistakes were made, but in hindsight this could be expected because this was a very early ERP implementation in state government.

Large-Scale ERP Design and Implementation:
A Case of Success but with a Lot of Hard Work

In 1999 the Commonwealth of Pennsylvania initiated a large-scale ERP implementation called Imagine PA, designed to integrate most of the state's many and diverse information systems across a wide variety of fifty-three different agencies, boards, and commissions, including sixteen data centers using a wide variety of different information systems.[8] At the start, the CIO presented the idea of a total ERP implementation to the state's CIO Advisory Council. A consulting firm, the Gartner Group, was brought in to validate this proposal, and it was finally approved by the Council with the support of the governor. A decision was made to partner with SAP and to use SAP R/3 "best practices" software because it was determined that the software would meet about 80 percent of the state's information systems requirements. "Best practices" in this context is a term that is used to describe the functionality of a software application. This means that the software is written in such a way as to meet the operational needs of an agency. For example, SAP R/3 ERP software supports governmental fund accounting methods as opposed to private-sector balance sheet accounting.

Then yet another consulting firm, BearingPoint, had to be called in because they had knowledge and expertise in implementing such a large-scale ERP system. They assigned over 250 full-time staff to help implement the project. Much of that assistance was in training the state agencies' staff to use the new software. Training is a critical component in any ERP implementation because the new system often requires entirely new ways of accomplishing old tasks.

Several of the systems development and implementation steps of the SDLC were used to design and implement the new ERP system. The functional areas targeted for integration included accounting, budgeting, payroll, human resources, and procurement. A timetable was established that contained several phases of implementation that would take thirty-three months. Requirements analysis was a major undertaking, consisting of 120 workshops conducted for 1,200 end users. Once designed, over 150 modifications in SAP's software modules had to be made to meet the business processes of the state. By July of 2003, three of the phases had been completed with over 92 percent of SAP's best practice requirements implemented in the software system, and portions of the system began to be phased in. As of 2004, the design and implementation of the system was on time and within budget and met over 90 percent of SAP's best practices. Overall the project is considered to be a success because it has resulted in reduced costs, increased data sharing—which leads to better data analysis and decision making—and high user satisfaction.

Problems and Issues with ERP Implementation

Managers in the public sector have encountered several problems and issues with the implementation of ERP systems. Some of those problems and issues are related to the unique ways that public agencies do business. Others are common across both the public and private sectors. The following are some of the more important problems and issues.

Rush to Implementation. While enterprise resource planning is partly a management strategy to achieve the integration of data in an organization, it also relies heavily on existing commercial off-the-shelf software developed in one organizational setting and then adapted to another. Because of the COTS component of ERP, there is a tendency to focus on the implementation phase of systems development to the neglect of the design phase. The assumption is that the software can be modified to meet the needs of the customer. This assumes that the customer's existing ways of doing business electronically are already efficient and effective. This is not always the case. Careful attention needs to be paid to the way that a legacy system functions: Does it capture the right data? Does it store the data in the right database? Does it properly transfer the data from one functional application area to another? Does it produce reports on screens and on paper containing the right data for operational, tactical, or strategic decision making? These are questions that have to do with the design phase of systems development and implementation. Unfortunately, they can be overlooked in a rush to implement a new ERP system.

This is precisely what happened in the case of the Commonwealth of Pennsylvania just described, but to their advantage. Early on, the developers of Imagine PA realized that they were not simply replacing legacy systems with new ERP systems. They needed to transform some of their business processes because the way they were conducted under the old legacy systems were inefficient and ineffective. In other words, the old legacy systems did not capture the right data, did not store it properly, and did not present it properly so that a user could make a well-informed decision based on the presented data. It took considerable time to redesign existing business processes, but doing so paid off in the end by providing a more efficient and effective integrated system.

Pay Attention to Change. Another frequent problem is that the way in which ERP software is constructed dictates how certain work processes are conducted. When you change the way that people do their work they may not like it. They may call for changes in the software to accommodate their accustomed ways of doing things. Called "customization" in the IT industry, it can be a dangerous endeavor for two reasons. First, rewriting code to make a system's module do something different is costly and is usually not figured into the original cost of the contract for services, so it becomes an expensive add-on. Second, because the modules of an ERP system are so tightly configured together, changing the programming code in one module can affect the performance of other modules, possibly making them operate improperly or not at all. Therefore, new code has to be written to make the other modules function properly—a task that also comes at an additional cost of time and programming charges.

Question Total Integration. Another potential problem with ERP implementation is the embrace of total integration. In a large public organization like a state's department of health or department of social services, or even an entire state, it is unreasonable to assume that all of the data contained in all of the possible functional applications need to be integrated. For example, do the data associated with a state's pension system need to be integrated with the state's data about the environmental quality of the state's water resources? Not likely.

For this, and many other possible real-world situations, the notion of "total integration" needs to be squashed. Some public managers and most vendors are aware of this, and this is why the current trend is to implement ERP systems incrementally as modules with a view to the appropriate systems that do need to be integrated. Examples would be financial and accounting systems that handle accounts receivables, accounts payable, and general ledger systems; or human resources systems that handle payroll, benefits, and pensions. Modules that address more specialized functional requirements such as fleet management can be added later, or they can even be taken away if they do not fit into the overall design and implementation of the ERP system.

This is precisely what happened in 2005 when the State of Arkansas decided to pull the performance-based budgeting tools out of its contract with SAP for total systems integration.[9] The budgeting tools would not work with the existing configuration of the total ERP system that supported line-item, not performance-based, budgeting techniques. The state's decision is currently under litigation, causing tensions between the state and SAP, highlighting the importance of proper contracting and contract management, which will be the topic of chapter 10. Furthermore, Arkansas's experience with its ERP system has not been rosy. The system cost the state $60 million, which is twice what was originally budgeted for at the start in February of 2000.[10]

Incremental Implementation. Incremental instead of "big bang" conversion seems to be the safest approach to ERP implementation. Louisiana's ISIS Project was broken up into seven phases, but the state still ran into problems in each of the seven phases with such things as the design of reports, the design and testing of interfaces between modules, data conversions, and the cleansing of data from old legacy systems. One can also question their rationale for implementing certain functionalities in the order that they did. Their DSS and EIS capabilities were implemented in Phase Three of the project while human resources and payroll were implemented in Phase Four. In hindsight, DSS and EIS are desirable additions to an information system, but the human resources and payroll module was mission critical, suggesting that this system should have been added earlier than the DSS and EIS modules.

What Will ERP Cost? The cost of ERP implementations in government is difficult to pin down for two reasons. First, no systematic research has been done on the actual costs of ERP implementations for agencies at any level of government. Second, the cost of an ERP implementation will depend upon what factors are figured into the project. Initially there is the cost of the software modules themselves, and perhaps the cost of additional hardware if the new software will not run on existing hardware platforms. Then there are the costs associated with installing the modules and testing them to see if they work right. There are costs associated with modifying the software to meet an agency's way of doing business. Conversely, there can be some serious costs associated with changing the way the agency does its business to fit the way the software operates. Training is a major cost that needs to be figured in, as are the costs of maintaining the system and adding upgrades to the system in the future. Finally, there are the costs associated with hiring consulting firms to manage the implementation and provide the training. Public agencies rarely have the staff on hand with the requisite knowledge and skill to manage an ERP implementation or to provide appropriate training for the new system.

The IT industry has come up with a concept called Total Cost of Ownership (TCO) to get a handle on all of the costs involved with an ERP implementation. TCO is usually placed within a life cycle model of the ERP system that includes the following stages: acquisition, implementation, operations, maintenance, and replacement. The Meta Group, a market research firm, did a survey of sixty-three companies in the private sector covering small, medium, and large firms.[11] They found the average TCO for an ERP system to be $15 million, with the highest cost being $300 million and the lowest cost being $400,000. These figures, coupled with the expenditure projections for ERP implementation in the federal government presented earlier, strongly suggest that ERP systems can be very expensive.

Never-Ending Implementation. How long will the implementation take? The vendors may tell you three months, six months, nine months, a year, eighteen months, two years, or more. It really depends upon the size and scope of the implementation and the occurrence of any unexpected problems like testing failures or modules not interacting properly, or unexpected customizations in the software or requirements creep as additional modules are added as an afterthought. This is where good project management comes into play. Unfortunately, most public agencies do not have good project managers on staff, so they have to be hired as consultants. If the project managers are familiar with the agency's processes, things should be fine, but if they are new to a particular agency and the work that it performs, expect a long learning curve.

In some circumstances the implementation never ends. Do not expect the internal people brought in to work on the implementation to return to their previous duties any time soon because these are the people who have learned how to make the ERP system work. They need to stay with the system for a long time during the maintenance phase to advise IT technicians on any needed refinements or changes to the system.

Rethink Your Processes. The most important thing that an ERP implementation offers is the opportunity to rethink how a public agency does its business. The real benefit of an ERP implementation comes from avoiding the rush to implementation and taking the time to go back to the design phase and ask the more fundamental question: "Are we going to simply replace an already inefficient and ineffective legacy stovepipe system, or are we going to see if we can restructure our work processes to make them more efficient and effective?" Oddly enough, it is the technology in the form of the ERP software modules that can force management to face this question. As noted before, ERP software can dictate how some business processes are performed by virtue of how the software is written for a particular application.

For example, a fleet management ERP software module might require an agency to keep track of its fleet of vehicles in a way that differs dramatically from the way the old software tracked the vehicles. One option is to tinker with the new ERP software module to make it emulate the old software system. As noted this can add to the cost of the implementation by necessitating the writing of new code for the new ERP module, which can result in even further changes in other ERP software modules that interface with the fleet management module, running the risk of introducing bugs in the new total ERP package.

The other option forces management to consider the more fundamental question of what its processes should be to manage its fleet of vehicles. Do the demands of the proposed ERP software module fit the agency's way of managing its vehicles? Or should it rethink its approach to vehicle management entirely? This seemingly mundane example leads us to the topic of the next section of this chapter—business process reengineering.

Business Process Reengineering

Business process reengineering (BPR) can be considered a revolutionary way of doing business, just another consultancy fad, or nothing more than a remembrance of Frederick Winslow Taylor's scientific approach to management. No matter which of these views one takes, there is no doubt that BPR has had a major impact on businesses and government agencies beginning in the early 1990s, and it will continue into the future for some time. Let us start with a few definitions of BPR, move on to its faddish qualities, and then move to the heart of what BPR has to do with improving the processes of public agencies.

Defining BPR

In the book that started it all, *Reengineering the Corporation*, Michael Hammer and James Champy define BPR as follows: "Reengineering is the fundamental rethinking and radical redesign of business processes to achieve dramatic improvements in critical, contemporary measures of performance, such as cost, quality, service, and speed."[12] The key to this definition lies in focusing on processes that deliver goods and services to customers and citizens instead of older views of organizations that focus on the functional structure of an organization and the specialized capabilities inherent in an organization's various departments.

In the context of the public sector, Sharon L. Caudle has defined BPR for the National Academy of Public Administration in the following way:

> Government business process reengineering is a radical improvement approach that critically examines, rethinks, and redesigns mission product and service processes within a political environment. It achieves dramatic mission performance gains from multiple customer and stakeholder perspectives. It is a key part of a process management approach for optimal performance that continually evaluates, adjusts or removes processes.[13]

BPR is not to be confused with just-in-time (JIT) inventory management systems or continuous process improvement (CPI) systems, or total quality management (TQM) programs. While such management reforms do focus on business processes in government and business, they advocate an incremental approach to process change—in other words, tinkering with an existing process to improve it by small changes. BPR is a radical approach calling upon us to throw out all old ways of doing things and creating brand-new ways of delivering goods and services to customers and citizens by focusing on the processes involved and not on organizational departments and units.

BPR as a Consulting Fad

According to some consulting gurus, BPR is all about radically changing the way an organization goes about its work processes with the aid of information technology. In an effort to point out the faddism of BPR, Paul Strassmann has collected the following quotes from Michael Hammer, who helped to start the BPR movement. The quotes come from a variety of books and journals. Strassmann uses them to describe the "Hocus Pocus of Reengineering":

- American managers . . . must abandon the organizational and operational principles and procedures they are now using and create entirely new ones. . . . Business reengineering means starting all over, starting from scratch. . . . It means forgetting how work was done. . . . Old job titles and old organizational arrangements . . . cease to matter. How people and companies did things yesterday doesn't matter to the business reengineer. . . . Reengineering . . . can't be carried out in small and cautious steps. It is an all or nothing proposition.
- In this journey we'll carry our wounded and shoot the dissenters. . . . I want to purge from the business vocabulary: CEO, manager, worker, job.
- It's basically taking an axe and a machine gun to your existing organization.
- What you do with the existing structure is nuke it!
- Reengineering must be initiated . . . by someone who has . . . enough status to break legs.
- You either get on the train or we'll run over you with the train. . . .
- The last thing in the world that reengineering does is enhance the manager's sense of self-importance, because one of the things that reengineering says is that managing isn't so important.
- Reengineering . . . will require a personality transplant . . . a lobotomy.
- Don't try to forestall reengineering. If senior management is serious about reengineering they'll shoot you.[14]

In place of such radical statements about BPR, Strassmann advocates business process improvement (BPI) as an incremental and evolutionary approach to process change rather than a revolutionary one. This involves taking existing work processes and examining them for possible minor changes that will improve the quality, cost, or speed of providing the finished product or service.

Despite Strassmann's efforts to soften the edge on BPR it has had a dramatic effect on organizations in the private sector as well as the public sector. Many small-, medium-, and large-scale BPR projects have been initiated in both the private and public sectors. Experience with BPR in the private sector has not been good. In the private sector, 50 to 70 percent of the projects failed to provide the desired improvements in quality, cost reduction, and speed. Also, BPR has received a bad reputation as being merely a euphemism for "downsizing" in corporate America. There have also been failures in the public sector, as will soon be noted.

BPR as Common Sense

Despite all of the hype surrounding BPR in both government and business, the concept behind BPR is merely a matter of common sense when viewed from a macro and micro perspective. Things change, so the ways we normally deal with things also need to change. In other words, from time to time we need to look at the way we are doing things to see if our processes are working properly and whether the processes are properly designed to meet the current demands placed on public agencies. From a macro perspective, the way public agencies did things in the 1960s, 1970s, 1980s, and 1990s need sto be reexamined in light of present-day and future demands of citizens, businesses, and politicians.

Consider a macro example from the private sector. Individually owned mom-and-pop five-and-dime stores have been largely replaced by megamarts that offer us wider choices in products and services at reduced prices. While those who are steeped in nostalgia may bemoan the passing of the five-and-dime stores, others gladly take advantage of the products, services, and cheaper prices offered by Super Wal-Marts, Super K-Marts, and Super Targets. For a public-sector example, consider how easy it is today to electronically file a tax return with the IRS and receive a refund in a matter of days instead of months. The megamarts (as well as many other businesses) and the IRS (as well as many other public agencies) have radically redesigned their processes in order to better serve the demands of their customers and citizens.

The micro perspective on BPR takes us to the level of software development. The way in which code is written for a particular software application will determine how a particular work process is performed. In new software development, the existing work process is examined and the code is written to fit the existing process. When customizing an off-the-shelf software module, the existing process is examined and the code is changed to meet the demands of the existing work process. All of this is fine if the existing process is efficient and effective and meets the needs of the end user and, ultimately, the citizen. If, however, the existing work process is inefficient or ineffective, it makes little sense to write new code for it or modify existing code to support it. At the micro level, BPR is radical in the sense that it looks beyond the particular software modules and their code to ask the more fundamental questions: Does the existing process make sense? Should the existing process be changed? These questions and the practical answers to them in actual public agencies go to the heart of BPR, wherein lies its value. BPR is first and foremost about people and processes or the way people do things to accomplish the work of a public agency. The technology only supports that work.

BPR in Government

Politicians, appointed officials, and public managers in the federal government were quick to pick up on BPR because it was introduced about the same time as the Clinton administration was initiating the Government Performance Results Act of 1993 and the National Performance Review initiative, both of which sought to improve the performance of the federal government by reinventing it.

In June of 1994 the General Accounting Office (GAO) convened a symposium on Reengineering Organizations. The GAO brought together executives from five Fortune 500 firms reputed to be successful in reengineering efforts in order to identify the basic principles behind successful reengineering:

- Top management must be supportive of and engaged in reengineering efforts to remove barriers and drive success.
- An organization's culture must be receptive to reengineering goals and principles.
- Major improvements and savings are realized by focusing on the business from a process rather than a functional perspective.
- Processes should be selected for reengineering based on a clear notion of customer needs, anticipated benefits, and potential for success.
- Process owners should manage reengineering projects with teams that are cross-functional, maintain a proper scope, focus on customer metrics, and enforce implementation timelines.[15]

The role of information technology was given only a brief mention in the symposium, but an important one nonetheless. The panelists believed that attention to process over function should come first before any consideration of technology and that existing information systems should be abandoned if they could not support reengineered processes.[16] These beliefs are consistent with the general philosophy behind BPR succinctly stated by Hammer as "Don't automate. Obliterate!" This does not, however, negate the important role of information technology as the enabler of reengineered processes.

The GAO subsequently came out with a *BPR Guide* for all federal agencies. It clearly states the importance of redesigning processes first and then acquiring technology to support those new processes. For example, the Guide states the following:

> When a reengineering project leads to new information requirements, it may be necessary to acquire new technology to support those requirements. It is important to bear in mind, however, that acquiring new information technology does not constitute reengineering. Technology is an enabler of process reengineering, not a substitute for it. Acquiring technology in the belief that its mere presence will somehow lead to process innovation is a root cause of bad investments in information systems.[17]

The GAO offers the following set of very high-level assessment questions posed as issues for agencies to resolve as they move through the process of reengineering some of their processes:

Assessment issue 1: Has the agency reassessed its mission and strategic goals?

Assessment issue 2: Has the agency identified performance problems and set improvement goals?

Assessment issue 3: Should the agency engage in reengineering?

Assessment issue 4: Is the reengineering project appropriately managed?

Assessment issue 5: Has the project team analyzed the target process and developed feasible alternatives?

Assessment issue 6: Has the project team completed a sound business case for implementing the new process?

Assessment issue 7: Is the agency following a comprehensive implementation plan?

Assessment issue 8: Are agency executives addressing change management issues?

Assessment issue 9: Is the new process achieving the desired results?[18]

Under each of the nine issues are listed several key activities that agencies should undertake to acquire information about processes and to manage risks associated with changing the processes. Note that these are high-level guidelines. The GAO recognizes that processes may vary across different types of agencies, so it is unwise to be much more specific in dictating more operational methods of reengineering.

There is no one single methodology for BPR. Indeed, there are controversies over whether there should be a single methodology and what steps should be included in a methodology. There are also competing methodologies. Nevertheless, the Prosci Reengineering Learning Center On-Line suggests the following general framework for a methodology for BPR efforts:

1. Project planning and launch (team selection, objective setting, scope definition, methodology selection, schedule development, consultant selection, sponsor negotiations, change-management planning, team preparation)
2. Current state assessment and learning from others (high-level process definition, benchmarking, customer focus groups, employee focus groups, technology assessment)
3. Solution design (process design, enabling technology architecture, organizational design, job design)

4. Business case development (cost and benefit analysis, business case preparation, presentation to key business leaders)
5. Solution development (detailed process definition, system requirements writing and system development, training development, implementation planning, operational transition plan, pilots and trials)
6. Implementation (larger-scale pilots and phased implementation, measurement systems, full implementation)
7. Continuous improvement (ongoing improvement and measurement of new processes and systems)[19]

From another perspective, the following steps are broadly derived from a variety of espoused BPR methodologies to simplify the process: (1) Define the project and determine its boundaries. Decide which processes will be included and which will not. (2) Create a clear vision of where the agency wants "to be" in terms of serving its customers. (3) Document "as-is" processes. Study the existing processes to see if and how they need to be changed. (4) Conduct a cost and benefit analysis of moving from the "as-is" to the "to-be" processes. (5) Redesign the existing processes and determine how technology will support them. (6) Plan and implement the new processes and systems. (7) Measure the performance of the new processes.

Steps 2 and 3 can be problematic. In step 2, people in an agency may be so steeped in traditional practices that they are unable to envision where they want the agency to be in terms of serving its citizens. They may need the help of external consultants to brainstorm new ideas about serving the citizen or they may turn to similar agencies to see what they are doing and how they are doing it. Step 3 can be a long and difficult process that inhibits creative thinking by focusing the team's attention on the existing "as-is" processes. Radical BPR gurus would skip this step entirely, advocating a "clean slate" approach, which can turn into an "open checkbook" approach. The "as-is" analysis provides the baseline to determine the gap between where the agency is and where it wants to be. This is the value of "as-is" analysis.

A BPR Example

The Virginia Department of Social Services (VDSS) has recently undertaken a major BPR initiative called the Virginia Social Services System (VSSS), which illustrates the importance of "as-is" analysis, "to-be" analysis, and a strong project management methodology.[20] First Data Government Solutions, a division of First Data Corporation, served as their BPR consultant.

The BPR team started off with a clear vision statement derived from the department's strategic planning process: "People helping people triumph over poverty, abuse, and neglect, to shape strong futures for themselves, their families, and communities."[21] Then the BPR team conducted an extensive study of the entire department that resulted in a list of deliverables:

- "As-is" discovery and identification of quick wins
- Documentation of baseline costs
- "As-is" documentation
- Identification of best practices
- Definition of high-level "to-be" business model
- Design of detailed business processes in the "to-be" model
- Change management plan
- Change management implementation plan

In project management terms, a deliverable is a finished product that can be handed off to someone who needs it in a chain of steps that make up the entire project from beginning to end.

The initial studies culminated in Deliverable No. 3, the as-is analysis contained in a 1,118-page document. The study portion of the research consisted of structured interviews, site visits, walkthroughs, and work observations involving over 150 staff members across 38 local offices. This resulted in the documentation of 20 work processes and 200 sub-processes, and the information systems supporting them. They found a complex maze of manual and automated work processes that frequently contained redundant tasks. They also found that locally acquired automated systems that did not interface with the central system caused unnecessary, expensive, and time-consuming manual conversion of data from the local systems to the central system. Overall, they discovered the following features of the as-is system:

- A thirty- to fifty-year-old business model
- Stovepipes and control
- Lack of shared information
- Lack of management information
- Imposition of inefficiencies on consumers
- Out-of-date job classes and compensation
- Redundancy and duplication
- Ineffective use of systems
- Failure to leverage new technologies
- Lack of auditability
- Lack of trust

As a result of the research they targeted over twenty stovepipe systems for reengineering. Some of the program systems included food stamps, child care, foster care, repatriation, state and local hospitalization, family and children's services, child protective services, adoption services, adult services, adult protective services, energy assistance, and refugee services, to name just a few. Three administrative support functions, including human resources, records preservation, and quality management evaluation were targeted for reengineering. Finally, twelve management support functions were targeted for reengineering: financial accounting, fiscal operations, statistical reporting, grants management, training, policy management, claims, appeals, forms and brochure management, fraud management, quality assurance, and customer contact.

The conclusion to the as-is report states that the BPR team will develop new models of doing business that will streamline existing processes and will require the support of new information technologies. Some operational units at the state level and at the local levels will have to adopt entirely new ways of doing things. This will require a careful change management plan that will move the agency incrementally to the "to-be" vision of operation. The date of the report from which this case example was drawn is August of 2005.[22] The VDSS is currently working on reengineering well over twenty processes in its efforts to achieve their "to-be" vision of what the agency can do to achieve its strategic mission to better serve its clients, which is what customer (or citizen) relations management is also all about.

Customer Relations Management

Customer relations management (CRM) emerged in the private sector during the late 1980s and early 1990s in response to extreme competition in a wide variety of markets. While information technology and related CRM software packages play a role in CRM, it is really a business strategy that attempts to gain a 360-degree picture of a firm's customers in the hope of retaining those customers for a long time. Anyone who has received an e-mail from a retail store offering the availability of a new item like a new line of clothing has experienced CRM. More than likely, the firm has maintained an electronic record of a customer's buying habits and uses the software to tell the customer about related or new items that he or she might be interested in. Financial services firms do the same thing by sending their clients e-mails about the performance of the stock market or a variety of mutual funds. Some governments have also turned to CRM as a strategy and a software package to provide better information to their citizens, sometimes calling this citizen or constituent relationship management.

In general, CRM technologies and software help agencies organize and manage their relationships with citizens through data collection, analysis, and call-routing features. They often provide "one-stop shopping" services such as a single phone number to call to get information from a public agency or to obtain a service from a public agency without the hassle of having to be bounced around from one department to another. CRM systems may contain a centralized searchable knowledge base of data on each citizen or constituent, eliminating the need for citizens to repeatedly provide the same data about themselves to a variety of different agencies. They can also offer case-management capabilities that can track the types of service and quality levels of service provided to citizens. All of this can improve services to citizens while reducing the labor costs of those services. Although the existence of non-interoperable legacy systems and security and privacy rules are impeding the development of CRM systems in the public sector, the future for such technologies looks hopeful.

CRM in government is an extension of e-government in the sense that it seeks to provide citizens with greater access to information and public services via the Internet. It is still in its infancy, but industry analysts project that public agencies will soon become a major market for CRM technologies. A 2004 article appearing on *Destination CRM*, the web site of the editors of *CRM Magazine*, reported that government purchases of CRM technology and services will reach $3 billion by 2007.[23] The same article mentioned that the cities of Baltimore and Las Vegas have instituted call centers that offer "one-stop shopping" for citizens, alleviating the need for citizens to call several different phone numbers in search of a particular service. Indianapolis has also recently instituted a new call center that consolidates citizen information, manages and tracks citizen requests, and is integrated across city departments to improve services to citizens and increase the accountability of city departments.[24] School districts are using CRM technologies to notify parents that their child is tardy or absent and to aggregate data on such things as test scores.[25] Finally, vendors are rushing into the market to provide off-the-shelf CRM software tailor-made for state and local governments. For example, Remedy, a call center vendor, has launched "Citizen Response," which tracks citizen phone, e-mail, in-person, and web inquiries. Siebel offers a similar package of technology called "Public Sector," and PeopleSoft offers "PeopleSoft CRM for Government," a pre-built, packaged portal for federal, state, and local governments.[26]

The Port of San Diego offers a CRM success story.[27] The Unified Port District, a special governmental entity, is charged with the responsibility of managing sixteen bayfront parks and various commercial properties occupied by about 350 businesses, protecting the bay and tidelands from pollution, and conserving the habitat of the bay and port area. The Unified Port District was faced with a communications problem. Phone calls from customers came into a central reception desk that had no standard way of referring the calls to the right departments of the District, resulting in calls being redirected from one department to another until the caller finally found the correct person to talk to. The District decided to apply the CRM philosophy and technologies to create a customer service center (CSC) specifically designed to put the customer first. Today, the CSC routes all phone calls to their proper destinations smoothly and quickly. In the process of implementing the CRM solution, management discovered that the majority of phone calls were inquiries about obtaining permits to use the various parks. As part of the CRM solution, the District established a web page that allows citizens to make inquiries about park permits and to obtain permits twenty-four hours a day, seven days a week, significantly reducing the number of calls coming into the CSC.

This case and the previously mentioned examples of CRM activities are just some "sign posts" that public agencies are moving in the direction of improving services to citizens via advancements in technology, services that make it easier for citizens to get the information or service that they are looking for—a transformation that is worth waiting for as public agencies learn how to exploit the technologies of citizen relationship management philosophies and software. The chapter on the Internet revolution clearly showed that governments across the world are moving to provide more e-government and e-democracy services to the public. Perhaps CRM will one day be a much more integral part of e-government and e-democracy.

However, some serious doubts remain about the use of CRM in the public sector. They have to do with privacy issues, which were addressed in chapter 4. Private firms collect information about customers. To what extent should public agencies collect personal information about citizens, even in efforts to provide them with better services? There are also statutory provisions in many states and localities that prevent agencies from sharing data about citizens even when those citizens are clients or customers of several different agencies.

Summary and a Look Forward

ERP, BPR, and, to some extent, CRM are private management initiatives strongly supported by information technology that have migrated to the public sector. ERP and BPR are already changing the way public agencies conduct their business. CRM has the potential to improve on government electronic initiatives to establish contact with the public and serve the public's interests, but with some privacy cautions. Part of the next chapter will also be about privacy issues—not the privacy of citizens but rather the privacy rights of government employees. This will be considered along with other issues related specifically to end users, namely ergonomics as well as telecommuting and telework.

9

End User Computing Issues

Innovations in technology have created issues related specifically to end users in public organizations, including employee privacy, telecommuting, and ergonomics. Admittedly, the three issues are unrelated except for the fact that they all arise from technology and all affect the end user. More important, however, all three issues represent major challenges for public administrators as management issues and public policy issues that will be addressed here.

Employee Privacy Rights

A public employee's right to privacy in a public agency is simultaneously a simple and a complex matter. Its simplicity rests with the fact that in the United States a public employee has little or no expectation of privacy whatsoever unless an agency specifically allows it. A public employer can collect and store just about any type of data about a current or prospective employee. The complexity of a public employee's right to privacy lies in the confusion arising from what the U.S. Constitution, state statutes, and common law torts have to say about an employee's right to privacy.

Here we will address privacy issues in general and then move on to a discussion of the policies that a public manager may wish to implement to deal with employee privacy issues that may affect the employee, the agency, and the public. The focus will be on the privacy rights of public employees as they pertain to the use of e-mail and the Internet. Although employee privacy rights is a far broader issue than e-mail and Internet access, these two issues are directly tied to information technology and present managerial challenges in managing the technology as well as the public workforce.

Background on Privacy Rights

Privacy is the right of an individual to prevent another person, group, corporation, or public agency from collecting information about him or her.[1] In our

167

modern society, it is virtually impossible to have total privacy. We could not function in society without sharing some information about ourselves such as our name, age, address, marital status, employment status, income, Social Security number, some medical information, and so on. The federal government and most of the states need some basic information about each citizen in order to collect taxes. Public agencies need information about their employees, such as their names, addresses, phone numbers, Social Security numbers, marital status, and number of dependents, to fulfill basic human resource management functions. Financial institutions need some basic information about people to provide them with checking and savings accounts, investment vehicles, loans, credit cards, and ATM cards. Physicians and medical institutions need basic information about people in order to provide them with proper health care. When you think about it, a society could not function at all if citizens were not willing to relinquish some of their rights to privacy to governments, businesses, and nonprofit corporations. The question then becomes, where should the sharing of private information stop and with whom should it stop?

Some countries, such as the member nations of the European Union, Canada, and Australia have established comprehensive laws that govern the collection, use, and dissemination of information about citizens.[2] They have also established oversight bodies to ensure compliance with those laws, providing considerable privacy protections to their citizens. Other countries, the United States in particular, rely on sectoral laws to deal with privacy issues. These laws include constitutions, state statutes, and tort laws to decide matters of privacy, but taken together these sectoral laws do not provide as much privacy as do the comprehensive laws of other nations.[3]

Most of the states recognize that citizens have certain rights to privacy based on state statutes or common law torts. The latter case includes the right not to have one's name or likeness appropriated by someone else; the right not to have embracing, private facts disclosed to someone else or the public; the right to seclusion, solitude, and private affairs; and the right to avoid publicity that places a person in a false light in the public eye. Yet, this sectoral approach to dealing with issues of privacy gives both public and private organizations wide latitude in establishing policies governing workplace privacy, especially policies governing e-mail and Internet use.

Privacy in the Workplace

In the United States, employees in both public and private organizations have very little privacy in the workplace. Employers can monitor just about everything an employee does while he or she is working. This monitoring extends to video surveillance, viewing the content of an employee's computer screen, keystroke logging, phone call monitoring, examination of e-mails, monitoring Internet activity, and even placing devices in chairs that measure the employee's wiggling behavior. Despite this wide latitude given to public managers to oversee what their employees are doing, it is important that management develop and disseminate explicit policies about employee privacy.

A Hypothetical Scenario

Let us consider the following hypothetical scenario to illustrate some of the managerial issues associated with employee privacy rights. Assume that you are an MPA student with an internship with a small city close to the university in which you are enrolled. It is a wonderful opportunity because your career plan is to become a city manager, and the year-long internship is also a paid one. You are working twenty hours a week and will receive six hours of credit toward your degree upon successful completion of the internship. You have been assigned to work as a special assistant to the current city administrator (CA). Because you have a host of IT knowledge and skill, the CA has assigned you to managing the city's network, e-mail system, and web page. You are particularly interested in the web page because it needs a lot of development work.

After two months on the job, the CA calls you into his office and asks you if you have noticed if any of the city's employees have been using the city's PCs and Internet connections for any unusual activities such as sending and receiving private e-mails, buying things on web sites like Amazon.com or eBay, downloading music from the Internet, or visiting sites with inappropriate content like pornography. You say that you have not noticed any of this. He asks if it is technically possible to monitor such activity. You assure him that it is possible; he asks if you will do it for him without telling anyone else. You agree. It is something that you have not done before, but you know that you can easily learn how to do it. You tell him that you will need some key-logging software to keep track of employee computer use. He agrees to get it for you.

You begin your investigation by checking out the employees' e-mail and web browsing habits. You soon discover that many of the city's workers are using e-mail to send jokes to one another and to others outside of the city offices; some are using e-mail to communicate with families and friends; one employee is using e-mail to carry on a romance with someone in another state; and a city council member is using her own PC to communicate with the director of public works to discuss the poor performance of the current CA and his possible removal.

As far as web site activity is concerned, most city employees regularly check a variety of sites that report on weather conditions; one employee regularly logs on to the city's library site to renew loans on books; some employees carry on nonagency business by engaging in instant messaging or talking in online chat rooms; one employee regularly downloads music from an illegal web site; and several employees regularly visit pornographic web sites. Once the key-logging software is installed you are able to determine that some workers are spending what seems to be an appropriate amount of time at their keyboards, while others seem to be spending not much time at all at their keyboards even though their work requires it.

By now you have mixed feelings about what you have found out. The seemingly innocent use of technology to send and receive jokes, send and receive e-mails from family members and friends, buy things off the Net, or renew books at the library does not really bother you. You do feel compelled to tell the CA about the cyber love affair, the downloading of illegal music, and the access to pornographic web sites, but you are worried about telling the CA about the e-mail exchanges between the council member and the public works director, and you worry about "ratting on" the workers who should be spending more time at their keyboards. Without naming names, except for the council member and public works director, you write a confidential memo to the CA and send it to him.

The next morning, the CA calls you into his office and closes the door. He demands the names of all employees who are using the office technology for all of the uses specified in your report. You agree to give him this information. Then he tells you that he wants you to closely monitor all e-mails between city council members and any city employees, and all e-mails from one city council member to another. You try to protest this last request because you suspect that it might be illegal. He reminds you that one call from him to the professor supervising your internship and it will be all over for you. You nod your head and leave the office.

You return to your office and ponder what to do. You call your professor and explain only the most innocent forms of Internet usage by city employees. She tells you to find the city's policy on Internet use. You go to the city attorney's office only to find out that the city has no written policy on Internet use. You send the CA the names of the city employees he requested, and then you start checking the e-mails of city council members and city employees, but you do not know what you should do with them. What the CA has asked for seems illegal, but you do not want to lose your internship.

Some Privacy Issues

This scenario is overly dramatic, but it does contain most of the issues that arise in public employee use of the Internet for nongovernmental purposes as well as some major managerial and privacy issues. For example, should a public employee be allowed to use the technology of a public agency for private purposes such as exchanging jokes, sending e-mails to family members and friends, renewing library books, and checking the weather? Well, the answer is "it depends." It depends on how strict a public agency wants to get about its Internet usage policy. Some public agencies are very strict and allow none of these simple practices because they detract from the work of the public employee. To carry this to the extreme, some agencies prohibit these practices even when an employee is on break time. Some strict agencies actually monitor this type of activity whether the employee is on agency time or break time. A more liberal agency's management might allow such innocuous use of the Internet as long as it does not get too out of hand in the belief that it boosts morale and increases productivity.

Such practices as buying merchandise over the Internet, carrying on romances via e-mail, downloading illegal music, and surfing pornographic sites certainly are not appropriate things to be doing with an agency's equipment, and certainly not on agency time. But in this case, the agency had no written policy forbidding these practices, although such practices could be covered by more general personnel policies that speak to what a public employee should be doing and not doing on agency time.

This city's lack of a written and published policy on Internet usage is the major managerial issue arising from this scenario. Such policies should be written and communicated to all employees in a public agency. They should be part of training programs for existing employees and part of orientation programs for new employees. In the absence of a written policy, neither employees nor management knows what to decide or how to act.

Examples of Internet Use and Privacy Policies

The following examples of actual government agency Internet use and privacy policies will show that some agencies are very strict about the use of the Internet, while others are more liberal.

The *Employee's Internet Usage Policy* of the City of Los Angeles California is quite clear and quite strict. It specifically states that "The use of Internet is restricted to 'official City business.' Personal use of or time spent for personal gain is strictly prohibited."[4] There is nothing else in the city's written policy that even hints at allowing city employees to use city equipment to access the Internet to send or receive private e-mails or even visit a site like Weather. com. The policy goes on to prohibit hacking (breaking into another web site using the city's equipment); sending messages that are threatening, slanderous, and racially or sexually harassing; copying or transferring electronic files without permission; downloading a file from the Internet without scanning it first for viruses; and sending chain letters. The policy also states in bold letters: "THERE IS NO EXPECTATION OF PERSONAL PRIVACY IN THE USE OF THE INTERNET AND E-MAIL." On the first page of the policy is a declaration stating that the employee has read the policy along with a place for a printed name and the employee's signature, followed by notification that the form and the policy will be included in the employee's personnel file. Note that all of the fictitious persons in the preceding hypothetical scenario would run afoul of this policy.

The Commonwealth of Virginia has a less strict policy on Internet and e-mail use for its employees. It allows for personal "incidental and occasional use of the Commonwealth's Internet access or electronic communication systems."[5] Personal use is prohibited, however, if "it interferes with the user's productivity or work performance, or with any other employee's productivity or work performance [or] adversely affects the efficient operation of the computer system." The policy does state certain prohibited uses:

- Accessing, downloading, printing, or storing information with sexually explicit content as prohibited by law.
- Downloading or transmitting fraudulent, threatening, obscene, intimidating, defamatory, harassing, discriminatory, or otherwise unlawful messages or images.
- Installing or downloading computer software, programs, or executable files contrary to policy.
- Uploading or downloading copyrighted materials or proprietary agency information contrary to policy.
- Uploading or downloading access-restricted agency information contrary to policy or in violation of agency policy.
- Sending e-mail using another's identity, an assumed name, or anonymously; permitting a non-user to use for purposes of communicating the message of some third-party individual or organization.
- Any other activities designated as prohibited by the agency.[6]

In the previous hypothetical scenario, this policy would appear to allow the sending and receiving of personal e-mail as well as occasional web surfing, but it does not define what is meant by "incidental and occasional use," nor does it define what it means by interfering with a worker's productivity or the productivity of other workers in the agency. Such judgments are best left to management.

Like the City of Los Angeles, the Commonwealth of Virginia clearly establishes no expectation of privacy:

> No user should have any expectation of privacy in any message, file, image or data created, sent, retrieved or received by use of the Commonwealth's equipment and/or access. Agencies have a right to monitor any and all aspects of their computer systems including, but not limited to, sites, instant messaging systems, chat groups, or news groups visited by agency users, material downloaded or uploaded by agency users, and e-mail sent or received by agency users. Such monitoring may occur at any time, without notice, and without the user's permission.[7]

Generally speaking, virtually all public agencies that have a stated policy on Internet use, e-mail use, or privacy maintain a "no expectation of privacy" policy.

Federal executive branch employees enjoy a little more freedom in the use of federal Internet-based technology. According to the policy set forth by the Chief Information Officer (CIO) Council, federal employees can "use government office equipment for personal needs if the use does not interfere with official business and involves minimal additional expense to the Government. This limited personal use of government office equipment should take place during the employee's non-work time." The policy acknowledges that this flexibility creates a more supportive work environment and specifically states that employees may use "government office equipment to check their Thrift Savings Plan or other personal investments, or to seek employment, or communicate with a volunteer charity organization" during non-work times, but it does prohibit the use of government equipment to run a personal business.[8]

Federal computer equipment and use policy covers other prohibited uses such as:

- Using the government systems as a staging ground or platform to gain unauthorized access to other systems.
- The creation, copying, transmission, or retransmission of chain letters or other unauthorized mass mailings regardless of the subject matter.
- Using government office equipment for activities that are illegal, inappropriate, or offensive to fellow employees or the public. Such activities include, but are not limited to: hate speech or material that ridicules others on the basis of race, creed, religion, color, sex, disability, national origin, or sexual orientation.
- The creation, download, viewing, storage, copying, or transmission of sexually explicit or sexually oriented materials.
- The creation, download, viewing, storage, copying, or transmission of materials related to illegal gambling, illegal weapons, terrorist activities, and any other illegal activities or activities otherwise prohibited.

- Use for commercial purposes or in support of "for-profit" activities or in support of other outside employment or business activity (e.g., consulting for pay, sales or administration of business transactions, sale of goods or services).
- Engaging in any outside fund-raising activity, endorsing any product or service, participating in any lobbying activity, or engaging in any prohibited partisan political activity.
- Use for posting agency information to external newsgroups, bulletin boards, or other public forums without authority. This includes any use that could create the perception that the communication was made in one's official capacity as a federal government employee, unless appropriate agency approval has been obtained.
- Any use that could generate more than minimal additional expense to the government.
- The unauthorized acquisition, use, reproduction, transmission, or distribution of any controlled information including computer software and data, which includes privacy information, copyrighted, trademarked, or other material with intellectual property rights (beyond fair use), proprietary data, or export-controlled software or data.[9]

Managerial Implications

Moving out of the realm of laws governing an employee's right to privacy and Internet use, it simply makes sense, from a managerial point of view, for all public agencies to establish and publish a set of policies governing e-mail privacy and Internet use, and make sure that employees have read and understood the policies.

With regard to e-mail policies, an agency must first decide if it will allow employees any use of agency equipment for private e-mail. Second, if it does allow for such use, policies should clearly state what an employee's right to privacy is. If there is some expectation of privacy it should be spelled out. For example, if the agency allows employees to send and receive private e-mails, the agency should specify this and place some limits on private e-mails. The agency should also indicate whether management has the right to simply monitor the amount of private e-mails that are sent or whether it has the right to actually examine the content of private e-mails. The agency should also clearly note whether the monitoring is constant, periodic, or random. Third, public managers should come to some agreement about the meaning of reasonable or acceptable private e-mail use. A handful of personal e-mails a day might be acceptable to some, but there has to be some generally understood limit. Certainly twenty to thirty personal e-mails a day might suggest that an employee is not paying enough attention to his or her work. Some standard needs to be imposed and declared so as to properly direct the private e-mail activities of employees. Fourth, the agency's managers must decide when personal e-mails can be composed, sent, received, and read: during working hours or only before and after work or on official breaks? Fifth, public employees should be told when and how their private e-mails will be monitored. If the content of the e-mail is to be monitored, they should be told that and advised to be careful in what they say in the e-mail. They should be warned about the use of racist, sexist, sexually explicit, or any other language or graphic content that might offend someone else. Sixth, there may also be prohibitions about sharing agency documents or software programs via e-mail, as well as private information about the citizens that the agency serves.

Establishing policies for Internet web surfing can be simple or complicated. A public agency may simply prohibit any and all web surfing and install hardware or software to prevent it. For agencies that try to foster a more positive workplace, this ban would probably be too strict. One can argue that there is little harm in allowing public employees to check a weather information site or a road conditions site in the event of inclement weather. One can also argue that there is nothing wrong with allowing public employees to visit other types of sites (e.g., eBay, a financial institution, or a public library) before and after work and while they are on breaks. One can argue convincingly that public employees should not have access to pornographic web sites using government equipment, on or off of government time. Prohibiting access to web sites becomes impractical when it is part of a public employee's job. Employees who are involved in research frequently need to access a wide variety of government and private-sector web sites to obtain needed information. Other public employees may need to access other government web sites in the performance of their jobs.

Fortunately, it is relatively easy to monitor the web sites employees visit, when they visit them, and how often they visit them. Again, an agency should develop and disseminate an official written policy regarding web surfing, whether it should be on or off of government time, when it can be done in the pursuit of professional responsibilities or private use, and what web sites are prohibited.

The Hypothetical Scenario Revisited

Let us return to the hypothetical scenario. You (the student intern) decide to visit several web sites dealing with employee privacy issues to learn about the issues at hand. After absorbing much of the foregoing information you decide to make some recommendations to the city administrator.

In a private meeting you tell the CA that the city may have the right to monitor employee e-mail and Internet access but that the city would be well advised to develop and disseminate an official policy regarding such practices. A formal policy would provide clear guidelines for city employees and protect the CA and the city in the event of a complaint. Otherwise, some employees could claim that they did not know that what they were doing was wrong. In the spirit of promoting a positive work environment, you suggest that such a policy might allow for limited personal e-mail use and limited web surfing, but it could also prohibit certain web surfing practices such as downloading music and visiting pornographic sites.

You also suggest that an official policy about no expectation of privacy should apply to the content of official and personal e-mails, and that e-mail traffic and e-mail content be monitored on a regular basis. These policies would probably put an end to the cyber romance and stop the public works director from discussing the performance of the CA with the council member via e-mail. You might also advise the CA that it would not be wise to monitor the council member's e-mail because it was generated from the council member's personal PC and could easily be construed as a violation of the council member's right to privacy and get the CA into a lot of trouble. Of course, you couch all of these recommendations as being in the best interest of the city, its employees, its citizens, and the administrator. Being a graduate of an MPA program, the CA knows the value of clearly stated policies and takes your recommendations.

Summary Comment on Privacy Issues in the Workplace

We have only touched upon some of the issues related to employee privacy in the workplace, namely e-mail and Internet privacy, which are immediately related to information technology. Other privacy issues, such as what types of information an employer can collect about employees (e.g., medical information) and who has access to that information, go beyond the scope of this chapter. If there is a single lesson to be learned about e-mail and Internet privacy in public agencies it is the necessity of having established and disseminated policies about proper e-mail and Internet use.

Telecommuting

More and more public agencies at all three levels of government are experimenting with telecommuting, also known as telework. Telecommuting is usually defined as working from home one or more days a week. It can also mean working from a remote location or locations away from the base office but not from home. Telecommuting has many advantages for the employee, the public agency, and the public in general. It also has some limitations, which makes telecommuting not for everyone. These advantages and limitations will be discussed here.

The Advantages of Telecommuting

We can turn to the web page of the American Telecommuting Association for a shameless plug in favor of telecommuting. They present nine major advantages associated with telework, noting that it can be a win-win solution for employees, employers, and society on the whole.

1. The individual benefits from telecommuting because he or she immediately eliminates the time, trouble, and expense of physically commuting to work. This gives the average person an extra hour per day, right off the top, to use for the thinking, the writing, the telephoning, the planning, and the reporting work that keeps the business organization moving forward.
2. The benefits of telecommuting also translate directly and immediately into more discretionary time, more time with the family, less stress, and general health improvements.
3. In addition, because the individual is working at home, he or she has more control over time, more flexibility to take a short break and change a diaper or drive a child to a friend's house, more freedom to cook a nice family meal, and less pressure to keep every minute crammed with useful activities.
4. Commuting costs are much lower for telecommuters, who tend to feel more in control of life than employees who travel to the same (distant) office five days a week.
5. The family generally likes having Mommy or Daddy around for that extra hour each telecommuting workday and presumably benefits from not getting dumped on by the physical commuter's unspent frustration accumulated during the trip home.
6. The employer benefits from telecommuting because of the extra productivity that results—consistently clocked at 10 to 15 percent in nearly every such study during the past two decades.
7. The organization also saves on expenses. For example, by having half your workforce telecommute one day a week, you cut down by 10 percent on your need for offices, desks and chairs, bathrooms, copy machines, parking spaces, heating and lighting, and all the rest.
8. In addition, telecommuting helps the best employees stay longer, saving on recruiting and training costs, and also makes it practical for the organization to reach out another ten, twenty, or thirty miles (or more) in finding qualified people to fill important posts.

9. Society benefits from telecommuting because it immediately cuts down on air pollution, use of nonrenewable energy sources, and traffic congestion.[10]

With the exception of Advantage 3, the rest of these statements about the benefits of telecommuting are accurate. Advantage 3 refers to childcare duties; some public agencies specifically prohibit telework as a replacement for childcare or even elder care because it can distract from work duties.

Background on Telecommuting

Telecommuting is not a new idea. It has been discussed in the transportation literature for over thirty years. The concept of the home worker was first introduced in 1957 and caught the eye of some transportation scholars during the 1960s. Interest in the potential benefits increased substantially in the 1970s as a result of the energy crisis and then waned as the crisis declined. By the mid-1990s, telecommuting became commonplace in the private sector with such corporate sponsors as AT&T, Pacific Bell, IBM, GTE, the Walt Disney Co., Blue Cross/Blue Shield, and American Express.[11]

In the early 1990s, the federal government and several state governments (e.g., Florida, Arizona, Colorado, Minnesota, and Oregon) began experimenting with pilot telecommuting projects that have since turned into existing programs.[12] The primary motives were a desire to reduce traffic congestion, conserve gasoline, reduce the stress of employee commuting, improve the productivity of workers, and provide job opportunities for people with disabilities. The latter was a 2001 initiative of the Bush administration that recognized that people with certain disabilities may not have the ability to commute to work but could still contribute valuable knowledge and skill in the federal workforce.

Telework Is Not for Everyone

Telecommuting is not for everyone. Its success depends upon the nature of the job, the nature of the employee, and the management style of the supervisor. Some jobs simply do not lend themselves to telecommuting, whether from home or from a remote location. It is not suited to employees who must work face to face with other employees or the public. Nurses, doctors, counselors, police officers, and firefighters would not be good candidates for telework. Nor is it suited to employees who work with special equipment such as laboratory workers, construction workers, computer operators, special equipment operators, receptionists, secretaries, human resource trainers, or employees who work with sensitive documents or special equipment that cannot be removed from the agency's office. It may or may not work for managers, depending on how often the manager must meet with people face to face or in meetings. However, some managers might find that working at home one day a week to complete written reports is feasible. This would classify as telework of a limited nature.

Then there is the nature of the employee. Not all public employees have the right knowledge, skills, abilities, and motivations to be an effective teleworker. The State of Arizona provides a questionnaire on its web site about their telecommuting program that allows employees and supervisors to identify if someone is a good candidate for telecommuting. A modified form of that questionnaire can be seen in Exhibit 9.1.

Successful telecommuting also requires a special type of supervisor—one who manages by results, not observation. Unfortunately, this can be a major barrier to successful telecommuting as reported by Arizona's Department of Administration. Traditional supervisors want to see people working at their desks; otherwise, they assume that people are not working. It takes a results-oriented supervisor to make telecommuting successful. This type of supervisor sets realistic goals and deliverables for the people they manage.

This management philosophy is clearly stated in Arizona's *Telecommuting Guide*. It says:

> Managing employees who are working in a variety of locations isn't new. But to ensure the success of telecommuting, be aware of the following: Managing by close, constant supervision isn't necessarily good supervision. You can achieve good supervision without proximity. In order for your telecommuters to succeed at working at home, you must succeed at supervising. Remember, this is a win-win situation for you and your employees. You will be managing by objectives and results, instead of by observation.[13]

The *Guide* goes on to explain that:

> One of the tools available to you—and one that is particularly effective with telecommuters—is management by objectives (MBO). You probably already know a good deal about this topic, but it's added here to provide some suggestions for working with telecommuters. Prepare an itemized list of what you expect from your telecommuter. The list can be done weekly, monthly, or quarterly. You have the flexibility to establish objectives in a format that will be easy for you to administer. Include your telecommuter in the process of establishing objectives, allowing the employee to have valuable input about his/her productivity. Clearly define what the telecommuter needs to accomplish to be rated as unsatisfactory, satisfactory, or excellent. Track

Exhibit 9.1
Are You a Candidate for Telecommuting?

Use the following survey to help you determine if telecommuting is for you.

Circle the answer that best describes you.

1. Are you self-motivated and self-disciplined? Can you complete work projects without constant supervision? Are you productive when no one is checking on you or watching you work? Successful telecommuters develop regular routines and are able to set and meet their own deadlines.

Yes   Somewhat   Not really

2. Do you have strong organizational and time-management skills? Are you results oriented? Will you remain focused on your work while at home and not be distracted by television, housework, or visiting neighbors? Do you manage your time and workload well, solve many of your own problems, and find satisfaction in completing tasks on your own? Are you comfortable setting priorities and deadlines? Do you keep your sights on results?

Yes   Somewhat   Not really

3. Are you comfortable working alone and disciplined to leave work at quitting time? Can you adjust to the relative isolation of working at home? Will you miss the social interaction at the central office on your telecommuting days? Do you have the self-control to work neither too much nor too little? Can you set a comfortable and productive pace while working at home?

Yes   Somewhat   Not really

4. Are you able to work independently, with minimal supervision and feedback? Can you accomplish work successfully without frequent feedback or approval? Are you able to make decisions independently?

Yes   Somewhat   Not really

5. Are you successful in your current position? Do you know your job well and have a track record of performance? Current job performance is a strong indicator of your potential success as a telecommuter. Consider how any problems or developmental needs evident in your last performance evaluation might affect your telecommuting experience.

Yes   Somewhat   Not really

6. Are you knowledgeable about your organization's procedures and policies? Have you been on the job long enough to know how to do your job in accordance with your organization's procedures and policies? Employees with more experience on the job likely will have fewer questions and less need to contact the central office. Do you have well-established work, communication, and social patterns at the central office? Telecommuters should have a good understanding of the organization's "culture."

Yes   Somewhat   Not really

7. Would you be sensitive to the effect on coworkers of any additional work required of them because of the telecommuting arrangement? Would you be willing to share some of your coworker's tasks to limit the effects, if any? Would you take particular care to provide support to coworkers while working at home? Do you have an effective working relationship with coworkers? When you're away from the central office and problems arise, it's important to know how to get help. Established relationships with coworkers enable both you and your coworkers to feel comfortable asking for assistance and to better understand each other's needs and concerns.

Yes   Somewhat   Not really

8. Are you adaptable to changing routines and environments? Have you demonstrated an ability to be flexible about work routines and environments? Telecommuting changes your daily routine, work environment, work flow, and personal interactions. While productivity usually increases at home, new distractions can present challenges to focusing on your work. Are you willing to come into the office on a regularly scheduled telecommuting day if your supervisor, coworkers, or customers need you there?

Yes   Somewhat   Not really

9. Are you an effective communicator and team player? Do you communicate well with your supervisor and coworkers? Are you able to express needs objectively and develop solutions? Successful telecommuting requires effective communication. You must develop ways to communicate regularly with your supervisor and coworkers on your telecommuting days. Telecommuters must take the initiative to keep up to date with coworkers and central office activities.

Yes   Somewhat   Not really

Check all that apply.

10. Do you have the right job for telecommuting?
___   Low face-to-face communication requirements; at least one day a week, communication can be handled by telephone, voice mail, or e-mail.
___   Responsibilities include large blocks of time handling information, such as writing, reading, analysis, planning, computer programming, word processing, data entry, and telephoning.
___   Minimal requirements for special equipment.
___   Clearly defined tasks and work products with measurable work activities and objectives.

11. Do you have an appropriate home/work environment?
___   A safe, comfortable workspace where it is easy to concentrate on work.
___   The required level of security.
___   The necessary office equipment.
___   A telephone, with a separate home office line, if required, and an answering machine or voicemail.
___   Household members who will understand you're working and will not disturb you.

If an employee answers "Yes" to a majority of these questions, then he or she is likely to be a good candidate for telework.

progress by results. If you are establishing weekly objectives, schedule a weekly meeting to review the telecommuter's accomplishments. Maintain a copy of the objectives in the employee's personnel file and make a copy for the employee.[14]

   This advice from the *Telecommuting Guide* clearly demonstrates that a telecommuting program in any public agency needs to be managed carefully. This is reinforced when we consider some of the issues that arise from telecommuting programs.

Some Telecommuting Issues

There are several issues related to telecommuting that are worthy of mention because they pose interesting questions for management. First, is a public employee covered by workman's compensation while working at home? In some states the answer is yes if the employee is actually performing work.

   Second, does the employee need to have a computer in order to telecommute? In some cases the answer is actually no. Telework can be accomplished without a computer, but computers have become so ubiquitous that they are usually employed in telework.

   Third, who provides the necessary equipment, the employee or the agency? The answer to that question varies across public agencies. In many instances where the public agency provides the equipment, the agency strives to ensure that the equipment is ergonomically designed so as to provide an efficient, effective, and safe working environment.

   Fourth, what should be the nature of the home office? The State of Florida provides an extensive checklist that defines the nature of the home office:

- Does the space seem adequately ventilated?
- Is the space reasonably quiet and free of distractions?
- Are all the stairs with four or more steps equipped with handrails?
- Are all circuit breakers and/or fuses in the electrical panel labeled as to intended service?
- Do circuit breakers clearly indicate if they are in open or closed position?
- Is all electrical equipment free from recognized hazards that would cause physical harm (e.g., frayed wires, bare conductors, loose wires, flexible wires running through walls, exposed wires fixed to the ceiling)?
- Are electrical outlets three pronged (grounded)?
- Is the computer equipment connected to a surge protector?
- Are aisles, doorways, and corners free from obstructions to permit movement?
- Are file cabinets and storage closets arranged so drawers and doors do not open into walkways?
- Is the space crowded with furniture?
- Are the phone lines, electrical cords, and extension wires secured under a desk or alongside the baseboard?
- Are floor surfaces clean, dry, level, and free from worn or frayed seams?

- Are carpets well secured to the floor and free from frayed or worn seams?
- Is there a fire extinguisher in the home, easily accessible from the home office?
- Is there a working smoke detector detectable from the workspace?[15]

Some states reserve the right to inspect an employee's home office.

Fifth, is a public employee's home office covered by Occupational Safety and Health Administration (OSHA) guidelines and regulations? This was a hotly debated issue in 2000[16] and still remains a general issue because of the existence of a variety of different state policies about occupational safety and health issues. As a practical matter, OSHA does not have the resources to inspect home offices, and there is some question as to whether the agency has the authority to require employers to do so. It does have the authority to promulgate voluntary guidelines about inspecting home offices. Some public agencies have chosen to apply those guidelines and inspect home offices; others have not. Whether they do or do not is usually contained in a written telecommuting agreement.[17]

Sixth, is telecommuting an employee right or a privilege? Public agencies have universally considered telecommuting to be a privilege and not a right. This is often explicitly stated in formal telecommuting agreements between public employees and their employers.

Seventh, most public agencies with telework programs have formal telecommuting agreements that both the employee and supervisor must sign. Such agreements usually stipulate such things as the location of the central worksite, the location of the alternate worksite, the duration of the telecommuting assignment, the number of days the employee is allowed to work from home, what equipment is provided by the employee and the employer, the conditions of the home workplace, whether the home workplace will be inspected, how time and attendance will be recorded, how frequently the employee should be in contact with his or her supervisor, and how overtime pay will be handled. These are just some of the issues that may be addressed in a telecommuting agreement. Such agreements protect both the employee and the employer and establish clear expectations for both parties.

Overall, the federal government, some states, and some localities have expressed overwhelming satisfaction with telecommuting arrangements for some of its employees. Although it is enabled by technology, telecommuting is actually a human resource management issue and requires considerable time and attention to implement and manage effectively.

Ergonomics

According to the International Ergonomics Association, ergonomics is defined as "the scientific discipline concerned with the understanding of interactions among humans and other elements of a system, and the profession that applies theory, principles, data and methods to design in order to optimize human well-being and overall system performance."[18] More generally, it is concerned with physical, cognitive, and organizational factors that influence human performance and well-being in the workplace.

Ergonomics became a "hot topic" in the popular press during the mid- to late 1990s. Today, its popularity seems to have waned a bit, but it is still an important issue in information technology and management circles because it can affect the comfort levels and productivity of public employees.

In the context of information technology, the issue of ergonomics most often arises from poorly designed workstations. Employees who spend most of their workday in front of a computer often complain of eye strain, headaches, backaches, neck strains, and wrist pain. The latter can lead to carpal tunnel syndrome (CTS), which presents with the following symptoms in the hands: tingling, pain, numbness, coldness, and loss of strength. Considerable scientific controversy exists over whether the connection between computer work and carpal tunnel syndrome is real.[19] Whether it be CTS or other forms of discomfort, poorly designed workstations can result in the loss of employee productivity.

The Occupational Safety and Health Administration (OSHA) was established in 1970 to prevent work-related injuries, illnesses, and deaths by issuing and enforcing standards for workplace safety and health. OSHA's original power to impose workplace safety standards on private firms has been significantly weakened over the years due to complaints from industry and commerce that these regulations would federalize the workplace and cost billions of dollars to change the nature of work as well as the design of machinery to comply with the imposed standards. It took OSHA ten years to develop standards, announced in 2000, to deal with ergonomic injuries in the workplace. By March of 2001, Congress repealed those standards in favor of voluntary compliance with guidelines. OSHA's scope of authority has never applied to public agencies, but most of the states have their own OSHA-type policies that cover public employees.

Many private businesses and public agencies have adopted voluntary minimal standards similar to OSHA's guidelines for ergonomic safety. In brief, OSHA's guidelines for "Good Working Positions" are as follows:

> To understand the best way to set up a computer workstation, it is helpful to understand the concept of neutral body positioning. This is a comfortable working posture in which your joints are naturally aligned. Working with the body in a neutral position reduces stress and strain on the muscles, tendons, and skeletal system and reduces your risk of developing a musculoskeletal disorder (MSD). The following are important considerations

when attempting to maintain neutral body postures while working at the computer workstation:

- Hands, wrists, and forearms are straight, in-line, and roughly parallel to the floor.
- Head is level, or bent slightly forward, forward facing, and balanced. Generally it is in line with the torso.
- Shoulders are relaxed and upper arms hang normally at the side of the body.
- Elbows stay in close to the body and are bent between 90 and 120 degrees.
- Feet are fully supported by the floor or a footrest.
- Back is fully supported with appropriate lumbar support when sitting vertical or leaning back slightly.
- Thighs and hips are supported by a well-padded seat and generally parallel to the floor.
- Knees are about the same height as the hips with the feet slightly forward.

Regardless of how good your working posture is, working in the same posture or sitting still for prolonged periods is not healthy. You should change your working position frequently throughout the day in the following ways:

- Make small adjustments to your chair or backrest.
- Stretch your fingers, hands, arms, and torso.
- Stand up and walk around for a few minutes periodically.[20]

Public managers should be well advised to follow these simple guidelines in setting up workstations to provide for the comfort, well-being, and productivity of public employees.

Summary and a Look Forward

As noted earlier, these issues of privacy, telecommuting, and ergonomics arise from developments in information technology, but they cross over from the field of IT into the domains of human resource management, public policy, and the law. They can have tremendous impacts on the lives of a wide variety of public employees. In the next chapter we will return, in part, to the realm of the IT specialist in relation to acquiring technology solutions for public agencies, but we will also encounter the fact that technology acquisition is an issue that is broader than just technology concerns. It involves competent government contracting and strong general managerial oversight.

10

Acquiring Technology Solutions

Acquiring technology solutions for public agency operations means dealing with government procurement and contracting processes. Unfortunately, these are two of the most complex facets of modern public administration. It takes years of education and training to become a competent contracting officer whether at the federal, state, or local level of government. Such persons need to have a firm understanding of the vast and complex rules and regulations that govern procurement and contracting as well as the technical knowledge and expertise to define precise specifications for the products and services they acquire for public agencies.

To make matters more complicated, procurement and contracting is governed by a variety of laws, statutes, prior practices, and regulations that can make doing business with the government appear to be an impenetrable maze in the eyes of a potential contractor looking to do some business with a public agency or in the eyes of a novice public purchasing officer. The federal government and each of the fifty states have their own sets of laws, statutes, prior practices, and regulations that are similar in nature but can often differ from one another in significant ways, making things difficult for both private sellers and public buyers. All of this gets even more complicated when one considers that local governments also have their own laws, statutes, prior practices, and regulations, some of which differ significantly from those of the states, the federal government, and other localities. This means that we can speak about the procurement and contracting for technology solutions only in the most general terms. But we can get a general sense of how important contracting and procurement procedures are in acquiring software solutions for public agencies.

This chapter is organized as follows. First, it provides a general conceptual background on procurement and contracting to provide a high-level picture of the complexity of the matter. Second, it focuses on the landscape of procurement and contracting at the federal, state, and local levels of government to get a general sense of the types of laws and regulations that govern procurement and contracting. Third, a managerial perspective on technology acquisition is taken by describing the Software Acquisition Capability Maturity Model (SA-CMM). The model is a powerful management tool for determining an agency's readiness to effectively acquire and develop software (and hardware) applications. Fourth, the outsourcing alternative is explored. This is a recent development in government procurement and contracting that has the potential to radically change the nature of public administration. We will consider how the federal government is using outsourcing to diminish the size of the federal workforce, and how state and local governments are using outsourcing to reduce costs and take advantage of technical knowledge and skill found in the private sector.

Background on Procurement and Contracting

This section provides some general background on how the federal government, some of the states, and some local governments address issues of procurement and contracting. This is a broad overview for three reasons: (1) there are similarities and differences in how public agencies acquire goods and services across all three levels of government; (2) procurement and contracting policies, procedures, rules, and regulations can be highly complex and at times unique to an agency or governmental entity; and (3) procurement and contracting policies, procedures, rules, and regulations are in a constant state of flux as various agencies at all three levels of government are undergoing procurement and contracting reforms. Here we will address the values that influence procurement and contracting, the exceptions for no-bid contracts and sole-source contracts, and the centralized and decentralized approaches to procurement and contracting, followed up with a hypothetical example of the contracting process.

A Competing Values Framework

To get a high-level conceptual sense of how government procurement and contracting works, it is useful to consider the values that have guided public policy and law about procurement and contracting. These values are contained in various statutes, court decisions, and administrative rules and regulations that have been established over fifty years or so, dating back to the late 1940s. We will also note how some of the values may come in conflict as guides to public action in certain situations.

Steven L. Schooner has identified nine values that influence government contracting and procurement.[1] They are: competition, integrity, transparency, efficiency, best value, customer satisfaction, wealth distribution, risk avoidance, and uniformity. Some of the values complement one another, making the procurement and contracting process run smoothly. Others conflict with one another, adding complexity to the procurement and contracting processes of public agencies.

Competition is a value because we live in a capitalist, free-market economy where private firms should have the right to compete with each other for the business of government, which is a gigantic market representing billions and billions of dollars. Competition helps to ensure that government gets the best value for its money in terms of price and quality of goods and services. The promotion of competition is also of general benefit to the robustness of the entire economy since government purchases funnel taxpayer dollars back into the economy. Speaking generally, public agencies should not be making the things that they use to conduct their day-to-day operations—for example, pens, pencils, paper, telephones, and, of course, computer technologies—if those goods are available in the private marketplace.

Integrity means that the procurement and contracting process should be conducted in such a way as to avoid unfair practices, favoritism, bribery, or corruption. Firms wishing to do business with the government should expect fair and equal treatment and a level playing field. As Phillip J. Cooper reminds us, during the latter part of the 1880s and the early 1900s, government purchasing, especially at the local levels of government, was beset with fraud, waste, abuse, and corruption.[2] Reformers during the Progressive Era (circa 1890s through the 1920s) did much to clean up the corruption associated with government contracting and procurement, instilling integrity into the process.

Transparency indicates that the procurement and contracting process is conducted in an open and impartial manner. This means that the rules and regulations governing procurements and contracts are open and known to all interested parties, even the general public, and that all opportunities to do business with the government are publicized. It also means that the government will be open about how all bids are evaluated and how the relevant rules and regulations were followed in the process of awarding a contract.

Efficiency refers to the expenditure of the least amount of resources in the process of obtaining a good or service. This means that the procurement and contracting process should employ the least number of government buyers (procurement or contracting officers) to obtain goods or services, and the length it takes to obtain a good or service should be as short as possible. This is one of the conflicting values because the rules and regulations that govern procurement and contracting usually make it a very lengthy and labor-intensive process, as we shall see shortly. Because of the length of the contracting process, some public agencies, most notably the federal government, allow for no-bid contracts in order to respond to emergencies in a timely fashion. No-bid contracts are controversial because they go against the value of competition, as will be discussed later.

Best value simply means that the government gets what it pays for at a fair or reasonable price for the taxpayers' money. Best value can be construed as the lowest bid for a product or service, but this may not always be the case. For example, purchasing the cheapest writing instrument at, say, ten cents per pen may make sense in some instances, but if the pens last only a few days before they dry out, this choice can be wasteful. In order to achieve best value at a fair price, purchasing officers need to articulate precise specifications for the products or services that their government customers desire. This means that a pen might end up costing fifty cents, but it may also last longer, thereby better satisfying the needs of a government customer.

Best value can compete with the value of customer satisfaction. Purchasing officers strive to satisfy the needs of their public customers. In other words, government employees should get the goods or services that they expect. This does not always mean the lowest-priced product or service. Sometimes the government customer desires a higher-quality good or service that comes at a higher price. Some purchasing regulations demand the lowest price; other regulations leave room for best value, which usually means a higher price and a higher-quality product or service. Best-value purchasing can also limit competition when a government customer demands a name-brand product or a named service provider. Best-value purchasing also conflicts with the value of efficiency because it usually involves extensive market research to find the right product or service as well as extensive negotiations with sellers in order to achieve the best value.

Procurement and contracting laws and regulations have been crafted to distribute wealth or, stated differently, to *re*distribute wealth. Preferential treatment is often given to small businesses, minority-owned business, women-owned businesses, and businesses owned by veterans as a matter of social policy. This value can conflict with the values of competition, best value, and customer satisfaction. For example, it can be argued that in some situations a small business does not have the experience or economies of scale that a large firm does to deliver a desired product for customer satisfaction at the best value, whether it be at the lowest price or at a higher price but with better quality.

Procurement and contracting systems should avoid risk. This usually means that government buyers need to be very precise in their statements about the design of a product or a service and in their performance specifications. For example, if an agency contracts for the delivery of a special piece of machinery, the agency should be precise in the design features of the machinery, making sure that it is safe to operate. Risk also arises in poorly worded contracts that allow for unwarranted or unanticipated cost overruns. Yet cost overruns are sometimes unavoidable when contracting for something that is in a research-and-development stage where it is impossible to foresee unknown costs. Poorly defined requirements is one of the primary reasons why technology acquisitions fail by going over budget or schedule or, in most cases, over both budget and schedule.

Another approach to risk avoidance can be found in a performance-based contract. With this type of contract an agency pays the contractor, only when measurable products, outputs, or outcomes are actually delivered. This method shifts the risk away from government and onto the private contractor, who must carefully calculate costs ahead of time so as not to run over budget and consequently lose money.[3]

Finally, there is the value of uniformity. This value demands that all of the agencies buy the same way, that they follow the same rules and regulations. This means that private sellers do not need to learn multiple sets of rules and regulations, and government buyers do not need to be trained on different procurement and contracting systems. This approach makes sense. Consider how confusing it would be if each agency in a state had a different procurement system for its own office supplies. The value of uniformity converges with the value of efficiency to make procurement and contracting run smoothly.

An additional value can be added to the list: the value of the contract itself, expressed in the structure of a well-written contract. Johnston, Romzek, and Wood observe that

> Successful contracting requires well-written contracts that specifically define all parties' roles and responsibilities, establish clear, meaningful, and measurable performance goals, outputs, and outcomes, and incorporate realistic incentives or sanctions. Such contracts minimize the potential for misunderstandings during the implementation phase and allow the contractor some flexibility to decide how best to achieve the desired outcomes and goals. This simple characteristic of contract structure—a well written contract—is actually a significant challenge in practice. It can be difficult to compose contractual language for complex governmental programs and services where "quality" and "efficiency" are hard to define and measure.[4]

Nothing ensures the success of an IT acquisition, whether for technologies or services, more than a well-written contract that clearly spells out all terms and conditions and satisfies both parties. A poorly written contract often leads to subsequent disputes and possibly even litigation.

While each of these values has influenced government procurement and contracting, it is easy to see that they can complicate the process, which will become even clearer as our discussion proceeds.

No-Bid Contracts and Sole-Source Contracts

Federal, state, and local governments usually have statutes or regulations in place that allow for no-bid contracts and sole-source contracts, but these are exceptions to other statutes or regulations requiring competitive bidding. The logic behind a no-bid contract is simple. There may be times when a public agency needs a product or a service quickly and the conventional competitive-bidding process would simply take too long to obtain the product or service. The logic behind a sole-source contract is also simple. There may be situations in which a public agency can find only one provider of a product or service in the marketplace. The presumption here is that there are no other qualified competitors for the desired product or service.

Because of the potential for fraud, abuse, and corruption, public agencies are usually very careful about signing no-bid contracts and entering into sole-source contracts. The statutes and regulations that govern these types of contracts usually require special written justifications for their use. The contracting officer must prove that speed is of the essence for no-bid contracts and that there are no other likely competitors for sole-source contracts.

Centralized and Decentralized Procurement and Contracting

Government contracting can be centralized, decentralized, or a mix of both. Traditionally, it was believed that the procurement and contracting functions of public agencies should be centralized into one unit. McCue and Pitzer observe that

> According to the National Institute of Governmental Purchasing (1989) and the National Association of State Procurement Officers (1997), a central procurement authority is desirable to limit the power of an agency, to assure professionalism, consistency and accountability and to provide for maximizing procurement planning, standardizing the purchase of commonly used goods and services and combining requirements to take advantage of economies of scale.[5]

Most public agencies at all three levels of government initially approached the procurement and contracting function with this view of centralization. It makes sense when an agency needs to acquire standard items such as pens, pencils, and paper that can be used by a wide variety of employees across an agency's various departments and offices. Bulk purchases of standard items usually come at much lower costs for an agency. It is also necessary when a public agency is faced with acquiring uniquely specialized goods and services such as information technology that require highly trained purchasing specialists who understand how to write product and service specifications and know how to measure purchasing performance. An example would be the acquisition of a new VoIP telephone system for an entire agency.

Logically, there can be a fully decentralized purchasing arrangement where there is no central purchasing department and an agency's various departments or units are responsible for all of their own purchasing under very broad policies. Such arrangements are very rare. A survey of county and city governments conducted in 2000 revealed that only 11 of the 314 respondents (3.5 percent) indicated that their procurement process was fully decentralized.[6] Decentralized purchasing makes sense when a unit or office needs something unique to meet its special needs. An example would be an art department of a state university that needs to acquire special canvases, brushes, paints, and pens that no other department in the university would require.

That same survey found a mixed model in which purchasing is simultaneously centralized and decentralized. It makes sense to centralize the purchasing function when an agency must acquire products or services that are highly specialized, technologically complex, and very expensive. An ERP system would be an example because it is a big-ticket item requiring highly specialized design specifications and the advice of either in-house or outside technical consultants. Purchasing other products or services such as office supplies could be decentralized because they are small-ticket items that can be acquired quickly. An example would be a purchasing card issued to secretarial staff in various departments of a public agency, although some public agencies centralize the purchasing of office supplies. This process may achieve greater economy by buying in large quantities. In this case, each department or unit within the agency places its order for supplies with a unit sometimes called "central stores." The central stores model carries an additional cost because supplies need to be kept in inventory, and maintaining inventories can be expensive and tie up operating cash. In other cases a public agency might sole-source the acquisition of office supplies to an office supply retailer such as OfficeMax or Office Depot that gives the agency a discounted price under a general contract.

A Hypothetical Example

The following hypothetical example will explain how the competing values, no-bid contracts, sole-source contracts, and centralized versus decentralized contracting might play out in the real world of government procurement.

Suppose a small city decides that its 150 five-year-old personal computers need to be replaced because they are slow and support only old software applications that have limited utility. Instead of replacing them one by one on a department-by-department basis, management feels it can get a better value if it buys centrally and in quantity from one seller. In this case, the city does not have a purchasing officer. So, the city's finance director assumes that responsibility and seeks the advice of the city's only information technology specialist to obtain specifications for the new PCs.

If the city has a sole-source purchasing agreement with a local office supply store, the acquisition of the new computers and related software would be a simple matter. The finance director and the technical person would simply go to the store and order the desired number of computers. However, the city might have a regulation in place that says that any purchase over a specified amount must go out for bid. In this case, replacing 150 personal computers and related hardware and software would probably exceed that limit. A savvy finance director might consider placing 150 separate orders, each of which would be below the specified limit, but this process could be viewed as an unethical bending of the procurement regulations of the city.

Under a no-bid contract, the city could go to a big box electronics store or directly to a manufacturer to solicit a price quote, but doing so would go against the value of competition, which is probably specified in some state statute, the city charter, a city ordinance, or a city policy. So, the finance director decides to put out a request for proposal (RFP), which is published in the local newspaper and on the city's web site. The RFP mentions the number of personal computers, their exact performance specifications, the types of monitors and printers that will come with the machines, the networking architecture, and the types of software applications that will come with the system. The RFP does not mention any of the specifications by brand name. For example, it does not specify an Intel Pentium 4 microprocessor, nor does it identify any of the software components by name, such as Microsoft Word or Corel WordPerfect. That specificity would give undue advantage to a potential supplier that uses differing chips and offers differing software packages.

Several sealed bids are received, some directly from the manufacturers of personal computers, some from large retailers, and one from a small local business. When the bids are examined, confusion arises. The lowest bid comes from the small local business, which satisfies the best value criteria, but it may not satisfy the customer satisfaction criteria because the proposed system would be built using "no name" microprocessors that may not have a track record of performance or dependability; they would come with software packages that the staff does not currently use, requiring additional training time to convert over to the new packages; and there is some doubt in the mind of the finance director about whether the small business will be around long enough to fulfill its ninety-day warranty, a risk-avoidance consideration.

Therefore, the finance director decides to go with a bid from one of the big electronics stores, which provides them the machines with known-quality microprocessors, known software packages, and an almost certain warranty guarantee. The small business is notified of the decision and files a protest, and the contracting process stops dead in its tracks. If the city has the right regulations in place, what might happen then is that the contracting process would begin again by opening negotiations with all of the bidders. Management would have the opportunity to more clearly express its needs and wants. The bidders would have a chance to try to address those needs and wants. The small business might choose to upgrade the microprocessors and offer more compatible software applications, but this would probably increase their costs and consequently their bid, in which case, the bids from the big box electronics stores or the direct manufacturer may be more appealing. In any case, the simple acquisition of PCs has become complex and the procurement process has become protracted.

The Procurement and Contracting Landscape

To get a sense of the complexity of government procurement and contracting, a brief look at the landscape at all three levels of government is in order. Here we will consider some of the laws, policies, and regulations that govern technology acquisition in the public sector.

Focus on the Federal Government

Oddly enough, the first federal laws governing contracting were not established until shortly after World War II. Of course the federal government had been involved in contracting with private firms for goods and services long before that time. Its authority to do so was implicitly stated in the preamble to the Constitution, which says that the government should promote the general welfare of the nation.

Prior to the contracting reform movement of the late 1940s, the United States, like many other nations, relied on a host of nongovernmental actors, often private firms, to do much of the government's work. Many Western European nations looked to private entities to collect taxes, manage public finances, build roads and modes of transportation like sailing ships, and establish empires. For example, the expeditions of the Spanish conquistadors were "private enterprises led by independent military contractors in pursuit of profit" and the British crown subcontracted colonization by issuing licenses and monopolies to private adventurers, who assumed the risks in speculative pursuit of profits.[7] Similarly, the United States, following many British common law ideas, relied on such firms as the Pinkerton Agency to provide law enforcement in some sections of the Wild West, and the State of Texas hired an independent band of gunfighters, the Texas Rangers, to bring peace to regions of the state. U.S. government contracting during World Wars I and II relied on a variety of commercial and common law precedents to guide the acquisitions of armaments and munitions. It was not until after World War II that the federal government realized that it needed to make federal contracting a more systematic and regulated endeavor as it faced the threats of the Cold War, the development of nuclear arms, and the exploration of space.

Three early congressional acts provide the statutory foundation of systematic federal government contracting. The Armed Services Procurement Act of 1947 (ASPA) governs the acquisition of all property (except land), construction, and services by defense agencies. The Federal Property and Administrative Services Act of 1949 (FPASA) governs similar civilian agency acquisitions. The latter allowed each executive agency to establish its own procurement and contracting policies, procedures, and regulations. Also in 1949, Congress established the General Services Administration (GSA) to be the major supplier of general goods and services to all federal agencies. As it has evolved, the GSA manages federal buildings and properties and supplies general-purpose goods and services such as office supplies and equipment, vehicles, scientific equipment, food services, and cleaning services to other federal agencies.

In 1984 Congress passed two major acts designed to reform federal government procurement and contracting. The Federal Acquisition Regulation (FAR) provides uniform policies and procedures for acquisitions by all federal agencies, military and civilian. It addresses nearly every procurement-related statute or executive policy.[8] The FAR was a major attempt to bring uniformity to federal contracting. Before the FAR, each executive agency had its own set of procurement and contracting regulations dating back to legislation in the late 1940s, violating the procurement value of uniformity. The Competition in Contracting Act (CICA) applies to both defense and civilian acquisitions. It requires all federal agencies to seek and obtain "full and open competition" wherever possible in the contract-award process. It was a response to perceived prior abuses in sole-source contracting or no-bid contracting. Contrary to simplifying federal procurement and contracting, both acts have resulted in confusion and complications.

By its enormous size and complexity, the FAR brings its own brand of confusion to the contracting table. As Vernon J. Edwards observes, the Government Printing Office's loose-leaf version of the first chapter of the FAR exceeds 2,200 pages, including the index.[9] It does not contain the cost accounting standards appendix, which contains another 288 pages. He further notes that many people rely on the Commerce Clearing House paperback FAR, which, in the January 2003 edition, runs to 1,858 pages, including an index but excluding the cost accounting standards. He then goes on to mention the many agency supplements that have been appended to the FAR that establish special regulations for different executive agencies. The supplements bring the total length of the FAR to in excess of ten thousand pages. In essence, these supplements take us back to the pre–FAR days when each agency had its own set of regulations, thus bending the procurement value of uniformity once more.

Edwards points out the absurdity of the complexity inherent in the FAR when he observes that

> FAR 1.602–1(b) says: "No contract shall be entered into unless the contracting officer ensures that all requirements of law, executive orders, regulations, and all other applicable procedures, including clearances and approvals, have been met." The command is absurd—the FAR alone is too big, its contents are too haphazardly organized, and many of its provisions are indecipherable. The FAR includes texts both ancient and modern, some of them dating back to the old Armed Services Procurement Regulation (c.1949–c.1978, R.I.P.). The rationale for, and the meaning of, some of these texts has been lost to all but the most dogged archivists, and some texts have been made obsolete by current practices.[10]

The FAR is testament to the need for increased training and education for federal contracting specialists.

The CICA was a noble effort to enhance competition for federal contracts, especially among minority-owned businesses, women-owned businesses, and small disadvantaged businesses that have difficulty competing with large private firms, but there have been exceptions. Existing regulations still allow for no-bid contracts between the federal government and the private sector in the belief that some contracts need to be awarded quickly to serve the public interest, thus bypassing lengthy competitive bidding. This practice has caused some controversy. For example, after the war in Iraq began in 2003, a no-bid contract in the amount of $2 billion was issued to the Halliburton Company for fuel distribution. Critics have pointed out that Vice President Dick Cheney was the former head of Halliburton. More recently, in the aftermath of Hurricane Katrina, the Bush administration has let several no-bid reconstruction contracts go to large private firms. Critics have argued that small firms, and especially minority firms, should have been given the opportunity to bid on these contracts. Awarding no-bid contracts is not unique to the Bush administration. Under the Clinton administration no-bid contracts were given to Halliburton for reconstruction efforts in Kosovo and Bosnia.

Competitive contracting can be a long and costly process for both the government and private firms wishing to contract with the government. Edwards points out that FAR requirements can create a lengthy ordeal, which he described as a "process model" containing fourteen steps that must be followed in sequence for most federal competitive contracts. The steps in the process are as follows:

1. Agency issues a request for proposals that solicits complete proposals from all competitors.
2. Agency receives competing proposals.
3. Agency convenes a panel or set of panels to evaluate the competing proposals.
4. Panels evaluate all proposals on the basis of the complete set of evaluation factors for award.
5. Panels report their findings to the decision maker in writing.
6. Decision maker either: (a) selects the contractor or (b) establishes a competitive range that includes all of the most highly rated competitors.
7. Agency negotiates ("conducts discussions") with the remaining competitors.
8. Agency asks remaining competitors to submit final proposal revisions.
9. Agency receives final proposal revisions.
10. Agency convenes panels to evaluate final proposal revisions.
11. Panels evaluate all final proposal revisions.
12. Panels report their findings to the decision maker in writing.
13. Decision maker selects the contractor.
14. Decision maker announces the award decision.[11]

These steps, especially the negotiations with competitors, can unreasonably prolong the time it takes for a federal agency to acquire hardware or software or information technology services. This is one source of the commonly heard industry complaint that once an agency has finally obtained a technology solution to a problem, the technology is already out of date.

There have been efforts to reform the problems caused by the FAR, and the GSA has tried to streamline technology acquisitions while keeping them open and competitive. GSA stands ready to provide other agencies, as well as states and local governments, with help in acquiring hardware, software, IT services, Internet services, wireless services, voice and data services, and consulting for integration of IT services. They do this through three basic mechanisms. First are Government Wide Acquisition Contracts (GWACs) for technology for one agency that can be used by other agencies. These include contracts for such things as online information services, all other information services, data-processing services, custom computer programming services, computer systems design services, computer facilities management services, and other computer-related services. Such services are provided by a list of approved vendors who have already established a contractual agreement with GSA under FAR regulations. Many of these vendors represent small businesses. Second are Technology Contracts (TCs). They cover a wide range of information technology solutions, from network services and information assurance to telecommunications and the purchase of hardware and software. Third, is IT Schedule 70 (ITS70), which is for large and small purchases by organizations that are self-sufficient in technical and contracting expertise. GSA offers prequalified resources to meet federal, state, and local government agency needs. It has more than 5,000 contracts for IT hardware, software, and telecommunications products and services available to federal, state, and local governments.

Despite the federal government's efforts to consolidate the procurement of IT products and services into a "one-stop shopping" location within GSA, other federal agencies often find loopholes within the FAR to procure and contract on their own. This practice has the potential to lead to unnecessary duplication of effort, but agencies are able to make the case that "one-size-fits-all" solutions do not meet their needs and they should be free to do their own procurement and contracting under the authority of the FAR and any special supplement to the FAR that exists for their agency. The classic example of this is the Department of Defense, which has its own supplementary regulations based on the argument that their needs for many goods and services are unique. For example, it is not likely that GSA has an established government-wide contract for submarines. Indeed, there are not many private firms, with the possible sole exception of the General Electric Corporation, that could supply the Navy with a submarine (unless the Department of Defense wants to open bidding to Russia or China, which is highly unlikely).

Consequently, federal procurement and contracting is both centralized and decentralized. The centralized portion seeks open competition and transparency while the decentralized portion may frequently seek expedience. The various agencies that turn to decentralized procurement and contracting often deal with established firms that have on-staff specialists for dealing with specific agency needs and wants.

Focus on the States

It is a little more difficult to get a handle on how all fifty states deal with procurement and contracting because historically each state has approached this somewhat differently, promulgating somewhat different policies, procedures, rules, and regulations. For example, it would not be unusual to find that in one state an agency could write a check for some piece of equipment that costs $100,000 without doing too much paperwork or complying with a lot of regulations about competitive bidding, while in another state all purchases exceeding $10,000 need to go through a formal bid process, handled by a centralized procurement office or agency.

Prior to the late 1990s, some states' regulations concerning procurement and contracting could have been described as lackadaisical while others would be the opposite—mired down in too many regulations, some of which were archaic and completely out of pace with rapid changes in the economy as well as technology. Fortunately, in 1996 the National Association of State Information Resource Executives (NASIRE) teamed up with the National Association of State Purchasing Officers (NASPO) and the National Association of State Directors of Administration and General Services (NASDAGS) to develop uniform policy recommendations on acquiring information technologies for the states. In general, these policy recommendations help to streamline IT acquisitions while retaining an open and competitive process.

In a report entitled *Buying Smart: Blueprint for Action,* the joint task force made five recommendations: (1) Simplify the procurement of commodity items and services; (2) build an infrastructure for electronic commerce; (3) procure information technology based on best value; (4) develop beneficial partnerships with vendors; and (5) solve problems with solicitations.[12] Simplification usually means raising the limits on what a state can pay for a technology product or service without having to go through a normal competitive-bidding process. This method saves time and speeds up the acquisition of the technology product or service. A brief explanation of the other recommendations follows.

An infrastructure for electronic commerce means e-procurement. This involves the use of information technology, especially telecommunications and Internet technology, in every stage of the purchasing process, from identification of requirements, to soliciting bids, to issuing RFPs, to conducting reverse auctions, to invoicing, to billing, to payment, and to contract management. The benefits of e-procurement include increased efficiency from the reduction of paperwork, improved relationships with vendors and suppliers, reduced costs for suppliers, increased competition, and reductions in bid protests. A specific example of e-procurement will be presented later in this chapter.

Best value moves governments away from the lowest bid to consider a broader range of variables, some of which may be intangible. Among those variables are total cost of ownership, including operational costs, training costs, and replacement costs, instead of simply the initial acquisition cost;

performance history of the vendor and the vendor's financial stability; the quality of goods and services; the timely delivery of goods and services; the proposed technical performance; the cost of training employees to use new technologies; the qualifications of consultants, vendors, or advisors proposed for a project; a realistic assessment of the risks of the proposed solution; and the availability and cost of technical support.

Because best-value procurement is far more complicated than lowest-price procurement, several conditions need to be in place. Agency personnel need to be trained in the philosophies, methods, and practices of best value. The vendor needs to be educated about how best-value procurement works, how the agency establishes evaluation criteria for goods and services, and how the agency applies the criteria to a formal bid for goods or services. Sources of reliable data for evaluating best-value contracts need to be identified. They might include information about the past performance of the vendors and the financial stability of the vendors. Agency staff should be educated about the total cost of acquiring and owning a system beyond the capital cost. Benchmark reports should be maintained so that the data used to evaluate the criteria for best value are well documented. Documentation will help an agency explain its decision making should a problem arise or if a bid is protested. Formal systems should be designed to evaluate the vendors, stating clear criteria for identifying performance beyond lowest price. These systems should be composed of evaluation committees including purchasing officers, financial officers, technical personnel, and end users.

Special attention should be paid to several possible issues:

- Best-value methodology involves subjective judgments, so careful attention should be paid to being fair and transparent in the process.
- The evaluation criteria that go into making the final decision must be clearly communicated to all possible vendors.
- The criteria used in selecting a proposal must be used consistently for all proposals.
- The data used to evaluate the criteria and factors must be reliable.
- All decisions must be documented to avoid protests and litigation.

Forming long-term partnerships with vendors is a major departure from traditional contracting. While the states have traditionally avoided partnerships in an effort to not show favoritism to any one vendor, they are learning that some partnerships work well. In a partnership where mutually beneficial goals are clearly understood, risk can be shared between the agency and the vendor, as opposed to having risk resting solely on the shoulders of the agency. Under traditional practices, a public agency buys a technology product or service, and once purchased, the vendor walks away. Under a long-term partnership arrangement, the vendor is there to provide assistance if something goes wrong in the interest of maintaining the partnership.

If a partnership is to succeed certain conditions must be met:

1. The vendors must have an interest or stake in the project. They must be willing to share the risks associated with the project.
2. The vendors must produce measurable results.
3. The relationship between the state and the vendor should be conducted under conditions of integrity, ethics, and trust.
4. The relationships should be long term. The state should know that the vendor will be there in the future if help is needed and what help will be provided.
5. Because this is a long-term relationship, both the state and the vendor should be looking out for each other's strategic interests.
6. Attention should be paid to continuing improvements in products and services.
7. Requirements should be openly communicated and the capabilities of both the state and the vendor should be clearly understood by both parties.
8. Because the financial health of the state's partner is important, financial specialists within the agency should be consulted.
9. States must have knowledge about the technology market and any rapid change in that market. This means that the state must have technology experts on hand either in-house or on a consulting basis.
10. States must know how to write and manage contracts. They cannot leave this to the vendor. A potential vendor may become a partner, but the partnership rests on a firm contract that the state should write and approve. This means having an experienced contracting staff on hand.

Problem-oriented bids (or solution solicitations) are radically different from traditional bids. Usually a state would write all of the specifications for a technology product or service. This is potentially dangerous when a state does not have personnel with the necessary knowledge and experience to write the right requirements. It can also be costly if a state has to hire a consultant with the necessary knowledge and experience to write the right requirements. Under problem-oriented bids, the state simply states the existence of a problem. For example: We need to integrate some of our data across several applications. This places the responsibility for writing the requirements to solve the problem on the shoulders of the vendors. It also shifts the risk to the vendors, who are responsible for designing an appropriate solution to a problem. In our example, the vendors would be writing the requirements for an ERP solution for the state, and it would make the vendor look bad if their proposed solution did not work.

This may sound like the state has little work to do other than to state a problem—this is far from the truth. The state must closely manage the proposed contracts as the requirements are developed by the vendors. Project management comes into play here as the state identifies concrete deliverables and delivery dates for various stages of the proposed solution. Risks should be identified if delivery dates slip or the deliverable is not what was originally desired or functions differently from what was originally promised. Careful attention must also be paid to costs. Problem-oriented bids are usually higher than traditional bids because the final product or service is usually more expensive but of higher quality; usually training and other services from the vendor are included in the problem-oriented bid. All of this means that the states will be in protracted negotiations with possibly several vendors as the details of the contract for technology and services are worked out.

These are some of the recommendations of the task force, but what is really going on in the states? In the summer of 2000, John R. Bartle and Ronnie LaCourse Korosec conducted a survey of all but two of the fifty states about their procurement and contracting processes.[13] They found considerable variability on the limits that states set before a product or service must be formally bid. In contracting for services, they found that some states such as Tennessee have very modest limits ($500) while other states such as Washington have very liberal limits ($250,000). For the majority of the states, the limit was $25,000. This is not a lot of money when contracting for technology services, which suggests that most service contracts go through competitive bidding. As for limits on the purchase of products, they found low limits of $2,000 in New Hampshire and Tennessee and relatively high limits of $75,000 in Oregon and Vermont, with the average limit for all of the states at $18,300. Although technology prices are famous for falling fast, these limits suggest that the purchase of most technology products must go out for competitive bidding. This also suggests that most states have not moved very far to simplify the procurement function as prescribed in the *Buying Smart* recommendations.

Focus on Local Government

The procurement and contracting landscape at local levels of government mirrors what is going on in the states, although it is difficult to get a comprehensive and firm handle on exactly what is going on because we are talking about thousands of counties, cities, school districts, and special districts. Generally, one can expect to find a single local government entity somewhere on a continuum between strict procurement and contracting regulations and relatively loose procurement and contracting regulations, with the likelihood that larger local governments will have more formal processes and smaller local governments will have less formal processes, although this may not hold in every instance. In a similar sense, any given local government could have a highly centralized system or a highly decentralized system or some combination of both.

In general most local governments mirror the states and the federal government in having statutes, common law court decisions, charters and constitutions, and formal regulations that govern procurements and contracts. In some cases state law dictates the rules and regulations governing local government procurement and contracting. Most local governments have provisions for competitive bidding and exceptions for no-bid contracts and sole-source contracts. Procurement and contracting can also be centralized, decentralized, or a mix of both.

Because local governments mirror the states in their procurement and contracting processes, a survey of what is going on in local government will not be presented. Instead, an example of how one local government, Miami-Dade County, handles its procurement and contracting through e-procurement will be presented. This will be an example of how many other local governments as well as the states and the federal government are relying on technology to improve their procurement and contracting processes.

The county's web page for procurement opens with the following statement: "Miami-Dade County's Department of Procurement Management (DPM) manages in excess of 1,100 active contracts valued at approximately $3 billion. Each year, DPM negotiates and awards contracts that exceed $900 million for the purchase of goods and services for the County's 47 departments and 15 offices. We use competitive methods and electronic procurement to provide our customers with the best service and value for their time and money."[14]

The county uses three vehicles for procurement: Invitation to Bid (ITB), Request for Proposals (RFPs), and Request for Qualifications (RFQs). The ITB is the standard method for acquiring goods and services using the lowest price as the primary criterion for selecting a bid. Exhibit 10.1 shows the steps in the ITB process.[15] Notice the "Cone of Silence." It is a mechanism to ensure fairness and transparency in the acquisition process by prohibiting any communication between a vendor and a city employee once a bid is advertised.

The county's procurement web site explains the logic and processes for RFPs and RFQs as follows:

Exhibit 10.1
Steps in the Invitation to Bid Process

Step 1. Bid Preparation. User department initiates a request, then researches the market, develops specifications, and submits electronic requisition to Department of Procurement Management.

Step 2. Procurement Review. After receiving an electronic requisition, Procurement Management reviews specifications for accuracy and completeness, drafts a bid for publication, sets a bid opening date/time, and mails bid solicitations.

Once the Bid Solicitation is issued, the Cone of Silence goes into effect. The Cone of Silence begins when the bid is advertised and ends when the County Manager or designee issues a written recommendation for award. Potential bidders cannot discuss any aspect of a bid that "is on the streets" with County personnel during the Cone of Silence. All communication must be in writing.

Step 3. Bid Opening. (Cone of Silence still in effect.)

- Bid proposals are opened and tallied.
- Important bid requirements are examined.
- Bid proposal must be typed or printed in ink.
- Firm's authorized agent must sign bid proposal.
- Completion of Disclosure Affidavits

Step 4. Bid Proposals Evaluated. (Cone of Silence still in effect.)

- Bid must be responsive and responsible.
- Responsive—A bidder who complies with all specifications and terms set forth in the Invitation to Bid (ITB).
- Responsible—A bidder whose reputation, past performance, and business and financial capabilities indicate the bidder is capable of satisfying the terms and conditions of the ITB.

Step 5. Award. Cone of Silence lifted once written recommendation has been made.

Step 6. Notification.

- Contracts valued at $100K or more—Recommendation for award received by mail.
- Contracts valued at less than $100K—Bid award posted on the first floor of Government Center outside Elections Satellite Office.

A Request for Proposals (RFP) process may be used when the scope of work cannot be completely defined by the County; the goods or services can be provided in several different ways; qualifications, experience, or the quality of the goods or services to be delivered are significant factors of consideration, in addition to price; and/or the responses may contain varying levels of service or alternatives, which lend themselves to negotiation.

A Request for Qualifications (RFQ) process may be used to determine the qualifications from proposers when the County cannot or has not completely established the scope of services. An RFQ may be used, for example, when creating a pool of qualified vendors to be used on a rotational basis, or in a two-step competitive basis where the scope of services is incomplete and only those firms selected in the qualification phase compete when a particular work order is established.[16]

Exhibit 10.2 shows the eleven steps taken to implement the acquisition for either an RFP or an RFQ. This is a clear example of best-value versus lowest-price procurement. The eleven steps allow the county to fairly evaluate the qualifications and experience of the bidder's staff; their methodology and management approach; their understanding of the project and the county's objectives; their technical superiority; and their financial stability and history of the firm. The county is proud of the fact that it developed its own e-procurement system in-house without having to contract with a vendor. They did it for $85,000, which was one-fourth of IBM's bid for the project.[17]

A press release from the county in September of 2005 reports that "For the second year in a row, the National Purchasing Institute has selected Miami-Dade County's Department of Procurement Management (DPM) to receive the prestigious Achievement of Excellence in Procurement Award. The award recognizes innovation, professionalism, e-procurement, productivity, and leadership in the field of procurement." The press release goes on to describe how the e-procurement system works:

A major turning point in County procurement came with the release of the County's first phase of its e-Procurement system. That phase included (1) the publication of solicitations online, and (2) a vendor enrollment system that enables vendors to select the goods and services they offer from a list of commodities. Using the e-mail address provided by vendors, the system automatically generates an e-mail alert to the vendor with a link to a downloadable solicitation document. More than 300,000 e-mail notifications have been sent to over 10,000 enrolled vendors. Over 40,000 enrolled and non-enrolled vendors have downloaded solicitations using our on-line, e-procurement tools. This has contributed significantly to enhancing competition and transparency in the procurement of goods and services.

Exhibit 10.2
Steps in the RFP/RFQ Process

1. User department requests RFP/RFQ.
2. Procurement Management prepares RFP/RFQ in conjunction with user department.
3. The Miami-Dade County Board of County Commissioners (BCC) approves the request to advertise.
4. RFP/RFQ is advertised.
5. Procurement Management holds pre-proposal conference.
6. Proposals are received.
7. Proposals are evaluated.
8. Negotiations take place.
9. County Manager recommends award.
10. BCC approves award or advises otherwise.
11. Contract administration.

The next phase of the County's e-Procurement system will include:

- automatic generation and distribution of Award Sheets to departments and municipalities;
- electronic distribution and receipt of vendor quotes;
- web-based Vendor Registration updates;
- Solicitation Builder and Collaboration Tools;
- Vendor Past Performance Database;
- Solicitation Tracking System.[18]

The procurement and contracting process of Miami-Dade County is not unique. Other local and state governments are moving in a similar direction. It is exemplary, however, in the clarity in which the procurement and contracting process is depicted on the county's web site, making this an excellent example of how e-procurement can work for public agencies.

The Software Acquisition Capability Maturity Model (SA-CMM)

Leaving behind the legal and public policy contexts and constraints on technology procurement and contracting, we can turn our attention to managerial considerations, namely the Software Acquisition Capability Maturity Model (SA-CMM) developed by the Carnegie Mellon Software Engineering Institute in the late 1990s in conjunction with the Department of Defense, other federal agencies, and private firms.[19] It is a comprehensive normative model containing a broad framework and many prescriptions about how to acquire and develop software applications. Many of the model's features and prescriptions can also apply to the acquisition of hardware to support the software acquisition development.

The following are the five levels of maturity in the Software Acquisition Capability Maturity Model:

1. *Initial.* The software acquisition process is characterized as ad hoc and occasionally even chaotic. Few processes are defined and success depends on individual effort. For an organization to mature beyond the initial level, it must install basic management controls to instill self-discipline.

2. *Repeatable.* Basic software acquisition project management processes are established to plan all aspects of the acquisition, manage software requirements, track project team and contractor performance, manage the project's cost and schedule baselines, evaluate the products and services, and successfully transition the software to its support organization. The project team is basically reacting to circumstances of the acquisition as they arise. The necessary process discipline is in place to repeat earlier successes on projects in similar domains. For an organization to mature beyond the level of self-discipline, it must use well-defined processes as a foundation for improvement.

3. *Defined.* The acquisition organization's software acquisition process is documented and standardized. All projects use an approved, tailored version of the organization's standard software acquisition process for acquiring their software products and services. Project and contract management activities are proactive, attempting to anticipate and deal with acquisition circumstances before they arise. Risk management is integrated into all aspects of the project, and the organization provides the training required by personnel involved in the acquisition. For an organization to mature beyond the level of defined processes, it must base decisions on quantitative measures of its processes and products so that objectivity can be attained and rational decisions made.

4. *Quantitative.* Detailed measures of the software acquisition processes, products, and services are collected. The software processes, products, and services are quantitatively and qualitatively understood and controlled.

5. *Optimizing.* Continuous process improvement is empowered by quantitative feedback from the process and from piloting innovative ideas

and technologies. Ultimately an organization recognizes that continual improvement (and continual change) is necessary to survive.[20]

The authors of the SA-CMM point out that it is highly generic and designed to be used by any type of organization, either public or private. It is broad enough to encompass many different approaches to software acquisition that may meet the unique needs of a particular organization. It is also broad enough to encompass the entire systems life cycle, recognizing that acquisitions can take place during the total life of a system, not merely at its inception. The SA-CMM also strongly endorses the adoption of rigorous project management and risk management methodologies to govern any acquisition activity.

Most federal agencies have tried to embrace the SA-CMM, some without much success, some with great success, and others needing considerable improvement. In 2002 the Mature Business Systems Modernization Office of the Internal Revenue Service was the first civilian agency to achieve CMM maturity level 2.[21] The Government Accountability Office has given mixed reviews to several Department of Defense units and some civilian agencies on their progress toward achieving different levels of maturity.[22] A 1999 survey conducted by the State of Texas of the states using best-practice models found that only Kansas, Michigan, Minnesota, North Carolina, Ohio, Tennessee, and Washington were using the SA-CMM.[23]

Most of the vendors that contract with federal, state, and local governments have adopted the SA-CMM, and many federal, state, and local agencies require their vendors to achieve some level of maturity using the model. However, a 2002 article in *Government Computing News* raised questions about the dependability of vendor claims to be qualified to help agencies to achieve a desired maturity level, noting that the Software Engineering Institute does not maintain a list of qualified organizations.[24] Also a 2004 article in *CIO Magazine* warns that many vendors overstate their CMM "qualifications," making it extremely difficult for government purchasing officials to objectively assess claims to CMM capabilities.[25]

It would seem that many public agencies are not following the most prescribed normative model of software acquisition and development, or they are not following it well. One wonders why this might be the case. Are they just flying by the seat of their pants? Or are they using some alternative, yet unspecified models of software development and acquisition?

The Outsourcing Alternative

Outsourcing, generally defined as the government relying on private firms to do some of the work of government, is not a new phenomenon. Consider that the colonial government outsourced some of American Revolution to Prussian military forces. Outsourcing should not be confused with a vendor relationship. While it is true that the Department of Defense has historically "outsourced" the making of such things as tanks, weapons, transport vehicles, ships, airplanes, and missiles to private firms, this is actually a vendor relationship in which commodities are purchased. Outsourcing means turning over management responsibility for some operation of government to a private or nonprofit organization. Today public agencies at all three levels of government are looking to outsource not only technology functions such as web page design and maintenance but also full technology support functions as well as some central business functions such as human resource management and even financial management and accounting functions.

The logic behind outsourcing is simple. It has two justifications that may occur independently or jointly. First, in some cases it is cheaper to rent than to own. For example, a city, county, or even a state may find that is simply cheaper to outsource its web page design and maintenance to a private contractor than it is to hire its own technical experts. There are many small- to medium-sized businesses that specialize in nothing but web page design and maintenance. Agencies may find that hiring them on contract is simply cheaper than dedicating agency staff to this function. Second, a public agency may not have the staff on hand with the necessary knowledge and skill to develop, implement, and maintain a specific application. Here we are talking about applications that can be much more complicated than simple web pages. Public agencies have outsourced such functions as human resource systems (including payroll, benefits, and basic database functions, accounting and financial systems, fleet-management systems, and even entire information systems). Agencies find that they do not have nor can they attract the highly skilled personnel to conduct such functions because they simply cannot offer the high salaries that theses positions can achieve in the private sector. Vendors have responded to this situation by offering these and other services at prices that some public agencies cannot turn down.

Outsourcing IT functions is controversial for three reasons. First, sometimes it is not done very well, leading to litigation between a public agency and a service provider over disputed contract provisions. Second, the federal government has made a major push to outsource not just IT functions but some core operational functions of agencies such as human resource systems, with the intent of significantly reducing the size of the federal workforce. Third, sometimes, but not always, public agencies outsource to firms either completely outside of the United States or to firms with substantial foreign operations. This situation became something of a political issue in the 2004 presidential election because, for some, it means taking jobs away from

American citizens. Here we will address the first two issues because they are of a more managerial concern.

The classic case of a public-sector outsourcing deal that went sour occurred in 1999 when San Diego County entered into an outsourcing contract with Pennant Alliance, a four-partner group of private-sector firms led by the Computer Services Corporation (CSC), to manage the county's entire IT processes for an initial estimated amount of $644 million for seven years.[26] The reasons behind the deal were simple. The county expected to save money by eliminating some 275 current IT employees and some 100 contractors, and CSC would assume the responsibility of dealing with the county's antiquated legacy systems. The plan was to replace the county's aged and dysfunctional telephone system that often failed to work, replace old 286 and 386 PCs that could not support modern software applications with modern workstations, replace an old LAN and a WAN that frequently went down, replace the IT staff who were knowledgeable about old mainframe technology but not modern client/server technology, replace old legacy applications with two new ERP systems (one for finance and one for human resources), and improve the functionality of the county's web portal. There were some initial successes. Some 2,000 new state-of-the-art PCs were installed, 1,000 phones were replaced, 533 of the county's legacy applications were assessed, the speed of the county's Internet was increased significantly, security vulnerabilities were fixed, and 22 help desks were consolidated into one help center.

In 2002, bitter contract disputes between the county and CSC emerged over additional costs, seemingly poor service from CSC, and a late ERP implementation.[27] From CSC's perspective, the project went $10 million over budget and required the addition of 300 extra staff assigned to the job. The Pennant Alliance was struck with a fine of $250,000 for failing to get all of the county's staff on a common e-mail system. Several service levels specified in the contract with the county were missed, resulting in fines to the Pennant Alliance and CSC in disputed amounts ranging from $2.1 million to $3.5 million. Finally, the county withheld $45 million in payments to the group because the ERP systems were not implemented on schedule. Although the county had built in safeguards in the contract that allowed them to opt out of the deal with CSC and the Pennant Alliance without any penalties, the county found itself stuck in the relationship because it no longer had the IT talent on hand to take back its IT processes. Relations between the county and the contractor were strained as both threatened litigation.

In January of 2006, San Diego signed a seven-year, $650-million contract with Northrop Grumman Information Technology to run the county's IT operations.[28] The county seems to have learned its lessons from its prior mistakes. The new contract is much more specific, containing many more definitions of acceptable service levels and clearly identified penalties if the contractor does not meet those service levels on time and to the county's satisfaction. Generally speaking, outsourcing IT functions in the public sector can work as long as a contract is well written and well managed.

Despite the troubles of San Diego County, government outsourcing of IT operations and services is expected to grow significantly in the coming years. The market research firm INPUT expects the state and local market for IT outsourcing to increase by 75 percent over the next ten years from $10 billion in fiscal year 2005 to $18 billion in fiscal year 2010.[29] They identify outdated information system infrastructures and an aging workforce as the primary reasons for the growth in IT outsourcing in state and local governments.

INPUT also expects the federal market for outsourcing to have a compound annual growth rate of 8 percent, representing an increase from $12.2 billion in fiscal year 2005 to $17.6 billion in fiscal year 2010.[30] The increase is motivated in part by OMB initiatives to privatize more federal functions as well as the need to supplement internal technical resources, acquire new technological capabilities, and reduce the cost of IT operations.

The growth in federal IT outsourcing is part of a larger policy initiative of "competitive sourcing," known as OMB Circular A-76, and it applies to a wide range of government operations, not just IT.[31] A-76 directs all executive agencies to identify government jobs that are not "inherently governmental" and to release those jobs so that private-sector firms may bid to perform them. The logic behind A-76 is simple: There are some federal government jobs that do not have to be performed by federal workers if the work can be performed by a private firm as effectively or more effectively than by a government worker and at a reduced cost to the federal government. Such jobs as food service, custodial service, and secretarial service do not necessarily have to be performed by federal workers. Often jobs like these can be performed by private firms at a significantly reduced cost to the federal government. Increasingly more professional jobs such as IT technicians, budget analysts, accountants, and policy analysts are being considered for outsourcing.

OMB's definitions of what constitute inherently governmental and inherently commercial job activities are presented in Exhibit 10.3. Generally speaking, an inherently governmental activity is one that is intimately tied to the public interest and requires considerable public policy discretion on the part of the jobholder in making decisions that bind the federal government to a commitment of funds or course of action. A commercial activity is one that can be performed under contract because it does not require a public policy decision or commit the government to an expenditure of funds or a new course of action.

The circular was introduced in 1983 and revised in 1999. As background,

Exhibit 10.3
Inherently Governmental or Commercial Provisions
of OMB Circular A-76

1. Inherently Governmental Activities. The CSO shall justify, in writing, any designation of government personnel performing inherently governmental activities. The justification shall be made available to OMB and the public upon request. An agency shall base inherently governmental justifications on the following criteria:

   a. An inherently governmental activity is an activity that is so intimately related to the public interest as to mandate performance by government personnel. These activities require the exercise of substantial discretion in applying government authority and/or in making decisions for the government. Inherently governmental activities normally fall into two categories: the exercise of sovereign government authority or the establishment of procedures and processes related to the oversight of monetary transactions or entitlements. An inherently governmental activity involves:

      (1) Binding the United States to take or not to take some action by contract, policy, regulation, authorization, order, or otherwise;
      (2) Determining, protecting, and advancing economic, political, territorial, property, or other interests by military or diplomatic action, civil or criminal judicial proceedings, contract management, or otherwise;
      (3) Significantly affecting the life, liberty, or property of private persons; or
      (4) Exerting ultimate control over the acquisition, use, or disposition of United States property (real or personal, tangible or intangible), including establishing policies or procedures for the collection, control, or disbursement of appropriated and other federal funds.

   b. While inherently governmental activities require the exercise of substantial discretion, not every exercise of discretion is evidence that an activity is inherently governmental. Rather, the use of discretion shall be deemed inherently governmental if it commits the government to a course of action when two or more alternative courses of action exist and decision making is not already limited or guided by existing policies, procedures, directions, orders, and other guidance that

(1) identify specified ranges of acceptable decisions or conduct and
(2) subject the discretionary authority to final approval or regular oversight by agency officials.

c. An activity may be provided by contract support (i.e., a private-sector source or a public reimbursable source using contract support) where the contractor does not have the authority to decide on the course of action but is tasked to develop options or implement a course of action, with agency oversight. An agency shall consider the following to avoid transferring inherently governmental authority to a contractor:

(1) Statutory restrictions that define an activity as inherently governmental;
(2) The degree to which official discretion is or would be limited, i.e., whether involvement of the private sector or public reimbursable provider is or would be so extensive that the ability of senior agency management to develop and consider options is or would be inappropriately restricted;
(3) In claims or entitlement adjudication and related services (a) the finality of any action affecting individual claimants or applicants, and whether or not review of the provider's action is de novo on appeal of the decision to an agency official; (b) the degree to which a provider may be involved in wide-ranging interpretations of complex, ambiguous case law and other legal authorities, as opposed to being circumscribed by detailed laws, regulations, and procedures; (c) the degree to which matters for decisions may involve recurring fact patterns or unique fact patterns; and (d) the discretion to determine an appropriate award or penalty;
(4) The provider's authority to take action that will significantly and directly affect the life, liberty, or property of individual members of the public, including the likelihood of the provider's need to resort to force in support of a police or judicial activity; whether the provider is more likely to use force,

especially deadly force, and the degree to which the provider may have to exercise force in public or relatively uncontrolled areas. These policies do not prohibit contracting for guard services, convoy security services, pass and identification services, plant protection services, or the operation of prison or detention facilities, without regard to whether the providers of these services are armed or unarmed;

(5) The availability of special agency authorities and the appropriateness of their application to the situation at hand, such as the power to deputize private persons; and

(6) Whether the activity in question is already being performed by the private sector.

2. Commercial Activities. A commercial activity is a recurring service that could be performed by the private sector and is resourced, performed, and controlled by the agency through performance by government personnel, a contract, or a fee-for-service agreement. A commercial activity is not so intimately related to the public interest as to mandate performance by government personnel. Commercial activities may be found within, or throughout, organizations that perform inherently governmental activities or classified work.

it states that "In the process of governing, the Government should not compete with its citizens. The competitive enterprise system, characterized by individual freedom and initiative, is the primary source of national economic strength. In recognition of this principle, it has been and continues to be the general policy of the Government to rely on commercial sources to supply the products and services the Government needs."[32]

The general policy of A-76 is explained in three paragraphs:

a. *Achieve Economy and Enhance Productivity.* Competition enhances quality, economy, and productivity. Whenever commercial-sector performance of a Government-operated commercial activity is permissible, in accordance with this Circular and its Supplement, comparison of the cost of contracting and the cost of in-house performance shall be performed to determine who will do the work. When conducting cost comparisons, agencies must ensure that all costs are considered and that these costs are realistic and fair.

b. *Retain Governmental Functions In-House.* Certain functions are inherently Governmental in nature, being so intimately related to the public interest as to mandate performance only by Federal employees. These functions are not in competition with the commercial sector. Therefore, these functions shall be performed by Government employees.

c. *Rely on the Commercial Sector.* The Federal Government shall rely on commercially available sources to provide commercial products and services. In accordance with the provisions of this Circular and its Supplement, the Government shall not start or carry on any activity to provide a commercial product or service if the product or service can be procured more economically from a commercial source.[33]

By some accounts, the policy of competitive sourcing has been successful. In 2003 OMB found that agencies that complied with the policy saved $1.1 billion, while in fiscal year 2004, agencies saved about $1.35 billion.[34] Another source reports a cumulative savings of $5.6 billion between fiscal years 2003 and 2005.[35] Overall, it simply makes sense to outsource some public agency functions if they are not inherently governmental and if the private sector can provide those functions efficiently, effectively, and at less cost to the taxpayer.

Summary and a Look Forward

Hopefully this chapter has communicated the fact that acquiring technology solutions for public agencies, whether hardware, software, or services, is not always easy. In many cases it is a very complex process requiring specialized knowledge of the specifications desired of the technology and specialized knowledge of government procurement and contracting, an extremely complex subject matter. The treatment of procurement and contracting presented here has been only cursory. It is a professional field that requires years of education and training, and entire books have been written about government procurement and contracting.[36] The key lessons to be learned here are that there are competing values that make procurement and contracting complex; there are multitudes of federal, state, and local laws, policies, procedures, and regulations that add to that complexity; and that any public manager who is contemplating a technology acquisition is well advised to acquire both expert information technology advice and expert procurement and contracting advice. The subject of the next chapter on information security is equally complex because of the technology that is involved, the often confusing and burdensome management policies and procedures governing information security, and the fact that some public managers may be aware of the importance of information security but are really not doing anything of substance to improve it.

11

Information Security

The field of information security is extremely complex. It ranges from highly technical and specialized fields of study and application such as cryptography and data encryption, to hardware and software technologies such as firewalls and spam filters to protect information systems from malicious software attacks, to managerial policies about who has authorized access to data or information. Furthermore, the IT industry uses a variety of terms such as data security, information security, information systems security, network security, cybersecurity, computer security, and computer insecurity to refer to the general concept of security. Some of the knowledge about security captured under each of these terms is the same and some of the knowledge is different. To further illustrate the complexity of the security issue consider that the federal government's National Security Telecommunications and Information Systems Security Committee has recently published the National Information Systems Security Glossary (Infosec), an eighty-page document consisting of hundreds of technical terms related to security issues in information technology.[1] Despite this effort to standardize the use of the terms, many IT security professionals often use their own unique terminology, leading to some confusion in the field.

Needless to say, this chapter can provide only the most general treatment of information security issues in government. The first part discusses the general concept of information security, which is in large part an idyllic myth given the apparent insecurity of government, corporate, and privately owned computers and information systems. The second part discusses the types of malicious software and human activities that pose threats to information security in both the public and the private sectors, bursting the myth of information security. The third part illustrates the severity of the information insecurity problem. The fourth part offers a brief assessment of the security of government information systems which, unfortunately, does not appear to be very good over all for federal agencies and many of the states.

Information Security in General

The *National Information Systems Security Glossary* defines information security as "the protection of information systems against unauthorized access to or modification of information, whether in storage, processing, or transit, and against the denial of service to authorized users or the provision of service to unauthorized users, including those measures necessary to detect, document, and counter such threats."[2] In this sense, information is always at risk and information security is inherently about risk management to ward off threats to information systems and the data they contain.[3]

For information to be secure it must possess several qualities: confidentiality, integrity, availability, and assurance. Confidentiality has been defined as the "assurance that information is not disclosed to unauthorized persons, processes, or devices."[4] More broadly it means ensuring that information is accessible only to those authorized to have access to it. This is usually accomplished by establishing secure, private computer access accounts and strong passwords. It is also one of the goals of cryptography, which is the field of study that focuses on securing communication usually through encryption. Encryption is the process of obscuring data and information by making it unreadable without an appropriate cipher or code. A cipher is a symbol or group of symbols that mask plain text so that it can be read only by the person who has the correct cipher. The use of encryption is important when sending sensitive or secret data over a network or the Internet. It is also important when storing sensitive or private data in a database. Unfortunately, most corporate and government data are not encrypted in either transmissions or databases because of the added costs of encryption.

Integrity refers to the condition that exists when data is unchanged from its source and has not been accidentally or maliciously modified, altered, or destroyed. At first glance this may seem to conflict with the first quality of confidentiality, but within the context of cryptography the process of unencrypting data should return data or information to its original state. More broadly, integrity refers to "the logical correctness and reliability of the operating system; the logical completeness of the hardware and software implementing the protection mechanisms; and the consistency of the data structures and occurrence of the stored data."[5] Both hardware and software controls can check the integrity of the data in an information system.

Two closely associated concepts, authorization and authentication, are associated with confidentiality as defined earlier. Authorization is a process whereby only authorized users are given access to a part of an information system. This is done through authentication, usually by providing the user with an identification number and a password. An example would be an ATM machine, which requires an authorized user to use a card with an account number embedded in it and a personal identification number (PIN) to gain access to his or her account information and make transactions. The card and the PIN serve as both authorization and authentication. A third concept called access control governs authorization and authentication in the sense that access must be given to a person to access a system. For example, only approved faculty and staff at a public university may be given access to electronic student records. This is done by listing those persons who are approved for access and providing them with identification numbers and passwords that enable authorization and authentication to gain access to student data.

The quality of availability is usually understood in the context of having an information system available—meaning operational and functional—so that an authorized person can get access to needed data or information.[6] Availability issues can arise from the existence of computer viruses or worms that disable information systems (see the following section). This is usually called denial of service, which means that an organization's computer systems have been made inoperable.

The quality of assurance is the "measure of confidence that the security features, practices, procedures, and architecture of an IS [information system] accurately mediates and enforces the security policy."[7] Thus, information system assurance is a broader management concept that looks to see if confidentiality, integrity, and availability qualities are met. Quality assurance is usually expressed in written policies, procedures, and rules that govern an agency's information security practices. As we will see, some federal agencies have taken steps to develop plans to ensure quality assurance, but much more work is needed to implement those plans.

While the qualities of confidentiality, integrity, availability, and assurance form the theoretical definition of a secure information system. There are several serious practical threats to information system security that can have devastating effects on the secure operation of information systems, making the theoretical definition of information security an idyllic dream, because computer systems in both the public and private sectors are constantly under attack by hackers, as we shall soon discover.

Threats to Information Systems

Threats to information systems are generally classified under the general term of *malware*, which is short for malicious software. Malware is associated with viruses, worms, Trojans, zombies, spyware, adware, spam, and phishing. The effects of malware can range from simply annoying, such as being inundated with unwanted spam e-mail, to significantly disastrous results, such as loss or theft of data, theft of money, identity theft, and the destruction of entire computer systems (technically termed a "denial of service attack"). The following is a brief description of the various forms of malware-associated threats to security.

Computer viruses were the earliest forms of malware. A virus is a computer program that can replicate and insert itself into executable programs, such as a word-processing program, and documents in a computer and then in other computers. Viruses can be transmitted by sharing floppy disks or sharing files over a network or the Internet, or by downloading documents, files, programs, or e-mails from a network or the Internet. They piggyback themselves on existing files or programs and replicate themselves whenever those files or programs are opened. For example, if someone were to give you a word-processing file with a virus attached to it and you opened that file, the virus would immediately spread to other programs and files on your hard disk. Viruses work in much the same way on mainframes and minis. For example, in 1999 the Melissa virus forced Microsoft and a host of other large companies to turn off their e-mail systems until the virus could be found and destroyed.[8] They can attack existing software programs on a computer, making them inoperable. Numerous antivirus software products are freely available in the marketplace to protect computer systems, but new viruses appear almost daily, requiring frequent virus updates.

Worms are similar to viruses in that they can replicate themselves, but they do not need to attach themselves to an existing software program to reproduce. They move around computer networks looking for security holes, and when they find them, they spread to other computers. MyDoom was perhaps the most famous worm. It infected about a quarter of a million computers in one day in January 2004.[9] Like viruses, worms can interfere with software programs on a computer, making them function in unusual ways or not at all. Unlike viruses, worms use up a tremendous amount of bandwidth in a network as they reproduce themselves, thus slowing down traffic on a network or the Internet. Antivirus software and firewalls help to protect against worms as well as viruses. Yet antivirus software needs to be updated constantly since new viruses and worms appear almost daily.

A Trojan, which is short for Trojan horse, is similar to a virus. It gets its name from the fact that a user may wish to download a desirable program from the Internet, but in doing so the user unknowingly also gets an undesirable Trojan. Some Trojans carry out spying functions, which makes them related to spyware. Such Trojans can seek out and steal sensitive or private information such as passwords (called password sniffing) on a computer system or network. Other Trojans can erase a hard drive, including all of its data and programs. Some Trojans can also create a backdoor on a computer system, which allows another computer system to take control, creating what is known as a zombie computer. Once a computer becomes a zombie, the other computer that made it a zombie can wreck havoc with the programs and data contained on the zombie.

Zombie computers are frequently used by spammers to send junk e-mail without the owner of the zombie computer knowing about it. It is estimated that 50 to 80 percent of all spam e-mail is transmitted by zombie computers. This spamming is essential for the spread of Trojans, because unlike viruses and worms, Trojans do not replicate themselves: They must be spread via e-mail spam. Antispam e-mail software helps to protect computers from Trojans.

Spyware is similar to a Trojan because it usually comes from surfing the Internet for legitimate purposes. It gets downloaded onto a hard drive, attaches itself to the computer's operating system, and tracks a person's surfing habits such as what web sites he or she visits on a regular basis. Unlike viruses and worms, spyware usually does not replicate itself. Some versions of spyware deliver unwanted pop-up advertisements; others are more malicious as they attempt to capture personal information, financial information, or credit card numbers. The least malicious thing that spyware does is slow down your computer because it runs in the background using up random access memory and processing power. Special software programs such as SpyBot are available to protect PCs from spyware infections, while "industrial strength" antispyware programs are available for mainframes and minis as well as client/server networks.

Adware is advertising-supported software that displays advertisements for a wide variety of products, usually on web browsers. The software usually comes along with an established software product downloaded from the Internet or purchased conventionally and helps to pay for the cost of the primary software product. Probably the least malicious of the malware threats, the ads, and sometimes accompanying pop-ups, are annoying and can slow down the speed at which a computer runs. Adware can become more malicious if it tracks someone's Internet surfing habits. Software programs such as AdAware are available for PCs while other similar integrated packages can protect government and commercial organizations from unwanted adware.

Spam is unsolicited bulk e-mail. It usually consists of offerings for products and services of dubious value as well as links to web sites containing pornographic content. While it can be a minor annoyance, it can also be very costly in terms of the amount of worktime that is used to delete the unwanted e-mail from agency e-mail systems. The most prevalent forms of spam are medical related, offering drugs that promise enhanced sexual performance, weight loss, and human growth hormones. The second most prevalent types of spam are e-mails containing links to pornographic web sites, while in third place are financial scams that try to get people to put their money into dubious investments. The best protection against spam is a spam e-mail filter, although they do not always work. The second-best protection is to teach people to simply ignore and delete spam.

Phishing is a deliberate attempt by someone to fool another person into revealing private information about himself or herself, such as a Social Security or credit card number. Technically it is not malware because it is not inherently malicious code, although it does rely on e-mail software to engage in fraudulent practices. Phishing is usually done by sending misleading e-mails to people that contain seemingly legitimate requests for private information. Phishing relies upon the fact that some people can be easily fooled into giving away private information. For example, someone might receive an e-mail from a phony source saying that his or her account at a legitimate business is about to be closed unless he or she updates the credit card number. Sophos, a major anti-malware provider, reports that phishers commonly try to imitate legitimate commercial sites such as PayPal, eBay, amazon.com, and major financial institutions.[10]

Hackers are usually responsible for these threats to computer security. They are people with the technical ability to alter software code to gain access to computer systems or create a host of malware threats to computer security. Malicious hackers, often called Black Hat Hackers, can be motivated by greed, personal or political revenge against a business or government agency, or simply by the challenge of cracking a computer system or creating malware. They can be inside or outside of an organization. White Hat Hackers, on the other hand, engage in hacking for altruistic purposes or for legitimate purposes such as helping an organization discover security problems with its computer systems. Many people have an image of a hacker as being some lonely computer geek or nerd working alone in some dingy basement hacking away simply for the fun of it. That may have been true in some cases, especially in the early days of computer hacking, but today some hackers have become highly organized professional criminals working within dark (underground) networks to breach the security of government and business computer systems.

Overall, the existence of these threats to data security makes the prior definition of information security an ideal myth rarely realized in practice. Government and business information systems across the world are constantly under threats of attack by hackers and spammers. In 2005, the Federal Bureau of Investigation along with the Computer Security Institute conducted a survey on "Computer Crime and Security." The research concluded that 56 percent of corporations and government agencies surveyed (N = 700) reported computer breaches within the past twelve months. Losses for most of the organizations amounted to $130,104,542, but that was for only 639 of the 700 respondents that were willing and able to estimate losses.[11] To make matters worse, the survey concluded that executives, middle-level managers, and first-line workers are simply not paying attention to information security threats.

The Severity of Security Threats

The threats to information security are quite severe. This is reflected in many industry, association, and government white papers and reports. Two of those reports will be outlined here to illustrate the severity of the threats.

A report published in 2005 by Sophos, a major provider of anti-malware software programs and hardware devices, indicates a staggering increase in the rate of growth in malware programs and some unique trends in computer hacking.[12] Sophos reports that

> The number of new threats has continued to grow at rates once thought by some to be unsustainable. By December 2005, Sophos Anti-Virus was identifying and protecting against over 114,000 different viruses, worms, Trojan horses and other malware.
>
> Over the period January–November 2005, the number of new virus, worm, Trojan horse and spyware threats rose by 48 percent as follows:
>
> - 2004: 10,724 new threats
> - 2005: 15,907 new threats
>
> What is most significant is the month-by-month increase in the number of new malware threats discovered. In November 2005 alone, there were 1,940 new malware threats—the biggest monthly increase in threats protected against by Sophos products since records began.[13]

The report goes on to characterize security threats for 2005 as follows:

- 48 percent increase in new malware threats over previous year.
- One in forty-four of all e-mails is viral.
- New Trojans outweigh Windows worms almost 2:1.
- Medical-related spam remains the most common, but pornographic content and pump-and-dump scams have surged.
- Cybercriminals have joined forces and attack using combined technology.[14]

The latter security threat is particularly vexing to the security industry because it reflects deliberate, coordinated, and planned attempts by organized criminals to target vital public and private information systems.

The Sophos report provides strong evidence that information system security threats are a serious problem, and Sophos is just one of a handful of security software and hardware providers who carefully study security threats. Other antivirus and security protection firms such as Symantec keep a similar vigilant watch for malware threats and publish their own surveys and reports on the extent of information system insecurity as well as long lists of existing and recent specific threats.[15]

For another view of the current state of information system insecurity consider that *Chief Security Officer Magazine* conducts an annual survey of computer crimes in partnership with the U.S. Secret Service and Carnegie Mellon University Software Engineering Institute's CERT Coordination Center. The latter (CERT stands for Computer Emergency Response Team) is a federally funded nonprofit organization tasked with the mission to conduct extensive studies of the varieties of Internet security threats and to provide expert advice on how public and private organizations can protect themselves from electronic security attacks. The results of the survey are based on a sample size of 819 public and private survey responses with a 95 percent confidence level and a margin of error of +/- 3.4 percent. The following are some of the highlights of the 2005 survey, which was conducted in March of 2005:[16]

- Respondents report an average loss of $506,670 per organization due to e-crimes and a sum total loss of $150 million.
- While the average number of e-crimes decreased year over year from 2003 to 2004, 68 percent of respondents report at least one e-crime or intrusion committed against their organization in 2004, and 88 percent anticipate an increase in e-crime during 2005. More than half (53 percent) expect monetary losses to increase or remain the same.
- When asked what e-crimes were committed against their organizations in 2004, respondents cite virus or other malicious code as most prevalent (82 percent), with spyware (61 percent), phishing (57 percent), and illegal generation of spam e-mail (48 percent) falling close behind.
- Phishing, a precursor to fraud and/or identity theft, jumps from 31 percent in the 2004 survey to 57 percent, the largest single percent increase of an e-crime year over year.
- Of those who experienced e-crimes, more than half of respondents (55 percent) report operational losses, 28 percent state financial losses, and 12 percent declare harm to reputation as a result. Interestingly, one-third (31 percent) of respondents do not have a formal process or system in place for tracking e-crime attempts, and 39 percent do not have a formalized plan outlining policies and procedures for reporting and responding to e-crimes, demonstrating room for improvement.

- Direction of Electronic Crime Losses: One in five respondents (22 percent) say that monetary losses caused by electronic crime increased in 2004 while 10 percent report a decrease and 21 percent say monetary losses caused by electronic crime stayed the same in 2004 compared to 2003. Nearly half (47 percent) could not say how monetary losses changed from year to year.
- When asked to predict the direction of monetary losses from electronic crime in 2005, over one-half of respondents (53 percent) expect monetary losses to either increase or remain the same. Only 13 percent expect monetary losses resulting from electronic crime to decrease, while one-third (34 percent) are unsure.
- Prevalence of Electronic Crime: The majority of respondents (88 percent) believe the prevalence of electronic crime in 2005 will increase compared to 2004. Only 1 percent expect that electronic crime will be less prevalent in 2005, 4 percent expect it to stay the same, and 7 percent are unsure.

These findings, along with the study results from Sophos, clearly indicate that information security will remain a significant problem for business and government in the near as well as distant future.

The Security of Government Information Systems

Numerous Government Accountability Office (GAO) reports testify to the fact that the information systems of most federal agencies are far from being secure. Very little is known about the security of state and local government information systems. This section will focus on the state of information security at the federal level of government, drawing on GAO reports and other sources. The following section will only hint at what the state and local governments are doing in the way of security practices.

A recent GAO report titled *Information Security: Weaknesses Persist at Federal Agencies Despite Progress Made in Implementing Related Statutory Requirements* (2005) opens with the following statement:

> Federal agencies have not consistently implemented effective information security policies and practices. Pervasive weaknesses exist in almost all areas of information security controls at twenty-four major agencies, threatening the integrity, confidentiality, and availability of information and information systems: Access controls were not effectively implemented, software change controls were not always in place, segregation of duties was not consistently implemented, and continuity of operations planning was often inadequate. These weaknesses exist because agencies have not yet fully implemented

strong information security management programs. As a result, federal operations and assets are at increased risk of fraud, misuse, and destruction. In addition, these weaknesses place financial data at risk of unauthorized modification or destruction, sensitive information at risk of inappropriate disclosure, and critical operations at risk of disruption.[17]

Access controls can be electronic or physical. The GAO found that twenty-three of the twenty-four agencies do not provide adequate electronic access controls with respect to passwords that are constructed simply out of common letters or words that can easily be guessed. They also found that many agencies did not deactivate unused accounts, leaving them open to vulnerability. With regard to physical controls they found that agencies often lack effective physical barriers to access, including locked doors, visitor screening, and effective use of access cards.[18] They conclude that "inadequate access controls diminish the reliability of computerized data and increase the risk of unauthorized disclosure, modification, and use. As a result, critical information held by the federal government is at heightened risk of access by unauthorized persons—individuals who could obtain personal data (such as taxpayer information) to perpetrate identity theft and commit financial crimes."[19]

Software change controls refer to software that has not been adequately tested for security but which is otherwise implemented on a day-to-day operational basis. Many software application programs provided by vendors are not adequately tested for security. By law they are required to be "fixed" or otherwise "changed" before being implemented by a federal agency. The GAO found that twenty-two of the major agencies had weaknesses in their software change controls. They included failure to make sure that the software was updated correctly, that changes to systems were properly approved for security purposes, that security testing was performed, and that documentation for implemented system changes was available. These findings led the GAO to conclude that "there is an increased risk that programming errors or deliberate execution of unauthorized programs could compromise security controls, corrupt data, or disrupt computer operations."[20]

Segregation of duties means that one single person cannot independently control all key aspects of an information system. Authority for access, use, and change to an information system must be shared to protect against unauthorized access. Dividing responsibility for access between two or more individuals or groups reduces the potential for errors and wrongdoing. The GAO found that at some of the agencies, individual users had free access to information systems and that they could authorize new accounts and provide those accounts with elevated access privileges without any oversight. Consequently, the information systems at these agencies are exposed to risk of fraud and loss.[21]

Continuity of operations means that plans should be in place to make sure that an agency can cope with the loss of an information system due to an accident, natural disaster, or sabotage. The GAO found that twenty of the agencies had very weak continuity of operations plans and that many of the agencies had not conducted tests or training exercises for their existing plans.[22]

Most important, the GAO found that none of the agencies had fully implemented agency-wide security plans. "Agencies often did not adequately assess risks, develop sufficient risk-based policies or procedures for information security, ensure that existing policies and procedures were implemented effectively, or monitor operations to ensure compliance and determine the effectiveness of existing controls."[23] This led the GAO to conclude that "until agencies effectively and fully implement agency-wide information security programs, federal data and systems will not be adequately safeguarded against unauthorized use, disclosure, and modification. Many of the weaknesses discussed have been pervasive for years; our reports attribute them to ineffective security program management."[24]

What can we conclude from this? Without being scientifically decisive, the GAO's findings suggest that the managers in federal agencies are probably not aware of the importance of information systems security or that information systems security is simply not a high priority on their management agenda despite the fact they are required to comply with the Federal Information Management Security Act of 2002 and any directives from the Office of Management and Budget, which oversees agency compliance with the act—a topic that will be addressed extensively in the following section of this chapter. Consequently, most information systems in the twenty-four major federal agencies are insecure and considered to be at high risk for attack.

This lack of awareness or focus of attention shows up in another GAO report titled *Information Security: Emerging Cybersecurity Issues Threaten Federal Information Systems* (2005).[25] The report begins by recognizing that

Spam, phishing, and spyware pose security risks to federal information systems. Spam is a problem not only because of the enormous resources it demands, but also because it now serves as a means for other types of attack. Phishing can lead to identity theft and loss of sensitive information; it can easily result in reduced trust in and therefore use of electronic government services, thereby reducing the efficiencies that such services offer. Phishers have targeted federal entities such as the Federal Bureau of Investigation (FBI), the Federal Deposit Insurance Corporation (FDIC), and the Internal Revenue Service (IRS). Spyware threatens the confidentiality, integrity, and availability of federal information systems by capturing and releasing sensitive data, making unauthorized changes to systems, decreasing system performance, and possibly creating new system vulnerabilities, all without the user's knowledge or consent. The blending of these threats creates additional risks that cannot be easily mitigated with currently available tools.[26]

The report goes on to state that agency awareness of these threats and how to deal with them vary widely across the federal government, and that many agencies are not following the information security program requirements of various security and privacy laws and directives. Furthermore agencies are not reporting the incidents of cyberattacks to the appropriate central federal entity. There seems to be some confusion about whom to report to since the Office of Management and Budget shares responsibility for reporting cyberattacks with the Department of Homeland Security. There is a definite lack of coordination and some confusion among the agencies about what incidents of attack to report and to whom to report them. This has become a major problem because the attacks are no longer random: They are coordinated and deliberately targeted at specific agencies such as the Federal Bureau of Investigation (FBI), the Federal Deposit Insurance Corporation (FDIC), and the Internal Revenue Service (IRS). Furthermore, many agencies are not taking adequate measures to educate employees about the dangers of spam, phishing, and spyware. The report observes that

> Several entities within the federal government and the private sector have begun initiatives directed toward addressing spam, phishing, and spyware. These actions range from targeting cybercrime to educating the user and private-sector community on how to detect and protect systems and information from these threats. While the initiatives demonstrate an understanding of the importance of cybersecurity and emerging threats and represent the first steps in addressing the risks associated with emerging threats, similar efforts are not being made to assist federal agencies.[27]

Ensuring Information Security

Hope is in sight for greatly increased information security at the federal level of government with the passage of the Federal Information Security Management Act of 2003 (FISMA). It, along with guidance documents developed by the National Institute of Standards and Technology (NIST), holds out promise for greater information security. Among other things, the Privacy Act requires that all executive agencies establish

> rules of conduct for persons involved in the design, development, operation, or maintenance of any system of records, or maintaining any record, and

instruct each such person with respect to such rules and the requirements of [the Privacy Act], including any other rules and procedures adopted pursuant to this [Act] and the penalties for noncompliance, and appropriate administrative, technical and physical safeguards to ensure the security and confidentiality of records and to protect against any anticipated threats or hazards to their security or integrity which could result in substantial harm, embarrassment, inconvenience or unfairness to any individual on whom information is maintained. (5 U.S.C. § 552a(e)(9)-(10)[28]

The Privacy Act also requires each of the executive agencies to submit an annual report to the Office of Management and Budget on its progress in meeting the security directives of the act.

Among other things, FISMA requires that the executive agencies report the following yearly findings to OMB:

- Inventory of Systems. FISMA continues the Paperwork Reduction Act of 1995 (44 U.S.C. §101 note) requirement for agencies to develop and maintain an inventory of major information systems (including national security systems) operated by or under the control of the agency. The inventory must be used to support monitoring, testing, and evaluation of information security controls.
- Contractor Operations and Facilities. FISMA requires federal agencies to provide information security for the information and information systems that support the operations and assets of the agency, including those provided or managed by another agency, contractor, or other source. When this condition is met, agencies must provide evaluations extending beyond traditional agency boundaries.
- Implementation of security configurations. FISMA requires each agency to determine minimally acceptable system configuration requirements and ensure compliance with them. In addition, agencies must explain the degree to which they implement and enforce security configurations.
- Plan of Action and Milestones. FISMA requires agencies to develop a process for planning, implementing, evaluating, and documenting remedial action to address any deficiencies in the information security policies, procedures, and practices of the agency.[29]

In addition, FISMA also requires the agencies to report incidences of cyberattacks (viruses, worms, Trojans, or spam), to test contingency plans if an information system is attacked and made inoperable in some fashion, to test security controls, to provide annual security awareness training for government workers and contractors, and to provide specialized training for government employees who have significant security responsibilities. The Act also requires something called certification and accreditation (C&A). Accreditation is a formal written authorization to allow the system to go online and actually process data and to formally accept the potential risks inherent in having the system functioning. This accreditation is accompanied by a formal written evaluation, called a "certification," of the management, operational, and technical controls established in an information system's security plan. Finally, agencies are required to develop plans and procedures to ensure the continuity of operations for information systems that support the activities of the agencies, assuming that an information system is breached. If so, there must be plans in place that show how the agency's operations will be continued, possibly with backup systems. This, of course, leads to the duplication of information systems which can be costly, but the cost might be worth it if the primary system is breached in some way and made inoperable.

The following are some highlights from the 2005 FISMA report to OMB. Agencies are required to establish effective plans of action and milestone processes (POA&M) to remediate IT security weaknesses. Nineteen agencies were determined to have effective POA&Ms in place; six did not, including the Departments of Agriculture, Commerce, Homeland Security, Interior, Transportation, and Treasury.[30]

Agencies are required to certify and accredit their approaches to information security. The 2005 report found that only one agency, the Social Security Administration, had an excellent certification and accreditation process. Four agencies were ranked as having good certification and accreditation processes, and twelve were ranked as having satisfactory processes. Eight agencies, including the Departments of Agriculture, Commerce, Defense, Energy, Homeland Security, Interior, the Nuclear Regulatory Commission, and the Smithsonian Institution, were ranked as having poor certification and accreditation processes.[31]

FISMA also requires the agencies to complete an inventory of information systems. The 2005 report found that two agencies, Agriculture and Defense, were only approximately complete in inventorying their information systems, defined as 0 to 50 percent complete in doing so. Two agencies, Energy and the Nuclear Regulatory Commission, were somewhere between 51 percent and 70 percent complete in inventorying their information systems. Eight agencies were 81 to 95 percent complete in inventorying their information systems, while thirteen agencies were somewhere between 96 percent and 100 percent complete. It may seem improbable that an agency does not know what systems it has, but considering the size of some agencies and their often decentralized structures it is possible to not have a complete account of all systems.[32]

FISMA and OMB require each agency to test its security controls annually. The 2005 report found that the agencies have tested the security controls on

Exhibit 11.1

Federal Computer Security Grades, 2001–2005

Agency	2005 Grade	2004 Grade	2003 Grade	2002 Grade	2001 Grade
Agriculture	F	F	F	F	F
AID	A+	A+	C–	F	F
Commerce	D+	F	C–	D+	F
DOD	F	D	D	D	F
Education	C–	C	C+	D	F
Energy	F	F	F	F	F
EPA	A+	B	C	D–	D+
GSA	A–	C+	D	D	D
HHS	F	F	F	D–	F
Homeland Security	F	F	F	—	—
HUD	D+	F	F	F	D
Interior	F	C+	F	F	D
Justice	D	B–	F	F	F
Labor	A+	B–	B	C+	F
NASA	B–	D–	D–	D+	C–
NRC	D–	B+	A	C	F
NSF	A	C+	A–	D–	B+
OPM	A+	C–	D–	F	F
SBA	C+	D–	C–	F	F
SSA	A+	B	B+	B–	C+
State	F	D+	F	F	D+
Transportation	C–	A–	D+	F	F
Treasury	D–	D+	D	F	F
VA	F	F	C	F	F
Government-wide Average	D+	D+	D	F	F

Source: Patience Wait, "FISMA Follies: Officials Claim Grades Suffer From Lack of Enterprise View of Security," *Washington Technology* 21 (April 11, 2006), www.washingtontechnology.com/news/21_7/federal/28347–1.html (accessed June 16, 2006).

72 percent of all known systems. This percentage was actually down from 76 percent in 2004, but the report did note that the agencies are trying to prioritize the testing of security controls.[33]

Overall, the 2005 FISMA report showed some improvements in some of the areas over the 2004 FISMA report, although a summary of the grade reports for the executive agencies for the past five years (2001–2005) paint an overall bleak picture of information security for the federal government, suggesting that many of the agencies are not taking information security seriously. (See Exhibit 11.1.) The grades were assigned based on answers to questions about each of FISMA's requirements as asked by Inspector Generals from OMB.

A deeper look into how the FISMA reporting process works raises some concerns that more emphasis is placed on making the reports look good than on actually improving information security. One report suggests that "agencies are drowning in mostly useless FISMA reports because they typically hire (Certification and Accreditation) contractors on a system-by-system basis, throwing money at contractors and allowing them to recycle generic report content." The same report went on to state that "agencies with bad grades catch flak from all sides, so they'll start spending money and shuffling the requisite papers until the grades improve, whether real improvements in security occur or not."[34] Another report observes that "FISMA has become a largely paperwork drill among the departments and agencies, consuming an inordinate amount of resources for reporting progress while putting in place very little in the way of actual security improvements."[35] So it would seem that doing the paperwork to cover up the security flaws has become more important than actually fixing the security problems.

A 2006 Government Accountability Office report titled *Information Security: Federal Agencies Show Mixed Progress in Implementing Statutory Requirements* evaluated the 2005 FISMA report to OMB and concluded generally that

- As we have previously reported, none of the twenty-four major agencies has fully implemented agency-wide information security programs as required by FISMA. Agencies often did not adequately assess risks, develop sufficient risk-based policies or procedures for information security, ensure that existing policies and procedures were implemented effectively, or monitor operations to ensure compliance and determine the effectiveness of existing controls. Moreover, as demonstrated by the 2005 FISMA reports, many agencies still do not have complete and accurate inventories of their major systems. Until agencies effectively and fully implement agency-wide information security programs, federal data and systems will not be adequately safeguarded against unauthorized use, disclosure, and modification.
- Agencies need to take action to implement and strengthen their information security management programs. Such actions should include completing and maintaining an accurate, complete inventory of major systems, and prioritizing information security efforts based on system risk levels. Strong incident procedures are necessary to detect, report, and respond to security incidents effectively.
- Agencies also should implement strong remediation processes that include processes for planning, implementing, evaluating, and documenting remedial actions to address any identified information security weaknesses. Finally, agencies need to implement risk-based policies and procedures that efficiently and effectively reduce information security risks to an acceptable level.[36]

The report goes on to note that there are weaknesses in

1. access controls, which ensure that only authorized individuals can read, alter, or delete data;
2. software change controls, which provide assurance that only authorized software programs are implemented;
3. segregation of duties, which reduces the risk that one individual can independently perform inappropriate actions without detection;
4. continuity of operations planning, which provides for the prevention of significant disruptions of computer-dependent operations; and
5. an agency-wide security program, which provides the framework for ensuring that risks are understood and that effective controls are selected and properly implemented.[37]

The final recommendation of the report has to do with physical protection of computer facilities including hardware and software. This is somewhat ironic since in May of 2006 the IRS lost a laptop containing data on 291 employees and job applicants,[38] and the Veterans Administration lost data files on 26 million veterans when they were stolen from an employee's home. The employee was not authorized to take the files home.[39]

So it would seem that data and information security are on the minds of some chief information officers, chief information security officers, and appointed officials within OMB and staff at the GAO, but information security within many federal agencies is still weak. It is hard to believe that managers in some agencies do not know how many information systems they have, suggesting that they do not know what those information systems do and what data they might contain. A lot more security work needs to be done at the federal level, considering the proliferation of new software systems applications, which may or may not have security holes due to poorly written programming code and the ever-increasing emergence of new malware threats.

Where are the states and localities when it comes to an awareness of data and information security threats, and what are the states and localities doing to protect theory systems and data? Unfortunately, this is an almost impossible question to answer because there is no central body or repository of information about what the states and localities are doing. We can, however, get some sense that the states and localities are aware of cybersecurity issues and that some of them are doing something about those issues by reviewing several stories from the *Government Technology* web site that is devoted to public policy and managerial issues at the state and local levels of government.

A 2002 article titled "Evolving Cyber Security" warns of a possible "digital Pearl Harbor" that would cripple the American technology infrastructure, but notes that there is a debate about how long it might take for one to occur.[40] The article goes on to mention the importance of firewalls and then discusses the policy decisions made by the State of Washington's Information Services Board. It identified three categories of security concern that the states should be aware of: (1) personnel security, which involves educating state personnel about the importance of passwords and keeping them secret as well as hiring practices and background checks on personnel; (2) physical security, which refers to where computer equipment is kept, especially laptops, and who has authorized access to computers; and (3) data security, which includes how data are entered into a system and how data are backed up, and obtaining software security patches in a timely fashion, testing for intrusions, and maintaining virus protection.

In October of 2003, an article titled "Security Steps" stated that the State of Ohio had invested $3.5 million over a two-year period to make its wide area network secure, and noted that Ohio state agencies had not done much in the way of assessing the security of their systems despite this investment. [41] The article also said that the State of Colorado was in the process of setting up an information security task force composed of state agency CIOs and other personnel. One function of the task force would be to accredit state agencies that are in compliance with the task force's security standards. The state was also establishing security officers in each of the agencies.

A June 2004 article titled "Internet Takedown" noted that the Georgia Technology Authority views hackers as the most immediate near-term threat to the state's information systems.[42] It notes that hackers find it easy to locate holes in software because it is often defective. The article goes on to say that the practice of housing data in just a few state data nodes is dangerous because they can be easily compromised and, because they are all linked together, one compromised node would most likely compromise all of the other nodes.

A November 2005 article titled "Cyber Security Summit Outlines Evolving Threats, Solutions" made some very interesting observations.[43]

- Hacking has become a major criminal activity, and spam and worms are often used by criminals to attack a company's computer systems and then extort money from the company to reverse the attack.
- Critical infrastructures have been attacked. For example, in 1998 a telephone system in Worchester, Massachusetts, was hacked that shut down the landing lights at the city's airport, while in 2000 a hacker in Queensland, Australia, broke into a wireless network and released sewage. Then in 2002, a worm shut down train signaling devices in several Midwestern states.

- Computer crime syndicates have emerged, mostly in Eastern Europe, that seek to capture credit card information and sell it in secondary criminal markets.
- Hackers have discovered how to break into wireless networks in order to break into the systems of businesses in order to commit acts of fraud. Such hacking can be done from a car via mobile networks.
- Because of the international nature of hacking, criminal activity is difficult to investigate and prosecute.

The article goes on to say that at the federal level, agencies have been pretty successful in dealing with the new threats but much work needs to be done at the state and local levels of government.

In February of 2006 a report in *Government Technology* announced a major assessment of state and local government investment in security measures.[44] While investment in security measures is not a direct measure of actual security, it is a fair surrogate. The survey was conducted by CDW-G, a leading vendor of security solutions to governments.[45] It classified the states into three categories: (1) early majority, including Colorado, Virginia, Georgia, Utah, Minnesota, North Carolina, Maryland, Texas, New Jersey, Tennessee, Pennsylvania, and Missouri, are states that have proven to be leaders with a firm grounding in policy and technology and have proven technology successes in securing data; (2) early investors, including Indiana, California, Oregon, Florida, Connecticut, and Illinois, who are knowledgeable about security best practices and adopt them appropriately, and have legislative or political support for security policies and technologies; and (3) lead investors, including Ohio, Michigan, Wisconsin, Washington, and Massachusetts, who understand the value of technology, are tolerant of risk and can manage it, have political or legislative support for technology and the risks associated with it, promote association or institutional support for IT security measures, and prioritize security expenditures. This leaves the rest of the states in a category of not being particularly invested in data or information security. Vendor surveys should be taken with some degree of skepticism, but this survey may give some idea of how well prepared the states are to handle threats to data and information security. It does not, however, give much indication of how localities are dealing with security measures.

We can conclude this chapter with a model framework of information security that localities and states that are just embarking on information security efforts might use as a guide. The Information Technology Association of America offers the practical tips shown in Exhibit 11.2 for securing information. They involve processes, people, and technology. They also seem to be matters of common sense, but given the high rates of successful attacks on computer systems one wonders if public managers are really taking security issues seriously.

Exhibit 11.2
Practical Steps for Enterprise Information Security:
On-Site and Teleworking

It's About Process, People, and Technology

Process

1. Regularly perform risk assessment and vulnerability analysis of enterprise information systems, both physical and electronic, and align security, incident response, and business continuity policies accordingly.
2. Develop a documented internal controls and audit policy for information management, such as:

   - How sensitive data are classified and prioritized.
   - Where and how sensitive data are stored.
   - How data are protected: physically, electronically, procedurally, in storage and in transit.
   - Who has access to what data, under what circumstances.
   - How data are used, transmitted, retained, and destroyed, and what data are not permitted to be transported over the Internet.

3. Integrate security requirements into budget planning and procurement process.

People

4. Appoint a chief information security officer with a direct line to a chief privacy officer and the CEO or agency head.
5. Establish, train, and enforce employee procedures for remote access, according to documented information management policies for physical, wireline, and wireless teleworking, including

   - Software download policies.
   - Use and transport of corporate- or agency-owned and configured computers, networking and security technology for access to business systems, versus employee-owned (personal) systems.
   - Use of external storage media (hard disk drives, thumb drives, CDs, and so on).

6. Make adherence to information security practices a performance objective.

Technology

7. Deploy and enforce strong (multifactor) authentication technology and procedures, and have a clear ID management policy in place.
8. Use intrusion-detection and intrusion-prevention technology to spot and stop hackers from getting into the network.
9. Use encryption or other technology to protect data from unauthorized access and exploitation.
10. Deploy strong remote access security features, including secure routers, virtual private networks with SSL or IPSec security features, device identity and authentication, firewalls, and antivirus and anti-spyware software.

Source: Information Technology Association of America, "Practical Steps for Enterprise Information Security: On-Site and Teleworking. It's About Process, People, and Technology," n.d., www.itaa.org/isec/docs/securitytips.pdf (accessed June 8, 2006).

Summary and a Look Forward

In some ways this chapter seems incomplete. For one, it simply cannot cover all of the technical details associated with data and information security in general, but hopefully it provides a general introduction to the technical, managerial, and public policy issues related to securing information systems. It also does not give a complete picture of how public agencies at all three levels of government are attempting to secure their data and their information systems. That information is simply not available, but we do have some idea of what federal agencies and some states are doing in the way of information security. Unfortunately, it looks like government information systems are a long way from being secure, and they may contain sensitive information about citizens that potential wrongdoers might easily acquire. It seems odd that the general public is not more up in arms about what data and information government agencies and private firms are collecting about them and the harm that could come to them if that data and information gets into the hands of the wrong people. The following and last chapter of this book will conclude with a discussion of the policy and management measures that some public agencies are undertaking to manage their information strategically.

12

Managing Information Strategically

The previous chapter ended with a generic model of information systems security that emphasized that security is about people, processes, and technology, and that, in a nutshell, is what managing information strategically is also all about. It is a high-level management philosophy and set of policies and practices that recognizes that information is a valuable resource for any public agency and that it should be managed just as effectively as financial, human, and material resources. This harkens back to chapter 1 where it was noted that NASPAA, the accrediting body for master's programs in public policy and administration, has recently incorporated the management of information into its "Common Curriculum Components" for graduate education in the field of public administration, joining the traditional components of human and financial management. It also resonates with the title of this book, *Managing Information in the Public Sector*, meaning that managing information is much more than just managing data, hardware, software, networks, and related technologies.

Managing information strategically focuses on four broad, unique, yet interrelated, subject areas within the field of information systems in general: (1) information resource management (IRM), which is a comprehensive approach to managing an agency's information, technology, processes, and people; (2) the role of the public agency Chief Information Officer, who is often tasked with overseeing IRM activities; (3) enterprise architectures (EAs), which are blueprints of how information facilitates the mission of an agency; and (4) knowledge management (KM), which is the recognition that agencies are composed of people who have valuable knowledge about the past, present, and future of the agency, and such knowledge should be systematically managed as an agency resource. This chapter will address each of those topics in turn, showing how they developed and how they play out in the day-to-day management of public agencies.

The focus in this chapter will be on the federal government. State and local governments also practice information resource management and have chief information officers, and some engage in building enterprise architectures. Some are also interested in knowledge management practices. Unfortunately, there is not enough room in this book to address what state and local governments are doing in these regards. Fortunately, what they are doing mirrors the logic of what the federal government is doing but only on a somewhat smaller scale. It is important to note, however, that the National Association of State Chief Information Officers has maintained a sustained effort to promote the concepts of IRM, CIO initiatives, EA activities, and KM practices across all three levels of government in recognition of their importance to managing information strategically.[1]

Information Resource Management

The Free Online Computer Dictionary (FOLDOC) (quoting Blass et al. 1991) provides a rather comprehensive definition of information resource management (IRM):

- IRM—A philosophical and practical approach to managing government information. Information is regarded as a valuable resource that should be managed like other resources and should contribute directly to accomplishing organizational goals and objectives. IRM provides an integrated view for managing the entire life cycle of information, from generation, to dissemination, to archiving and/or destruction, for maximizing the overall usefulness of information, and improving service delivery and program management.
- IRM views information and Information Technology as an integrating factor in the organization; that is, the various organizational positions that manage information are coordinated and work together toward common ends. Further, IRM looks for ways in which the management of information and the management of Information Technology are interrelated and fosters that interrelationship and organizational integration.
- IRM includes the management of (1) the broad range of information resources, for example, printed materials, electronic information, and microforms; (2) the various technologies and equipment that manipulate these resources; and (3) the people who generate, organize, and disseminate those resources. Overall the intent of IRM is to increase the usefulness of government information both to the government and to the public.[2]

Two things should be observed from this rather broad and extensive definition of IRM. First, in its generality, it covers all of the topics previously addressed in this book, indicating that it is a holistic, or global, approach to managing information, people, processes, and technologies. Second, it specifically mentions IRM in the context of the operation of government agencies where the concept first took hold.

The IRM concept emerged during the 1970s through the work of Forrest Woody Horton[3] and events leading up to the Federal Paperwork Reduction Act (PRA) of 1980,[4] although the Diebold Group, a consulting firm, claims to have introduced the IRM concept in the private sector in 1977,[5] and the private sector currently practices IRM alongside the public sector. Horton claims that the basic idea behind IRM actually dates back to 1887 and the Cockrell Committee, headed up by U.S. Senator Francis Marion Cockrell of Missouri to look into the high cost of copying documents. Although Norton notes that the modern concept of IRM emerged with the Paperwork Reduction Act.

IRM gained the attention of the information systems community of professionals at the 1981 meeting of the Association of Computing Machinery (ACM), which was the first professional society devoted to computing and information technology and management. At that meeting, Horton and several other IS professionals presented some of the first published papers on the IRM concept. In a paper presented by Horton, he observes that information has not been regarded as a valuable organizational resource like money or people, although it should be and it should be managed accordingly. He explains that

> In short, IRM is a parallel or analogous approach to the planning, management, and control of information resources, in the same way the organization has usually established a financial management function, a personnel management function, a facilities (properties and inventories) management function, and so on. Since major differences exist between information and other assets, the same approaches between resources must be adopted and tailored to the uniqueness of the situation.[6]

Other papers presented at that conference endorsed the same view of IRM, creating a whole new discipline within the information systems community of academicians and professionals.[7]

The Paperwork Reduction Act of 1980 reflects the philosophy of IRM. It established the Office of Information and Regulatory Affairs (OIRA) within the Office of Management and Budget and required its director to

- Establish a system for integrating information management practices with the information policies of this Act;
- Identify initiatives to improve productivity in Federal operations using information processing technology;

- Develop a program to enforce Federal information processing standards and to revitalize the standards development program;
- Complete action on recommendations of the Commission on Federal Paperwork;
- Consult with the Administrator of General Services, to develop a five-year plan for meeting the automatic data processing and telecommunication needs of the Government; and
- Submit to the President and Congress legislative proposals to remove inconsistencies in laws involving privacy, confidentiality, and disclosure of information.[8]

It also required each agency to

- Carry out information management activities in an efficient, economical manner;
- Designate a senior official or officials to carry out agency responsibilities under this Act including the acquisition of automatic data processing equipment and services;
- Inventory its major information systems and review, periodically, its management activities;
- Ensure that its systems do not overlap each other or duplicate systems of other agencies;
- Develop procedures for assessing the paperwork burden of its collection activities; and
- Ensure that each information-collection request submitted to nine or fewer persons contains a notice that it is not subject to the provisions of this Act.[9]

This set the stage to bring the management of information out of the back offices of federal agencies and into the forefront of top-level management concerns. It was also the beginning of the end for such antiquated terms as "ADP," or automated data processing, and "EDP," electronic data processing, terms that are rarely used today in light of significant developments in information management. Federal agencies responded to the PRA by establishing personnel positions with the title of Information Resource Manager and entire departments within agencies devoted to IRM.

How well has the federal government implemented IRM? It had a very rocky start. Early progress reports from the GAO noted that agencies were slow to respond to the new mandates for managing information. For example, in testimony before the Subcommittee on Legislation and National Security of the House Committee on Government Operations on Implementation of the Paperwork Reduction Act Public Law 96–511, Charles A. Bowsher, the comptroller general of the United States, said

> A sufficiently high priority has not been given to implementing the Act. Little or no effort has been directed to key requirements of this Act. As recently as October 16, 1981, OMB had approved no formal plans for implementing the Act. Resources have been allocated to other functions, and a growing workload of paperwork clearances is resulting in little or no effort being devoted to other key requirements of the Act. Many of the agencies' plans for implementing the Act are inadequate and generally failed to lay an adequate groundwork for the more substantive efforts to follow. No progress has been made toward developing the Federal Information Locator System, a key management tool required by the Act. The General Services Administration and the Department of Commerce, both of which have key responsibilities under the Act, have not been involved in the limited planning which has occurred. Critical Government-wide information management programs in both agencies are facing budget cuts, which may render them incapable of performing the functions envisioned by the Act.[10]

Furthermore, agency computer personnel with old mind-sets about mainframe computing never really caught on to the realities of trying to understand how information is vital to performing the missions of the agencies, partly because they never really understood those missions. Of course they understood computers and software programming, but not the business functions of the agencies. They lacked a high-level management perspective to effectively implement the IRM philosophies and practices. OIRA was given sweeping authority to impose those mandates but with the addition of few new resources to do so. A search on the GAO's web site for "information resource management" turned up no less than 940 reports or testimonies from 1980 to May of 2006 indicating that a wide variety of federal agencies were making some progress toward meeting the ideals of IRM, but there were also many areas of concern about the agencies fully implementing IRM policies and procedures, as well as some concerns about the security of agency information systems. This is not to say that improvements have not been made. They have. Federal information is being managed more effectively today than in 1980, but not without some additional help in the form of the Clinger-Cohen Act of 1996, which created the role and function of the Chief Information Officer within Federal agencies.

Chief Information Officer

The Information Technology Management Reform Act of 1996, which is also known as the Clinger-Cohen Act (or CCA), was co-authored by U.S. Representative William Clinger and Senator William Cohen in 1996.[11] Prior to the act, Cohen—well, actually his staff—had published the *Computer Chaos Report*, detailing the massive amounts of waste involved in federal government purchases of computer systems, services, and related technologies.[12]

What was the state of information management in the federal government prior to the introduction of CCA? One GAO report makes the following two observations:

- On the whole, the federal government's track record in delivering high-value information technology solutions at acceptable cost is not a good one. Put simply, the government continues to spend money on systems projects that far exceed their expected costs and yield questionable benefits to mission improvements. Familiar examples, such as the Federal Aviation Administration's Air Traffic Control modernization and the Internal Revenue Service's Tax Systems Modernization projects, serve as stark reminders of situations where literally billions of dollars have been spent without clear results. Moreover, agencies have failed to take full advantage of IT by failing to first critically examine and then reengineer existing business and program-delivery processes.
- Federal agencies lack adequate processes and reliable data to manage investments in information technology. Without these key components, agencies cannot adequately select and control their technology investments. As the GAO's financial and information management audits have demonstrated over the last decade, it is sometimes impossible to track precisely what agency IT dollars have actually been spent for or even how much has been spent. Even more problematic, rarely do agencies collect information on actual benefits to the organization accruing from their investments. More often than not, results are presented as descriptions of outputs and activities rather than changes in performance or program outcomes.[13]

Obviously the prior Paperwork Reduction Act of 1980 did little to improve the management of federal information, related technologies, and policies and practices.

Cohen's *Computer Chaos Report* concluded with the following recommendations presented in Exhibit 12.1.[14]

The CCA was designed to improve the way the federal government acquires and manages information technology. It required the agencies and individual programs to use performance-based management principles for acquiring IT. These principles included capital planning for major IT investments instead of

Exhibit 12.1
Recommendations of the *Computer Chaos Report*

Congress and federal agencies should consider the following options to remedy the problems that exist in the way the federal government buys computer systems:

- Emphasize early oversight and planning: Target oversight of computer acquisitions during the early phases of programs to encourage agencies to reevaluate how they do business before spending money on automation.
- Reduce bureaucratic barriers to purchases: Replace the Delegation of Procurement Authority process with an approach that provides meaningful oversight over early planning. Establish one forum for reviewing all contract protests, and streamline internal agency review processes, which add months to purchasing time and result in the acquisition of outdated technology. If the government cannot reduce the time it takes to competitively buy computers before they are obsolete, it should consider alternatives such as leasing, task order contracts, and privatization of federal computer services and operations.
- Avoid reinventing existing technology: Ensure that developing unique systems is the exception rather than the rule. It should be rare for the government to purchase anything but commercially available hardware and software.
- Size projects to manageable levels: The government should address automation in manageable segments that are compatible with other systems and easily cancelled if they run into any cost or schedule difficulties.
- Encourage innovation: Establish pilot programs to try new procurement ideas. As technology changes, what is appropriate in today's buying environment may be obsolete tomorrow. No one has a monopoly on good ideas, and the government needs to be flexible in incorporating new technology.
- Create incentives for the government and contractors to perform: Allocate agency information budgets based on past management performance in meeting cost, schedule, and performance goals. While cost should remain a significant factor, the government should select computer contractors as much as possible based on past performance and reputation.

- Communicate lessons learned: Encourage the foundation of inter-agency advisory groups to share experiences with federal computer system acquisitions. Industry-government communications should be enhanced during all phases of the acquisition cycle. An online database with agency comments on contractor performance should be established and made available to agencies buying computer systems.
- Reevaluate existing procurements and halt new procurements until the computer acquisition process is improved: Suspend and review existing large computer system acquisitions to determine if current agency plans for automation will achieve the best value for the taxpayer. Halt new large computer procurements until the government improves the computer acquisition process and can ensure effective planning, cost effectiveness, and timely delivery of new systems.

Note: The recommendations of Cohen's *Computer Chaos Report* have been reproduced in the following article: "Computer Chaos 8 Recommendations," *Federal Computer Week Online,* n.d., www.fcw.com/article89088–06–06–05-Web (accessed June 12, 2006).

"fly by" acquisitions of technology; the examination and revisions of business process reengineering (BPR) before investing in new technologies to support those processes; enforcement of accountability standards for the performance of new IT-enabled business processes; the use of standards for the acquisition of technology products; and an increased reliance on commercial technology as opposed to in-house development of technology. It also took away much of the control that the General Services Administration had over the acquisition of technology and technology services, giving the agencies more autonomy in acquiring technology solutions for business processes.

The act also created the position of Chief Information Officer (CIO). Despite the fact that agencies had Information Resource Managers in place thanks to the PRA of 1980, each agency was now required to establish a CIO office and position of even greater authority to oversee all of the agency's information needs and information-related technologies, policies, and practices. This was yet another intentional move to elevate the management of information and technology out of the back office of the agencies and into the front office of top management, a move that emulated trends in the private sector. The CIO was supposed to have the same authority and responsibility as chief financial officers (CFOs), chief executive officers (CEOs), and chief operating officers (COOs). The CIO was supposed to report directly to the head of the agency on all manner of issues related to information management and related technologies. Many states and localities mimicked the federal government by creating their own CIO positions. A CIO council was also established and comprised CIOs from various agencies as well as the private sector to advise the OMB and the agencies on the proper role and functioning of the CIOs within the agencies.[15]

Unfortunately, the CIO initiative also got off to a shaky start. As early as 1996, the GAO observed that the National Aeronautics and Space Administration (NASA) CIO position was actually started in 1995—before the Clinger-Cohen Act was passed. NASA's program offices and field centers were left with considerable autonomy over their own information systems. The GAO recommended strengthening NASA's CIO's authority over the program offices and field centers in order to settle disputes and improve standardization of technology operations agency-wide.[16]

In 1997 the GAO issued another report indicating that several agencies had acting CIOs who did not have the technical or managerial qualifications to be CIOs, and that in some agencies, the CIOs did not report to the head of the agency.[17] The GAO also observed that some CIOs had other major management responsibilities that distracted them from their CIO duties. The report also found that in some agencies it was unclear that the CIO's duties were actually to manage the agency's information resources. In some large agencies it is difficult to invest all of the duties of a CIO into just one person, suggesting that there should be more CIO staff in those larger agencies.

The same report recognized that the CIO Council—established by an executive order, not the CCA—has a major role to play in improving the management of information and technology across the federal government. It has the potential to

- develop recommendations for government-wide information technology management policies, procedures, and standards;
- share experiences, ideas, and promising practices for improving information technology management;
- promote cooperation in using information resources;
- address the federal government's hiring and professional development needs for information management; and
- make recommendations and provide advice to OMB and the agencies on the government-wide strategic plan required under the PRA.[18]

Although the CIO Council was in its early formative stage of development, the report strongly recommended that all agencies follow the leading advice and recommendations of the council. However, some agencies, approximately half of them, were slow to respond.

Then, in 1998, the GAO focused its attention on the U.S. Department of Agriculture, opening its remarks about the agency's lack of attention to implementing the CIO position properly by observing that

> As we testified before this Subcommittee last spring, USDA has a long history of problems in managing its substantial investments in IT. We chronicled many cases dating back to 1981 in which the department had not effectively planned major computer modernization activities or managed IT resources. Such ineffective IT planning and management have resulted in USDA's wasting millions of dollars.[19]

Noting that the Department of Agriculture is not atypical of many federal agencies, the GAO also observed that

> over time, the department has invested hundreds of millions of dollars in hundreds of systems that are not interoperable with others in the agency and that actually inhibit the use and sharing of information. In fact, data are often inaccessible and underutilized outside of and even within USDA's individual agencies for identifying problems, analyzing trends, or assessing crosscutting programmatic and policy issues.[20]

As for the role of the CIO in the USDA, the report observed that the CIO responsibilities had been handed to a deputy director of the agency who had other responsibilities, and that the CIO responsibilities for the deputy director had not been delineated. In addition, there was no plan to establish an independent CIO position reporting to the director of USDA.[21] Furthermore, the agency was supposed to develop an information architecture (a blueprint of where the agency is with regard to information management, with a view to where it should be in the future with regard to information management). The USDA did so with a draft version that still needed considerable work.[22] To make matters worse, the USDA is one of those agencies with many strategic subcomponents, and various persons had been given CIO responsibilities within those subcomponents, but the lead CIO person could not keep track of them all.[23]

Also in 1998, the GAO examined the U.S. Department of Veterans Affairs (VA) only to find that the VA had not developed an overall business process improvement strategy or an information architecture, nor did it have a disciplined process for selecting, controlling, or evaluating technology investments. Furthermore, its investment portfolio for technology products was incomplete.[24] Finally, the VA did not have a sole person in charge of the CIO function. Those responsibilities were given to the Assistant Secretary for

Management and Chief Financial Officer (CFO). Consequently, information resource issues were not addressed promptly.[25]

NASA, the USDA, and the VA are just three examples of several agencies that the GAO identified as not being in compliance with many of the CIO requirements of the CCA. Since 2000 the GAO has released seven individual guides on how to effectively implement the CIO provisions of the CCA, suggesting that the agencies are not doing a very good job of it, and consequently, the strategic management of information in the federal government can be significantly improved. One of those reports, titled *Federal Chief Information Officers: Responsibilities, Reporting Relationships, Tenure, and Challenges*, tells a compelling story of what it is like to be a federal agency CIO.

First, the report lists the following thirteen major responsibilities of an agency CIO:

- **IT/IRM strategic planning.** CIOs are responsible for strategic planning for all information and information technology management functions—thus, the term IRM strategic planning [44 U.S.C. 3506(b)(2)].
- **IT capital planning and investment management.** CIOs are responsible for IT capital planning and investment management [44 U.S.C. 3506(h) and 40 U.S.C. 11312 & 11313].
- **Information security.** CIOs are responsible for ensuring compliance with the requirement to protect information and systems [44 U.S.C. 3506(g) and 3544(a)(3)].
- **IT/IRM workforce planning.** CIOs have responsibilities for helping the agency meet its IT/IRM workforce or human capital needs [44 U.S.C. 3506(b) and 40 U.S.C. 11315(c)].
- **Information collection/paperwork reduction.** CIOs are responsible for the review of agency information collection proposals to maximize the utility and minimize public "paperwork" burdens [44 U.S.C. 3506(c)].
- **Information dissemination.** CIOs are responsible for ensuring that the agency's information dissemination activities meet policy goals such as timely and equitable public access to information [44 U.S.C. 3506(d)].
- **Records management.** CIOs are responsible for ensuring that the agency implements and enforces records management policies and procedures under the Federal Records Act [44 U.S.C. 3506(f)].
- **Privacy.** CIOs are responsible for compliance with the Privacy Act and related laws [44 U.S.C. 3506(g)].
- **Statistical policy and coordination.** CIOs are responsible for the agency's statistical policy and coordination functions, including ensuring the relevance, accuracy, and timeliness of information collected or created for statistical purposes [44 U.S.C. 3506(e)].

- **Information disclosure.** CIOs are responsible for information access under the Freedom of Information Act [44 U.S.C. 3506(g)].
- **Enterprise architecture.** Federal laws and guidance direct agencies to develop and maintain enterprise architectures as blueprints to define the agency mission and the information and IT needed to perform that mission.
- **Systems acquisition, development, and integration.** We have found that a critical element of successful IT management is effective control of systems acquisition, development, and integration [44 U.S.C. 3506(h)(5) and 40 U.S.C. 11312].
- **E-government initiatives.** Various laws and guidance direct agencies to undertake initiatives to use IT to improve government services to the public and internal operations [44 U.S.C. 3506(h)(3) and the EGovernment Act of 2002].[26]

This is a rather daunting list of required activities, and it is easy to see how it would be difficult for one government executive to perform all thirteen alone, especially if that official has other major duties.

All twenty-seven of the federal CIOs were surveyed about their involvement in these required activities. Generally, all of the CIOs were responsible for most of the areas. All of the CIOs were responsible for the first five of the required activities: capital planning and investment management, enterprise architecture, information security, IT/IRM strategic planning, and IT/IRM workforce planning. Twenty-five of the CIOs were responsible for major e-gov initiatives, and twenty-five were responsible for systems acquisition, development, and integration. Twenty-two were responsible for information collection/paperwork reduction; twenty-one for records management; twenty for information dissemination; seventeen for privacy; nine for information disclosure/freedom of information; and eight for statistical policy and coordination. Most of the CIOs said they were comfortable with other units in the agencies handling some of these required duties, but the GAO noted that it was against the law and commented that it could impede the full integration of technology management functions.[27]

Another area in which some of the CIOs were not in compliance with the law was in their reporting relationships to the agency heads. Only nineteen out of twenty-seven of the CIOs reported directly to agency heads. The others reported to deputies. There were mixed feelings among the CIOs about the importance of reporting to the agency head, but most of them said that it was very important to forge such an alliance.[28]

Another set of interesting facts emerged from the survey about the CIOs' job tenure. The median time in office for a CIO is only two years, and it is generally believed that it can take three to five years for a CIO to effectively implement his or her agenda. Reasons cited for the turnover were competition for better-paying jobs in the private sector, the political environment of the CIOs, and the challenging nature of the job of a CIO.[29] These results suggest that private-sector executives are leery of political hassles, the daunting nature of the work, and the relatively low salaries offered to federal CIOs.

Is the CIO initiative for improving the management of information and related technologies a success? It is difficult to make a decision about that because there are no real benchmarks by which to judge the success of CIOs, except possibly to hold them to the myriad of reports they must complete and submit to OMB and the CIO Council. As we have seen it has been a troubled endeavor. Agencies were slow to respond to the initiative. The GAO was highly critical of several federal agency CIO policies and practices, noting that they were not in compliance with the law. The thirteen major responsibilities of the CIOs are daunting—no wonder not all CIOs are responsible for all of them. Finally, the median time in office and the high turnover rate among federal CIOs does not bode well for the initiative.

Outsiders have noticed this, too. An article appearing in *CIO Magazine. com* in May of 2006 titled "Federal IT Flunks Out" contains the following observation:

> Federal IT systems are still failing at an alarming rate nearly 10 years after Clinger-Cohen was signed into law by President Clinton. For example, of 16 IT projects in the Federal Aviation Administration's massive 25-year-old modernization program, 13 are over budget, ranging from $1.1 million to $1.5 billion, according to the Government Accountability Office. The Army's Future Combat System—a fully integrated set of networks to deliver real-time information to the battlefield through sensors that pinpoint high-tech weapons—could come in as much as $130 billion over its original 2001 budget estimate of $70 billion. The Interior Department's IT systems have proved so insecure that over the past three years a federal judge has repeatedly ordered the department to shut down all its Internet access. The list goes on, with the IRS's repeated failures to modernize and the disaster of the FBI's virtual case file system merely two of the most well-publicized examples.[30]

The article does not place the blame for the failure of the Clinger-Cohen Act on the CIOs themselves, noting that many are very competent individuals. Instead the blame is placed on the provisions of the act itself, which hampers the effectiveness of the CIOs. First, they have very little authority but a lot of responsibility. Their roles in the agencies are not taken seriously enough by top managers and elected officials. Second, politics has come to rule the appointments of CIOs. The CIO position was originally envisioned to be a career position, but the Bush administration has made several political appointments to those positions of people having no technical background in IT. The third reason is the bureaucracy itself, which impedes strong executive decision making and precludes the implementation of new business practices such as sound project management disciplines and the development of strong business cases for proposed IT projects. Finally, the entire CIO initiative is buried in paperwork. There are simply too many reports to write dealing with minor issues rather than strategic concerns. This will be evidenced in the next section when we address the biggest report of all—the enterprise architecture.

Enterprise Architectures

The Clinger-Cohen Act also mandated that the agencies, under the direction of the CIOs, develop enterprise architectures, a concept borrowed from the private sector. An enterprise architecture (EA) is a blueprint or model that attempts to align an agency's data, technology, business processes, lines of business, strategic goals, and finally its overall mission. As such, it becomes an extremely complex document and a very time-consuming product to develop (some wags say it was simply developed to give CIOs something to do), but it is supposed to optimize all of an agency's functioning in terms of organizational structure, organizational processes, financial processes, personnel processes, and information processes.

Enterprise architectures can become quite complex. Each of the twenty-seven federal agencies has one for the entire agency and is supposed to have one for each of its own discrete lines of business or program areas. For example, the Department of Defense has an EA for the entire department and one for each branch of the service; within each branch are supposed to be EAs for virtually every conceivable functional operation, right on down to each and every army or naval base. Ideally, all of these EAs can be nested together to get a total picture of the Department of Defense, but because of the complexity of that picture, one wonders about how much use it would be.

The Department of Defense's definition of an EA gives some sense of what it is and what an enormous undertaking it can be.

> An architecture description is a representation of a defined domain, as of a current or future point in time, in terms of its component parts, what those parts do, how the parts relate to each other, and the rules and constraints under which the parts function. What constitutes each of the elements of this definition depends on the degree of detail of interest. For example, domains

can be at any level, from DoD as a whole down to individual functional areas or groups of functional areas. Component parts can be anything from "U.S. Air Force" as a component of DoD, down to a "satellite ground station" as a component part of a communications network, or "workstation A" as a component part of system "x." What those parts do can be as general as their high-level operational concept or as specific as the lowest-level action they perform. How the parts relate to each other can be as general as how organizations fit into a very high-level command structure or as specific as what frequency one unit uses in communicating with another. The rules and constraints under which they work can be as general as high-level doctrine or as specific as the e-mail standard they must use.[31]

Sounds complicated? Well, it is, but IT professionals place great store in the value of an EA in enhancing the performance of any organization, public or private.

The GAO provides a simpler and more useful definition of an EA that can be used to develop a more general sense of what an EA can do for an agency. According to the GAO:

In simple terms, an enterprise can be viewed as any purposeful activity, and an architecture can be characterized as the structure (or structural description) of any activity. Building on this, EAs can be viewed as systematically derived and captured structural descriptions—in useful models, diagrams, and narrative—of the mode of operation for a given enterprise, which can be (1) a single organization or (2) a functional or mission area that transcends more than one organizational boundary (e.g., financial management, homeland security).[32]

The need for enterprise architectures arose out of the fact that as public and private organizations became more and more dependent on data and information systems, and as data and information systems began to proliferate throughout the organization, both the IS administrators and the general managers needed a way to get a handle on them. This meant developing conceptual frameworks, which became known as architectures, that incorporated data, technology, lines of business, business processes, organizational goals, and strategic missions. In this respect, enterprise architectures are almost analogous to traditional organizational charts that show the functional breakdown of all of the specialized activities conducted by the various divisions or departments of a public agency in order to achieve the agency's mission. What makes them different from traditional organizational charts is that they focus on the flow of data and information throughout an agency as it conducts its day-to-day operations in support of its mission. John Zachman pioneered the concept of architectures in the mid- to late 1980s to deal with the fact that information systems were growing in size, complexity, and numbers, so much so that some logical construct, what he called an architecture, was needed for making decisions about data and data flows throughout an agency. These architectures should be holistic as well as precise in detail, particularly when the components of information systems need to be integrated in order to function properly.[33]

Zachman proposed a framework, which is now in the public domain, that looks at an organization from a variety of perspectives at different levels of abstraction to give a full picture of how the organization operates from an information processing point of view. Those perspectives include: (1) the strategic planner who views the scope of the enterprise, (2) the system owner who views the business model of the enterprise, (3) the system designer who views the system model of the enterprise, (4) the system developer or builder who views the technology model of the enterprise, (5) the subcontractor who views the detailed representations of the enterprise, and finally (6) the system itself, which is a fully functional view of the enterprise system. Zachman added six other models, or views, to each of these perspectives to create a multidimensional model of the enterprise. Those views include: (1) what the enterprise uses to operate (the data), (2) how the enterprise operates (the function), (3) where the enterprise operates physically (the network), (4) who operates the enterprise (the people), (5) when the enterprise operations occur (time), and (6) why the enterprise operates (motivation).[34]

Then Zachman combined the perspectives with the views to obtain a total enterprise architecture framework consisting of a matrix view of the enterprise (see Exhibit 12.2). The task of the enterprise architects then becomes one of filling in all of the detailed information into the appropriate cells of the matrix in order to get a holistic view of the entire enterprise from an information processing perspective. This can be a very daunting task for a large public agency but an important one for reasons that soon will be provided.

The Zachman framework can be applied to an entire agency at a very high level of abstraction, or it can be applied to various departments, offices, programs, subunits, or basic operational entities at increasingly lower levels of abstraction with increasingly more detail about how the smaller enterprises operate. As noted, the framework is analogous to an organizational chart of an agency showing how the various units and subunits are related to one another as data flows between them, and then one can drill down into the chart to see how the various units are organized and use their data.

Since Zachman's pioneering work in developing his EA framework, several other frameworks have been developed. DOD's framework has already been introduced. In September 1999, the federal CIO Council published the Federal

Exhibit 12.2

The Zachman Enterprise Architecture Framework

	Data (What)	Function (How)	Network (Where)	People (Who)	Time (When)	Motivation (Why)
Objective/ Scope Planner's View	List of things important to the enterprise	List of processes the enterprise performs	List of locations where the enterprise operates	List of organizational units	List of business events/ cycles	List of business goals/ strategies
Model of the Business Owner's View	Entity relationship diagram (including m:m, n-ary attributed relationships)	Business process model (physical data flow diagram)	Logistics network (nodes and links)	Organization chart, with roles; skill sets; security issues	Business master schedule	Business rules
Model of the Information System Developer's View	Data model (converged entities, fully normalized)	Essential Data flow diagram; application architecture	Distributed system architecture	Human interface architecture (roles, data, access	Dependency Diagram, entity life history (process structure)	Business rule model
Technology Model Builder's View	Data architecture (tables and columns); map to legacy data	System design: structure chart, pseudocode	System architecture (hardware, software types	User interface (how the system will behave); security design	"Control flow" diagram (control structure)	Business rule design
Detailed Representation Subcontractor's View	Data design (denormalized), physical storage design	Detailed Program Design	Network architecture	Screens, security architecture	Timing definitions	Rule specification in program logic
Functioning System Functioning Enterprise View	Converted data	Executable programs	Communications facilities	Trained people	Business events	Enforced Rules

Source: David C. Hay, *The Zachman Framework: An Introduction* available at www. tdan.com/i001fe01.htm (accessed November 29, 2006). Originally introduced in: John Zachman, "A Framework for Information Systems Architecture," *IBM Systems Journal,* Vol. 26, No. 3, 1987.

Enterprise Architecture Framework (FEAF) as a guide to facilitate common frameworks across all federal agencies. OMB also has its own recommended EA framework.[35] Apparently the various agencies are free to choose which framework they will use and modify it to their own unique situation as long as they have some framework in place.

In general, the advantages of an EA framework follow:

- It acts as a way to pass from chaos and disagreement to order and structure.
- It enables an integrated vision and a global perspective of informational resources.
- It enables the discovery and elimination of redundancy in the business processes reducing information systems complexity.
- It contributes to having information systems that reflect common goals and performance measures for all managers, to encourage cooperation rather than conflict, and competition within organizations.
- It becomes the bridge between the business and technical domains.[36]

Currently, the OMB is prescribing five reference models for the development of agency EAs. They include the following:

- The Business Reference Model is intended to describe the business operations of the federal government independent of the agencies that perform them, including defining the services provided to state and local governments.
- The Performance Reference Model is to provide a common set of general performance outputs and measures for agencies to use to achieve business goals and objectives.
- The Data and Information Reference Model is to describe, at an aggregate level, the type of data and information that support program and business line operations, and the relationships among these types.
- The Service Component Reference Model is to identify and classify IT service (i.e., application) components that support federal agencies and promote the reuse of components across agencies.
- The Technical Reference Model is to describe how technology is supporting the delivery of service components, including relevant standards for implementing the technology.[37]

Taken together, these models summarize the relationships among business processes, performance outputs and measures, data and information that support operations, the applications that support operations, and finally the technologies involved in delivering services to provide an overall picture of how an agency operates from an enterprise architecture point of view.

It is well beyond the scope of this chapter to go into the complex details of how EAs are developed and used by federal agencies. We can, however, say that EAs are being developed by a wide variety of agencies with some degree of success, but not enough success to satisfy GAO audits that find much room for improvement.[38] We can note that the Food and Drug Administration has had some considerable successes with its EA activities.[39] It achieved significant cost savings by consolidating IT functions and eliminating redundant IT-related activities. Its EA is also being used to document and standardize business processes resulting in the streamlining of work. It improves communication within units of the agency and simplifies operational and strategic decision making. It has also improved strategic planning, capital investment control, and control over the systems development life cycles of information systems projects. Other public agencies at all three levels of government could receive the same benefits as the FDA by using enterprise architectures.

Developing and implementing an enterprise architecture for a public agency of any considerable size is a formidable undertaking requiring considerable time, money, and personnel. Yet it can have tremendous benefits. It can provide an agency with a comprehensive inventory of its data and the information systems in which the data is contained. This can lead to the identification of duplicate and redundant data as well as duplicate and redundant information systems within an agency that can subsequently be eliminated to reduce operating costs. It can also identify gaps within an organization where data and information systems are needed to achieve the agency's goals. Most importantly, it provides a holistic and comprehensive view of an agency's data and information systems that can be linked to the agency's lines of business and ultimately its overall mission. As a logical and practical extension of information resource management it goes a long way to achieving the goal of managing an agency's data and information as an important organizational resource. In the next section we will see how IT professionals are taking this one step further to manage not only data and information but also the knowledge contained in modern public organizations.

Knowledge Management

The need for strategic knowledge management initiatives in both public- and private-sector organizations can be summed up in one statement: "Organizations do not know what they know." Stated differently, managers of public agencies do not know what knowledge is contained in their agencies that could be used to make the agency operate more efficiently and effectively.

Consequently, they do not know what they need to know in order to make the organization more successful. In other words, there is a lot of knowledge about the history of an agency, how it operates, why it operates, and how it can operate better that is most often located in the minds of its employees, but management does not really know what that knowledge is, nor does management know how vital it is to the functioning of the agency.

Here is an example from the private sector. A major firm in the business of electronically processing literally millions of credit card transactions each day is looking for a way to cut costs. A decision is made to downsize the organization and lay off a lot of mature computer programmers because they are not knowledgeable about modern software programming languages like C++. The firm soon discovers that the new and younger programmers have little or no knowledge of COBOL programming, which supports the majority of the firm's legacy application software systems. The firm has lost the knowledge base of COBOL programming that supports the major infrastructure of their firm. It tries to hire back the old programmers only to discover that the best of them have been scooped up by other firms, leaving the firm with the only choice of hiring back less-than-the-best COBOL programmers.

Sound implausible? No, it is not, but the firm will not be named. The firm did not know what its employees knew and that placed the firm at a competitive disadvantage within its market domain. Proper attention was not paid to the knowledge that was required to run the business effectively. The federal government, as well as state and local governments, is facing this same problem but in a different way. Its IT workforce is aging and beginning to retire, taking with it valuable knowledge about how agency information systems work. This problem extends not only to IT professionals but also other professionals with specialized and needed knowledge in other functions of government as well. Consider that 46 percent of U.S. government employees are forty-five years old or older, and that 45 percent of the U.S. public employees will be at retirement age within the next five years—hence the need for knowledge management initiatives.[40] However, the aging demographics of the public workforce are not the sole reason for effective knowledge management policies and practices. The rapid growth in specialized knowledge requirements in a variety of professional domains requires effective knowledge management. This is particularly true in government, where the vast majority of workers are knowledge workers.

Various definitions of knowledge management (KM) and knowledge itself exist in the relevant literature. Wikipedia defines knowledge management most generally as referring to "the ways organizations gather, manage, and use the knowledge that they acquire."[41] Wikipedia goes on to explain that "the term also designates an approach to improving organizational outcomes and organizational learning by introducing into an organization a range of specific processes and practices for identifying and capturing knowledge, know-how, expertise and other intellectual capital, and for making such knowledge assets available for transfer and reuse across the organization," and that "knowledge management programs are typically tied to specific organizational objectives and are intended to lead to the achievement of specific targeted results such as improved performance, competitive advantage, or higher levels of innovation."

Understanding what knowledge is exactly is not particularly easy. Consider our very early conversation in chapter 2 when we distinguished between data and information. Recall that data are nothing more than meaningless facts. They do not become information until they are recognized by a person, understood by a person, and placed into a meaningful context in which the person can use the data as information. In a similar sense, information by itself is not knowledge. Knowledge has been defined as "a fluid mix of framed experience, values, contextual information and expert insight that provides a framework for evaluation and incorporating new experiences and information."[42] As such, it is more than just information. It is what people know, to put it simply, but it is still not simple. Consider that Michael Polanyi drew a distinction between explicit and tacit knowledge.[43] Explicit knowledge is what a person knows and can readily communicate to others in a conversation, or perhaps in a professor's lecture, or even in the writing of an article or a book. Tacit knowledge is implicit. It is knowledge of a personal quality that resides in a person and is difficult to articulate. Consider, for example, the type of knowledge that a person has that allows him or her to ride a bicycle. Such knowledge is hard to communicate to others. Although one might be able to write up a set of instructions on how to ride a bicycle, it still takes a special type of knowing to actually learn how to ride a bike. Knowledge management tries to capture both types of knowledge, oftentimes with great difficulty, especially in the case of tacit knowledge.

Knowledge management is not about technology. It is a business or management policy and set of practices that strive to capture the knowledge of the employees of an organization, although this may sometimes be enabled by some forms of technology. In 1997, David J. Skyrme conducted a yearlong study of international best practices in knowledge management in which he found some of the following common KM activities:

- Creation of knowledge databases—best practices, expert directories, and market intelligence.
- Effective information management—gathering, filtering, classifying, and storing.

- Incorporation of knowledge into business processes, for example, through the use of help screens or access to experts from icons.
- Development of knowledge centers—focal points for knowledge and skills and facilitating knowledge flow.
- Reuse of knowledge at customer support centers, for example, via case-based reasoning.
- Introduction of collaborative technologies, especially intranets or group-ware for rapid information access.
- Knowledge webs—networks of experts who collaborate across and beyond an organization's functional and geographic boundaries.
- Augmentation of decision support processes, such as through expert systems or group decision support systems.[44]

In addition to this list of technology-enabled KM practices, there are also socially based initiatives known as communities of practice.[45] These are either informal or formal groups of people who come from a common disciplinary background, similar work activities, or similar skills formed to share their knowledge, experiences, and skills.

It is difficult to get a clear picture of how well or how extensively federal executives have embraced knowledge management practices. One way to get a handle on it is to trace the history of some, but not all, of the news articles appearing in *Government Computer News*, one of the IT industry's major trade papers, focusing on knowledge management.

A November 1999 article reported that "agencies are looking beyond chief information officers to take advantage of the reams of information stored in a multitude of systems. To meet the challenge, some agencies are creating a new post: chief knowledge officer. Knowledge management has been a buzz phrase in industry for more than a year, but it only recently began to take hold in the federal government."[46] The article went on to note that the General Services Administration and the U.S. Coast Guard had both appointed chief knowledge officers (CKOs) and quoted one of them as saying, "Knowledge management is a good development because it changes our focus from tech-nology to how we use information. . . . We can get our hands on technology so people are comfortable with it, but what we really need is the knowledge and focus on what we've learned."[47]

A May 2000 article reported that "knowledge management is moving to the front office, where it should affect customer service in a big way. . . . Knowledge management concept is drawing interest from organizations that want to improve service to the public, as well as those that want to improve service to their own users. . . . Until now, knowledge management had been largely focused on data mining and data warehousing for internal use. But moving it to the front office signals a shift in focus from internal to external services. For government, . . . it [is] a shift from an agency-centric to a customer-centric view."[48]

A November 2000 article announced that the U.S. Army was building a knowledge management portal that will give personnel access to e-mail, real-time collaborative software applications, data warehouses, and subject matter experts.[49] Several later articles tracked the development of the Army's web portal–based KMS.

A March 2001 article began by observing that "knowledge management initiatives are on the upswing as managers at all government levels face mounting pressure to work smarter and faster while wrestling with the demands of electronic government and a shrinking workforce."[50] Oddly enough, on the same day in March of 2001, *Government Computer News* issued a story titled "What Is Knowledge Management?" and offered three very short definitions of it.[51] Obviously the publication thought it was important to define knowledge management for readers who might not be familiar with it.

Then, in April of 2001, an article reported that the U.S. Department of State was working on the development of a global, multiagency network for sharing information and knowledge.[52] Subsequently, the GAO reported on the State Department's development of its KM system and gave it some considerable praise, noting that it greatly facilitates the sharing of knowledge worldwide.[53]

A few other articles followed, noting some KM initiatives and developments, until September of 2001 when an article appeared titled "KM: Difficult to Define But Here to Stay." The article went on to say that "this is not some big, new fad. . . . It's a way of focusing on intellectual capital and how we apply that in this new world where everybody is connected and has access to everything, so there's an exponential increase in data and information. In this new virtual world, how are we going to handle the complexity of decision-making? That's what it's all about."[54] That article also mentioned the fact that the Federal CIO Council's KM working group had recently published a white paper titled "Managing Knowledge @ Work" and noted that the working group now had its own web site, www.km.gov, promoting KM policies and practices. That web site reports on several KM initiatives undertaken by the KM working group, in particular the establishment of several communities of practice so professionals and specialists in several domain areas can share knowledge with one another.

Seventeen other articles followed over the next couple of years, noting a variety of different KM initiatives, until a May 2006 article reported that the market research firm INPUT predicted that federal spending on KM software and hardware will grow from $965 million in fiscal year 2005 to $1.3 billion in fiscal year 2010.[55] That is a relatively small amount of money to spend on KM compared to the federal government's overall spending on information technologies, but it suggests that federal agencies are starting to address the strategic importance of knowledge management.

A final way to get a sense of the federal government's interest in KM policies and practices is to consider some of the strategies for facilitating KM offered in an article published in the February 2006 issue of *Government Technology's Public CIO*.[56] It offers the ten suggestions for "Better Knowledge Management" presented in Exhibit 12.3.

These are well-thought-out guidelines to develop the knowledge management capabilities of federal agencies as they move in yet another way to manage information strategically. They can also apply equally well to state and local government agencies.

Review

This chapter provides a fitting end to this book. A strategic perspective on information management and the management of related technologies covers the full range of topics addressed in this book but at a much higher level of abstraction. Information resource management, CIO policies and activities, enterprise architectures, and knowledge management rely on most of the technologies previously addressed in this book, including hardware, software, decision making systems, telecommunications, the Internet, databases and database management systems, system development methods, ERP, BPR, CRM, procurement of technology solutions, and a concern for the security of information and information systems. The strategic management of information as a vital organizational resource in the public sector begins with the basics of data, moves on to the technologies that store, manipulate, and transform data into useful information, then addresses the public policies as well as the organizational policies and procedures for managing data, information, and knowledge.

As we have seen, the management of information in the public sector can be a very complex matter. The complexity stems from the technology that is involved, which is the realm of highly trained and educated technology experts, to public managers who must effectively manage not only information but related technologies and also the people who support those technologies, and to end users who use the technologies and the information to carry out the work of the agency. Information and its related technologies have, in the minds of some practitioners and academicians, finally become an organizational resource of equal importance in serving the public as are financial, human, and material resources.

Exhibit 12.3
Better Knowledge Management

1. Identify high-risk business processes likely to produce negative outcomes if errors are made or critical employees leave. The critical business processes of an organization are logical places to seek "pain points" needing solutions.
2. Take a user-centric approach to knowledge management. Technology often starts with a structure or methodology requiring users to learn how to take advantage of it. Good KM allows user experience to drive all KM implementations and tailors projects to the way jobs are done.
3. Apply business case analysis methods and information to a KM, to predict its usefulness. The use of authoritative, third-party research can help document return on investment for senior management.
4. Build consensus and ownership. KM initiatives are typically an iterative process, requiring feedback from stakeholders at every major stage of the process. CIOs can align theory and practice by gaining input from stakeholders, including experts, management, technologists, and workers closest to business processes.
5. Identify information users who "do." This means gathering information about how knowledge supports business goals and concluding with knowledge Strengths, Weaknesses, Opportunities, and Threats (SWOT) analysis. To decide which information is valuable, determine what people really want to know rather than what management thinks it needs to know.
6. Identify the knowledge experts who "know." CIOs need to develop a formal process for identifying institutional experts, and discover roles and responsibilities other than those listed in a job description (e.g., a person's job is described as "IT specialist," but her expertise includes professional photography and photo archiving for her region's agency).
7. "Connect people versus collect information" is a false argument. KM pundits often argue whether the resulting knowledge from Communities of Practice (CoPs) is more valuable than codifying knowledge through the collection of best-of-breed documents. In practice, implementing KM requires multiple approaches.
8. Help people find information more easily by structuring it. A taxonomy provides entry and connection points to users: It classifies, structures, and manages information, making it easier to find what

is there. A taxonomy that anticipates user needs and responses, together with a well-designed underlying information architecture, is the infrastructure behind good search results. Reducing time spent searching for information creates a more productive organization.

9. Use technology judiciously to embed KM in the organization. Just-in-time delivery of knowledge changes the existing ways of doing things; it is not a separate activity requiring additional time and effort. When access to knowledge is easy, it becomes intuitive or instinctive and improves performance.

10. Develop metrics and usage statistics to measure success. Test to find out what works and what doesn't. Metrics are critical to evaluate project success/failure, to provide feedback for improvement, or to plan the next phase of a project.

Notes

Notes to Chapter 1

1. This observation is based on firsthand knowledge of the author, who served on several NASPAA committees dealing with common curriculum issues. Older versions of NASPAA's Curriculum Standards can be obtained from NASPAA itself. National Association of Schools of Public Affairs and Administration, 1120 G Street, NW, Suite 730, Washington, DC 20005, Phone: 202.628.8965, Fax: 202.626.4978 naspaa@naspaa.org.

2. NASPAA's Common Curriculum Components Standard 4.21, www.naspaa.org/accreditation/seeking/reference/standards.asp (accessed May 8, 2006).

3. Ellen Perlman, "Technotrouble," in *Governing: Issues and Applications from the Front Lines of Government,* ed. Alan Ehrenhalt (Washington, DC: CQ Press, 2002): 72–76.

4. Ibid., 72.

5. Ibid., 73.

6. W. Wayt Gibbs, "Software's Chronic Crisis," *Scientific American* (September, 1994): 86–97. Tod Newcombe, "Large Project Software Scare," *Government Technology* (December 1, 1995). Available at www.govtech.net/magazine/story.print.php?id=96116 (accessed June 26, 2006).

7. Kirk Johnson, "Denver Airport Saw the Future. It Didn't Work," *The New York Times* (August 27, 2005). Available at www.nytimes.com/2005/08/27/national/27denver.html?ei=5090&en=c1a4a185ddb79852&ex=1282795200&partner=rssuserland&emc=rss&pagewanted=print (accessed June 26, 2006).

8. Newcombe, "Large Project Software Scare."

9. Katherine Barrett and Richard Greene, "Grading the States 1999: A Management Report Card," *The Government Performance Project, Governing.com.* Available at www.governing.com/gpp/1999/gp9intro.htm (accessed June 26, 2006).

10. Ibid.

11. This observation comes from the author's professional experience.

12. Bruce Rocheleau, "Governmental Information System Problems and Failures: A Preliminary Review," *Public Administration and Management: An Interactive Journal,* n.d., 9. Available at www.pamij.com/roche.html (accessed June 26, 2006).

13. Gibbs, "Software's Chronic Crisis," 92.

14. Dan Eggen, "FBI Pushed Ahead with Troubled Software," *Washingtonpost.com* (June 6, 2005): A01. Available at www.washingtonpost.com/wp-dyn/content/article/2005/06/05/AR2005060501213_pf.html (accessed June 26, 2006).

15. Government Performance Project. Available at www.results.gpponline.org/ (accessed May 8, 2006).

16. U.S. General Accounting Office, *Executive Guide: Improving Mission Performance Through Strategic Information Management and Technology: Learning From Leading Organizations* (Washington. DC: GAO, May 1994).

17. See for example some of the following GAO reports on the weaknesses of some executive agency information systems: U.S. General Accounting Office, *Information Technology Investment: Agencies Can Improve Performance, Reduce, Costs, and Minimize Risk* (Washington, DC: GAO, September 30, 1996); U.S. General Accounting Office, *Information Technology Investment Management: A Framework for Assessing and Improving Process Maturity, Exposure Draft* (Washington, DC: GAO, May 2000); U.S. General Accounting Office, *United States Postal Service: Opportunities to Strengthen IT Investment Management Capabilities* (Washington, DC: GAO, October 15, 2002); U.S. General Accounting Office, *Information Technology: DLA Needs to Strengthen Its Investment Management Capability* (Washington, DC: GAO, March 15, 2002); U.S. General Accounting Office, *Information Technology: INS Needs to Strengthen Its Investment Management Capability* (Washington, DC: GAO, December 29, 2000).

18. U.S. Office of Management and Budget Memorandum M-04–08, *Maximizing Use of SmartBuy and Avoiding Duplication of Agency Activities with the President's 24 E-Gov Initiatives* (Washington, DC: OMB, February, 2004). Available at www.whitehouse.gov/omb/memoranda/fy04/m04–08.pdf (accessed May 8, 2006).

19. U.S. General Accounting Office, *Information Technology: Agencies Need to Improve the Accuracy and Reliability of Investment Information* (Washington, DC: GAO, January 12, 2006): 1. Also see the following OMB Press Release: *President's 2006 Information Technology Budget Supports National Priorities And Focuses On Results* (Washington, DC: OMB, February 8, 2006), available at www.whitehouse.gov/omb/pubpress/2005/2005–04.pdf (accessed May 8, 2006).

20. INPUT. "INPUT Forecasts Federal IT Spending to Surpass \$93 Billion by FY11," (March 28, 2006). Available at www.input.com/corp/press/detail.cfm?news=1177 (accessed May 8, 2006).

21. "U.S. State and Local Government Technology Spending on the Rise," *Datamonitor* (August 31, 2005). Available at www.industryanalystreporter.com/research/ News.asp?id=5710 (accessed May 8, 2006).

22. Dibya Sarkar, "State and Local IT Spending on the Rise: After a Dry Spell, Governments Look to Technology," *Federal Computer Week.Com* (September 12, 2005). Available at www.fcw.com/article90731–09–12–05-Print (accessed May 8, 2006).

23. *OASIG Survey,* 1995, available at www.it-cortex.com/Stat_Failure_Rate.htm#The%200ASIG%20Study%20 (accessed on May 8, 2006).

24. *KPMG Canada Survey,* 1997. Available at www.it-cortex.com/Stat_Failure_Rate.htm#The%20KPMG% 20Canada%20Survey%20 (accessed May 8, 2006).

25. *Conference Board Survey,* 2001. Available at www.it-cortex.com/Stat_Failure_Rate.htm#The%20Conference%20Board%20Survey (accessed May 8, 2006).

26. The Standish Group International, *The Chaos Report, 1994* (West Yarmouth, MA: The Standish Group International, Inc., 1994), p. 1. Available at www.standishgroup.com/sample_research/chaos_1994_1.php (accessed May 8, 2006).

27. Ibid., p. 3.

28. Ibid., p. 4.

29. Frank Hayes, "Chaos is Back," *Computerworld* (November 8, 2004). Available at www.computerworld.com/managementtopics/management/project/story/0,10801,97283,00.html (accessed May 8, 2006).

30. Wilson P. Dizzard III, "FBI Plans To Build New Case Management System From Scratch," *Government Computer News* (December 30, 2004). Available at www.gcn.com/online/vol1_no1/31432–1.html (accessed May 7, 2006).

Notes to Chapter 2

1. Jim Gray and Andreas Reuter, *Transaction Processing: Concepts and Techniques* (San Francisco: Morgan Kaufman Publishers, 1993).

2. See generally: Daniel J. Power, *Decision Support Systems: Concepts and Resources for Managers* (Westport, CT: Quorum Books, 2002); Steven Alter, *Decision Support Systems: Current Practice and Continuing Challenge* (Reading, MA: Addison-Wesley, 1980).

3. Ralph H. Sprague and Eric D. Carlson, *Building Effective Decision Support Systems* (Englewood Cliffs, NJ.: Prentice-Hall, 1982).

4. See for example: Jon William Toigo, "Decision Support Systems Make Gains in Government," *Washington Technology* (Washington, DC: May 24, 1999), www.washingtontechnology.com /news/144/tech_features/530–1.html (accessed April 6, 2006); and Victoria Mabin, Malcolm Menzies, Graeme King, and Karen Joyce, "Public Sector Priority Setting Using Decision Support Tools," *Australian Journal of Public Administration,*" 60 (2001): 44–59.

5. For an extended discussion of group decision support systems, see: Paul Gray, "The SMU Decision Room Project," *Transactions of the 1st International Conference on Decision Support Systems* (1981): 135–62; Paul Gray, "Group Decision Support Systems," *Decision Support Systems, The International Journal*, 3 (September 1987): 233–42; Gerardine DeSanctis and R. Brent Gallupe, "A Foundation for the Study of Group Decision Support Systems, *Management Science,* 33 (May, 1987): 589–609; Gerardine DeSanctis and R. Brent Gallupe, "Group Decision Support Systems: A New Frontier," *ACM SIGMIS Database Archive,* 16 (Winter 1984): 3–10; and Leonard M. Jessup and Joseph S. Valacich, eds., *Group Decision Support Systems: New Perspectives* (New York: Macmillan, 1993).

6. State of Colorado's Water Management DSS. Available at www.cdss.state.co.us/index.asp (accessed April 8, 2006).

7. University of Arizona's Cow Culling DSS. Available at www.ag.arizona.edu/AREC/cull/culling.html (accessed April 8, 2006).

8. City College of San Francisco's Student Management DSS. Available at www.research.ccsf.edu/HTM/decision_what.htm (accessed April 8, 2006).

9. Chittenden County Regional Planning Commission (CCRPC) and the Chittenden County Metropolitan Planning Organization (CCMPO) Land use and Transportation DSS. Available at www.ccmpo.org/modeling/dss.html. Available at (accessed April 8, 2006).

10. For a general discussion of executive information systems and their derivation for decision support systems, see: Paul Gray, *Decision Support and Executive Information Systems* (Englewood Cliffs, NJ: Prentice Hall, 1994).

11. Gary H. Anthes, "Notes System Sends Federal Property Data Nationwide," *Computer World* (1994). Available at www.computerworld.com/news/1994/story/ 0,11280,7668,00.html (accessed April 6, 2006).

12. University of Nebraska Medical Center EIS. www.meditech.com (accessed April 6, 2006).

13. These examples were found on the web site of the Department of Computer Science of the University of Indonesia. Available at www.cs.ui.ac.id/ (accessed April 8, 2006).

14. Leo Yonghong Liang and Rowan Miranda, "Dashboards and Scorecards: Executive Information Systems for the Public Sector," *Government Finance Review* (2001): 14–19.

15. Peter F. Drucker, *Landmarks of Tomorrow: A Report on the New "Post-Modern" World* (New York: Harper, 1959).

16. There are many books about expert systems and their relationship to artificial intelligence, many of which are not written with the public manager or layperson in mind.

The following three books provide relatively clear explanations of expert systems and their relation to artificial intelligence: Patrick H. Winston and Karen A. Prendergast, eds. *The AI Business: The Commercial Uses of Artificial Intelligence* (Cambridge: MIT Press, 1984); William B. Gevarter, *Artificial Intelligence, Expert Systems, Computer Vision, and Natural Language Processing* (Park Ridge, NJ: Noyes Publications, 1984); and Robert I. Levine, Diane E. Dranf, and Barry Edelson, *A Comprehensive Guide to AI and Expert Systems* (New York: McGraw-Hill, 1986).

17. "HR eXpert," New South Wales Australia Expert System. Available at www. premiers.nsw.gov.au/hrexpert/hrx.htm (accessed May 12, 2006).

18. "Logist," Israeli Ministry of Finance Expert System. Available at www.mof.gov. il/micun/prof.htm (accessed April 6, 2006). For "Logist" expert system applications in general see the corporate web page of Expert Solutions International. Available at www. esi-knowledge.com/busrules.asp (accessed November 21, 2006). See also the companion web site for the human resource expert system available at www.hrsoftwaredownload. com/workforcemanagement/logist.htm (accessed November 21, 2006).

19. From November of 1999 until May of 2006, there have been 310 news items posted on the web site of *Government Computer News* concerning the initiation and oftentimes troubled implementation of the NMCI. See their web site for a listing of those news items at: www.appserv.gcn.com/cgi-bin/texis/scripts/gcn-search/+lwwFqnNTgfxzmwwxIqFqA5BdGOe6DwwBnmFqnmn5qozmwwxeamww/search.html (accessed April 8, 2006). The Department of the Navy's informational site about the NMCI can be found at www.nmci.navy.mil/ (accessed April 8, 2006). The Electronic Data Systems Corporation's (EDS) informational web site about NMCI can be found at www.eds.com/sites/nmci/ (accessed April 8, 2006).

Notes to Chapter 3

1. Most of the mainstream introductory textbooks on information systems or management information systems classify the types of computers by size, processing speed, and capabilities. See, for example: Uma Gupta, *Information Systems: Success in the 21st Century* (Upper Saddle River, NJ: Prentice-Hall, 2000; Kenneth C. Loudon and Jane P. Loudon, *Essentials of Management Information Systems: Managing the Digital Firm* (Upper Saddle River, NJ: Prentice-Hall, 2003); and Stephen Haag, Maeve Cummings, and James Dawkins, *Management Information Systems for the Information Age* (New York: Irwin/McGraw-Hill, 2000).

2. *Wikipedia, The Free Online Encyclopedia* provides an extensive history of computers along with hardware and software. See: www.en.wikipedia.org/wiki/History_of_computing_hardware (accessed June 8, 2006). There are also several good books detailing the history of computers. Some of them include: Nicholas Metropolis, J. Howlett, and Gian-Carlo Rota, eds., *A History of Computing in the Twentieth Century* (New York: Academic Press, 1980); René Moreau, *The Computer Comes of Age: The People, the Hardware, and the Software* (Cambridge: MIT Press, 1984); and Brian Randell, *The Origins of Digital Computers* (New York: Springer-Verlag, 1982).

3. Doris Langley Moore, *Ada: Countess of Lovelace* (London: John Murray, 1977); Joan Baum, *The Calculating Passion of Ada Byron* (New York: Archon Books, 1986); Betty A. Toole, *Ada, the Enchantress of Numbers* (Mill Valley, CA: Strawberry Press, 1992).

4. C. Thomas Wu, *Introduction to Object-Oriented Programming* (New York: McGraw-Hill, 2004): 2–3.

5. Geoffrey D. Austrian, *Herman Hollerith, Forgotten Giant of Information Processing* (New York: Columbia University Press, 1982).

6. "ENIAC Story." Available at http://ftp.arl.mil/~mike/comphist/eniac-story.html (accessed May 22, 2006).

7. "The Univac." Available at www.csif.cs.ucdavis.edu/~csclub/museum/items/univac.html (accessed May 22, 2006).

8. "History of IBM." Available at www-03.ibm.com/ibm/history/history/history_intro.html (accessed May 22, 2006).

9. "Introduction to Supercomputers." Available at www.thocp.net/hardware/super-computers.htm (accessed May 22, 2006).

10. For a general discussion of programming languages, see: Ruknet Cezzar, *A Guide to Programming Languages: Overview and Comparison* (Boston: Artech House, 1995).

11. Bob Sutor, Director, Web Services Strategy, IBM. 2004. "Something Old, Something New: Integrating Legacy Systems," *EBIZ: The Insider's Guide to Business Integration* (October 18). Available at www.ebizq.net/topics/legacy_integration/features/5229.html (accessed December 6, 2006).

12. See the entry for "operating system" in FOLDOC (*Free On-line Dictionary of Computing*). Available at www.foldoc.org/foldoc.cgi?query=operating+system&action=Search (accessed May 22, 2006).

13. See entry for "system software" in FOLDOC (*Free On-line Dictionary of Computing*), www.foldoc.org/foldoc.cgi?query=system+software&action=Search; see also "System Software" in *Wikipedia, The Free Online Encyclopedia* at www.en.wikipedia.org/wiki/System_software (both accessed May 22, 2006).

14. See: Ed Watson, et al., *ERP Implementation in State Government* (Hershey, PA: Idea Group Pub., 2003); and Fiona Fui-Hoon Nah, *Enterprise Resource Planning: Solutions and Management* (Hershey, PA: IRM Press, 2002).

15. See: "Commercial Off-the-Shelf-Software," from *Wikipedia, The Free Online Encyclopedia*, www.en.wikipedia.org/wiki/Commercial_off-the-shelf (accessed May 22, 2006); and U.S. General Accounting Office, *Information Technology: Selected Agencies' Use of Commercial Off-the-Shelf Software for Human Resources Function* (Washington, DC: GAO, July 2000).

16. Andrew Schiff and Tigineh Mersha, "An Innovative Adaptation of General Purpose Accounting Software for a Municipal Social Services Agency," Case Study #IT5514 (Hershey, PA: Idea Group Publishing, 2000). Available at www.idea-group.com. (accessed May 22, 2006).

17. Ibid., 5–6.

18. For a comprehensive introduction to open source software, see: Stefan Koch, ed., *Free Open Source Software Development* (Hershey, PA: Idea Group, 2005). For a discussion of open source software in the public sector, see: Robert W. Hahn, ed., *Government Policy Toward Open Source Software* (Washington, D.C.: AEI-Brookings Joint Center for Regulatory Studies, 2002).

19. *Open Source Initiative*, www.opensource.org/ (accessed May 22, 2006).

20. John McCormick, "Power User: For Agencies, It's Firefox No, Openoffice Yes," *Government Computer News* (May 15, 2005). Available at www.gcn.com/print/24_11/35780–1.html (accessed May 22, 2006).

21. Rishi Sood, "Across the Digital Nation: U.S. Watches World Governments Try Open Source Software," *Washington Technology* (Washington, DC: September 1, 2003). Available at www.washingtontechnology.com/news/18_11/statelocal/21583–1.html (accessed May 22, 2006).

22. IDABC, *Chinese Government Opts For Open Source Software* (November 21, 2005). Found at: www.europa.eu.int/idabc/en/document/5138/469 (accessed May 22, 2006). IDABC stands for "Interoperable Delivery of European eGovernment Services to

Public Administrations, Businesses and Citizens." It is a community program managed by the European Commission's Enterprise and Industry Directorate General.

23. The FLOSS study and report can be found at www.infonomics.nl/FLOSS/report/index.htm (accessed May 22, 2006).

24. William Welsh, "State, Local Government Warm to Open Source Research Firm Finds," *Government Computer News* (June 17, 2005). Available at www.appserv.gcn.com/cgi-bin/udt/im.display.printable?client.id=gen_daily&story.id=36115 (accessed May 22, 2006). See also: Joab Jackson, "Open Source Software in Government," *Washington Technology* (October 30, 2003). Available at www.washingtontechnology.com/news/forum/forums/22028–1.html (accessed May 22, 2006).

25. Jay Layman, "Open Source Winning in Federal Government, Slowly," *NewsForge: The Online Newspaper for Linux and Open Source* (July 28, 2004). Available at www.trends.newsforge.com/article.pl?sid=04/07/23/2335201 &tid=152&tid=136&tid =110&tid=91 (accessed May 22, 2006).

26. U.S. Office of Management and Budget Memorandum M-04–16. *Federal Procurement Policy* (Washington DC: July 1, 2004).

27. Welsh, "State, Local Government Warm to Open Source Research Firm Finds.".

28. William Welsh, "Mass. Open Standards Official," *Washington Technology* (January 14, 2004). Available at www.washingtontechnology.com/news/1_1/daily_news/22524–1.html (accessed May 22, 2006).

Notes to Chapter 4

1. For a comprehensive introduction and overview of databases and database management systems see: Raghu Ramakrishnan and Johannes Gehrke, *Database Management Systems* (New York: McGraw-Hill, 2002); and Donald K. Burleson, *Inside the Database Object Model* (Boca Raton, FL: CRC Press, 1999).

2. W. Frawley, G. Piatetsky-Shapiro, and C. Matheus, "Knowledge Discovery in Databases: An Overview," *AI Magazine* (Fall 1992): 213–28.

3. Phillip Britt, "Trends in Database Management Systems Technology," *Information Today* 23 (May 2006): 1–20.

4. Jan L. Harrington, *Relational Database Design Clearly Explained* (New York: Morgan Kaufmann Publishers, 2002).

5. For a general introduction and explanation of object-oriented programming, see: James Keogh and Mario Giannini, *OOP Demystified* (New York: McGraw-Hill/Osborne, 2004).

6. R.C. Goldstein and J. B. McCririck, "What Do Data Administrators Really Do?" *Datamation* 26 (August 1980): 131–34.

7. Arizona State University, "Policy on data administration." Available at www.asu.edu/data_admin/data_administration.htm (accessed June 8, 2006).

8. Forest Service of British Columbia, Canada, "Purposes and Principles of Data Administration." Available at www.for.gov.bc.ca/his/datadmin/dapurp.htm (accessed June 8, 2006).

9. For a general introduction to online analytical programming, data warehouses, and data mining, see: Surajit Chaudhuri and Umeshwar Dayal, "An Overview of Data Warehousing and OLAP Technology," *ACM SIGMOD* 26 (March 1997): 65–74, www.doi.acm.org/10.1145/248603.248616 (accessed May 26, 2006)

10. Frawley, Piatetsky-Shapiro, and Matheus, 214.

11. "Data Miners: New Software Instantly Connects Key Bits of Data that Once Eluded Teams of Researchers," *Time Magazine*. (December 23, 2002). Available at www.time.com/time/globalbusiness/article/0,9171,1101021223-400017,00.html (accessed June 13, 2006).

12. U.S. Governmental Accountability Office, *Data Mining: Federal Efforts Cover a Wide Range of Uses* (Washington, DC: GAO, May 2004).

13. Tod Newcombe, "Opening the Doors to the Data Warehouse," *Government Technology* (October 1, 1995). Available at www.govtech.net/magazine/story.php?id=96051&issue=10:1995 (accessed May 26, 2006).

14. Tod Newcombe, "Planting Data Gardens," *Government Technology* (April 6, 2002). Available at www.govtech.net/magazine/story.php?id=8093 &issue=2:2002 (accessed May 26, 2006).

15. Ibid.

16. Alan Day, "Government Technology: Data Warehouses," *American City & County. Com* (Jan 1, 2004). Available at www.americancityandcounty.com/mag/government_data_warehouses/index.html (accessed May 26, 2006).

17. GAO, *Data Mining*, 8.

18. The home page for the Electronic Privacy Information Center can be found at: www.epic.org/ (accessed May 26, 2006).

19. From EPIC's web pages, www.epic.org/privacy/profiling/tia/ (accessed May 26, 2006).

20. Ibid.

21. Multistate Anti-Terrorism Information Exchange. Available at www.fdle.state. fl.us/press_releases/20050415_matrix_project.html (accessed May 26, 2006).

22. Jeffrey W. Seifert, "Data Mining and Homeland Security: An Overview," *CRS Report for Congress* (Washington, DC: Congressional Research Service, January 27, 2006): 21.

23. Ibid., 22.

24. EPIC, www.epic.org/privacy/budget/fy2006/ (accessed May 26, 2006).

25. See ChoicePoint's web site, www.choicepointgov.com/strategic.htm (accessed May 26, 2006).

Notes to Chapter 5

1. For basic definitions of telecommunications, see: "Telecommunications," *Wikipedia, The Free Encyclopedia*, www.en.wikipedia.org/wiki/Telecommunications (accessed May 27, 2006) and "Telecommunications," *Webopedia*, www.webopedia.com/TERM/t/tele-communications.html (accessed May 27, 2006). The following books provide the basics of telecommunications: George Reynolds, *Introduction to Business Telecommunications* (Columbus, OH: Charles E. Merrill Publishing Company, 1984); and Annabel Z. Dodd, *The Essential Guide to Telecommunications* (Upper Saddle River, NJ: Prentice Hall, 2002).

2. Information about how telephones work was obtained from Marshall Brain, "How Telephones Work," in *Howstuffworks*, www.howstuffworks.com/telephone.htm, n.d. (accessed on May 27, 2006); Arthur C. Clarke, et al., eds., *The Telephone's First Century—And Beyond: Essays on the Occasion of the 100th Anniversary of Telephone Communication* (New York: Crowell, 1977); and Herbert N. Casson, *The History of the Telephone* (1910; reprint, Fairfield, IA: 1st World Library, 2004).

3. "Europe #1 in Per Capita Cell Phone Usage." 2006. Press release (February 28). Arlington Heights, IL: Computer Industry Almanac, Inc. Available at www.c-i-a.com/pr0206.htm (accessed on May 27, 2006); and Bradley Johnson, "Wireless Generation Eager for Innovation," *Television Week* 25 (March 27, 2006): 20.

4. For a discussion of disruptive technologies see: Clayton M. Christensen, *The Innovator's Dilemma* (New York: Harpers Business, 1997); and Clayton M. Christensen and Michael E. Raynor, *The Innovator's Solution* (Boston: Harvard Business School Press, 2003).

5. For a discussion of how cellular phones function see: Ian Poole, *Cellular Com-*

munications Explained: From Basics to 3G (London: Elsevier Science and Technology Books, March 2006); and Julia Layton, Marshall Brain, and Jeff Tyson, "How Cell Phones Work," *Howstuffworks.com*, n.d. Available at www.howstuffworks.com/cell-phone.htm (accessed on May 27, 2006).

6. Edmund X. DeJesus, "Handhelds Rival Laptops—But Choose Carefully," *Washington Technology* 20 (February 7, 2005). Available at www.washingtontechnology. com/news/20_3/emerging-tech/25469-1.html (accessed May 27, 2006).

7. For a detailed discussion of the basics of telecommunications, see: Roger L. Freeman, *Telecommunication System Engineering* (Hoboken, NJ: Wiley-Interscience, 2004); and Jeff Rutenbeck, *Tech Terms: What Every Telecommunications and Digital Media Professional Should Know* (London: Elsevier Science and Technology Books, 2006). The detailed facts about the technologies associated with telecommunication systems were drawn from these two sources.

8. "Local Area Network," www.webopedia.com/TERM/l/local_area_network_LAN. html (accessed May 27, 2006) and "Wireless Local Area Network," www.webopedia. com/TERM/W/WLAN.html (accessed May 27, 2006).

9. Ray Panko, *Business Data Networks and Telecommunications* (Upper Saddle River, NJ: Prentice Hall, 2006).

10. "Protocols," www.webopedia.com/TERM/p/protocol.html (accessed May 27, 2006). Also see E. Byran Carne, *A Professional's Guide to Data Communications in a TCP/IP World* (Norwood, MA: Artech House, 2004).

11. "Ethernet," www.webopedia.com/TERM/E/Ethernet.html (accessed May 27, 2006). Also see: Gilbert Held, *Ethernet Networks: Design, Implementation, Operation, Management* (New York: John Wiley & Sons, 2003).

12. "Servers," www.webopedia.com/TERM/s/server.html (accessed May 27, 2006). Also see: René J. Chevance, *Server Architectures: Multiprocessors, Clusters, Parallel Systems, Web Servers, Storage Solutions* (London: Elsevier Science and Technology Books, 2004).

13. "Network Typologies," www.webopedia.com/TERM/n/network.html (accessed on May 27, 2006). For an extended discussion of network architectures, see: James D. McCabe, *Network Analysis, Architecture and Design* (San Francisco: Morgan Kaufmann Publishers, 2003).

14. Rohit Rampal, "Design and Implementation of a Wide Area Network: Technological and Managerial Issues," Case Study #T2525 (Hershey, PA: Idea Group Publishing, 2002). Available at www.idea-group.com (accessed on May 22, 2006).

15. For an explanation of intranet technology see: D. Keith Denton, *Empowering Intranets to Implement Strategy, Build Teamwork, and Manage Change* (Westport, CT: Praeger, 2002).

16. Meeta Gupta, *Building a Virtual Private Network* (Cincinnati, OH: Premier Press, 2003).

17. Tony Zecca, "Pilot Program Shares the Cost of Personal Cell Phones for Government Use," *Access America E-Gov E-Zine*, n.d. Available at www.govinfo.library.unt. edu/accessamerica/docs/mobilecommunications.html, 1–3 (accessed May 29, 2006).

18. Ibid., 3.

19. "The Lowdown on VOIP," *Government Computer News* (January 10, 2005). Available at www.gcn.com/print/24_1/34754-1.html (accessed May 27, 2006).

20. Olivier Hersent, Jean-Pierre Petit, and David Gurle, *Beyond VoIP Protocols: Understanding Voice Technology and Networking Techniques for IP Telephony* (Hoboken, NJ: John Wiley, 2005).

21. William Jackson, "Census Bureau Runs VOIP over Upgraded, High-Quality Network," *Government Computer News* (March 21, 2005). Available at www.gcn.com/ print/24_6/35292-1.html (accessed May 27, 2006).

22. Brad Grimes, "Defense Department Certifies Cisco VoIP," *Washington Technology* (September 27, 2004), www.washingtontechnology.com/news/1_1/defense/24628-1.html (accessed May 27, 2006).

23. Brad Grimes, "With Wireless, It's Good to Learn from Others," *Government Computer News* (July 25, 2005). Available at www.gcn.com/print/24_20/36441-1.html (accessed May 27, 2006).

24. Dan Tynan, "Arizona Hears the Call of IP Telephony," *Government Computer News* (August 29, 2005). Available at www.gcn.com/print/24_25/36789-1.html (accessed May 27, 2006).

25. Corey McKenna, "Internet Telephony Keeps Baton Rouge Hospital in Touch When Hurricane Hits," *Government Technology* (August 2005). Available at www.govtech.net/digitalcommunities/story.php?id=96493 (accessed May 27, 2006).

26. "Voice over Internet Protocol," Federal Communications Commission. Available at www.fcc.gov/voip/ (accessed May 27, 2006).

27. William Jackson, "Carriers Need More Time to Develop Ways to Find, Map 911 Call Locations," *Government Computer News* (August 13, 2001). Available at www.gcn.com/print/20_23/16770-1.html (accessed May 27, 2006).

28. U.S. Government Accountability Office, *Telecommunications: Uneven Implementation of Wireless Enhanced 911 Raises Prospect of Piecemeal Availability for Years to Come* (Washington, DC: GAO, November 2003): 11–12.

29. William Jackson, "Nebraska City Extends Wired Municipal Network," *Government Computer News* (September 22, 2004). Available at www.gcn.com/online/vol1_no1/27376-1.html (accessed May 27, 2006).

30. Thomas Davies, "Eye on the States: Lessons in Wireless from the Little Guys," *Washington Technology* 19 (November 8, 2004). Available at www.washingtontechnology.com/news/19_16/statelocal/24922-1.html (accessed May 27, 2006).

31. "Grand Haven Goes WiFi," *Washington Technology* 19(10) (August 16, 2004). Available at www.washingtontechnology.com/news/19_10/datastream/24223-1.html (accessed May 27, 2006).

32. Brad Grimes, "Philly's Wireless Network Rolls On," *Government Computer News* (June 8, 2005). Available at www.gcn.com/online/vol1_no1/36017-1.html (accessed May 27, 2006).

33. "City of Alexandria Launches 'Wireless Alexandria,'" *Government Technology* (August 26, 2005). Available at www.govtech.net/magazine/channel_story.php/96394 (accessed on May 27, 2006).

34. See Intel's web site for more information about their promotion of "Digital Communities." Available at www.intel.com/business/bss/industry/government/digital-communities.htm (accessed on May 27, 2006).

35. Trudy Walsh, "New Bill Would Aid Municipal Broadband Nets," *Government Computer News* (August 26, 2005). Available at www.gcn.com/print/24_17/36283-1.html (accessed on May 27, 2006).

Notes to Chapter 6

1. Walt Howe, "A Brief History of the Internet" (last updated on November 7, 2005). Available at www.walthowe.com/navnet/history.html (accessed May 30, 2006).

2. Sources of information about the Internet are plentiful. The following book is quite informative: J. R. Okin, *The Internet Revolution: The Not-for-Dummies Guide to the History, Technology, and Use of the Internet* (Winter Harbor, ME: Ironbound Press, 2005). The World Wide Web is also an excellent source of information about the history of the Internet, especially the web site of the Internet Society (ISOC), which contains the

following detailed history of the Internet: Barry M. Leiner, et al., *A Brief History of the Internet*, www.isoc.org/internet/history/brief.shtml (accessed May 30, 2006).

3. For a concise history of the WWW and Tim Berners-Lee's involvement in its development, along with numerous links to additional web pages about the history of the Internet and the WWW, see Wikipedia's article on the World Wide Web. www.en.wikipedia.org/wiki/World_Wide_Web (accessed May 30, 2006).

4. For information about Internet Relay Chat (IRC) see: David Caraballo and Joseph Lo, *The IRC Prelude, version 1.1.5*, updated June 1, 2000. Available at www.irchelp.org/irchelp/new2irc.html (accessed May 29, 2006).

5. For a discussion of USENET, see Wikipedia's article on USENET located at: www.en.wikipedia.org/wiki/Usenet (accessed May 30, 2006).

6. For information about the Internet Corporation for Assigned Names and Numbers (ICANN), visit their web page: www.icann.org/ (accessed May 30, 2006).

7. For further information about the Internet Engineering Task Force (IETF), see their web page at www.ietf.org/ (accessed May 30, 2006).

8. Ibid.

9. Internet Society (ISOC): www.isoc.org/isoc/mission/principles/ (accessed May 29, 2006).

10. Ibid.

11. For information about the W3C, see their web site: www.w3.org/ (accessed May 29, 2006).

12. *Internet World Stats: Usage and Population Statistics*. Available at www.internet-worldstats.com/stats.htm (accessed May 29, 2006).

13. Darrell M. West, *Global E-Government, 2005*. Available at www.insidepolitics.org/egovt05int.pdf (accessed May 29, 2006).

14. Ibid., 3.

15. Accenture, *eGovernment Leadership: High Performance, Maximum Value*, 2004. Available at www.accenture.com/Global/Research_and_Insights/By_Industry/Government/HighValue.htm (accessed May 29, 2006).

16. Ibid., 9.

17. United Nations, *UN Global E-government Readiness Report 2005: From E-government to E-inclusion*, UNPAN/2005/14 (New York: United Nations): xi–xiii.

18. U.S. Office of Management and Budget, *E-Government Strategy,* 2002. Available at www.whitehouse.gov/omb/inforeg/egovstrategy.pdf (accessed May 29, 2006).

19. Ibid., 5.

20. Ibid., 15.

21. Ibid., 4.

22. State and Local Government on the Net, www.state localgov.net (accessed May 29, 2006); and FirstGov, www.firstgov.gov/ (accessed May 29, 2006).

23. Darrell M. West, *State and Federal E-Government in the United States, 2005*. Available at www.insidepolitics.org/egovt05us.pdf (accessed May 29, 2006).

24. Ibid., 4.

25. Ibid., 4.

26. Ibid., 3.

27. Ibid., 3.

28. Thomas B. Riley, "eDemocracy in a Changing World," *EGov Monitor* (August 12, 2002). Available at www.egovmonitor.com/features/rileyA.html (accessed May 29, 2006).

29. There are many web sites devoted to e-democracy in Switzerland. The following are just a few of the more informative ones. See: "E-Democracy." *BBC World Home Page* (December 18, 2003), www.bbcworld.com/content/clickonline_archive_50_2003.asp?pageid=666&co_pageid=3 (accessed May 29, 2006); "E-Democracy Center," www.

lake-geneva.net/Telecom/FHomePageTelecom.aspx?tokenPage=v2nIFkxE2WMid4vCSp-0xLs1WaY8xxt9j0TmAQHDaKw%29%29 (accessed May 29, 2006); Swiss Politics.org, www.swisspolitics.org/en/links/index.php?page=links&catid=53&linktopcat=demokratie (accessed May 29, 2006).

30. The original Minnesota E-Democracy site has been merged into a larger e-democracy site comprising many political jurisdictions domestic and foreign. It can be found at www.e-democracy.org/. The Minnesota specific site can be found at www.e-democracy.org/mn-politics/ (accessed May 29, 2006).

31. R. Michael Alvarez and Thad E. Hall, *Point, Click, and Vote: The Future of Internet Voting* (Washington, DC: Brookings Institution Press, 2004).

32. The Secure Electronic Registration and Voting Experiment (SERVE) was an experimental Internet-based voting system built for the U.S. Department of Defense's FVAP (Federal Voting Assistance Program). The program's web site was at www.serveusa.gov/, but because SERVE was never implemented, the web site was eventually taken down.

33. David Jefferson, et al., *A Security Analysis of the Secure Electronic Registration and Voting Experiment (SERVE)* (January 21, 2004). Available at www.servesecurityreport.org/paper.pdf, 2–3 (accessed May 29, 2006).

34. The full report of the California Internet Voting Task Force where these recommendations are found is located at the following web page: www.ss.ca.gov/executive/ivote/ (accessed May 29, 2006).

35. See: "CH: Internet Referendum Successfully Held in Switzerland." *eGovernment News* (September 28, 2004), ec.europa.eu/idabc/en/document/3311; and *Kable: Public Sector Research, Publishing, and Events Services*, "Swiss Roll Out E-vote." (September 21, 2004), www.kablenet.com/kd.nsf/Frontpage/22756CE2CE33701180256F16003918D6?OpenDocument (both accessed May 29, 2006).

36. "Information Rich and Information Poor," *BBC News*. Available at www.news.bbc.co.uk/1/hi/special_report/1999/10/99/information_rich_information_poor/466651.stm) (accessed May 29, 2006).

37. National Telecommunications and Information Administration, *Falling Through the Net* (Washington, DC: U.S. Department of Commerce, 1998), xiii. Available at www.ntia.doc.gov/ntiahome/fttn99/FTTN.pdf (accessed May 29, 2006).

38. Mark Cooper, *Expanding the Digital Divide and Falling Behind on Broadband: Why a Telecommunications Policy of Neglect Is Not Benign*, Washington, DC: Consumer Federation of America and Consumers Union (October 2004): www.consumersunion.org/pub/ddnewbook.pdf: 2 (accessed May 29, 2006).

39. Ibid.

40. Ibid., p 1.

41. Lennard G. Kruger and Angele A. Gilroy, *Broadband Internet Access and the Digital Divide: Federal Assistance Programs* (Washington, DC: Congressional Research Service, January 17, 2006), i. Available at www.usembassy.it/pdf/other/RL30719.pdf (accessed June 16, 2006).

42. National Telecommunications and Information Administration, *A Nation Online: Entering the Broadband Age* (Washington, DC: U.S. Department of Commerce, 2004). Available at www.ntia.doc.gov/reports/anol/NationOnlineBroadband04.pdf (accessed May 29, 2006).

Notes to Chapter 7

1. The "waterfall" method of systems development and implementation, also known as the systems development life cycle (SDLC), has been around for a long time. For a

comprehensive overview of this and other approaches to systems development and implementation, see: James A. Senn, *Analysis and Design of information Systems* (New York: McGraw-Hill Book Company, 1984).

2. U.S. Department of Justice (DOJ), *The Department of Justice Systems Development Life Cycle Guidance Document* (Washington, DC: Department of Justice, Justice Management Division, January 2003). Available at www.usdoj.gov/jmd/irm/lifecycle/table.htm (accessed May 30, 2006).

3. Ibid., chapter 1, section 1.3.

4. The Standish Group International, *The Chaos Report*, p. 3.

5. John A. Benamati and Ram Pakath, "Mismanaging a Technology Project: The Case of A.B.C., Inc." Case No. IT5565 (Hershey, PA: Idea Group Publishing, n.d.). Available at www.idea-group.com/ (accessed May 8, 2006).

6. Winston W. Royce, "Managing the Development of Large Software Systems: Concepts and Techniques," *Proceedings of IEEE WESCON* (August 1970): 1–9. Reprinted in *Proceedings of the 9th International Conference on Software Engineering* (Monterey, CA: International Conference on Software Engineering, 1987): 328–38.

7. Prototyping as an alternative approach to systems development was introduced in the early to mid-1980s. Credit for introducing the idea of prototyping is frequently given to Barry W. Boehm. See his seminal article: Barry W. Boehm, "A Spiral Model of Software Development and Enhancement," *ACM SIGSOFT Software Engineering Notes* 11 (August 1986): 14–24. Also see: Marius A. Janson and L. Douglas Smith, "Prototyping for Systems Development: A Critical Appraisal," *MIS Quarterly* (December 1985): 305–16; Kenneth E. Lantz, *The Prototyping Methodology* (Upper Saddle River, NJ: Prentice Hall, 1986); and Daniel E. Klingler, "The Ten Commandments of Prototyping," *Journal of Information System Management* (Summer 1988): 66–72.

8. Rapid applications development (RAD) was developed in part by James Martin. See his seminal work: James Martin, *Rapid Application Development* (Upper Saddle River, NJ: Prentice Hall, 1991). Also see: Malcolm Eva, "Requirements Acquisition for Rapid Applications Development," *Information & Management* 39 (2002): 101–9.

9. The small informal group of software developers and engineers turned into a non-profit company called Agile Alliance (www.agilealliance.com, accessed May 31, 2006). For an explanation of how the agile approach works, see: Kevin Aguanno, ed., *Managing Agile Projects* (Lakefield, Ontario: Multi-Media Publications, Inc., 2004).

10. Kent. Beck, *Extreme Programming Explained: Embrace Change* (Boston: Addison-Wesley, 1999).

11. Matt Stephens and Doug Rosenberg, *Extreme Programming Refactored: The Case Against XP* (Berkeley, CA: Apress, 2003).

12. University of Texas at Austin, Human Resource Services, "Joint Application Development (JAD)—What Do You Really Want?" Available at www.utexas.edu/ecs/trecs/hris/pub/jad.php#what(accessed May 31, 2006).

13. Alistair Sutcliffe and Nikolay Mehandjiev, "End-User Development," *Communication of the ACM* 47 (September 2004): 31–32.

14. Megan Santosus, "Application Development. Making It on Their Own. End User Developers Are Everywhere. The Key Is Getting Them to Work for You," *CIO Magazine* (May 15, 2005). Available at www.cio.com/archive/051505/et_article.html (accessed May 31, 2006).

15. Jack Cooper and Matthew Fisher, eds. *Software Acquisition Capability Maturity Model* (SA-CMM) Version 1.03, CMU/SEI-2002-TR-010, ESC-TR-2002–010 (Pittsburgh, PA: Carnegie Mellon Software Engineering Institute, March 2002).

16. Christine B. Tayntor, *Successful Packaged Software Implementation* (Boca Raton, FL: Auerbach Publications, 2006).

Notes to Chapter 8

1. For a general introduction to enterprise resource planning (ERP), see: Ellen F. Monk and Bret J. Wagner, *Concepts in Enterprise Resource Planning* (Boston: Thomson Course Technology, 2006); and Daniel Edmund O'Leary, *Enterprise Resource Planning Systems: Systems, Life Cycle, Electronic Commerce, and Risk* (Cambridge: Cambridge University Press, 2000).

2. Data Management Group, www.datamanagementgroup.com/PublicSector/Public-Sector.asp (accessed June 15, 2006).

3. SAP, www.sap.com/usa/industries/publicsector/index.epx (accessed June 15, 2006).

4. Lisa Terry, "Feds, States Lean on ERP as E-Gov Pillar," *Washington Technology* 15(3) (September 9, 2000): 1. Available at www.washingtontechnology.com/news/15_13/cover/1804–1.html (accessed June 15, 2006).

5. INPUT, "Federal ERP Spending to Grow 37 Percent by 2009," (August 23, 2004). Available at www.input.com/corp/community/detail.cfm?news=959 (accessed June 15, 2006).

6. Ed Watson, et al., "ERP Implementation in State Government," *Annals of Cases on Information Technology* 5 (Hershey, PA: Idea Group Publishing, 2003).

7. Ibid.

8. William Wagner and Yvonne L. Antonucci, "An Analysis of the Imagine PA Public Sector ERP Project" *Proceedings of the 37th Hawaii International Conference on System Sciences* (2004): 1–8. Also see the official web site of Imagine PA, located at the Commonwealth of Pennsylvania's Office of Administration, www.ies.state.pa.us/imaginepa/cwp/view.asp?a=4&Q=125583&PM=1 (accessed June 15, 2006).

9. Marc Songini, "Arkansas Set to Pull the Plug on ERP-driven Budgeting Approach," *Computerworld* (February 7, 2005). Available at www.computerworld.com/softwaretopics/erp/story/0,10801,99578,00.html (accessed June 15, 2006).

10. Ibid.

11. As reported by Christopher Koch in, "The ABCs of ERP," *CIO.com,* n.d. Available at www.cio.com/research/erp/edit/erpbasics.html#erp_costs (accessed June 15, 2006).

12. Michael Hammer and James Champy, *Reengineering the Corporation: A Manifesto for Business Revolution* (New York: HarperCollins, 1993): 32.

13. Quoted in "Reengineering: A Radical Approach to Business Process Redesign," www.dod.mil/comptroller/icenter/learn/reeng.htm: 3 (accessed June 15, 2006). Original source: Sharon L. Caudle, *Reengineering for Results: Keys to Success from Government Experience* (Washington, DC: National Academy of Public Administration, 1995). Available at www.71.4.192.38/NAPA/NAPAPubs.nsf/17bc036fe939efd685256951004e37f4/1fb41dbc8efe764c85256886007eb48f/$FILE/94-11-Reengineering+for+Results.pdf (accessed June 15, 2006).

14. Paul A. Strassmann, "The Hocus-Pocus of Reengineering," *Across the Board* (June 1994), 35–38. Available at www.strassmann.com/pubs/hocus-pocus.html (accessed June 15, 2006).

15. U.S. General Accounting Office, *Reengineering Organizations: Results of a GAO Symposium* (Washington, DC: GAO, Dec. 13, 1994): 2.

16. Ibid., 10.

17. U.S. General Accounting Office, *Business Process Reengineering Assessment Guide* (Washington, DC: GAO, 1997): 10.

18. Ibid., 3–4.

19. Prosci Reengineering Learning Center On-Line, "Recommended Approach," n.d. Available at www.prosci.com/project-planning.htm (accessed June 15, 2006).

20. The Virginia Department of Social Services, "The Virginia Social Services System (VSSS)." Available at www.dss.virginia.gov/about/bpr/index.cgi (accessed June 15, 2006).

21. Ibid., 8.

22. The document can be found in PDF form at: www.dss.virginia.gov/about/bpr/files/deliverables/as_is_report/deliverable.pdf (accessed June 15, 2006).

23. David Myron, "CRM.GOV: No Longer the Bailiwick of the Private Sector, CRM is a Prime Focus of Government Agencies," *Destination CRM* (July 1, 2004). Available at www.destinationcrm.com/print/default.asp?ArticleID=4187 (accessed June 15, 2006).

24. Colin Beasty, "The City of Indianapolis Turns to Citizen Relationship Management," *Destination CRM* (March 15, 2005). Available at www.destinationcrm.com/articles/default.asp?articleid=4957 (accessed June 15, 2006).

25. Joshua Weinberger, "School Districts Use CRM to Balance the Needs of Their Constituents," *Destination CRM* (August 2, 2004). Available at www.destinationcrm.com/articles/default.asp?articleid=4282 (accessed June 15, 2006).

26. Myron, "CRM.GOV," see note 23.

27. SAP, *Port of San Diego: mySAP™ CRM Enables a Vision of World-Class Customer Service and Drives Excellence in Public Service.* n.d. Available at www.sap.com/industries/publicsector/pdf/CS_Port_San_Diego.pdf (accessed June 15, 2006).

Notes to Chapter 9

1. Privacy is notoriously difficult to define precisely in any meaningful way. *The American Heritage Dictionary of the English Language* (fourth edition, 2000) defines privacy narrowly to mean:

1a. The quality or condition of being secluded from the presence or view of others.
   b. The state of being free from unsanctioned intrusion: a person's right to privacy.
2. The state of being concealed; secrecy.

The definition presented here is expanded to cover a wider range of information technology issues. This is not inconsistent with other treatments of privacy in academic literature. For example, see: Frederick Lane, *The Naked Employee: How Technology Is Compromising Workplace Privacy* (New York: AMACOM, 2003); William S. Hubbartt, *The New Battle Over Workplace Privacy: How Far Can Management Go? What Rights Do Employees Have? Safe Practices to Minimize Conflict, Confusion, and Litigation* (New York: AMACOM, 1998); and Ellen Alderman and Caroline Kennedy, *The Right to Privacy* (New York: Vintage Books, 1997).

2. Background information on privacy rights in general can be found on the web site of Privacy International, especially a discussion of the difference between comprehensive laws and sectoral laws that govern a citizen's right to privacy, at www.privacyinternational.org/article.shtml?cmd[347]=x-347-82589 (accessed June 20, 2006).

3. Ibid.

4. The City of Los Angeles' "Internet Policies and Guidelines." Available at www.ci.la.ca.us/policy/intpolgu.htm (accessed June 20, 2006).

5. The Commonwealth of Virginia's formal policy on Internet and e-mail usage can be found at: www.vsdbs.virginia.gov/VSDB_IT_Acceptable_Use_Policy.pdf: 2 (accessed June 20, 2006).

6. Ibid.

7. Ibid.

8. Federal CIO Council, *Recommended Executive Branch Model Policy/Guidance on "Limited Personal Use" of Government Office Equipment Including Information Technology* (1999). Available at www.cio.gov/documents/peruse_model_may_1999.pdf (accessed June 20, 2006).

9. Ibid.

10. The American Telecommuting Association's definition of telecommuting and its list of advantages are located at: www.knowledgetree.com/ata-adv.html (accessed June 20, 2006).

11. The background material on telecommunicating was taken from Vaishali Punamchand Vora and Hani S. Mahmassani, *Development and Implementation of a Telecommuting Evaluation Framework, and Modeling the Executive Telecommuting Adoption Process* (Austin, TX: Center for Transportation Research, Bureau of Engineering Research, University of Texas at Austin, February 2002).

12. University of South Florida, *Public Sector Telework Sample Policies and Agreements* Available at www.nctr.usf.edu/clearinghouse/teleworksamples.htm.

13. State of Arizona Telework Program. Available at www.teleworkarizona.com (accessed June 20, 2006).

14. Ibid.

15. State of Florida, Department of Management Services, "Telecommuting Checklist for the Home Office." Available at www.dms.myflorida.com/dms/media/hrm_files/state_employee_telecommuting_program/telecommuting_checklist_for_the_home_office (accessed June 20, 2006).

16. Gil E. Gordon, *The OSHA Episode: How Molehills Become Mountains* (January 29, 2000). Available at www.gilgordon.com/telecommuting/osha.html (accessed June 20, 2006).

17. Gil E. Gordon, "Suggestions for Employers" (January 29, 2000). Available at www.gilgordon.com/telecommuting/osha_suggestion.html (accessed June 20, 2006).

18. International Ergonomics Association, www.iea.cc/ergonomics/ (accessed June 20, 2006).

19. Research suggests that there may be only a very tenuous link between carpal tunnel syndrome and computer use. See: A. Hedge, "Computer Use and Risk of Carpal Tunnel Syndrome," *JAMA* 290 (14) 2003: 1854; and J. C. Stevens, et al., "The Frequency of Carpal Tunnel Syndrome in Computer Users at a Medical Facility," *Neurology* 56 (11) (2001): 1568–70.

20. U.S. Department of Labor, Occupational Safety and Health Administration, "Computer Workstations: Good Working Positions," n.d. Available at www.osha.gov/SLTC/etools/computerworkstations/positions.html (accessed June 20, 2006).

Notes to Chapter 10

1. Steven L. Schooner, "Desiderata: Objectives for a System of Government Contract Law," *Public Law and Legal Theory Working Paper No. 37* (Washington, DC: George Washington University Law School, 2002).

2. Phillip J. Cooper, *Governing by Contract: Challenges and Opportunities for Public Managers* (Washington, DC: CQ Press, 2003).

3. Jocelyn M. Johnston, Barbara S. Romzek, and Curtis H. Wood, "The Challenges of Contracting and Accountability Across the Federal System: From Ambulances to Space Shuttles," *Publius: The Journal of Federalism* 34 (Summer 2004): 161.

4. Ibid., 160.

5. Clifford P. McCue and Jack T. Pitzer, "Centralized vs. Decentralized Purchasing: Current Trends in Governmental Procurement Practices," *Journal of Public Budgeting, Accounting & Financial Management* 12 (Fall 2000): 400–1.

6. Ibid., 411.

7. Dan Guttman, "Governance by Contract: Constitutional Visions; Time for Reflection and Choice," *Public Contract Law Journal* 33 (2004): 4.

8. The Federal Acquisition Regulation (FAR), Available at www.arnet.gov/far/ (accessed June 18, 2006).

9. Vernon J. Edwards, "A Modest Proposal," *Where Is Federal Contracting?* (February 2004): 1. Available at www.wifcon.com/analmodest.htm (accessed June 18, 2006).

10. Ibid.

11. Vernon J. Edwards, "Competitive Processes in Government Contracting: The FAR Part 15 Process Model and Process Inefficiency," *Where Is Federal Contracting?* (April 2003): 2. Available at www.wifcon.com/analcomproc.htm (accessed June 18, 2006).

12. The National Association of State Purchasing Officials (NASPO), the National Association of State Information Resource Executives (NASIRE), and the National Association of State Directors of Administration and General Services (NASDAGS), *Buying Smart: State Procurement Reform Saves Millions* (September 1996). Available at www. naspo.org/whitepapers/buyingsmart2.cfm (accessed June 18, 2006).

13. John R. Bartle and Ronnie LaCourse Korosec, "A Review of State Procurement and Contracting," *Journal of Public Procurement* 3 (2003): 192–214.

14. The Miami-Dade County Procurement web site, www.miamidade.gov/dpm/home. asp (accessed June 18, 2006).

15. An explanation of the Miami-Dade County procurement process can be found at www.miamidade.gov/dpm/solicitation-process.asp (accessed June 18, 2006).

16. An explanation of the Miami-Dade County logic for using requests for proposals and requests for qualifications can be found at www.miamidade.gov/dpm/rfp-process.asp (accessed June 18, 2006).

17. Bea Garcia, "Big Blue Loses Job to Miami-Dade's IT department," *The Miami Herald* (February 26, 2002). Available at www.co.miami-dade.fl.us/dpm/Miami_Herald_022502.asp (accessed June 18, 2006).

18. "County Recognized for Procurement Excellence," Press release, Miami-Dade County Department of Procurement Management (September 02, 2005). Available at www.co.miami-dade.fl.us/dpm/releases/05–09–02_dpm-award.asp (accessed June 18, 2006).

19. Jack Cooper and Matthew Fisher, eds., *Software Acquisition Capability Maturity Model* (SA-CMM) Version 1.03, CMU/SEI-2002-TR-010, ESC-TR-2002–010 (Pittsburgh, PA: Carnegie Mellon Software Engineering Institute, March 2002): I-5.

20. Ibid., I-5–I-6.

21. Lloyd Anderson, Matt Fisher, and Jon Gross, *Case Study: IRS Business System Modernization Process Improvement,* Technical Report CMU/SEI-2004-TR-002 ESC-TR-2004–002 (Pittsburgh, PA: Software Engineering Institute, Carnegie Mellon University, March 2004).

22. See, for example: U.S. General Accounting Office, *Customs Service Modernization: Ineffective Software Development Processes Increase Customs System Development Risks* (Washington, DC: February 11, 1999); U.S. General Accounting Office, *District of Columbia: Software Acquisition Processes for a New Financial Management System* (Washington, DC: April 30, 1998); U.S. General Accounting Office, *Social Security Administration: Software Development Process Improvements Started But Work Remains* (Washington, DC: January 28, 1998); U.S. General Accounting Office, *Defense Computers: Technical Support Is Key to Naval Supply Year 2000 Success.* (Washington, DC: October

21, 1997); U.S. General Accounting Office, *Defense Financial Management: Immature Software Development Processes at Indianapolis Increase Risk* (Washington, DC: June 6, 1997); U.S. General Accounting Office, *Medicare Transaction System: Success Depends Upon Correcting Critical Managerial and Technical Weaknesses* (Washington, DC: May 16, 1997); U.S. General Accounting Office, *Air Traffic Control: Immature Software Acquisition Processes Increase FAA System Acquisition Risks* (Washington, DC: March 21, 1997); U.S. General Accounting Office, *Air Traffic Control: Complete and Enforced Architecture Needed for FAA Systems Modernization* (Washington, DC: February 3, 1997); U.S. General Accounting Office, *Air Traffic Control: Improved Cost Information Needed to Make Billion Dollar Modernization Investment Decisions* (Washington, DC: January 22, 1997); U.S. General Accounting Office, *Tax Systems Modernization: IRS Needs to Resolve Certain Issues With Its Integrated Case Processing System* (Washington, DC: January 17, 1997); U.S. General Accounting Office, *Software Capability Evaluation: VA's Software Development Process Is Immature* (Washington, DC: June 19, 1996).

23. George Brotbeck, Tom Miller, and Joyce Statz, *A Survey of Current Best Practices and Utilization of Standards in the Public and Private Sectors* (December 1999). Available at www.dir.state.tx.us/eod/qa/bestprac.htm#figure1 (accessed June 18, 2006).

24. Susan M. Menke, "Feds Must Weigh Worth of Vendors' CMM Claims," *Government Computer News* (August 12, 2002). Available at www.appserv.gcn.com/cgi-bin/udt/im.display.printable?client.id=gcn&story.id=19576 (accessed June 18, 2006).

25. Christopher Koch, "Bursting the CMM Hype," *CIO Magazine.com* (Mar. 1, 2004). Available at www.cio.com/archive/030104/cmm.html (accessed June 18, 2006).

26. "High Anxiety," *CIO Magazine.com* (September 1, 2000). Available at www.cio.com/archive/090100/anxiety.html (accessed June 18, 2006).

27. "You Can't Outsource City Hall," *CIO Magazine.com* (September 15, 2002). Available at www.cio.com/archive/061502/govt.html (accessed June 18, 2006).

28. Stephanie Overby, "San Diego Tries to Learn from Contract Mistakes," *CIO Magazine.com* (May 1, 2006). Available at www.cio.com/archive/050106/tl_outsourcing.html?action=print (accessed June 18, 2006).

29. INPUT, "State and Local IT Outsourcing Spending to Grow 75 Percent by FY10," (January 23, 2006). Available at www.input.com/corp/press/detail.cfm?news=1132 (accessed June 18, 2006).

30. INPUT, "INPUT Predicts Federal IT Outsourcing Market to Reach Nearly $18 Billion by FY10," (January 11, 2006). Available at www.input.com/corp/press/detail.cfm?news=1127 (accessed June 18, 2006).

31. U.S. Office of Management and Budget, "Circular A-76," Revised 1999, original date August 4, 1983. (Washington, DC: OMB, 1999), www.whitehouse.gov/omb/circulars/a076/a076.html (accessed June 18, 2006).

32. Ibid.

33. Ibid.

34. Jason Miller, "Coming Report: A-76 Continues to Produce Savings," *Washington Technology* (January 18, 2005). Available at www.washingtontechnology.com/cgi-in/udt/im.display.printable?client.id=wtdaily-test&story.id=25336 (accessed June 18, 2006).

35. Matthew Weigelt, "OMB Touts the Value in Best-Value: Administration Wants Congress to Remove Its A-76 Restrictions," *Federal Computer Week* (May 1, 2006). Available at www.fcw.com/article94224-05-01-06-Print (accessed June 18, 2006).

36. Steven Kelman has written one of the best books on federal procurement. See his book: *Procurement and Public Management: The Fear of Discretion and the Quality of Government Performance* (Washington, DC: AEI Press, 1990).

Notes to Chapter 11

1. National Security Telecommunications and Information Systems Security Committee, *National Information Systems Security (Infosec) Glossary* (Ft. Meade, MD: National Security Agency, 2003). Available at www.cnss.gov/Assets/pdf/cnssi_4009.pdf (accessed June 8, 2006).

2. Ibid., 33.

3. Bruce Schneier, *Secrets and Lies* (New York: John Wiley and Sons, 2000).

4. *Infosec*, 34.

5. Ibid., 5.

6. Ibid., 3.

7. CERT is a center of Internet security expertise, located at the Software Engineering Institute, a federally funded research and development center operated by Carnegie Mellon University. They study Internet security vulnerabilities, research long-term changes in networked systems, and develop information and training to help improve security; see www.cert.org/advisories/CA-1999–04.html (accessed June 8, 2006).

8. For a history of the Melissa virus see: the "Melissa (computer worm)," *Wikipedia: The Free Encylopedia*. Available at en.wikipedia.org/wiki/Melissa_worm

9. BBC News, "Mydoom Virus 'Biggest in Months'" (January 27, 2004). Available at www.news.bbc.co.uk/1/hi/technology/3432639.stm (accessed June 8, 2006).

10. Sophos is one of the industry leaders in integrated security threat management, providing protection to governments and businesses against viruses, spyware, Trojans, phishing, and spam; see www.sophos.com (accessed June 8, 2006).

11. Computer Security Institute, *CSI/FBI Computer Crime and Security Survey*, 2005. Available at www.gocsi.com/awareness/publications.jhtml (accessed June 8, 2006).

12. Sophos, "Sophos Security Threat Management Report," 2005, www.sophos.com/security/whitepapers/SophosSecurity2005-mmuk (accessed June 8, 2006).

13. Ibid., 4.

14. Ibid., 4–8.

15. Various reports from Symantec, www.symantec.com/avcenter/global/index.html (accessed June 8, 2006).

16. *Chief Security Officer Magazine*, U.S. Secret Service, and CERT Coordination Center, "2005 E-Crime Watch Survey—Survey Results." Available at www.csoonline.com/info/ecrimesurvey05.pdf (accessed June 8, 2006).

17. U.S. Government Accountability Office, *Information Security: Weaknesses Persist at Federal Agencies Despite Progress Made in Implementing Related Statutory Requirements* (Washington, DC: GAO, July 2005).

18. Ibid., 2.

19. Ibid., 11.

20. Ibid., 19.

21. Ibid., 12.

22. Ibid., 13.

23. Ibid., 13.

24. Ibid., 14.

25. U.S. Government Accountability Office, *Information Security: Emerging Cybersecurity Issues Threaten Federal Information Systems* (Washington, DC: GAO, May 2005).

26. Ibid., 4.

27. Ibid., 4.

28. U.S. Office of Management and Budget, *Safeguarding Personally Identifiable Information*, Memorandum for the Heads of Departments and Agencies, M-06–15 (Washington, DC: OMB, May 22, 2006): 1.

29. U.S. Office of Management and Budget, FY 2005 Report to Congress on Implementation of the Federal Information Security Act of 2002 (Washington, DC: OMB, March 1, 2006): 2.

30. Ibid., 6.

31. Ibid., 7.

32. Ibid., 8.

33. Ibid., 4.

34. David Perera, "FISMA Fizzles," *Govexec.Com* (March 15, 2006). Available at www.govexec.com/story_page.cfm?articleid=33605&printerfriendlyVers=1& (accessed June 8, 2006).

35. INPUT, "INPUT Says FISMA Fails to Improve Overall Security," (March 16, 2006). Available at www.input.com/corp/press/detail.cfm?news=1168 (accessed June 16, 2006.

36. U.S. Government Accountability Office, *Information Security: Federal Agencies Show Mixed Progress in Implementing Statutory Requirements* (Washington, DC: GAO, March 16, 2005): 23–24.

37. Ibid., 24.

38. Mary Mosquera, "IRS Missing Laptop with Employee Data," *Government Computer News* (June 6, 2006). Available at www.appserv.gcn.com/cgi-bin/udt/im.display.printable?client.id=gcn_daily&story.id=40966 (accessed June 8, 2006).

39. Mary Mosquera, "VA Data Files on Millions of Veterans Stolen," *Government Computer News* (May 22, 2006). Available at www.appserv.gcn.com/cgi-bin/udt/im.display.printable?client.id=gcn_daily&story.id=40840 (accessed June 8, 2006).

40. Jim McKay, "Evolving Cyber Security," *Government Technology* (April 16, 2002). Available at www.govtech.net/magazine/story.print.php?id=8029 (accessed June 8, 2006).

41. Shane Peterson, "Security Steps," *Government Technology* (October 28, 2003). Available at www.govtech.net/magazine/story.print.php?id=75049 (accessed June 8, 2006).

42. Jim McKay, "Internet Takedown," *Government Technology* (June 3, 2004). Available at www.govtech.net/magazine/story.print.php?id=90471 (accessed June 8, 2006).

43. Wayne Hanson, "Cyber Security Summit Outlines Evolving Threats, Solutions," *Government Technology* (November 16, 2005). Available at www.govtech.net/magazine/story.print.php?id=97301 (accessed June 8, 2006).

44. "CDW-G Releases Assessment of State and Local Government Security Investment," *Government Technology* (February 22, 2006). Available at www.govtech.net/magazine/story.print.php?id=98511 (accessed June 8, 2006).

45. CDW-G, "State and Local Government Technology Investment Curve (TIC)" (February 20, 2006). Available at www.newsroom.cdwg.com/features/feature-02–20–06.html (accessed June 8, 2006).

Notes to Chapter 12

1. To learn more about what the National Association of State Chief Information Officers is doing to promote the strategic management of information, visit their web site at www.nascio.org (accessed June 18, 2006).

2. Free Online Computer Dictionary (www.foldoc.org), s.v. "Information Resource Management," quoting Gary D. Blass et al., "Finding Government Information: The Federal Information Locator System (FILS)," *Government Information Quarterly* 8 (1): 11–32.

3. Forest Woody Horton, Jr., "Information Resources Management (IRM): Where Did It Come from and Where Is It Going?" *Proceedings of the 1981 Association of Computing Machinery Conference* (1981): 277–78.

4. Paperwork Reduction Act of 1980 (P.L. 96–511). Available at www.thomas.loc. gov. (accessed June 18, 2006).

5. Boulton B. Miller, "Information Resource Management: Theory Applied," *Proceedings of the 1981 Association of Computing Machinery Conference* (1981): 279–80.

6. Horton, 277.

7. John F. Schrage, "Information Resource Management (IRM): Theory Applied to Three Environments. Overview of Presentations," *Proceedings of the 1981 Association of Computing Machinery Conference* (1981): 274.

8. Paperwork Reduction Act of 1980, 2.

9. Ibid., 2.

10. U.S. General Accounting Office, *Statement of Charles A. Bowsher, Comptroller General of the United States Before the Subcommittee on Legislation and National Security of the House Committee on Government Operations on Implementation of the Paperwork Reduction Act Public Law 96–511.* (Washington, DC: GAO, October 21, 1981): 3.

11. Information Technology Management Reform Act of 1996. (P.L. 104–106).

12. William S. Cohen, *Computer Chaos: Billions Wasted Buying Federal Computer Systems.* Investigative Report of Senator William Cohen, Ranking Minority Member, Subcommittee on Oversight of Government Management, Senate Government Affairs Committee (Washington DC: U.S. Senate, 1994).

13. U.S. General Accounting Office, *Information Management Reform: Effective Implementation Is Essential for Improving Federal Performance.* (Washington, DC: GAO, July 17, 1996): 2.

14. The recommendations of Cohen's *Computer Chaos Report* have been reproduced in the following article: "Computer Chaos 8 Recommendations," *Federal Computer Week Online*, n.d. Available at www.fcw.com/article89088–06–06–05-Web (accessed June 12, 2006).

15. The CIO Council's web page can be found at www.cio.gov/ (accessed June 18, 2006).

16. U.S. General Accounting Office, *NASA Chief Information Officer: Opportunities to Strengthen Information Resources Management* (Washington, DC: GAO, August 15, 1996).

17. U.S. General Accounting Office, *Chief Information Officers: Ensuring Strong Leadership and an Effective Council* (Washington, DC: GAO, October 27, 1997): 4–5.

18. Ibid., 10.

19. U.S. General Accounting Office, *USDA Information Management: Proposal to Strengthen Authority of the Chief Information Officer* (Washington, DC: GAO, March 3, 1998): 2.

20. Ibid., 2.

21. Ibid., 4.

22. Ibid., 4.

23. Ibid., 5–6.

24. U.S. General Accounting Office, *VA Information Technology: Improvements Needed to Implement Legislative Reforms* (Washington, DC: GAO, July 7, 1998): 2.

25. Ibid., 3.

26. U.S. Government Accountability Office, *Federal Chief Information Officers: Responsibilities, Reporting Relationships, Tenure, and Challenges* (Washington, DC: GAO, July 21, 2004): 10–11.

27. Ibid., 16.

28. Ibid., 18.

29. Ibid., 20.

30. Allan Holmes, "Federal IT Flunks Out: Ten Years After the Clinger-Cohen Act Was Passed to Fix Federal IT, Federal IT Remains Broken. Government CIOs Tell Us Why," *CIO Magazine* (May 15, 2006). Available at www.cio.com/archive/051506/federal_IT.html?action=print (accessed June 18, 2006).

31. U.S. Department of Defense, *DoD Architecture Framework, Version 1.0. Volume I: Definitions and Guidelines.* (Washington, DC: DOD, February 9, 2004). Available at www.defenselink.mil/nii/doc/DoDAF_v1_Volume_I.pdf (accessed June 18, 2006).

32. U.S. General Accounting Office, *Information Technology: A Framework for Assessing and Improving Enterprise Architecture Management (Version 1.1).* (Washington, DC: GAO, April 2003): 1.

33. John A. Zachman, "A Framework for Information Systems Architecture," *IBM Systems Journal* 26, no. 3 (1987): 276–92.

34. The Zachman framework is explained in great detail on his web site, *The Zachman Institute for Framework Advancement,* available at www.zifa.com/ (accessed June 18, 2006).

35. The Chief Information Officers Council, *Federal Enterprise Architecture Framework Version 1.1,* (Washington, DC: Office of Management and Budget, September 1999.) Available at https://secure.cio.noaa.gov/hpcc/docita/files/federal_enterprise_arch_framework.pdf (accessed November 24, 2006).

36. Carla Marques Pereira and Pedro Sousa, "A Method to Define an Enterprise Framework Using the Zachman Framework," *ACM Symposium on Applied Computing* (2004): 1366.

37. Full and comprehensive details about all five reference models can be found on the following OMB web site: www.whitehouse.gov/omb/egov/a-2-EAModelsNEW2.html (accessed November 24, 2006).

38. U.S. Government Accounting Office, *Information Technology: A Framework for Assessing and Improving Enterprise Architecture Management (Version 1.1)*: 2.

39. This information was drawn from a case study of the Food and Drug Administration's successful efforts to develop an EA. "Enterprise Architecture in Action: FDA Uses EA to Standardize and Save With Consolidation Effort," U.S. Office of Management and Budget, n.d. Available at www.whitehouse.gov/omb/egov/documents/FDA_FINAL.pdf (accessed June 18, 2006).

40. Judith Ribbler, "Enhancing Government's DNA," *Government Technology's Public CIO* (February 9, 2006). Available at www.public-cio.com/story.print.php?id=2006.02.09-98399 (accessed June 18, 2006).

41. "Knowledge management," *Wikipedia, The Free Encyclopedia,* www.en.wikipedia.org/wiki/Knowledge_management (accessed June 18, 2006).

42. T. H. Davenport and L. Prusak, *Working Knowledge: How Organizations Manage What They Know* (Boston, MA: Harvard Business School Press, 1997).

43. Michael Polanyi, *The Tacit Dimension* (Garden City, NY: Doubleday, 1967).

44. David J. Skyrme, "Knowledge Management Solutions: The IT Contribution," *ACM SIGGROUP Bulletin* 19, no. 1 (April 1998): 34.

45. David R. Millen, Michael A. Fontaine, and Michael J. Muller, "Understanding the Benefit and Costs of Communities of Practice," *Communications of the ACM* 45 (April 2002): 69–73.

46. Shruti Daté, "Agencies Create CKO Posts to Get in the Know," *Government Computer News* (November 8, 1999). Available at www.appserv.gcn.com/cgi-bin/udt/im.display.printable?client.id=gcn&story.id=950 (accessed June 18, 2006).

47. Ibid.

48. Wallace O. Keene, "Another View," *Government Computer News* (May 8, 2000). Available at www.appserv.gcn.com/cgi-bin/udt/im.display.printable ?client.id=gcn&story.id=1829 (accessed June 18, 2006).

49. Susan M. Menke, "Army Lures People to Portal," *Government Computer News* (November 20, 2000).Available at www.appserv.gcn.com/cgi-bin/udt/im.display. printable?client.id=gcn&story.id=3291 (accessed June 18, 2006).

50. Trish Williams, "Knowledge Management Initiatives Gain Foothold in Government," *Government Computer News* (March 9, 2001). Available at www.appserv.gcn. com /cgi-bin/udt/im.display.printable?client.id=gcn_daily&story.id=3784 (accessed June 18, 2006).

51. Trish Williams, "What Is Knowledge Management?" *Government Computer News* (March 9, 2001). Available at http//appserv.gcn/cig-bin/udt/im.display.printable?client. id=gcn_daily&story,id=3785 (accessed June 18, 2006).

52. Dawn S. Onley, "State Starts Work on Global, Multiagency Network," *Government Computer News* (April 2, 2001). Available at www.appserv.gcn.com/cgi-bin/udt/im.display. printable?client.id=gcn&story.id=3921 (accessed June 18, 2006).

53. U.S. General Accounting Office, *Information Technology: State Department Led Overseas Modernization Program Faces Management Challenges* (Washington, DC: GAO, November 16, 2001).

54. Richard W. Walker, "KM: Difficult to Define but Here to Stay," *Government Computer News* (September 24, 2001). Available at www.gcn.com/print/20_29/17173–1.html (accessed June 18, 2006).

55. David Essex, "In the Know—Knowledge Management Software," *Government Computer News* (May 8, 2006). Available at www.appserv.gcn.com/cgi-bin/udt/im.display. printable?client.id=gcn&story.id=40654 (accessed June 18, 2006).

56. Judith Ribbler, "Enhancing Government's DNA."

Bibliography

Aguanno, Kevin, ed. 2004. *Managing Agile Projects.* Lakefield, ON: Multi-Media Publications, Inc.

Alderman, Ellen, and Caroline Kennedy. 1997. *The Right to Privacy.* New York: Vintage Books.

Alter, Steven. 1980. *Decision Support Systems: Current Practice and Continuing Challenge.* Reading, MA: Addison-Wesley.

Alvarez, R. Michael, and Thad E. Hall. 2004. *Point, Click, and Vote: The Future of Internet Voting.* Washington, DC: Brookings Institution Press.

Anderson, Lloyd, Matt Fisher, and Jon Gross. 2004. *Case Study: IRS Business System Modernization Process Improvement.* Technical Report CMU/SEI-2004-TR-002ESC-TR-2004–002 (March). Pittsburgh, PA: Software Engineering Institute, Carnegie Mellon University.

Anthes, Gary H. 1994. "Notes System Sends Federal Property Data Nationwide." *Computer World* 28 (32): 45.

Austrian, Geoffrey D. 1982. *Herman Hollerith, Forgotten Giant of Information Processing.* New York: Columbia University Press.

Barrett, Katherine, and Richard Greene. 1999. "Grading the States 1999: A Management Report Card." *The Government Performance Project, Governing.com* (February). Available at www.governing.com/gpp/1999/gp9intro.htm. (accessed June 26, 2006).

Bartle, John R., and Ronnie LaCourse Korosec. 2003. "A Review of State Procurement and Contracting." *Journal of Public Procurement* 3: 192–214.

Blass Gary D., et al., "Finding Government Information: The Federal Information Locator System (FILS)," *Government Information Quarterly* 8 (1): 11–32.

Baum, Joan. *The Calculating Passion of Ada Byron.* 1986. New York: Archon Books.

Beasty, Colin. 2005. "The City of Indianapolis Turns to Citizen Relationship Management." *Destination CRM* (March 15). Available at www.destinationcrm.com/articles/default.asp?articleid=4957 (accessed June 25, 2006).

Beck, Kent. 1999. *Extreme Programming Explained: Embrace Change.* Boston, MA: Addison-Wesley.

Benamati, John A., and Ram Pakath. n.d. "Mismanaging a Technology Project: The Case of A.B.C., Inc." Case No. IT5565. Hershey, PA: Idea Group Publishing. Available at www.idea-group.com/ (accessed May 8, 2006).

Boehm, Barry W. 1986. "A Spiral Model of Software Development and Enhancement." *ACM SIGSOFT Software Engineering Notes,* 11, No. 4 (August): 14–24.

Brain, Marshall. n.d. "How Telephones Work." Available at www.electronics.how-stuffworks.com/telephone.htm (accessed on May 27, 2006).

Britt, Phillip. 2006. "Trends in Database Management Systems Technology." *Information Today,* 23 (May): 1–20.

Brotbeck, George, Tom Miller, and Joyce Statz. 1999. *A Survey of Current Best Practices and Utilization of Standards in the Public and Private Sectors.* Austin, TX: State of Texas, Department of Information Services. Available at www.dir.state.tx.us/eod/qa/bestprac.htm (accessed June 25, 2006).

Burleson, Donald K. 1999. *Inside the Database Object Model.* Boca Raton, FL: CRC Press.

Carne, E. Byran. 2004. *A Professional's Guide to Data Communications in a TCP/IP World.* Norwood, MA: Artech House.

Casson, Herbert N. 1910. *The History of the Telephone.* Reprint, Fairfield, IA: 1st World Library, 2004.

Caudle, Sharon L. 1995. *Reengineering for Results: Keys to Success from Government Experience.* Washington, DC: National Academy of Public Administration. Available at www.71.4.192.38/NAPA/NAPAPubs.nsf/17bc036fe939efd685256951004e37f4/1fb41dbc8efe764c85256886007eb48f/$FILE/94–11—Reengineering+for+Results.pdf (accessed June 15, 2006).

Cezzar, Ruknet. 1995. *A Guide to Programming Languages: Overview and Comparison.* Boston: Artech House.

"CH: Internet Referendum Successfully Held in Switzerland." *eGovernment News* (September 28, 2004). Available at ec.europa.eu.int/idabc/en/document/3311 (accessed May 29, 2006).

Chaudhuri, Surajit, and Umeshwar Dayal. 1997. "An Overview of Data Warehousing and OLAP Technology," *ACM SIGMOD* 26 (March): 65–74.

Chevance, René J. 2004. *Server Architectures: Multiprocessors, Clusters, Parallel Systems, Web Servers, Storage Solutions.* London: Elsevier Science and Technology Books.

Christensen, Clayton M. 1997. *The Innovator's Dilemma.* New York: Harpers Business.

Christensen, Clayton M., and Michael E. Raynor. 2003. *The Innovator's Solution.* Boston: Harvard Business School Press.

"City of Alexandria Launches 'Wireless Alexandria.'" 2005. *Government Technology.* (August 26). Available at www.govtech.net/magazine/channel_story.php/96394 (accessed May 27, 2006).

Clarke, Arthur C., Michael L. Dertouzos, Morris Halle, Ithiel de Sola Pool, and Jerome B. Wiesner, eds. 1977. *The Telephone's First Century—And Beyond: Essays on the Occasion of the 100th Anniversary of Telephone Communication.* New York: Thomas Y. Crowell.

Cohen, William S. 1994. *Computer Chaos: Billions Wasted Buying Federal Computer Systems.* Investigative Report of Senator William Cohen, Ranking Minority Member, Subcommittee on Oversight of Government Management, Senate Government Affairs Committee. Washington DC: U.S. Senate.

"Commercial Off-the-Shelf-Software." n.d. *Wikipedia, The Free Encyclopedia.* www.en.wikipedia.org/wiki/Commercial_off-the-shelf (accessed May 22, 2006).

"Computer Chaos 8 Recommendations." 1994. *Federal Computer Week.* www.fcw.com/article89088–06–06–05-Web (accessed June 12, 2006).

Computer Security Institute. 2005. *CSI/FBI Computer Crime and Security Survey.* San

Francisco, CA: Computer Security Institute. Available at www.gocsi.com/aware-ness/publications.jhtml (accessed June 8, 2006).

Cooper, Jack, and Matthew Fisher, eds. 2002. *Software Acquisition Capability Maturity Model* (SA-CMM) Version 1.03, CMU/SEI-2002-TR-010, ESC-TR-2002–010. Pittsburgh, PA: Carnegie Mellon Software Engineering Institute.

Cooper, Mark. 2004. *Expanding the Digital Divide and Falling Behind on Broadband: Why a Telecommunications Policy of Neglect is Not Benign.* Washington, DC: Consumer Federation of America. Available at www.consumersunion.org/pub/ddnewbook.pdf (accessed May 29, 2006).

Cooper, Phillip J. 2003. *Governing by Contract: Challenges and Opportunities for Public Managers.* Washington, DC: CQ Press.

"County Recognized for Procurement Excellence." 2005. Press release, Miami-Dade County Department of Procurement Management (September 2). Available at www.co.miami-dade.fl.us/dpm/releases/05–09–02_dpm-award.asp (accessed June 25, 2006).

Daté, Shruti. 1999. "Agencies Create CKO Posts to Get in the Know." *Government Computer News.* (November 8). Available at www.appserv.gcn.com/cgi-bin/udt/im.display.printable?client.id=gcn&story.id=950 (accessed June 25, 2006).

Davenport, Thomas H., and Laurence Prusak. 1997. *Working Knowledge: How Organizations Manage What They Know.* Boston, MA: Harvard Business School Press.

Davies, Thomas. 2004. "Eye on the States: Lessons in Wireless From the Little Guys." *Washington Technology* 19 (November 8). Available at www.washingtontechnology. com/news/19_16/statelocal/24922–1.html (accessed May 27, 2006).

Day, Alan. 2004. "Government Technology: Data Warehouses." *American City & County.Com.* (January 1). Available at www.americancityandcounty.com/mag/government_data_warehouses/index.html (accessed May 26, 2006).

DeJesus, Edmund X. 2005. "Handhelds Rival Laptops—But Choose Carefully." *Washington Technology.* 20 (February 7). Available at www.washingtontechnology. com/news/20_3/emerging-tech/25469–1.html (accessed May 27, 2006).

Denton, D. Keith. 2002. *Empowering Intranets to Implement Strategy, Build Teamwork, And Manage Change.* Westport, CT: Praeger.

DeSanctis, Gerardine, and R. Brent Gallupe. 1987. "A Foundation for the Study of Group Decision Support Systems." *Management Science* 33 (May): 589–609.

———. 1984. "Group Decision Support Systems: A New Frontier." *ACM SIGMIS Database Archive* 16 (Winter): 3–10.

Dizzard, III. Wilson P. 2004. "FBI Plans to Build New Case Management System from Scratch." *Government Computer News.* (December 30). Available at www.gcn.com/online/vol1_n01/31432–1.html (accessed May 7, 2006).

Drucker, Peter F. 1959. *Landmarks of Tomorrow: A Report on the New "Post-Modern" World.* New York: Harper.

Edwards, Vernon J. 2004. "A Modest Proposal." *Where Is Federal Contracting?* (February). Available at www.wifcon.com/analmodest.htm (accessed June 25, 2006).

———. 2003. "Competitive Processes in Government Contracting: The FAR Part 15 Process Model and Process Inefficiency," *Where Is Federal Contracting?* (April). Available at www.wifcon.com/analcomproc.htm (accessed June 25, 2006).

Eggen, Dan. 2005. "FBI Pushed Ahead with Troubled Software." *Washington Post* (June 6): A01. Available at www.washingtonpost.com/wp-dyn/content/article/2005/06/05/AR2005060501213_pf.html (accessed June 26, 2006).

Eom, S.B., S.M. Lee, E.B. Kim, and C. Somarajan. 1998. "A Survey of Decision

Support System Applications." *Journal of the Operational Research Society* 49 (22): 109–120.

Essex, David. 2006. "In the Know—Knowledge Management Software." *Government Computer News* (May 8). Available at www.appserv.gcn.com/cgi-bin/udt/im.display.printable?client.id=gcn&story.id=40654 (accessed June 13, 2006).

"Ethernet" n.d. *Webopedia.* www.webopedia.com/TERM/E/Ethernet.html (accessed June 13, 2006).

"Europe #1 in Per Capita Cell Phone Usage." 2006. Press release (February 28). Arlington Heights, IL: Computer Industry Almanac, Inc. Available at www.c-i-a.com/pr0206.htm (accessed on May 27, 2006).

Eva, Malcolm. 2002. "Requirements Acquisition for Rapid Applications Development." *Information & Management* 39 (2): 101–9.

Federal CIO Council. 1999. *Recommended Executive Branch Model Policy/Guidance on "Limited Personal Use" of Government Office Equipment Including Information Technology.* Washington, DC: General Services Administration, General CIO Council. Available at www.cio.gov/documents/peruse_model_may_1999.pdf (accessed June 15, 2006).

Franklin, Daniel. 2002. "Data Miners: New Software Instantly Connects Key Bits of Data that Once Eluded Teams of Researchers." *Time* (December 23). Available at www.time.com/time/globalbusiness/article/0,9171,1101021223–400017,00.html (accessed June 13, 2006).

Frawley, W., G. Piatetsky-Shapiro, and C. Matheus. 1992. "Knowledge Discovery in Databases: An Overview." *AI Magazine* (Fall): 213–28.

Freeman, Roger L. 2004. *Telecommunication System Engineering.* Hoboken, NJ: Wiley-Interscience.

Fui-Hoon Nah, Fiona. 2002. *Enterprise Resource Planning: Solutions and Management.* Hershey, PA: IRM Press.

Garcia, Bea. 2002. "Big Blue Loses Job to Miami-Dade's IT Department." *The Miami Herald,* (February 26). Available at www.co.miami-dade.fl.us/dpm/Miami_Herald_022502.asp (accessed June 16, 2006).

Gevarter, William B. 1984. *Artificial Intelligence, Expert Systems, Computer Vision, and Natural Language Processing.* Park Ridge, NJ: Noyes Publications.

Gibbs, W. Wayt. 1994. "Software's Chronic Crisis." *Scientific American* (September): 86–97.

Goldstein, R.C. and J.B. McCririck. 1980. "What Do Data Administrators Really Do?" *Datamation* 26 (8) (August): 131–34.

Gordon, Gil E. 2000a. *The OSHA Episode: How Molehills Become Mountains.* (January 29). Available at www.gilgordon.com/telecommuting/osha.html (accessed June 25, 2006).

———. 2000b. "Suggestions for Employers." *The OSHA Episode: How Molehills Become Mountains.* Available at www.gilgordon.com/telecommuting/osha_suggestion.html (accessed June 26, 2006).

"Grand Haven Goes WiFi." 2004. *Washington Technology* 19 (10) (August 16). Available at www.washingtontechnology.com/news/19_10/datastream/24223–1.html (accessed May 27, 2006).

Gray, Jim, and Andreas Reuter. 1993. *Transaction Processing: Concepts and Techniques.* San Francisco: Morgan Kaufman Publishers.

Gray, Paul. 1981. "The SMU Decision Room Project." *Transactions of the 1st International Conference on Decision Support Systems* (Atlanta, GA, June 8–10): 122–29.

————. 1987. "Group Decision Support Systems," *Decision Support Systems, The International Journal* 3 (September): 233–42.

————. 1994. *Decision Support and Executive Information Systems.* Englewood Cliffs, NJ: Prentice Hall.

Grimes, Brad. 2004. "Defense Department Certifies Cisco VOIP." *Washington Technology* (September 27). Available at www.washingtontechnology.com/news/1_1/defense/24628–1.html (accessed May 27, 2006).

————. 2005a. "Philly's Wireless Network Rolls On." *Government Computer News* (June 8). Available at www.gcn.com/online/vol1_no1/36017–1.html (accessed May 27, 2006).

————. 2005b. "With Wireless, It's Good to Learn From Others." *Government Computer News* (July 25). Available at www.gcn.com/print/24_20/36441–1.html (accessed May 27, 2006).

Gupta, Meeta. 2003. *Building a Virtual Private Network.* Cincinnati, OH: Premier Press.

Gupta, Uma. 2000. *Information Systems: Success in the 21st Century.* Upper Saddle River, NJ: Prentice Hall.

Guttman, Dan. 2004. "Governance by Contract: Constitutional Visions; Time for Reflection and Choice." *Public Contract Law Journal* 33 (2): 1–44. Available at www.papers.ssrn.com/s013/papers.cfm?abstract_id=488345 (accessed June 25, 2006).

Haag, Stephen, Maeve Cummings, and James Dawkins. 2000. *Management Information Systems for the Information Age.* New York: Irwin/McGraw-Hill.

Hahn, Robert W., ed. 2002. *Government Policy Toward Open Source Software.* Washington, DC: AEI-Brookings Joint Center for Regulatory Studies.

Hammer, Michael, and James Champy. 1993. *Reengineering the Corporation: A Manifesto for Business Revolution.* New York: HarperCollins.

Hanson, Wayne. 2005. "Cyber Security Summit Outlines Evolving Threats, Solutions." *Government Technology,* (November 16). Available at www.govtech.net/magazine/story.print.php?id=97301 (accessed June 25, 2006).

Harrington, Jan L. 2002. *Relational Database Design Clearly Explained.* New York: Morgan Kaufmann Publishers.

Hayes, Frank. 2004. "Chaos Is Back." *Computerworld.* (November 8). Available at www.computerworld.com/managementtopics/management/project/story/0,10801,97283,00.html (accessed May 8, 2006).

Hedge, A. 2003. "Computer Use And Risk of Carpal Tunnel Syndrome." *JAMA* 290 (14): 1854.

Heeks, Richard, and Anne Davies. 2000. "Different Approaches to Information Age Reform." In *Reinventing Government in the Information Age.* Edited by Richard Heeks. London: Routledge.

Held, Gilbert. 2003. *Ethernet Networks: Design, Implementation, Operation, Management.* New York: John Wiley & Sons.

Hersent, Olivier, Jean-Pierre Petit, and David Gurle. 2005. *Beyond VOIP Protocols: Understanding Voice Technology and Networking Techniques for IP Telephony* Hoboken, NJ: John Wiley.

"High Anxiety." 2000. *CIO Magazine.* (September 1). Available at www.cio.com/archive/090100/anxiety.html (accessed June 25, 2006).

"History of Computing Hardware." n.d. *Wikipedia, The Free On-line Encyclopedia.* Available at www.en.wikipedia.org/wiki/History_of_computing_hardware (accessed June 25, 2006).

Holmes, Allan. 2006. "Federal IT Flunks Out: Ten Years After the Clinger-Cohen Act Was Passed to Fix Federal IT, Federal IT Remains Broken. Government CIOs Tell Us Why." *CIO Magazine* (May 15). Available at www.cio.com/archive/051506/federal_IT.html?action=print (accessed June 13, 2006).

Horton Jr., Forest Woody. 1981. "Information Resources Management (IRM): Where Did It Come from and Where Is It Going?" *Proceedings of the 1981 Association of Computing Machinery Conference*: 277–78.

Hubbartt, William S. 1998. *The New Battle Over Workplace Privacy: How Far Can Management Go? What Rights Do Employees Have? Safe Practices to Minimize Conflict, Confusion, and Litigation*. New York: AMACOM.

IDABC. 2005. *Chinese Government Opts for Open Source Software* (November 21). Available at www.europa.eu.int/idabc/en/document/5138/469 (accessed May 22, 2006).

"Information Rich and Information Poor: Bridging the Digital Divide." 1999. BBC News. Available at www.news.bbc.co.uk/1/hi/special_report/1999/10/99/information_rich_information_poor/466651.stm (accessed June 13, 2006).

Information Technology Association of America (ITAA). n.d. "Practical Steps for Enterprise Information Security: On-site and Teleworking. It's About Process, People, and Technology." Available at www.itaa.org/isec/docs/securitytips.pdf (accessed June 8, 2006).

INPUT. 2004. "Federal ERP Spending to Grow 37 Percent by 2009." (August 23). Available at www.input.com/corp/community/detail.cfm?news=959 (accessed June 15, 2006).

———. 2006a. "INPUT Predicts Federal IT Outsourcing Market to Reach Nearly $18 Billion by FY10" (January 11). Available at www.input.com/corp/press/detail.cfm?news=1127 (accessed June 25, 2006).

———. 2006b. "State & Local IT Outsourcing Spending to Grow 75 Percent by FY10." (January 23) www.input.com/corp/press/detail.cfm?news=1132 (accessed June 15, 2006).

———. 2006c. "INPUT Says FISMA Fails to Improve Overall Security." (March 16). Available at www.input.com/corp/press/detail.cfm?news=1168 (accessed June 16, 2006.

———. 2006d. "INPUT Forecasts Federal IT Spending to Surpass $93 Billion by FY11." (March 28). www.input.com/corp/press/detail.cfm?news=1177 (accessed May 8, 2006).

Jackson, Joab. 2003. "Open Source Software in Government." *Washington Technology.* October 30). Available at www.washington=technology.com/news/forum/forums/22028-1.html (accessed May 22, 2006).

Jackson, William. 2001. "Carriers Need More Time to Develop Ways to Find, Map 911 Call Locations." *Government Computer News* (August 13). Available at www.gcn.com/print/20_23/16770–1.html (accessed May 27, 2006).

———. 2004. "Nebraska City Extends Wired Municipal Network." *Government Computer News.* (September 22). Available at www.gcn.com/online/vol1_no1/27376–1.html (accessed May 27, 2006).

———. 2005. "Census Bureau Runs VOIP over Upgraded, High-Quality Network." *Government Computer News* (March 21). Available at www.gcn.com/print/24_6/35292–1.html (accessed May 27, 2006).

Janson, Marious A., and L. Douglas Smith. 1985. "Prototyping for Systems Development: A Critical Appraisal." *MIS Quarterly* 9(4) (December): 305–16.

Jefferson, David, Aviel D. Rubin, Barbara Simons, and David Wagner. 2004. *A Security Analysis of the Secure Electronic Registration and Voting Experiment (SERVE).* (January 21). Available at www.servesecurityreport.org/paper.pdf (accessed May 29, 2006).

Jessup, Leonard M., and Joseph S. Valacich, eds. 1993. *Group Decision Support Systems: New Perspectives.* New York: Macmillan.

Johnson, Bradley. 2006. "Wireless Generation Eager for Innovation." *Television Week* 25 (March 27): 20.

Johnston, Jocelyn M., Barbara S. Romzek, and Curtis H. Wood. 2004. "The Challenges of Contracting and Accountability Across the Federal System: From Ambulances to Space Shuttles." *Publius: The Journal of Federalism* 34 (Summer): 155–82.

Johnson, Kirk. "Denver Airport Saw the Future. It Didn't Work." 2005. *The New York Times* (August 27): A1. Available at www.nytimes.com/2005/08/27/national/27denver.html?ei=5090&en=c1a4a185ddb79852&ex=1282795200&partner=rssuserland&emc=rss&pagewanted=print (accessed June 26, 2006).

Kable Ltd. 2004. "Swiss Roll Out E-vote." (September 21). London: Kable Ltd. Available at www.kablenet.com/kd.nsf/Frontpage/22756CE2CE33701180256F16003918D6?OpenDocument (accessed May 29, 2006).

Keene, Wallace O. 2000. "Another View." *Government Computer News* (May 8). Available atwww.appserv.gcn.com/cgi-bin/udt/im.display.printable?client.id=gcn&story.id=1829 (accessed June 25, 2006).

Keogh, James, and Mario Giannini. 2004. *OOP Demystified.* New York: McGraw-Hill/Osborne.

Klingler, Daniel E. 1988. "The Ten Commandments of Prototyping." *Journal of Information System Management* (Summer): 66–72.

"Knowledge Management." n.d. *Wikipedia, The Free Encyclopedia.* Available at www.en.wikipedia.org/wiki/Knowledge_management (accessed June 25, 2006).

Koch, Christopher. 2004. "Bursting the CMM Hype." *CIO Magazine* (March 1). Available at: www.cio.com/archive/030104/cmm.html (accessed June 25, 2006).

———. n.d. "The ABCs of ERP." Available at www.cio.com/research/erp/edit/erp-basics.html#erp_costs (accessed June 15, 2006).

Koch, Stefan, ed. 2005. *Free Open Source Software Development.* Hershey, PA: Idea Group.

Kruger, Lennard G., and Angele A. Gilroy. 2006. *Broadband Internet Access and the Digital Divide: Federal Assistance Programs.* Washington, DC: Congressional Research Service. Available at www.usembassy.it/pdf/other/RL30719.pdf (accessed June 16, 2006).

Lane, Frederick. 2003. *The Naked Employee: How Technology Is Compromising Workplace Privacy.* New York: AMACOM.

Lantz, Kenneth E. 1986, *The Prototyping Methodology.* Upper Saddle River, NJ: Prentice Hall.

Layman, Jay. 2004. "Open Source Winning in Federal Government, Slowly." *NewsForge: The Online Newspaper for Linux and Open Source* (July 28). Available at www.trends.newsforge.com/article.pl?sid=04/07/23/2335201&tid=152&tid=136&tid=110&tid=91 (accessed May 22, 2006).

Layton, Julia, Marshall Brain, and Jeff Tyson. n.d. "How Cell Phones Work." Available at www.electronics.howstuffworks.com/cell-phone.htm (accessed on May 27, 2006).

Leiner, Barry M., Vinton G. Cerf, David D. Clark, Robert E. Kahn, Leonard Kleinrock, Daniel C. Lynch, Jon Postel, Larry G. Roberts, and Stephen Wolff. 2003. *A*

Brief History of the Internet. Reston, VA: The Internet Society (ISOC). Available at www.isoc.org/internet/history/brief.shtml (accessed May 30, 2006).

Levine, Robert I., Diane E. Dranf, and Barry Edelson. 1986. *A Comprehensive Guide to AI and Expert Systems*. New York: McGraw-Hill.

Liang, Leo Yonghong, and Rowan Miranda. 2001. "Dashboards and Scorecards: Executive Information Systems for the Public Sector." *Government Finance Review* (December): 14–19.

"Local Area Network." n.d. *Webopedia*. Available at www.webopedia.com/TERM/1/local_area_network_LAN.html (accessed May 27, 2006).

"Logist." Israeli Ministry of Finance Expert System. www.mof.gov.il/micun/prof. htm. (accessed April 6, 2006).

Loudon, Kenneth C., and Jane P. Loudon. 2003. *Essentials of Management Information Systems: Managing the Digital Firm*. Upper Saddle River, NJ: Prentice Hall.

"Lowdown on VOIP." 2005. *Government Computer News* (January 10). Available at www.gcn.com/print/24_1/34754–1.html (accessed May 27, 2006).

Mabin, Victoria, Malcolm Menzies, Graeme King, and Karen Joyce. 2001. "Public Sector Priority Setting Using Decision Support Tools." *Australian Journal of Public Administration* 60 (2): 44–59.

Martin, James. 1991. *Rapid Application Development*. Upper Saddle River, NJ: Prentice Hall.

McCabe, James D. 2003. *Network Analysis, Architecture and Design*. San Francisco, CA: Morgan Kaufmann Publishers.

McCormick, John. 2005. "Power User: For Agencies, It's Firefox No, Openoffice Yes." *Government Computer News* (May 15). Available at www.gcn.com/print/24_11/35780–1.html (accessed May 22, 2006).

McCue, Clifford P. and Jack T. Pitzer. 2000. "Centralized vs. Decentralized Purchasing: Current Trends in Governmental Procurement Practices." *Journal of Public Budgeting, Accounting & Financial Management*, 12 (Fall): 400–20.

McKay, Jim. 2002. "Evolving Cyber Security." *Government Technology* (April 16). Available at www.govtech.net/magazine/story.print.php?id=8029 (accessed on June 8, 2006).

———. 2004. "Internet Takedown." *Government Technology* (June 3). Available at www.govtech.net/magazine/story.print.php?id=90471 (accessed June 25, 2006).

McKenna, Corey. 2005. "Internet Telephony Keeps Baton Rouge Hospital in Touch When Hurricane Hits." *Government Technology* (August). Available at www.govtech.net/digitalcommunities/story.php?id=96493 (accessed May 27, 2006).

Menke, Susan M. 2000. "Army Lures People to Portal." *Government Computer News* (November 20). Available at www.appserv.gcn.com/cgi-bin/udt/im.display.printable?client.id=gcn&story.id=3291 (accessed June 25, 2006).

———. 2002. "Feds Must Weigh Worth of Vendors' CMM Claims." *Government Computer News* (August 12). Available at www.appserv.gcn.com/cgi-in/udt/im.display.printable?client.id=gcn&story.id=19576 (accessed June 25, 2006).

Metropolis, Nicholas, J. Howlett, and Gian-Carlo Rota, eds. 1980. *A History of Computing in the Twentieth Century*. New York: Academic Press.

Millen, David, R., Michael A. Fontaine, and Michael J. Muller. 2002. "Understanding the Benefit and Costs of Communities of Practice." *Communications of the ACM* 45 (April): 69–73.

Miller, Boulton B. 1981. "Information Resource Management: Theory Applied."

Proceedings of the 1981 Association of Computing Machinery Conference (November 9–11): 279–80.

Miller, Jason. 2005. "Coming Report: A-76 Continues to Produce Savings." *Washington Technology* (January 18). Available at www.washingtontechnology.com/cgi-bin/udt/im.display.printable?client.id=wtdaily-test&story.id=25336.

Monk, Ellen F., and Bret J. Wagner. 2006. *Concepts In Enterprise Resource Planning.* Boston, MA: Thomson Course Technology.

Moore, Doris Langley. 1977. *Ada: Countess of Lovelace.* London: John Murray.

Moreau, René. 1984. *The Computer Comes of Age: The People, the Hardware, and the Software.* Cambridge: MIT Press.

Mosquera, Mary. 2006a. "IRS Missing Laptop with Employee Data." *Government Computer News* (June 6). Available at www.appserv.gcn.com/cgi-bin/udt/im.display.printable?client.id=gcn_daily&story.id=40966 (accessed June 8, 2006).

———. 2006b. "VA Data Files on Millions of Veterans Stolen." *Government Computer News* (May 22). Available at www.appserv.gcn.com/cgi-bin/udt/im.display.printable?client.id=gcn_daily&story.id=40840 (accessed June 8, 2006).

"Mydoom Virus 'Biggest in Months'." 2004. BBC News (January 27). Available at www.news.bbc.co.uk/1/hi/technology/3432639.stm (accessed on June 8, 2006).

Myron, David. 2004. "CRM.GOV: No Longer the Bailiwick of the Private Sector, CRM is a Prime Focus of Government Agencies." *Destination CRM* (July 1). Available at www.destinationcrm.com/print/default.asp?ArticleID=4187 (accessed June 15, 2006).

National Association of State Purchasing Officials (NASPO), National Association of State Information Resource Executives (NASIRE), and National Association of State Directors of Administration and General Services (NASDAGS). 1996. *Buying Smart: State Procurement Reform Saves Millions.* Available at www.naspo.org/whitepapers/buyingsmart2.cfm (accessed June 25, 2006).

National Security Telecommunications and Information Systems Security Committee. 2003. *National Information Systems Security (Infosec) Glossary.* Ft. Meade, MD: National Security Agency. Available at www.cnss.gov/Assets/pdf/cnssi_4009.pdf (accessed on June 8, 2006).

National Telecommunications and Information Administration. 1998. *Falling Through the Net.* Washington, DC: U.S. Department of Commerce. Available at www.ntia.doc.gov/ntiahome/fttn99/FTTN.pdf (accessed May 29, 2006).

———. 2004. *A Nation Online: Entering the Broadband Age.* Washington, DC: U.S. Department of Commerce. Available at www.ntia.doc.gov/reports/anol/NationOnlineBroadband04.pdf (accessed May 29, 2006).

Newcombe, Tod. 1995a. "Large Project Software Scare." *Government Technology* (December 1). Available at www.govtech.net/magazine/story.print.php?id=96116 (accessed June 26, 2006).

———. 1995b. "Opening the Doors to the Data Warehouse." *Government Technology* (October 1). Available at www.govtech.net/magazine/story.php?id=96051&issue=10:1995 (accessed May 26, 2006).

———. 2002. "Planting Data Gardens." *Government Technology* (April 6). Available at www.govtech.net/magazine/story.php?id=8093&issue=2:2002 (accessed May 26, 2006).

Okin, J.R. 2005. *The Internet Revolution: The Not-for-Dummies Guide to the History, Technology, and Use of the Internet.* Winter Harbor, ME: Ironbound Press.

O'Leary, Daniel Edmond. 2000. *Enterprise Resource Planning Systems: Systems, Life*

Cycle, Electronic Commerce, and Risk. Cambridge: Cambridge University Press.

Onley, Dawn S. 2001. "State Starts Work on Global, Multiagency Network." *Government Computer News* (April 2). Available at www.appserv.gcn.com/cgi-bin/udt/im.display.printable?client.id=gcn&story.id=3921 (accessed June 25, 2006).

Overby, Stephanie. 2006. "San Diego Tries to Learn from Contract Mistakes." *CIO Magazine.* (May 1). Available at www.cio.com/archive/050106/tl_outsourcing.html?action=print (accessed June 25, 2006).

Panko, Ray. 2006. *Business Data Networks and Telecommunications.* Upper Saddle River, NJ: Prentice Hall.

Pereira, Carla Marques, and Pedro Sousa. 2004. "A Method to Define an Enterprise Framework Using the Zachman Framework." *Proceedings of the 2004 ACM Symposium on Applied Computing,* March 14–17, Nicosea, Cyprus: 1366–1371.

Perera, David. 2006. "FISMA Fizzles." (March 15). Available at www.govexec.com/story_page.cfm?articleid=33605&printerfriendlyVers=1& (accessed June 8, 2006).

Perlman, Ellen. 2002. "Technotrouble." In *Governing: Issues and Applications from the Front Lines of Government,* Alan Ehrenhalt, ed. Washington, DC: CQ Press.

Peterson, Shane. 2003. "Security Steps." *Government Technology* (October 28). Available at www.govtech.net/magazine/story.print.php?id=75049 (accessed June 25, 2006).

Polanyi, Michael. 1967. *The Tacit Dimension.* Garden City, NY: Doubleday.

Poole, Ian. 2006. *Cellular Communications Explained: From Basics to 3G.* London: Elsevier Science and Technology Books.

Power, Daniel J. 2002. *Decision Support Systems: Concepts and Resources for Managers.* Westport, CT: Quorum Books.

"Protocols." n.d. *Webopedia.* www.webopedia.com/TERM/p/protocol.html (accessed May 27, 2006).

Ramakrishnan, Raghu, and Johannes Gehrke. 2002. *Database Management Systems.* New York: McGraw-Hill.

Rampal, Rohit. 2002. "Design and Implementation of a Wide Area Network: Technological and Managerial Issues." Case Study #T2525. Hershey, PA: Idea Group Publishing. Available at www.idea-group.com (accessed on May 22, 2006).

Randell, Brian. 1982. *The Origins of Digital Computers.* New York: Springer-Verlag.

Ribbler, Judith. 2006. "Enhancing Government's DNA." *Washington Technology's Public CIO.* (February 9). Available at www.public-cio.com/story.print.php?id=98399 (accessed June 25, 2006).

Riley, Thomas B. 2002. "eDemocracy in a Changing World." *EGov Monitor* (August 12). Available at www.egovmonitor.com/features/rileyA.html (accessed May 29, 2006).

Rocheleau, Bruce. n.d. "Governmental Information System Problems and Failures: A Preliminary Review." *Public Administration and Management: An Interactive Journal.* Available at www.pamij.com/roche.html (accessed June 26, 2006).

Royce, Winston W. 1970. "Managing the Development of Large Software Systems: Concepts and Techniques" *Proceedings of IEEE WESCON* (August 1970): 1–9. Reprinted in *Proceedings of the 9th International Conference on Software Engineering* (Monterey, CA: International Conference on Software Engineering, 1987): 328–38.

Santosus, Megan. 2005. "Application Development. Making It on Their Own. End User Developers Are Everywhere. The Key Is Getting Them to Work for You." *CIO Magazine.* (May 15). Available at www.cio.com/archive/051505/et_article. html (accessed May 31, 2006).

SAP. n.d. *Port of San Diego: mySAP™ CRM Enables a Vision of World-Class Customer Service and Drives Excellence in Public Service.* Available at www.sap.com/industries/publicsector/pdf/CS_Port_San_Diego.pdf (accessed June 15, 2006).

Sarkar, Dibya. "State and Local IT Spending on the Rise: After a Dry Spell, Governments Look to Technology." 2005. *Federal ComputerWeek.Com* (September 12). Available at www.fcw.com/article90731-09-12-05-Print (accessed May 8, 2006).

Schiff, Andrew, and Tigineh Mersha. 2000. "An Innovative Adaptation of General Purpose Accounting Software for a Municipal Social Services Agency." Case Study #IT5514. *Annals of Cases on Information Technology,* vol. 2. Hershey, PA: Idea Group Publishing.

Schneier, Bruce. 2000. *Secrets and Lies.* New York: John Wiley and Sons.

Schooner, Steven L. 2002. "Desiderata: Objectives for a System of Government Contract Law." *Public Law and Legal Theory Working Paper No. 37.* Washington, DC: George Washington University Law School.

Schrage, John F. 1981. "Information Resource Management (IRM): Theory Applied to Three Environments. Overview of Presentations." *Proceedings of the 1981 Association of Computing Machinery Conference*: 274.

Seifert, Jeffrey W. 2006. "Data Mining and Homeland Security: An Overview." *CRS Report for Congress* (January 27). Washington, DC: Congressional Research Service.

Senn, James A. 1984. *Analysis and Design of Information Systems.* New York: McGraw-Hill.

Skyrme, David J. 1998. "Knowledge Management Solutions: The IT Contribution," *ACM SIGGROUP Bulletin,* 19, no. 1 (April), 34–39.

Songini, Marc. 2005. "Arkansas Set to Pull the Plug on ERP-driven Budgeting Approach." *Computerworld* (February 7). Available at www.computerworld.com/softwaretopics/erp/story/0,10801,99578,00.html (accessed June 15, 2006).

Sood, Rishi. 2003. "Across the Digital Nation: U.S. Watches World Governments Try Open Source Software." *Washington Technology* (September 1). Available at www.washingtontechnology.com/news/18_11/statelocal/21583–1.html (accessed May 22, 2006).

Sophos. 2005. "Sophos Security Threat Management Report." 2005. Available for download at www.sophos.com/security/whitepapers/SophosSecurity2005-mmuk (accessed on June 8, 2006).

Sprague, Ralph H. and Eric D. Carlson. 1982. *Building Effective Decision Support Systems.* Englewood Cliffs, NJ: Prentice Hall.

Standish Group International. 1994. *The Chaos Report, 1994.* West Yarmouth, MA: The Standish Group International, Inc. Available at www.standishgroup.com/sample_research/chaos_1994_1.php (accessed May 8, 2006).

Stephens, Matt, and Doug Rosenberg. 2003. *Extreme Programming Refactored: The Case Against XP.* Berkeley, CA: Apress.

Stevens, J. Clarke, John C. Witt, Benn E. Smith, and Amy L. Weaver. 2001. "The Frequency of Carpal Tunnel Syndrome in Computer Users at a Medical Facility." *Neurology* 56 (11): 1568–70.

Strassmann, Paul A. 1994. "The Hocus-Pocus of Reengineering." *Across the Board* (June): 35–38. Available at www.strassmann.com/pubs/hocus-pocus.html (accessed June13, 2006).

Sutcliffe, Alistair, and Nikolay Mehandjiev. 2004. "End-User Development." *Communication of the ACM* 47 (9) (September): 31–32.

Sutor, Bob. 2004. "Something Old, Something New: Integrating Legacy Systems," *EBIZ: The Insider's Guide to Business Integration* (October 18). Available at www. www.ebizq.net/topics/legacy_integration/features/5229.html (accessed December 6, 2006).

"System Software." n.d. *Wikipedia, The Free Encyclopedia.* www.en.wikipedia. org/wiki/System_software (accessed May 22, 2006).

Tayntor, Christine B. 2006. *Successful Packaged Software Implementation.* Boca Raton, FL: Auerbach Publications.

"Telecommunications." *Wikipedia, the Free Encyclopedia.* www.en.wikipedia.org/ wiki/ Telecommunications (accessed June 25, 2006).

Terry, Lisa. 2000. "Feds, States Lean on ERP as E-Gov Pillar." *Washington Technology* 15 (September 25). Available at www.washingtontechnology.com/news/15_13/ cover/1804–1.html (accessed June 15, 2006).

"Tim Berners-Lee." *Wikipedia, The Free Internet Encyclopedia.* www.en.wikipedia. org/wiki/World_Wide_Web (accessed May 30, 2006).

Toigo, Jon William. 1999. "Decision Support Systems Make Gains in Government." *Washington Technology* (May 24). Available at www.washingtontechnology.com /news/144/tech_features/530–1.html (accessed April 6, 2006).

Toole, Betty A. 1992. *Ada, the Enchantress of Numbers.* Mill Valley, CA: Strawberry Press.

Tynan, Dan. 2005. "Arizona Hears the Call of IP Telephony." *Government Computer News* (August 29). Available at www.gcn.com/print/24_25/36789–1.html (accessed May 27, 2006).

U.S. Department of Defense. 2004. *DoD Architecture Framework, Version 1.0. Volume I: Definitions and Guidelines.* Washington, DC: Department of Defense. Available at www.defenselink.mil/nii/doc/DoDAF_v1_Volume_I.pdf (accessed June 25, 2006).

U.S. Department of Justice. 2003. *The Department of Justice Systems Development Life Cycle Guidance Document.* Washington, DC: Department of Justice, Justice Management Division. Available at www.usdoj.gov/jmd/irm/lifecycle/table.htm (accessed May 30, 2006).

U.S. General Accounting Office. 1981. *Statement of Charles A. Bowsher, Comptroller General of the United States Before the Subcommittee on Legislation and National Security of the House Committee on Government Operations on Implementation of the Paperwork Reduction Act Public Law 96–511.* Washington, DC: U.S. General Accounting Office.

———. 1994a. *Executive Guide: Improving Mission Performance Through Strategic Information Management and Technology; Learning From Leading Organizations.* Washington. DC: U.S. General Accounting Office.

———. 1994b. *Reengineering Organizations: Results of a GAO Symposium.* Washington, DC: U.S. General Accounting Office.

———. 1996a. *Information Management Reform: Effective Implementation is Essential for Improving Federal Performance.* Washington, DC: U.S. General Accounting Office.

———. 1996b. *Information Technology Investment: Agencies Can Improve Performance, Reduce, Costs, and Minimize Risk.* Washington, DC: U.S. General Accounting Office.

———. 1996c. *NASA Chief Information Officer: Opportunities to Strengthen Information Resources Management.* Washington, DC: U.S. General Accounting Office.

———. 1996d. *Software Capability Evaluation: VA's Software Development Process Is Immature.* Washington, DC: U.S. General Accounting Office.

———. 1997a. *Air Traffic Control: Complete and Enforced Architecture Needed for FAA Systems Modernization.* Washington, DC: U.S. General Accounting Office.

———. 1997b. *Air Traffic Control: Immature Software Acquisition Processes Increase FAA System Acquisition Risks.* Washington, DC: U.S. General Accounting Office.

———. 1997c. *Air Traffic Control: Improved Cost Information Needed to Make Billion Dollar Modernization Investment Decisions.* Washington, DC: U.S. General Accounting Office.

———. 1997d. *Business Process Reengineering Assessment Guide.* Washington, DC: General Accounting Office.

———. 1997e. *Chief Information Officers: Ensuring Strong Leadership and an Effective Council.* Washington, DC: U.S. General Accounting Office.

———. 1997f. *Defense Computers: Technical Support Is Key to Naval Supply Year 2000 Success,* Washington, DC: U.S. General Accounting Office.

———. 1997g. *Defense Financial Management: Immature Software Development Processes at Indianapolis Increase Risk.* Washington, DC: U.S. General Accounting Office.

———. 1997h. *Medicare Transaction System: Success Depends upon Correcting Critical Managerial and Technical Weaknesses.* Washington, DC: U.S. General Accounting Office.

———. 1997i. *Tax Systems Modernization: IRS Needs to Resolve Certain Issues with Its Integrated Case Processing System.* Washington, DC: U.S. General Accounting Office.

———. 1998a. *District of Columbia: Software Acquisition Processes for a New Financial Management System.* Washington, DC: U.S. General Accounting Office.

———. 1998b. *Social Security Administration: Software Development Process Improvements Started But Work Remains.* Washington, DC: U.S. General Accounting Office.

———. 1998c. *USDA Information Management: Proposal to Strengthen Authority of the Chief Information Officer.* Washington, DC: U.S. General Accounting Office.

———. 1998d. *VA Information Technology: Improvements Needed to Implement Legislative Reforms.* Washington, DC: U.S. General Accounting Office.

———. 1999. *Customs Service Modernization: Ineffective Software Development Processes Increase Customs System Development Risks.* Washington, DC: U.S. General Accounting Office.

———. 2000a. *Information Technology Investment Management: A Framework for Assessing and Improving Process Maturity, Exposure Draft.* Washington, DC: U.S. General Accounting Office.

———. 2000b. *Information Technology: INS Needs to Strengthen Its Investment Management Capability,* Washington, DC: U.S. General Accounting Office.

————. 2000c. *Information Technology: Selected Agencies' Use of Commercial Off-the-Shelf Software for Human Resources Function.* Washington, DC: U.S. General Accounting Office.

————. 2001. *Information Technology: State Department Led Overseas Modernization Program Faces Management Challenges.* Washington, DC: U.S. General Accounting Office.

————. 2002a. *Information Technology: DLA Needs to Strengthen Its Investment Management Capability.* Washington, DC: U.S. General Accounting Office.

————. 2002b. *United States Postal Service: Opportunities to Strengthen IT Investment Management Capabilities.* Washington, DC: U.S. General Accounting Office.

————. 2003a. *Information Technology: A Framework for Assessing and Improving Enterprise Architecture Management (Version 1.1).* Washington, DC: U.S. General Accounting Office.

————. 2003b. *Telecommunications: Uneven Implementation of Wireless Enhanced 911 Raises Prospect of Piecemeal Availability for Years to Come.* Washington, DC: U.S. General Accounting Office.

————. 2004a. *Data Mining: Federal Efforts Cover a Wide Range of Uses.* Washington, DC: U.S. General Accounting Office.

————. 2004b. *Federal Chief Information Officers: Responsibilities, Reporting Relationships, Tenure, and Challenges.* Washington, DC: U.S. General Accounting Office.

————. 2005a. *Information Security: Emerging Cybersecurity Issues Threaten Federal Information Systems.* Washington, D.C: U.S. General Accounting Office.

————. 2005b. *Information Security: Federal Agencies Show Mixed Progress in Implementing Statutory Requirements.* Washington, DC: U.S. General Accounting Office.

————. 2005c. *Information Security: Weaknesses Persist at Federal Agencies Despite Progress Made in Implementing Related Statutory Requirements.* Washington, DC: U.S. General Accounting Office.

————. 2006. *Information Technology: Agencies Need to Improve the Accuracy and Reliability of Investment Information.* Washington, DC: U.S. General Accounting Office.

U.S. Office of Management and Budget. 1999. "Circular A-76," revised 1999, original date August 4, 1983. Washington, DC: Office of Management and Budget. Available at www.whitehouse.gov/omb/circulars/a076/a076.html (accessed May 29, 2006).

————. 2002. *E-Government Strategy.* Washington, DC: Office of Management and Budget. Available at www.whitehouse.gov/omb/inforeg/egovstrategy.pdf (accessed May 29, 2006).

————. 2004a. *Federal Procurement Policy.* Memorandum M-04–16. Washington DC: Office of Management and Budget.

————. 2004b. *Maximizing Use of SmartBuy and Avoiding Duplication of Agency Activities with the President's 24 E-Gov Initiatives.* Memorandum M-04–08. Washington, DC: Office of Management and Budget. Available at www.whitehouse.gov/omb/memoranda/fy04/m04–08.pdf (accessed May 8, 2006).

————. 2006a. *FY 2005 Report to Congress on Implementation of the Federal Information Security Act of 2002.* Washington, DC: Office of Management and Budget.

————. 2006b. *President's 2006 Information Technology Budget Supports National*

Priorities And Focuses On Results. Washington, DC: Office of Management and Budget. Available at www.whitehouse.gov/ omb/pubpress/2005/2005–04.pdf (accessed May 8, 2006).

———. 2006c. *Safeguarding Personally Identifiable Information.* Memorandum for the Heads of Departments and Agencies, M-06–15. Washington, DC: Office of Management and Budget.

"U.S. State and Local Government Technology Spending on the Rise." 2005. New York: Datamonitor USA. Available at www.tekrati.com/research/News-Archives.asp?q=%22technology+spending%22&id=5658 (accessed November 1, 2006).

United Nations. *UN Global E-government Readiness Report 2005: From E-government to E-inclusion.* UNPAN/2005/14. New York: United Nations Department of Economic and Social Affairs.

"USENET." *Wikipedia, The Free Internet Encyclopedia.* www.en.wikipedia.org/wiki/Usenet (accessed May 30, 2006).

Vora, Vaishali Punamchand, and Hani S. Mahmassani. 2002. *Development and Implementation of a Telecommuting Evaluation Framework, and Modeling the Executive Telecommuting Adoption Process.* Austin, TX: Center for Transportation Research, Bureau of Engineering Research, University of Texas at Austin.

Wagner, William, and Yvonne L. Antonucci. 2004. "An Analysis of the Imagine PA Public Sector ERP Project." *Proceedings of the 37th Hawaii International Conference on System Sciences,* 2004: 1–8.

Wait, Patience. 2006. "FISMA Follies: Officials Claim Grades Suffer from Lack of Enterprise View of Security." *Washington Technology* 21 (April 11). Available at www.washingtontechnology.com/news/21_7/federal/28347–1.html (accessed June 16, 2006).

Walker, Richard W. 2001. "KM: Difficult to Define but Here to Stay." *Government Computer News* (September 24). Available at www.gcn.com/print/20_29/17173–1.html (accessed June 13, 2006).

Walsh, Trudy. 2005. "New Bill Would Aid Municipal Broadband Nets." *Government Computer News* (August 26). www.gcn.com/print/24_17/36283–1.html (accessed May 27, 2006).

Watson, Ed, Sylvia Vaught, Dan Gutierrez, and Dan Rinks. 2003. "ERP Implementation in State Government." *Annals of Cases on Information Technology* 5: 302–18.

Weigelt, Matthew. 2006. "OMB Touts the Value in Best-Value: Administration Wants Congress to Remove Its A-76 Restrictions." *Federal Computer Week, FCW.com* (May 1). Available at www.fcw.com/article94224–05–01–06-Print (accessed June 18, 2006).

Weinberger, Joshua. 2004. "School Districts Use CRM to Balance the Needs of Their Constituents" *Destination CRM.* (August 2). Available at www.destinationcrm.com/articles/default.asp?articleid=4282 (accessed June 15, 2006).

Welsh, William. 2004. "Mass. Open Standards Official." *Washington Technology* (January 14). Available at www.washingtontechnology.com/news/1_1/daily_news/22524–1.html (accessed May 22, 2006).

———. 2005. "State, Local Government Warm to Open Source Research Firm Finds." *Government Computer News* (June 17). Available at www.appserv.gcn.com/cgi-bin/udt/im.display.printable?client.id=gen_daily&story.id=36115 (accessed May 22, 2006).

West, Darrell M. 2005a. *Global E-Government, 2005.* www.insidepolitics.org/egovt05int.pdf (accessed May 29, 2006).

———. 2005b. *State and Federal E-Government in the United States,* 2005. Available at www.insidepolitics.org/egovt05us.pdf (accessed May 29, 2006).

Williams, Trish. 2001a. "Knowledge Management Initiatives Gain Foothold in Government." *Government Computer News* (March 9). Available at www.appserv.gcn.com/cgi-bin/udt/im.display.printable?client.id=gcn_daily&story.id=3784 (accessed June 25, 2006).

———. 2001b. "What Is Knowledge Management?" *Government Computer News,* (March 9, 2001). http//appserv.gcn/cig-bin/udt/im.displayprintaable?client.id=gcn_daily&story,id=3785 (accessed June 18, 2006).

Winston, Patrick H., and Karen A. Prendergast, eds. 1984. *The AI Business: The Commercial Uses of Artificial Intelligence.* Cambridge: MIT Press.

"World Wide Web." *Wikipedia. The Free Encyclopedia.* www.en.wikipedia.org/wiki/World_Wide_Web (accessed May 30, 2006).

Wu, C. Thomas. 2004. *Introduction to Object-Oriented Programming.* New York: McGraw-Hill.

"You Can't Outsource City Hall." 2002. *CIO Magazine.com* (September 15). Available at www.cio.com/archive/061502/govt.html (accessed June 18, 2006).

Zachman, John A. 1987. "A Framework for Information Systems Architecture." *IBM Systems Journal* 26 (3): 276–92.

Zecca, Tony. n.d. "Pilot Program Shares the Cost of Personal Cell Phones for Government Use." *Access America E-Gov E-Zine,* 1–3. Available at www.govinfo.library.unt.edu/accessamerica/docs/mobilecommunications.html (accessed May 29, 2006).

Web Sources

Accenture. 2004. *eGovernment Leadership: High Performance, Maximum Value.* Available at www.accenture.com/Global/Research_and_Insights/By_Industry/Government/HighValue.htm (accessed May 29, 2006).

Adler, Jim. www.votehere.net/blog.php (accessed May 29, 2006).

Agile Alliance. www.agilealliance.com (accessed May 31, 2006).

American Telecommuting Association. www.knowledgetree.com/ata-adv.html (accessed June 18, 2006).

Arizona State University, "Policy on Data Administration." www.asu.edu/data_admin/data_administration.htm (accessed June 18, 2004).

California Internet Voting Taskforce. www.ss.ca.gov/executive/ivote/ (accessed May 29, 2006).

Caraballo, David, and Joseph Lo, *The IRC Prelude, version 1.1.5.* www.irchelp.org/irchelp/new2irc.html (accessed May 29, 2006).

"CDW-G Releases Assessment of State and Local Government Security Investment." *Government Technology* (February 22, 2006). www.govtech.net/magazine/story.print.php?id=98511 (accessed June 25, 2006).

CDW-G, "State & Local Government Technology Investment Curve (TIC)." (February 20, 2006). www.newsroom.cdwg.com/features/feature-02-20-06.html (accessed June 8, 2006).

CERT. www.cert.org/advisories/CA-1999–04.html (accessed June 8, 2006).

Chief Security Officer Magazine, U.S. Secret Service, and CERT Coordination Center, "2005 E-Crime Watch Survey–Survey Results." www.csoonline.com/info/ecrime-survey05.pdf (accessed June 8, 2006).

Chittenden County Regional Planning Commission (CCRPC) and the Chittenden County Metropolitan Planning Organization (CCMPO) land use and transportation DSS. www.ccmpo.org/modeling/dss.html (accessed April 8, 2006).

ChoicePoint. www.choicepointgov.com/strategic.htm (accessed May 26, 2006).

CIO Council. www.cio.gov (accessed June 25, 2006).

City College of San Francisco's Student Management DSS. www.research.ccsf.edu/HTM/decision_what.htm (accessed April 8, 2006).

City of Los Angeles. "Internet Policies and Guidelines." www.ci.la.ca.us/policy/intpolgu.htm (accessed May 29, 2006).

Commonwealth of Virginia. "Policy on Internet and E-mail Usage." www.vsdbs.virginia.gov/VSDB_IT_Acceptable_Use_Policy.pdf (accessed June 25, 2006).

Conference Board Survey, 2001. www.it-cortex.com/Stat_Failure_Rate.htm#The%20Conference%20Board%20Survey (accessed May 8, 2006).

Data Management Group. www.datamanagementgroup.com/PublicSector/Public Sector.asp (accessed June 15, 2006).

Department of Computer Science, University of Indonesia. www.cs.ui.ac.id (accessed April 8, 2006).

"Digital Communities." www.intel.com/business/bss/industry/government/digital-communities.htm (accessed on May 27, 2006).

"E-Democracy." BBCWorld.com (December 18, 2003) www.bbcworld.com/content/clickonline_archive_50_2003.asp?pageid=666&co_pageid=3 (accessed May 29, 2006).

"E-Democracy Center." www.lake-geneva.net/Telecom/FHomePageTelecom.aspx?t okenPage=v2nIFkxE2WMid4vCSp-0xLs1WaY8xxt9j0TmAQHDaKw%29%29 (accessed May 29, 2006).

Electronic Data Systems. NMCI Website. www.eds.com/sites/nmci (accessed April 8, 2006).

Electronic Privacy Information Center (EPIC). www.epic.org/.

"ENIAC Story." www.ftp.arl.mil/~mike/comphist/eniac-story.html (accessed May 22, 2006).

"Enterprise Architecture in Action: FDA Uses EA to Standardize and Save with Consolidation Effort." Available at www.whitehouse.gov/omb/egov/documents/FDA_FINAL.pdf (accessed June 25, 2006).

Extreme Programming (XP) FAQ. "The Twelve Principles of Extreme Programming." www.jera.com/techinfo/xpfaq.html (accessed May 31, 2006).

Federal Acquisitions Regulations (FAR). www.arnet.gov/far (accessed June 15, 2006).

FirstGov. www.firstgov.gov (accessed May 29, 2006).

Forest Service of British Columbia, Canada. "Purposes and Principles of Data Administration" www.for.gov.bc.ca/his/datadmin/dapurp.htm (accessed June 25, 2006).

"Free/Libre and Open Source Software: Survey and Study" (FLOSS)." www.infonomics.nl/FLOSS/report/index.htm (accessed May 22, 2006).

Government Computer News. (Various articles on NMCI) www.appserv.gcn.com/cgi-bin/texis/scripts/gcn-search/+lwwFqnNTgfxzmwwxIqFqA5BdGOe6 DwwBnmFqnmn5qozmwwxeamww/search.html (accessed April 8, 2006).

Government Performance Project. www.results.gpponline.org (accessed May 8, 2006).

History of IBM. www.www-03.ibm.com/ibm/history/history/history_intro.html (accessed May 22, 2006).

Howe, Walt. "A Brief History of the Internet." www.walthowe.com/navnet/history.html (accessed May 30, 2006).

HR eXpert. New South Wales Australia Expert System. www.premiers.nsw.gov.au/hrexpert/hrx.htm (accessed May 12, 2006).

Imagine PA. www.ies.state.pa.us/imaginepa/cwp/view.asp?a=4&Q=125583&PM=1 (accessed June 15, 2006).

Information Technology Management Reform Act of 1995. (Public Law 104–106). Available at http://.irm.cit.nih.gov/itmra/itmra96.html.

International Ergonomics Association. www.iea.cc/ergonomics (accessed June 25, 2006).

Internet Corporation for Assigned Names and Numbers (ICANN). www.icann.org (accessed May 30, 2006).

The Internet Engineering Task Force (IETF). www.ietf.org (accessed May 30, 2006).

Internet Society (ISOC) www.isoc.org/isoc/mission/principles (accessed May 29, 2006).

Internet World Stats: Usage and Population Statistics. www.internetworldstats.com/stats.htm (accessed May 29, 2006).

"Introduction to Supercomputers." www.thocp.net/hardware/supercomputers.htm. (accessed May 22, 2006).

Israeli Ministry of Finance expert system. www.mof.gov.il/micun/prof.htm (accessed April 6, 2006).

KPMG Canada Survey. 1997. www.it-cortex.com/Stat_Failure_Rate.htm#The%20KPMG% 20Canada%20Survey%20(1997) (accessed May 8, 2006).

Miami-Dade County Procurement. www.miamidade.gov/dpm/home.asp (accessed June 25, 2006).

Miami-Dade County Procurement Process. www.miamidade.gov/dpm/solicitation-process.asp (accessed June 25, 2006).

Miami-Dade County Requests for Proposals and Requests for Qualifications. www.miamidade.gov/dpm/rfp-process.asp (accessed June 25, 2006).

Minnesota E-Democracy. www.e-democracy.org/(accessed May 29, 2006).

Multistate Anti-Terrorism Information Exchange. www.fdle.state.fl.us/press_releases/20050415_matrix_project.html (accessed May 26, 2006).

National Association of Schools of Public Affairs and Administration. Common Curriculum Components Standard 4.21. www.naspaa.org/accreditation/seeking/reference/standards.asp (accessed May 8, 2006).

National Association of State Chief Information Officers. https://www.nascio.org. (accessed June 25, 2006).

New South Wales Australia expert system "HR eXpert." www.premiers.nsw.gov.au/hrexpert/hrx.htm (accessed May 12, 2006).

OASIG Survey, 1995. www.it-cortex.com/Stat_Failure_Rate.htm#The%200ASIG%20Study%20 (accessed May 8, 2006).

Open Source Initiative. www.opensource.org/docs/definition.php (accessed May 22, 2006).

Paperwork Reduction Act of 1980 (P.L. 96–511). www.thomas.loc.gov (accessed June 25, 2006).

"Principles Behind the Agile Manifesto." www.agilemanifesto.org/principles.html (accessed May 31, 2006).

Privacy International. www.privacyinternational.org/article.shtml?cmd[347]=x-347–82589 (accessed June 16, 2006).

Prosci Reengineering Learning Center On-Line. "Recommended Approach," www.prosci.com/project-planning.htm (accessed June 15, 2006).

"Reengineering: A Radical Approach to Business Process Redesign" www.dod.mil/comptroller/icenter/learn/reeng.htm (accessed June 15, 2006).

SAP. www.sap.com/usa/industries/publicsector/index.epx (accessed June 15, 2006).

Sophos. www.sophos.com (accessed on June 8, 2006)

State and Local Government on the Net. www.statelocalgov.net (accessed May 29, 2006).

State of Arizona Telework Program. www.teleworkarizona.com (accessed June 25, 2006).

State of Colorado's Water Management DSS. www.cdss.state.co.us/index.asp (accessed April 8, 2006).

State of Florida, Department of Management Services, "Telecommuting Checklist for the Home Office." www.dms.myflorida.com/dms/media/hrm_files/state_employee_telecommuting_program/telecommuting_checklist_for_the_home_office (accessed June 25, 2006).

Swiss Politics.org. www.swisspolitics.org/en/links/index.php?page=links&catid=53&linktopcat=demokratie (accessed May 29, 2006).

Symantec. www.symantec.com/avcenter/global/index.html (accessed June 8, 2006).

"The Univac." www.csif.cs.ucdavis.edu/~csclub/ museum/items/univac.html (accessed May 22, 2006).

University of Arizona, "Cow Culling DSS": www.ag.arizona.edu/AREC/cull/culling.html (accessed April 8, 2006).

University of Nebraska Medical Center. MEDTECH EIS: www.meditech.com (accessed April 6, 2006).

University of South Florida, *Public Sector Telework Sample Policies and Agreements.* www.nctr.usf.edu/clearinghouse/teleworksamples.htm (accessed June 25, 2006).

University of Texas at Austin, Technology Resources for Employee and Campus Services, "Joint Application Development." www.utexas.edu/hr/is/pubs/jad.html (accessed May 31, 2006).

U.S. Department of Defense. The Secure Electronic Registration and Voting Experiment (SERVE). Federal Voting Assistance Program. (FVAP), www.serveusa.gov (accessed June 13, 2006).

U.S. Department of Labor, Occupational Safety and Health Administration, "Computer Workstations: Good Working Positions." www.osha.gov/SLTC/etools/computer-workstations/positions.html (accessed June 25, 2006).

U.S. Department of the Navy. NMCI Website: www.nmci.navy.mil (accessed April 8, 2006). Virginia Department of Social Services. "The Virginia Social Services System (VSSS)." www.dss.virginia.gov/about/bpr/index.cgi (accessed June 15, 2006).

"Voice Over Internet Protocol." Federal Communications Commission. www.fcc.gov/voip/ (accessed May 27, 2006).

Webopedia™, online dictionary and search engine for computer and internet technology definitions: www.webopedia.com.

World Wide Web Consortium (WEC). www.w3.org (accessed May 29, 2006).

Zachman Institute for Framework Advancement. www.zifa.com (accessed June 25, 2006).

Index

Boldface page references indicate figures. *Italic* references indicate boxed text and tables.

About the Author

Jay D. White is the Reynolds Professor of Public Affairs and Community Service at the University of Nebraska–Omaha. He teaches master's courses in managing information, organizational behavior and development, and human resource management; and doctoral seminars in the philosophy of science and advanced public management theory. He is the author of numerous scholarly articles, book chapters, and books in public administration. He is a former Fulbright Scholar at the University of Leiden in the Netherlands.